12th Edition

GENERAL BUSINESS
For Economic Understanding

Anne Scott Daughtrey　　Professor, School of Business
Old Dominion University

Robert A. Ristau　　Professor of Administrative Services and Business Education
Eastern Michigan University

S. Joseph DeBrum　　Professor Emeritus, School of Business
San Francisco State University

Published by

G15　　**SOUTH-WESTERN PUBLISHING CO.**

CINCINNATI　WEST CHICAGO, ILL.　DALLAS　PELHAM MANOR, N.Y.
PALO ALTO, CALIF.

ISBN: 0-538-07150-8

Library of Congress Catalog Card Number: 80-53571

    5 6 7 8 9 D 9 8 7 6 5

Printed in the United States of America

PREFACE

All Americans enjoy the privilege of participating in a free enterprise economy. Yet in order to get the greatest benefit from our system, each of us needs to understand the business and economic environment in which we assume our roles of consumer, worker, and citizen. As consumers we depend on business to satisfy our needs and wants. As workers we derive our incomes from business or from sources that depend on business. And as citizens we engage in activities and make decisions that affect our economic welfare.

In order to play these roles well, each American needs to understand free enterprise. This twelfth edition of *General Business for Economic Understanding* is dedicated to helping students develop an understanding of our business system and the economic setting in which it functions.

IMPROVING ECONOMIC CITIZENSHIP

One of the major purposes — if not *the* major purpose — of a course in general business is to improve economic citizenship through the study of the business and economic environment in which we live and work. We interpret economic citizenship in this context to mean the development of individuals who are:

1. competent in managing their personal business affairs;
2. skillful in selecting and using the goods and services that are available from business, industry, and government;
3. knowledgeable about the American business system as a part of our total economic society; and
4. aware of the world of work and concerned about career opportunities, career preparation, and job success and satisfaction.

Stated very simply, we can say that an up-to-date course in general business is concerned with four aspects of economics: (1) the economics of personal business management, (2) consumer economics, (3) social economics, and (4) the economics of the world of work and career selection. The units in this revision deal with these four phases of economics.

FEATURES OF THE TWELFTH EDITION

This edition thoroughly updates the widely used previous edition. Based on successful experience and on the response to a survey of many users, much of the significant and tested content of the preceding edition has been retained and made current. Some of the topics treated in previous editions have been eliminated or reduced in coverage to make greater use of material that is of more value to today's students. The writing style emphasizes forceful and idiomatic language, and careful attention has been given to making the text free from ethnic- and sex-stereotyping. An entirely new selection of photographs and many new graphs and charts have been included. Also, an added dimension has been given to this edition in the use of full-color printing and new formatting.

This revision contains 48 parts which are divided into 12 broad topical units. All parts have been edited and revised to give a fresh approach to the basic content and to add relevant and timely material. One important new feature in this revision is that the free enterprise system is introduced as a separate part in Unit 1, followed by a part which stresses the importance of the economic roles each person plays in our system. Another improvement is that the entire text is performance-based, with learning objectives stated at the beginning of each unit and part. A description of these new major features follows:

The Free Enterprise System. Because the free enterprise system is guided in a large measure by the economic decisions of every citizen, all persons should have a basic understanding of how the system works. Part 1 of Unit 1 introduces students to the basic economic problem of limited resources and unlimited wants. Part 2 presents the free enterprise system as the way our country is organized to solve the basic economic problem. This part discusses the features of free enterprise, the economic freedoms it provides, and the basic differences between our system and other economic systems. Part 3 helps the student examine the economic roles played by each citizen and shows how the economy is affected by individual decisions. Part 4 then presents several ways used to measure the growth of our economy.

Performance Objectives. Measuring achievement in general business has often been difficult and subjective. This task will be much easier for users of the twelfth edition. Performance objectives are included at the beginning of each unit and part and are keyed to text material, end-of-part activities, and achievement tests. Both the student and the teacher will know the minimal goals to be achieved for each topic. A matrix included in the teacher's manual identifies the relationship between each performance objective and the end-of-part activities and test questions which measure its achievement.

STUDENT ACTIVITIES

At the end of each part of *General Business for Economic Understanding* are activities carefully planned for teaching and learning. These activities involve students in writing, investigating, interviewing, problem solving, demonstrating, computing, explaining, reporting, and other behavioral responses. These varied and challenging experiences allow teachers to provide for a wide range of student abilities and interests. As already noted, activities are keyed to the performance objectives; in addition, there are many activities which will provide opportunities for enrichment beyond the minimal achievement. The end-of-part activities are divided into the following sections:

1. Increasing Your Business Vocabulary. This section fulfills an important goal — that of increasing word power by expecting students to identify definitions of commonly used business and economic terms.
2. Understanding Your Reading. This section measures students' comprehension through oral or written responses to questions directly related to the content of each part.
3. Using Your Business Knowledge. Through the activities in this section, students apply what they have learned in problem situations relevant to their everyday lives.
4. Solving Problems in Business. By solving the business-economic problems in this section, students strengthen and refine their basic mathematics abilities. Problems vary in

level of difficulty; the first two in each section are designed for easy and quick solution. Beginning with Part 8, each set of problems contains a metric activity to familiarize students with the metric system.

5. Expanding Your Understanding of Business. The activities in this section are intended mainly as optional experiences for students. The solutions require the students to exercise careful thought, to investigate sources of information beyond the textbook, and in some cases to conduct studies using basic and practical research methods. Students may be expected to report on their findings and to make decisions or recommendations. This section is designed particularly, but not exclusively, for the more able or resourceful students.

ACKNOWLEDGMENTS

Specialists from all levels of the teaching profession have read manuscripts, offered suggestions, and otherwise contributed to the improvement of this book. Authorities from business and government helped significantly in updating content and illustrations relating to insurance, banking, social security, labor, credit, investments, and other topics.

Many pages would be required to give deserving and proper recognition to each individual who has contributed in some way to the production of this textbook. Although it is not possible to give credit to all contributors individually, we acknowledge with deep appreciation the special assistance received from Dr. Steve Eggland of the University of Nebraska, Dr. Bruce Heatwole of Glendale High School, and Dr. Barry Van Hook of the University of Colorado.

Anne Scott Daughtrey
Robert A. Ristau
S. Joseph DeBrum

CONTENTS

Unit 9

Protecting Yourself with Insurance

Unit 10

Moving People, Ideas, and Goods

Unit 11

Government and Labor in Your Economy

Unit 12

Starting Your Career

ACKNOWLEDGMENTS

For permission to reproduce the photographs on the pages indicated, acknowledgment is made to the following:

UNIT 1   p. 2: Roger Webster/Environmental Communications. p. 4: Kings Island. p. 7: Photo Courtesy Westvaco Corporation. p. 7: Courtesy of International Paper Company. p. 8: Webb/Magnum Photos, Inc. p. 20: Mead Corporation. p. 31: Ford Motor Company. p. 39: Albertsons, Inc. p. 41: Springman/Black Star.

UNIT 2   p. 48: Environmental Communications and Venturi & Rauch. p. 50: Burlington Industries. p. 52: Burt Glinn/Magnum Photos, Inc. p. 57: Photo Courtesy Westvaco Corporation. p. 72: Webb Photos. p. 82: Courtesy of Nabisco, Inc. p. 89: Photo Courtesy, Digital Equipment Corporation. p. 97: Swiss Bank Corporation. p. 99: Reprinted with permission of Morgan Guaranty Trust Company of New York. p. 103: Photograph courtesy of Cincinnati Reds, Inc.

UNIT 3   p. 110: Michael Collier/Stock, Boston. p. 114: Genstar Limited. p. 115: Wyle Laboratories. p. 116: Courtesy Du Pont Company. p. 123: Shaw-Walker. p. 124: Courtesy of Phelps Dodge. p. 125: Shaw-Walker. p. 127: Charles Harbutt/Magnum Photos, Inc. p. 133: Boy Scouts of America. p. 137: Courtesy of Carter Hawley Hale Stores, Inc.

UNIT 4   p. 149: Celanese Corporation. p. 163: Lima Druskis/Editorial Photocolor Archives. p. 164: Burlington Industries.

UNIT 5   p. 188: Photri. p. 190: © Angel Franco/Vision. p. 193: Photo Courtesy of Ethyl Corporation.

UNIT 6   p. 232: Craig Sherburne. p. 234: Photo by Joe Aker Photography, Houston, Texas. p. 236: Courtesy of Bank America Corporation. p. 237: The Northern Trust Company. p. 279: The Central Trust Company, N.A. p. 303: American Express Company.

UNIT 7   p. 314: © 1978 Joel Gordon. p. 317: Shell Oil Company. p. 341: Charles Harbutt/Magnum Photos, Inc.

UNIT 8   p. 370: Honeywell. p. 372: Girl Scouts of the U.S.A. p. 384: LeFebure, Division of Walter Kidde & Company, Inc. p. 395: The securities trading room of Investors Diversified Services. p. 405: Courtesy of United States Gypsum Company. p. 409: Century 21 Real Estate Corporation.

UNIT 9   p. 416: © Four by Five, Inc. p. 418: Arthur Tress/Magnum Photos, Inc. p. 421: American Express Company. p. 428: Photri. p. 441: Photo courtesy of Gamble-Skogmo, Inc. p. 452: Bristol-Myers Company/Burt Glinn. p. 461: Charles Steinhacker/Black Star. p. 465: Photo by Ken Kaminsky. p. 473: Social Security Administration.

UNIT 10   p. 482: © William Rivelli 1978. p. 485: United Air Lines Photo. p. 487: The Greyhound Corporation. p. 497: Steelcase Inc. p. 498: Photo courtesy of Western Union. p. 500: Photo courtesy of Western Union. p. 518: Courtesy of the Illinois Central Gulf Railroad, and IC Industries Company. p. 519: The Martin-Brower Company. p. 520: The Dun & Bradstreet Corporation. p. 522: Dennis Stock/Magnum Photos, Inc. p. 528: Photo courtesy of Western Union.

UNIT 11   p. 530: Lukas/Editorial Photocolor Archives. p. 532: Cincinnati Recreation Commission. p. 545: 3M Company. p. 547: U.S. Customs Service. p. 559: Ben Weaver/Camera 5. p. 559: Arthur Grace/Sygma.

UNIT 12   p. 571: Burt Glinn/Magnum Photos, Inc. p. 573: The Culinary Institute of America. p. 578: Boy Scouts of America.

UNIT 1
Your Economic System

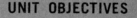

UNIT OBJECTIVES

After studying the parts in this unit, you will be able to:

1. Explain the basic economic problem.

2. Describe several characteristics of the free enterprise system.

3. Give an example to show how each of your economic roles plays a part in our economic system.

4. Discuss three ways to measure our economic progress.

1 MEETING YOUR NEEDS AND WANTS

PART OBJECTIVES

After studying this part and completing the end-of-part activities, you will be able to:
1. Explain what economics means.
2. Give two examples to show that human wants are unlimited.
3. Give two examples to show that economic resources are limited.
4. State the role business plays in satisfying our needs and wants.
5. Give one example of each of the three kinds of economic resources that are essential in producing goods and services.
6. Explain the importance of human resources in production.
7. Explain why the basic economic problem forces you to make choices.
8. Tell why it is important for everyone to understand how our system for meeting needs and wants operates.

How would you feel if someone told you that you could have anything you wanted? You would probably be able to think of a number of things to ask for right away — a stereo, a motorbike, or a guitar. But there are lots of other things you would probably want too, if you thought about it. You might ask for a bigger house or apartment for your family, or an even greater variety of stores and restaurants to choose from. Or you might ask for a new part-time job after school, or a chance to take tennis lessons. The number of things you need or want is unlimited. Supplying

3

you with as many of those things as possible is what economics is all about.

Economics deals with producing and making available the products and services that will satisfy as many of our wants as possible. It also deals with ways you can earn money to buy these products and services. And economics is concerned, too, with helping you to choose wisely from the many things you are offered and to use well the things that you buy.

YOUR NEEDS AND WANTS

You are not alone in needing and wanting things. Everyone does. **Needs** are things we must have to stay alive — things like food, clothing, and housing. **Wants** are things which we could live without, but which add comfort and pleasure to our lives.

Often it is hard to tell the difference between needs and wants. A car may be a need for you to get to your job. And it may also be thought of as a want — or even a luxury — if you used it for visiting friends or just riding around. A TV set would generally be considered as a want, but some people might call it a need in order to keep up with local, national, and world events. All of us need clothing to help keep us warm, protected, and clean. But most of us also want — but do not really need — additional or special clothing for appearance, style, and variety.

Illus. 1-1

A ride on a roller coaster may be one of your many wants.

UNLIMITED WANTS

We never stop wanting and needing things. You may eat a very satisfying lunch but by dinner time you are ready to eat again. Or you may have bought a great pair of jeans that you have wanted for some time. Then before long you want something else to wear because you have outgrown the jeans, or they are no longer in style, or you simply are tired of them. A young family may want to move from a small house to a larger one when the family size increases. Or the family may want to move because its income has increased and it can afford a better house. The owner of a large car may want to buy a smaller one which uses less gas in order to save money and conserve energy.

As new products are made available, you may discover wants that you were not aware of last week or last year. You may want a product because it is useful or just because it is new. Also, satisfying one want usually brings up new ones. Buy a camera, and you want film. Then you may want a flash attachment, a tripod, and perhaps a developing outfit.

As you can see, your wants are always changing for many reasons. That is also true for everyone else. It is not possible to satisfy all the wants and needs people have; wants are unlimited.

WANTING GOODS AND SERVICES

When you say you want something, you usually mean that you want "goods" or "services." These are key words in the study of business and economics and you will use them often. **Goods** are tangible things — things that you can touch — that you use in everyday life. Goods are also called products. Some goods, like a pizza or a bar of soap or a package of notebook paper, are used up in a short time. Other goods, like a car or a typewriter or a stereo, can be used over a much longer period of time.

When you pay someone to do something for you or to show you how to do something, you are buying **services**. When you ride a bus, use your telephone, enjoy rides at an amusement park, get a haircut, or take karate lessons, you are using services.

SUPPLYING GOODS AND SERVICES

Supplying all of us with goods and services is what business is all about. We satisfy most of our needs and wants by buying goods and services from stores, offices, and factories. A **business** is an establishment or "enterprise" that supplies us with goods and services in exchange for payment in some form. Businesses vary in nature and size from small neighborhood stores to giant automotive companies.

As a buyer and user of goods and services, you are a **consumer**. So is every person you know. Schools, government agencies, and other organizations are also consumers. Your school buys and uses paper, chairs, lab equipment, and many other products. Your local government buys many things, including fire engines and the services of fire-fighting crews.

Businesses which supply goods and services to you are also consumers. The owner of a service station, for example, buys and uses goods supplied by other businesses — a cash register, display cases, gasoline pumps, and other items.

As you can see, businesses and other organizations are producers when they supply us with goods and services. But they are also consumers when they buy goods and services themselves to use in production.

THREE ECONOMIC RESOURCES

Goods and services don't just come out of thin air. You cannot create goods from nothing or provide services without some effort. The means or sources of help through which things needed and wanted are produced are known as **economic resources**. These are also commonly called **factors of production**. There are three kinds of economic resources: natural resources, capital resources, and human resources.

Natural resources are raw materials supplied directly by nature. Natural resources include all mineral, animal, and plant products that come from the earth, the sea, and the air. We mine iron ore from the earth to use in making steel. We grow vegetables in the soil and take fish from the sea for food. And we use oxygen from the air for patients in hospitals and to make other products, such as carbonated water. All of the goods used today began with one or more raw materials.

Capital resources include tools, machinery, and other equipment used in producing goods and services. Factory buildings, power plants, tractors, computers, and typewriters are examples of capital resources. If you need a bicycle to deliver newspapers, your bicycle is a capital resource because it is equipment you use to provide the newspaper delivery service.

The word **capital** is often used in place of capital resources, especially when referring to the factors of production. Capital is also thought of as money that is needed to run a business. A person may say she or he is trying to raise "$40,000 capital" to expand a business or that she or he has a "$10,000 capital investment" in a store operated by friends. Capital has a variety of meanings, but here the word is used in its economic sense to include equipment and other facilities needed to produce goods and services.

Illus. 1-2

Lumber, a natural resource, and machinery, a capital resource, are important economic resources.

Human resources are the people who work to produce goods and services. **Labor** is another name for human resources. Human resources include the people who run our farms, mines, and factories, who transport products to places where they are needed, who perform business and government services for other people, and who manage businesses. Natural and capital resources would have little value without human resources to use them in producing goods and services.

Illus. 1-3
Without human resources, we could not produce goods and services.

LIMITED RESOURCES

You already know that you want many things that you cannot have because you do not have enough resources to exchange for everything you want. This is true for people everywhere. Resources that can be turned into goods and services are limited.

We do not have an endless supply of coal, oil, timber, and other such raw materials. We are also realizing that, because of pollution, we do not have an endless supply of clean air, water, and land. In addition, we will probably never have enough dentists, nurses, accountants, secretaries, and other persons with the skills and education to satisfy our unlimited wants. And since our natural and human resources are limited, our manufactured capital resources are also limited.

THE BASIC ECONOMIC PROBLEM

Just as meeting unlimited wants with limited resources is a problem for you, so it is for everyone — your family, your school club, your city and state, the nation, and all other nations. That is why economists call the conflict between unlimited wants and limited resources the **basic economic problem**.

Your family members may not be able to afford many things they want because the wages of your father or mother must be used to buy food and clothing and to pay such expenses as the mortgage and electric bill. Your school club might want to hire a band to play for its annual dance, but it may not have enough money and might have to use stereo tapes instead.

Towns and cities must also deal with the basic economic problem. Your town may wish to give a large wage increase to its police officers and fire fighters; but because taxes may not provide enough money, the increase might have to be smaller in order to also provide other needed services to the citizens. All governments face the same problem: how to use their limited resources to satisfy the many things their citizens want.

MAKING ECONOMIC CHOICES

Because you cannot have everything you want, you must choose which of the things you want most and can afford. You need to be "economical" in using your limited resources so that you can satisfy as many of your unlimited wants as possible. Making wise economic decisions is as necessary for you as it is for the nation.

As a consumer, you decide how best to use your personal income to satisfy your needs and wants. Suppose you earn $10. If you spend it for bowling after school, you won't have enough left to go to the movie Friday night. So you must make an economic decision. You have to decide which want — bowling with your friends or the movie — is more important to you.

All countries have a shortage of economic resources. Some have fewer economic resources than others. A major problem facing every nation is how best to use its limited economic resources so that it satisfies as many as possible of its people's needs and wants.

PREPARING TO MAKE WISE ECONOMIC DECISIONS

Every person needs to have a basic understanding of the way needs and wants are met. Everyone must make economic decisions, and these decisions should be made wisely. Many activities in your life will call for economic decision making. Now and in the future you will be managing your limited resources while trying to satisfy as many of your unlimited wants as possible. You will be earning, spending, saving, and investing money. You will be making decisions about the kinds and amounts of goods and services you will buy. This course will help prepare you to make these economic decisions in a way that will bring you the greatest benefit and enjoyment.

In addition, you will be reading about the problems that businesses and governments face as they try to make wise use of resources to provide you with the goods and services you demand. And later, when you vote, you will be helping to make decisions on a variety of economic issues. This course will help prepare you for this important responsibility.

It is the purpose of this book to introduce you to the American system for meeting needs and wants. You will learn how businesses operate and how to be a wise consumer and manager of your personal business affairs within the system.

INCREASING YOUR BUSINESS VOCABULARY

The following terms should become part of your business vocabulary. For each numbered statement, find the term that has the same meaning.

basic economic problem
business
capital resources or capital
consumer
economic resources or
    factors of production
economics

goods
human resources or labor
natural resources
needs
services
wants

1. One who buys and uses goods and services.
2. An establishment that supplies us with goods and services in

exchange for payment in some form.

3. The means or sources of help through which we produce the things we need and want.
4. The problem of satisfying unlimited wants with limited resources which faces individuals, businesses, organizations, and governments.
5. Raw materials supplied directly by nature.
6. The study of producing and making available products and services to help satisfy as many of our wants as possible.
7. The tangible things you use in everyday life.
8. Tools, machinery, and other equipment used in producing goods and services.
9. Those things we must have to stay alive, such as food, clothing, and housing.
10. The people who work to produce goods and services.
11. Those things which we can live without but which can add pleasure and comfort to living.
12. Those things that you pay others to do for you or to show you how to do.

UNDERSTANDING YOUR READING

1. What is economics about? Give three concerns of economics.
2. Can you easily tell the difference between needs and wants? Explain.
3. Give three examples that show why people can never satisfy all their wants and needs.
4. What role does business play in satisfying our wants and needs?
5. Are business firms and government agencies consumers? Explain.
6. Give at least two examples each of natural resources, capital resources, and human resources.
7. Is it possible to produce goods by using only capital resources and human resources? Explain.
8. Explain the importance of human resources in the production of goods and services.
9. Give two examples to show that economic resources are limited.
10. What is the basic economic problem? Explain.
11. Why does the basic economic problem force us to make choices?
12. Why should every person understand how our system for meeting needs and wants operates?

USING YOUR BUSINESS KNOWLEDGE

1. List at least four different goods and services that are supplied by businesses for two of the following: your school's football team, your family car, a family pet, or a hobby which you enjoy.
2. "Satisfying one want often brings up other wants." Give an example from your experience or your family's experiences to support this statement.
3. List four businesses in your community that sell goods; four that sell services; and four that sell both goods and services.
4. All goods begin with raw materials. Name the raw materials which went into making at least three objects that you own. The objects might be articles of clothing, sports equipment, furniture, or other goods.
5. Several examples of limited resources were given in this part. In addition to those in the text, give two examples of limited resources for each of the three economic resources.
6. For each of the following, give one example to show that each had to face the basic economic problem recently: your family, your local government, your school district, your state. What economic choice was made in each case?

SOLVING PROBLEMS IN BUSINESS

1. Mrs. Martin bought the things below to help satisfy some of the everyday needs and wants of her family.

   1 quart milk, 69¢
   2 dozen eggs, 75¢ a dozen
   1 plastic measuring cup, 44¢
   6 cans soup, 32¢ each
   1 10-pound bag potatoes, $2.89
   1 toothbrush, 97¢

   What is the total cost of Mrs. Martin's purchases?
2. The actual land of the United States is one of its most important economic resources. The area of land in our country is listed below:

Privately owned land	1,367,000,000 acres
Land owned by the federal government	761,000,000 acres
Land owned by the states	116,000,000 acres
Land owned by counties and cities	20,000,000 acres

   (a) What is the total acreage of land in our country?
   (b) What is the total acreage of public land — owned by federal, state, and local governments?

(c) Which is larger, the total acreage of privately owned land or the total acreage of public land?

3. In a recent year, the federal government spent the following amounts of its $450.8 billion budget on natural resources and the environment:

Pollution control	$4.0 billion
Water resources	3.5 "
Conservation and land management	2.0 "
Recreational resources	1.4 "
Other natural resources	1.2 "

(a) What was the total budget amount for natural resources and the environment?

(b) What percent of the total federal budget was spent for natural resources and the environment? (Round your answer to the nearest whole percent.)

(c) On what natural resource category was the greatest amount of money spent? What percent is that amount of the total that you calculated in part (a) of this problem? (Round your answer to the nearest whole percent.)

EXPANDING YOUR UNDERSTANDING OF BUSINESS

1. Select a product that you often eat or use. Show how each of the three basic economic resources was necessary for the production of that product.

2. Natural resources, capital resources, and human resources are the three basic economic resources. What do you think would happen if any of these three resources were not available to us?

3. We buy most of the goods and services we want from various kinds of businesses, but many of the things we want come from government. Make a list of the wants that are satisfied by local, state, and national government agencies. How do we pay for these wants?

4. During the next three or four days, be alert to things that you read or hear about that are said to be scarce. Make a list of these and bring it to class. Combine the lists of all the class members and discuss ways in which you think people can cope with the scarcity of the items.

2 THE FREE ENTERPRISE SYSTEM

PART OBJECTIVES

After studying this part and completing the end-of-part activities, you will be able to:

1. State the three basic economic questions that must be answered by every society.
2. Identify four freedoms and rights that Americans enjoy under the free enterprise system.
3. Defend the statement that people are entitled to make profits from their business ventures.
4. Give two reasons in addition to profit for going into business.
5. Explain why competition generally results in better services and more goods at lower prices.
6. Tell who owns or controls the economic resources under capitalism, socialism, and communism.

When the Milledge family moved to a different city, they learned that the small yard at their new home would not provide space for everything each member of the family wants. Mrs. Milledge wants a vegetable garden to help cut food costs. Bob, 12, agrees; he wants to plant enough so that he can sell vegetables to earn spending money. Mr. Milledge and Janet, 15, want to plant and care for flowers. Scott, 17, is on the basketball team and wants to mount a basketball hoop. Janet likes that idea also.

14

What decision regarding use of the yard will the family make? Should they use the small yard to grow flowers or food? Who will make the decision? Will Mrs. Milledge simply announce that she will have a garden? If a garden is chosen, who will decide what vegetables to plant and how much of each? How will the garden be cared for? How will the labor be divided? These are some of the questions the Milledge family must consider in deciding how best to use their limited resource — the small yard.

Nations must also make decisions about resource use. Each nation must decide how to use its scarce resources to produce the goods and services its citizens want. Let's now look at how a country makes such decisions.

THREE BASIC ECONOMIC QUESTIONS

In order to decide how to use its scarce resources, each nation must answer three basic economic questions: (1) What goods and services are to be produced? (2) How should goods and services be produced? (3) For whom should goods and services be produced? A nation's plan for answering those questions is called its **economic system** or economy.

What goods and services should be produced? A society's people must decide which goods and services are most important to them. The limited economic resources are then used to produce these goods and services. A nation might decide to go all out to produce space ships and to explore other planets. But if it does this, there likely won't be enough resources left to provide better medical care or housing or many cars, TV sets, and other such things for its people. The nation must decide which kinds of goods and services it values most.

How should goods and services be produced? Economic resources can be combined in different ways to produce the same goods and services. For example, a country could hire many workers to use picks and shovels in building a road. Or it could hire a few workers to run machines such as bulldozers and power shovels. In the first case, the country is making great use of human resources and little of capital resources. In the second case, it is making great use of capital resources and little of human resources. In either case, the road will get built. But the second combination is more efficient, and the road should be finished much sooner.

For whom should goods and services be produced? This really means: How should goods and services be divided among the people? Some people believe that the goods and services a society produces should be shared equally by all the people. Most people, though, believe that people who contribute more to producing the goods and services should be able to get a larger share of them. In our economic system, the share of goods and services that you are able to have is largely determined by the amount of money you have to spend. The amount of money that you receive in wages is affected by many factors, including your abilities and how you use them.

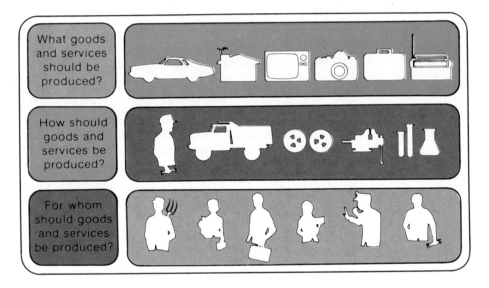

Illus. 2-1

The three basic economic questions must be answered by every society.

CAPITALISM

Because nations answer the three basic economic questions in different ways, they have different economic systems. The three major economic systems in the world today are capitalism, communism, and socialism. The main differences among these systems are in who owns the economic resources and who makes the decisions about production.

Capitalism is one name used to identify the system in the United States; it means that economic resources are mostly owned by individuals rather than by government. Since individuals own most of the resources, they are free to decide what they will produce with those resources. That is one reason why a more common name for our economy is the **free enterprise system**. Both terms mean about the same thing — private ownership and use of economic resources with limited government control. This private ownership means that in a free enterprise system, the three basic economic questions are usually answered by individuals. A look at some of the main features of free enterprise, or capitalism, will help you understand how our system differs from socialism and communism, which are discussed later in this part.

THE RIGHT OF PRIVATE ENTERPRISE

In some countries, the Milledges might not have a choice about how to use their yard; someone in government might make the decision for them. In the United States, however, the decision is theirs. If the family does have a vegetable garden, Bob might choose to set up a produce stand to sell the extra vegetables. And he can set whatever prices he wants. As long as he does not break any law, he is free to operate his enterprise in any way he chooses.

In a free enterprise system, you may start or invest in any business, or enterprise, you wish as long as you obey the law in doing so. You are free to choose what you will do to earn a living. You are free to be a bricklayer, minister, business owner, lawyer, dancer, karate instructor, or anything you wish. As a business person you are generally free to offer goods and services at times, prices, and places of your choice. The right to choose what business to enter and what to produce is the right of **private enterprise**. Because of the importance of this right, our economic system is also called private enterprise. Some people prefer the term "private enterprise system" as the best label for our economy.

Of course, there are some regulations that prevent you from doing things that would harm others. A supermarket may not sell spoiled food. Nor can you practice surgery unless you have been granted a surgical license by the medical profession. These regulations are not designed to limit freedom but to protect people from harmful practices.

18

Illus. 2-2

In a free enterprise system, you may choose to start your own business.

THE RIGHT OF PRIVATE PROPERTY

In some economic systems, the Milledge family may not be allowed to own its house or its yard. In the United States, you may own any home you can afford to buy.

The right of **private property** is the right to own, use, or dispose of things of value. You may dispose of things you own by selling them, giving them away, willing them to anyone you wish when you die, or even by throwing them away. In our country, you can own any item and do what you want with it, so long as you do not break a law. You also have the right to own, use, and sell what you invent or create.

Business people also have the right to own property. This property includes land, buildings, tools, and the goods they produce. Business people also have the right to use and dispose of their property in any lawful way, just as individuals do.

THE PROFIT MOTIVE

Bob Milledge wants to sell vegetables in the hope of making some money. If he sets up his produce business, he is free to keep what he makes and to spend it as he wishes. If he thought he would not make some money, he probably would not want to put the time and energy into the project. **Profit** is the difference between what it costs a person to run a business and the amount sales bring in. Profit is what free enterprise is all about. Business owners are entitled to profits because, when they start a business, they run the risk of losing the money they have invested. Also, extra work and extra headaches go with owning and running a business.

The desire to work for profit is often called the **profit motive**. It helps make our economic system strong. Because of the profit motive, people invest money in businesses and business leaders develop new products to satisfy consumers' needs and wants. But the profit motive is not the only reason for putting time, money, and effort into businesses. Some people take great pride in bringing out new products or improving existing ones. Many people get pleasure from knowing that the goods or services they produce make other people's lives happier. Other people thrive on the excitement of starting and running new businesses. But the profit motive is the heart of free enterprise.

THE IMPORTANCE OF COMPETITION

If Bob Milledge's neighbor sets up a vegetable stand next door and takes some of Bob's customers, Bob might decide to lower prices or add delivery service to keep his customers. In other words, he would compete.

Look at the ads you see in newspapers and magazines and on billboards and TV. All urge you to buy this or that. The rivalry among businesses to sell their goods and services to buyers is called **competition**. Competition gives you the opportunity to make choices among countless goods and services that are available. You make these choices by comparing prices, quality, appearance, and usefulness of things you buy. And if you are not satisfied with one purchase, you will take your money somewhere else the next time you buy. Competition encourages business owners to improve products, give better service, keep prices in line, and produce new things.

Illus. 2-3

Competition gives you the chance to choose from many products.

FREEDOM OF CHOICE

You have learned that free enterprise gives you the right to enter a business of your choice, to own property, to make a profit, and to compete with other businesses. You also have other rights that give you economic freedom of choice. Here are some of them:

1. You have the right to buy where and what you please, except for those things that the government declares to be harmful to you. If you do not like the goods and services of one business, you can go to another.
2. You have the right as a worker to organize with other workers. Through organization, you can strive to improve working conditions.
3. You have the right to travel when and where you please in this country and in many other countries.
4. You have the right to express your opinions in newspapers, over radio and television, and in talking with others.

OTHER ECONOMIC SYSTEMS

As you read earlier in this part, there are basically three different economic systems. If you studied each system in detail, however, you would find that it is very hard to define capitalism, socialism, and communism and explain how they work. This is true partly because none of them exists anywhere in a pure form. Under pure capitalism, for example, all enterprises would be privately owned and managed. Under pure communism, all enterprises would be owned and run by the government.

Under **socialism** today, the government may own and operate such basic enterprises as steel mills, railroads and airlines, power plants, radio and TV stations, and banks. However, the extent of government ownership and control is decided by the people. If they want more government control, they can vote for it. If they want less, they can vote against it. Some enterprises are also privately owned, but there is less chance for private business ownership than in our country.

Under **communism**, the government has tight control over the economic resources. Farms, mines, factories, stores, newspapers, railroads, telephone services — all are owned and run by the government. Government decides what goods and services are to be produced, and it decides how they are to be produced. It is true that people are free to buy whatever goods and services are offered for sale. But the prices and supply of such products as clothing, TV sets, watches, and cars are set by the government.

Most people living under communism do not have the freedom to decide how far they will go in school or what job they will have. Job opportunities and wages to be paid are mostly fixed by government. Government may even tell a person how large an apartment or house he or she may live in.

MIXED ECONOMIC SYSTEMS

An economic system usually gets its name from the way its economic resources are owned and controlled. But most modern economic systems cannot be easily and neatly placed under such labels as capitalism, socialism, or communism. As you have learned, there is no pure form of any of these systems in any country today. In general it is better to think of most nations as having mixed economic systems because they combine some of the features from each system.

In our country, there is some government regulation of business. There are also some government-operated enterprises such as post offices and schools. Our economic system is not pure capitalism, so it is often called modified or mixed capitalism. In Unit 11, you will learn about how government and business work together in our economic system.

INCREASING YOUR BUSINESS VOCABULARY

The following terms should become part of your business vocabulary. For each numbered statement, find the term that has the same meaning.

capitalism or
   free enterprise system
communism
competition
economic system

private enterprise
private property
profit
profit motive
socialism

1. The rivalry among businesses to sell their goods and services to buyers.
2. The difference between what it costs to run a business and the amount sales bring in.
3. An economic system in which government owns most of the property and has tight control over the production and distribution of goods and services.
4. An economic system in which the government owns and operates a number of basic industries and provides for some degree of private property and private enterprise.
5. The right to own, use, or dispose of things of value.
6. An economic system in which most of the economic resources are owned by individuals rather than by the government.
7. The desire to benefit financially from investing time and money in a business.
8. The right of individuals to choose what business to enter and what to produce.
9. The plan that a nation has for making decisions on what to produce, how to produce, and how to distribute goods and services.

UNDERSTANDING YOUR READING

1. What are three basic economic questions that every economic system must answer?
2. Who owns and manages most capital resources in the system of capitalism?
3. Why are business owners entitled to profits from their business ventures?
4. In addition to the profit motive, what are two other reasons that might encourage people to invest their time and money in operating their own businesses?
5. What are four important rights, in addition to those of private property and private enterprise, that give us economic freedom of choice?
6. State at least three ways in which consumers may benefit from competition among businesses.
7. Tell how the ownership of resources differs under capitalism, socialism, and communism.
8. Are people free to buy whatever is offered for sale in a communist country? Why or why not?
9. Why is it more nearly accurate to refer to our economic system as modified or mixed capitalism rather than as capitalism?

USING YOUR BUSINESS KNOWLEDGE

1. How is the problem of what goods and services to produce chiefly determined under capitalism, socialism, and communism?
2. Can you think of ways in which competition among businesses might work to the disadvantage of consumers?
3. Select two of the rights mentioned on page 20. If these rights were taken away from you and other Americans, what changes would take place in the way you live?
4. We have the freedom to own and use property as we wish, so long as we don't interfere with the rights of others. Can you think of some restrictions that are placed upon the use of property we own? Who imposes these restrictions? Why?
5. Americans enjoy many freedoms, among them the right to choose almost any kind of work we want to do for a living. Why, then, don't individuals have the freedom to open a law office, be a pharmacist, practice medicine, or be an airline pilot when they believe they are ready to do so?
6. If you could not sell or dispose of your property in any way you wish, what effect would this have on the right of private property?

SOLVING PROBLEMS IN BUSINESS

1. Norma Mendoza was shopping for fresh fruit as part of her weekly marketing. She saw a sign in the window of the Glenway Fruit Mart that said, "Apples — 3 pounds for $1.98." Then she noticed that Cline's Market across the street was selling apples for 69¢ a pound. At which store would Norma find the better bargain for apples?

2. Greg Peery was offered $395 for his used motorcycle. He decided that he could get a much better price if he made some repairs on the motorcycle. He did the work himself after buying these parts:

Item	Price
Clutch cable	$ 4.95
Front tire and tube	31.20
Drive chain	17.38
Spark plugs	2.80

Greg was then able to sell his motorcycle for $675.

(a) How much more money did Greg receive when he sold his motorcycle than he would have if he had not made the repairs?

(b) How much did Greg spend on parts?

(c) How much of a profit did Greg make on his motorcycle, after allowing for expenses for parts?

3. In Russia, consumer goods are not as plentiful as they are in this country. Most items, especially home furnishings and appliances, are very expensive when compared with costs in the United States. Assume that to earn enough money to buy a 23-inch color TV set, the average Russian worker would have to put in 960 working hours. Assume that the average American worker would have to put in 120 hours to earn enough to buy a similar TV set.

(a) The Russian worker has to work how many times as long as the American worker to earn enough money to buy the TV set?

(b) How many 8-hour days of work are required for each of the two workers to buy the TV?

(c) If the American worker receives $5.60 an hour, what would be the cost of the TV to him or her?

(d) If the American worker had to put in as many hours as the Russian worker, how much would she or he be paying for the set?

1. Interview a person in your community who owns and manages a business. Find out why that person has invested money and time in operating his or her own business. Ask the business owner if it would not be easier and less worrisome to work for someone else at a salary. If the business owner agrees, find out why he or she doesn't seek such a position.

2. Select a foreign country to study, particularly with regard to its business and economic life. You can get information from reference books, travel guides, and other printed materials. Try also to talk with someone who has lived or traveled in that country. Find out how the country compares with the United States in as many ways as you can. The topics listed below are some you may want to cover, and you can probably think of more.

   Advantages or disadvantages in natural resources
   Characteristics of the economic system
   Amount of goods and services that are available to consumers
   Ability of people to buy the things they need and want
   Economic and political freedom
   Educational opportunities

3. Countries in which the economic resources are owned and controlled by the government are sometimes referred to as "centrally planned economies."

   (a) Using library resources, find the following information:
      (1) Which two countries are identified as the largest centrally planned economies in the world today?
      (2) What is the population of each of these two countries?
      (3) What percent of the world's population lives in each?
      Prepare your information in table form to present to the class. The three headings for a simple table would be "largest centrally planned economies," "population," and "% of world population."

   (b) Give an example of a decision regarding resource use which would be made one way in these countries and a different way in the United States.

3

YOUR ROLES IN THE ECONOMY

PART OBJECTIVES

After studying this part and completing the end-of-part activities, you will be able to:
1. Identify three economic roles each person plays.
2. Explain why our economic system is called a market economy.
3. Give an example to show how dollar votes help create demand.
4. Name four things that affect prices.
5. Explain how your worker role supports your consumer role.
6. Give two examples of economic citizenship.

On her way to work, Joan Tollino stopped at a service station to get gas for her car. She also stopped at the dry cleaners to leave her jacket to be cleaned. Then she drove to her job where she fills orders for a firm that makes electronic calculators. After work, she voted on a bond issue which would give the city permission to borrow money to build a new school.

On this day, Joan Tollino played three economic roles. As a consumer, she purchased goods (gasoline) and services (dry cleaning). As a worker, she helped provide a product (calculators), for which she would receive wages. And, as a citizen, she voted on an economic issue.

YOUR ROLES AS CONSUMER, WORKER, AND CITIZEN

You and everyone you know will play many different roles in life. You may become a famous recording star or a business executive or perhaps even President of the United States. Your best friend may become a professional dancer, an electrician, a minister, or a worker for a company that produces television sets. While you and your friend may follow different careers, some of the roles you play will be the same.

The three basic roles that all people share are those of consumer, worker, and citizen. As you play these roles, you will make decisions that affect not only you but the entire economy as well. Understanding how the free enterprise system works will help you make better decisions in each of your important economic roles.

In the remainder of this part, you will have a chance to look at how the American economy works and how your roles fit into the picture.

MAKING DECISIONS IN THE MARKETPLACE

One of the most interesting things about the free enterprise system is the important role you will play as a consumer. It may seem to you that the free enterprise system is a big, unorganized system where everyone does about as he or she pleases. You may wonder how the system can work when each business makes its own decisions about what to produce and each buyer makes his or her own decisions about what to buy. But it does work, and it works well.

Most of the economic decisions are made by buyers and sellers in the marketplace. **Marketplace** is a term that means any place where buyers and sellers exchange goods, services, and money. You are operating in the marketplace when you buy food at a grocery store. When an airline orders a new jet plane or the federal government buys trucks to carry the mail, each is also working in the marketplace. No one tells you what to buy and no one tells a business to sell a certain product or service. Each makes a decision based on his or her own interests. These self-interest decisions provide all of us with a marketplace full of products of all kinds from which to choose — homes, television sets, plastic cups, cars, and baseball games, to name a few. Because the economic decisions are freely made by buyers and sellers in the marketplace, the free enterprise system is often called a **market economy**.

Your role as a consumer is so important that the market economy has been described as one in which the consumer is the boss. Your buying decisions have a great influence on our market economy, since you and other consumers like you buy over two thirds of all the goods and services produced in the country.

Illus. 3-1

In your role as a consumer, you have an important effect on the economy.

CREATING DEMAND BY DOLLAR VOTES

As a consumer, you help businesses make their decisions. You do this by buying — or not buying — certain goods and services. When you buy something, you are casting a **dollar vote** or **economic vote**. You are saying to a business, "I like your product or service, and I'm willing to pay for it." When a business sees your dollar votes and those of all other consumers, it knows the demand for a product. **Demand** means the amount of a product or service that consumers are willing and able to buy. Knowing the demand tells a business what products and services to produce and how much of each.

HOW DEMAND AND SUPPLY AFFECT PRICES

In addition to deciding what to produce, a business must set a price on the product or service. Have you ever wondered how a business decides what price to charge for a product or service? Why does a sweater cost $25 or a new car cost $5,000? Generally speaking, prices are very carefully determined after a good deal of study.

One thing that affects the price of a product is its demand. If many people want (demand) a particular product or service, its price will tend to go up. When demand is low, prices usually are low.

Another thing that affects price is the supply of a product or service. **Supply** means the amount of a product or service that businesses are willing and able to provide at a particular price. Suppliers usually will produce a product as long as it can be sold for enough to cover the costs of making it, plus provide a reasonable profit. If a supplier of jogging shoes, for example, sets a price too high, people won't buy them; so the supplier will have to lower the price in order to sell the shoes. Of course, if the price is set too low, the supplier will lose money and soon go out of business. All this means that the supplier must produce a good product in an efficient way. This helps cause prices to be set at reasonable levels so that you and other consumers will be willing and able to buy the products.

Illus. 3-2

One factor that determines the price of a product is the available supply.

The prices of some things tend to stay high because the materials from which they are made are limited by nature. For example, diamonds have been found in only a few countries of the world. Therefore, the price of diamonds is very high. In recent years the people of the United States have also come to understand how scarce the world's supply of oil is. As the supply of oil continues to be used up, the price will probably rise.

COMPETITION'S EFFECT ON PRICES

Earlier it was said that suppliers set the prices to cover the costs of production and earn some profit. But what is to prevent a seller from charging an unreasonably high amount in order to get larger profits? The answer is that competition keeps a supplier from charging extremely high prices. You will remember from Part 2 that competition is one of the main features of free enterprise. If one store offers stereo tapes for $15 but another offers them for less, you would probably say to the merchant with the higher price, "Forget it. I can buy that same tape at a store down the street for $8.95." If the owners of the store keep the price at $15, they will soon go out of business because not many people will buy tapes from them. Competition, then, aids the consumer by helping keep prices and profits at reasonable levels.

YOUR WORKER ROLE SUPPORTS YOUR CONSUMER ROLE

Now that you have considered some of the ways your decisions as a consumer help make the free enterprise system work, it would be good to see how your role as a worker fits into the picture. No matter what price is set on products and services in the marketplace, you cannot enjoy them unless you have the money to buy them. Most people earn their money by working. Of course, people work for many reasons. But probably the main reason you will work is to get money to buy things you need and want. While your parents may be supplying most of your needs and wants now, before long you will begin thinking about what you will do for a living.

When you begin your worker role, you will join over 100 million other workers in the United States. These workers produce the goods and services that consumers demand. One of the reasons this country has progressed so far in such a short time is that it has had a varied and skilled work force.

In Part 2, you learned that in this country you are free to choose any occupation you wish. Deciding what kind of work you will do is one of the most important economic decisions you will have to make. Usually your work determines your level of income, and income usually determines how many wants and needs you can satisfy. Your worker role and your consumer role, as you can see, work together.

Illus. 3-3

Workers earn money to satisfy their consumer needs and wants.

YOUR ROLE AS A CITIZEN

There are some needs and wants that you will not be able to obtain for yourself. Some of them you will gain through your role as an economic citizen. For example, you probably will not earn enough money to have your own fire department to protect your home. Or, you probably will not make enough to build your own highways on which to drive your car. In addition to these, there are many other things, such as schools, courts, and police protection, that neither individuals nor businesses can usually provide. In your role as an economic citizen you will join with others and pay taxes so that government can provide these goods and services.

You will also help decide which goods and services the government will furnish. When Joan Tollino voted for the bond issue which would give her city permission to borrow money to build a new school, she helped the city decide which of the many needed goods and services would be provided. In voting on economic issues as Joan did, you will be fulfilling a part of your economic citizenship role.

THE IMPORTANCE OF YOUR ECONOMIC DECISIONS

The decisions you make in your three economic roles are important to you and the way you will live. In your consumer role, for example, if you are wise in the way you cast your dollar votes, you will be able to enjoy more and better quality goods and services. To prepare for your worker role, you need to study a variety of jobs so that you can choose a career that will suit your needs and interests. If you choose the right career, you will probably be a more productive worker, which will benefit both you and the economy. And in your economic citizenship role, you should remember that the government cannot supply all that the people want. It, too, must make choices as to which goods and services it can afford to provide. By voting you will be helping to make some of those decisions.

INCREASING YOUR BUSINESS VOCABULARY

The following terms should become part of your business vocabulary. For each numbered statement, find the term that has the same meaning.

demand   *marketplace*
dollar or economic vote   *supply*
market economy

1. Expressing approval of a product by buying it.
2. The amount of a product or service that consumers are willing and able to buy.
3. The amount of a product or service that businesses are willing and able to provide at a particular price.
4. Any place where buyers and sellers exchange goods, services, and money.
5. A term used to describe the freedom of buyers and sellers to make economic decisions in our free enterprise system.

UNDERSTANDING YOUR READING

1. You learned in this part that most people play the same three economic roles in life. What are the roles?
2. Give an example of the way dollar votes help create demand.
3. Give an example of the way demand can affect prices.
4. Suppliers usually set their prices to cover what two things?
5. If a business has an oversupply of a product, would it be likely to raise or lower the price of the product?
6. Would prices of a product made with scarce natural resources tend to be high or low?
7. Give an example to show how competition affects prices.
8. In what way might your selection of a career affect your future standard of living?
9. Give two examples of activities you perform in your economic citizenship role.

USING YOUR BUSINESS KNOWLEDGE

1. If you buy a set of encyclopedias in your own home from a salesperson who calls, are you trading in the marketplace? Explain.
2. When the demand for small cars increases, what might the suppliers of large cars do to sell cars?
3. Give two examples of products whose prices are usually high because they are made from scarce natural resources.
4. Someone has described the free enterprise system as one in which the "consumer is sovereign." Explain the term.
5. Explain why choosing a career is one of the most important economic decisions a person makes.

SOLVING PROBLEMS IN BUSINESS

1. Margo Tate, owner of Tate's Sport Shop, bought ten dozen pairs of ice skates at $25 per pair to sell during the Christmas season.
   (a) How many pairs of ice skates did Margo buy?
   (b) How much did it cost to buy all of the skates?
2. In December, Margo Tate still had two thirds of her supply of skates left (see problem 1).
   (a) How many pairs of skates were still unsold?
   (b) If she sold the remaining skates for $30 per pair, how much would Margo receive in sales?
3. The table on the next page shows how consumers recently spent each $100 they had after taxes and savings:

Food, beverages	$ 20.70
Foreign travel	.40
Religion, welfare activities	1.30
Personal care	1.40
Tobacco	1.50
Private education, research	1.50
Housing	15.30
Household operation	14.60
Transportation	13.70
Medical care	9.70
Clothing, including care	8.20
Recreation	6.60
Personal business	5.10
	$100.00

(a) For what 5 items was the most money spent?
(b) What percent of each $100 is used for these 5 items combined?

4. Below is a table showing the production of gold during a recent year in the United States and in the three states where most of the gold is produced.

Total U.S. Production	1 million ounces
Nevada	238,000 ounces
South Dakota	286,000 ounces
Utah	235,000 ounces

(a) What was the total ounces of gold produced in the three states?
(b) What was the total amount of gold produced elsewhere in the United States during that year?
(c) If the price at that time was $228 per ounce, what was the value of the gold produced in South Dakota?
(d) A few years later the world demand for gold had pushed the price per ounce to $800. At that price, what was the value of the gold produced in South Dakota during the first year?

5. Below is a table showing information about the voting activity of young people in two recent national elections. Study the data and answer the questions which follow.

Year	No. of persons 18–20 years old	No. of persons reporting they voted
1976	12,100,000	4,600,000
1978	12,200,000	2,400,000

(a) How many young people did not vote in 1976?

(b) In what year was the larger number of 18- to 20-year-olds eligible to vote?

(c) What percent of eligible voters reported that they voted in 1976 and in 1978? (Round to nearest whole percent.)

EXPANDING YOUR UNDERSTANDING OF BUSINESS

1. If all stores in your area charged the same price for an electric hair dryer, there would be no competition among the stores on the basis of price. And if all the hair dryers were exactly the same, the customer would have no reason to choose one hair dryer over another. If these conditions were true, what other forms of competition could stores use in order to get customers to buy hair dryers from them?

2. Interview the manager of a local supermarket. Ask the manager how prices are determined in the store. Find out whether there have been any items recently for which there was a surge of demand. If so, did the store have enough of the item to supply the demand? Did the price change? Ask the manager to explain also how such things as spoilage, bad checks, and theft affect prices in the store.

3. Interview five seniors in your school who are or soon will be 18 years old. Find out how they feel about voting. Suggested questions: What is your age? If you are 18, have you registered to vote? Why or why not? Do you plan to register before the next election? Do you think 18-year-olds should vote? Why or why not? Report your findings to the class.

4. Look through your local newspaper and clip articles dealing with economic citizenship. Try to find at least one article on taxes and one dealing with voting on an economic issue. Write a brief statement of your views on each article and justify your position.

4

MAKING ECONOMIC PROGRESS

PART OBJECTIVES

After studying this part and completing the end-of-part activities, you will be able to:

1. Explain how GNP is used as a measure of economic growth.
2. Tell the difference between per capita output and output per worker-hour.
3. Tell how a person's life-style is determined.
4. List three economic problems which our country faces.

Shawn O'Brien's parents can tell how much taller Shawn has grown each year. They can do so by looking at a tape measure they attached to the wall of his room when he was one year old. On each birthday, Shawn stands next to the tape and his father places a mark to show his new height. From this record, the O'Briens can tell many things about their son's growth. They can compare his height from one birthday to another. They can point to years in which he grew a lot and others in which his growth was slower. In addition, they can figure his total growth and his average annual growth.

The O'Briens could also use other methods of checking Shawn's growth. They can, of course, see that he has grown taller and stronger. But they could also measure his growth by recording his weight or the size of his clothes.

CHECKING THE GROWTH
OF THE ECONOMY

Just as the O'Briens could use different ways to measure Shawn's growth, so can we use different methods to check on the growth of the economy. For example, a high rate of employment and a low rate of business failures would indicate that our economy is doing well. However, the most important ways by which we can measure how well we are doing relate simply to how much we produce to help satisfy the needs and wants of our people. Today more than 100 million Americans work in thousands of different jobs and produce thousands of different goods and services. Hamburgers, snowmobiles, garbage collection, nail polish, hair styling, fire engines, carry-out chicken dinners, concerts — you could name many more. The total of all the goods and services that Americans produce is the output or production of our nation. We have only about 7 percent of the world's land and about 5.4 percent of the world's population, but our output accounts for about 25 percent of all goods and services produced in the world.

MEASURING NATIONAL OUTPUT

One way to find out how well our economy is doing is to compare output from year to year. The federal government collects information from producers and estimates our national output. The most widely used estimate is the **gross national product** or **GNP**. The GNP is the total value of all goods and services produced in our country during a year.

GNP includes what consumers spend for food, clothing, and housing. It includes what businesses spend for buildings, equipment, and supplies. It also includes what government agencies spend to pay employees and buy supplies. If the GNP increases from year to year, this is a good sign that our economy is growing. Even though we have had some bad years, our economy has enjoyed a steady climb over its history.

There is one big difficulty in comparing a country's GNP from year to year. Prices of what we produce do not stay the same from year to year. Prices go up and down — mainly up. So in order to make comparisons that are fair and accurate, we need to take the current prices and adjust them each year so that they are equal in value over a period of years. Let's look at a very easy example.

Suppose the tiny make-believe country of Posterland produced only colorful wall posters of recording stars, as shown in the table below.

YEAR	NO. OF POSTERS PRODUCED	CURRENT PRICE PER POSTER	GNP AT CURRENT PRICES	PRICES ADJUSTED TO 1960	GNP AT CONSTANT PRICE
1960	1,000	$ .50	$ 500	$.50	$500
1970	1,000	$1.00	$1,000	$.50	$500
1980	1,000	$1.50	$1,500	$.50	$500

Note that under current prices, the GNP for 1980 is reported at $1,500. On this basis you could say that the GNP (or total output) increased three times since 1960. This would be wrong. Actually, Posterland made no progress in producing wall posters. In each of the years, 1,000 posters were produced. If prices had remained the same, the dollar value would have been $500 each year.

Now let's look at a different example for Posterland.

YEAR	NO. OF POSTERS PRODUCED	CURRENT PRICE PER POSTER	GNP AT CURRENT PRICES	PRICES ADJUSTED TO 1960	GNP AT CONSTANT PRICE
1960	1,000	$ .50	$ 500	$.50	$ 500
1970	1,500	$1.00	$1,500	$.50	$ 750
1980	3,000	$1.50	$4,500	$.50	$1,500

A look at the figures above shows that in 1980 Posterland produced three times as many posters as in 1960. But if the current prices are compared, the GNP increase in 1980 was nine times that of 1960 ($4,500 ÷ $500 = 9). However, in "constant" prices, the GNP in 1980 was three times that of 1960 — exactly the same as the actual increase in the total number of posters produced.

MEASURING OUTPUT
PER PERSON

An even better way than GNP to measure economic growth is to find out what the **per capita** (or per person) **output** is. For example, suppose that there is no change in GNP this year over last. But suppose that the population increases. You can see that the same output would have to be divided among more people. So each person would produce and have, on the average, less than before.

The per capita output can easily be found by dividing the GNP by the total population. An increase in per capita output usually means that our economy is growing. A decrease may mean that our economy is having troubles.

Illus. 4-1

Output per person can be used to measure economic growth.

MEASURING OUTPUT
PER HOUR

Another important measure of how our economy is growing is the **output per worker-hour** or **productivity**. This is the amount of goods that one worker, on the average, can produce in one hour. In a recent ten-year period, our output per worker-hour increased about 20 percent. And as workers produce more goods and services per hour, our economic studies show that workers earn more per hour. For example, in the same ten-year period just mentioned, wages more than doubled — which is about five times the increase in productivity.

Our ability to produce more and more has also made it possible to reduce the number of hours in a work week. In the early 1890's, an average worker put in about 60 hours a week. Today the average work week is a little less than 40 hours. But even though we work fewer hours and have more leisure time, we produce more and earn more than our labor force ever has before. We can produce more in less time because we use modern equipment and efficient work methods, and we have many highly skilled workers.

IMPROVING OUR WAY OF LIVING

A different and more personal way than measuring output to find out if we are making economic progress is to check on how we live. Each of us has a **life-style** or way of living. In part, a life-style is measured by the amount, quality, and variety of goods and services you have. Life-style also includes the amount of leisure time you have. Certainly most of us want to have as many as possible of the goods and services that can make living more comfortable and pleasant. And since there is growth in our output of goods and services, this can mean that more and more of us will enjoy a higher life-style in the future. But in order to share in our increasing output, people need money to buy the available goods and services. You can see, therefore, that your life-style also depends a great deal on how much you earn and how smart you are in spending what you earn.

Your life-style is also greatly influenced by your personal values, likes, and dislikes. One person may thoroughly enjoy going to a ballet but not to a professional football game. Another person may feel just the opposite. A person may prefer to have an inexpensive apartment but an expensive car — or just the reverse. We all have different ways to spend our leisure time.

These kinds of things are difficult to count in numbers or measure in dollars. Yet they are very important.

BUILDING THE ECONOMIC FUTURE

What lies ahead for our economy? No one knows for sure. Robots doing most of the routine work in factories? Housekeeping done entirely by machines? Farming under the ocean? Space colonies on the moon? Two-way pocket telephones and three-dimensional TV? Germproof, tornadoproof, earthquakeproof, soundproof, fireproof, burglarproof houses? These are some of the things scientists have predicted for the year 2000.

We've come a long way under our private enterprise system. We know it works well. We also know it can be made to work even better. In our country, there are still some people who do not have good food, decent housing, and proper health care. All of us are being harmed by what is happening to our environment. Air and water are being polluted by gases, smoke, and waste coming from industry and from the products we buy and use. This is one problem that we must solve. Government now is

Illus. 4-2

One danger to our environment is the pollution caused by oil spills.

responding to the people's demand for action, and businesses are cooperating so that we can keep our environment healthy for future Americans.

Another challenge is that of providing proper housing for all our people, especially in large cities. Already much slum housing is being remodeled or torn down and rebuilt. Efforts are also being made to solve traffic problems in large cities, and new shopping and cultural centers are being built.

As Americans, we realize that we have some shortcomings. And as a nation, we are working to eliminate economic hardship for our people. Much needs to be done to control disease and reduce human suffering. There are great responsibilities to find new sources of energy and to conserve all our natural resources. Ideas are needed on how to continue to improve our government and on how to live in peace with everyone. Much remains to be done in education, mass transportation, and human relations.

To provide for a better life for everyone, each of us has the responsibility of gaining a basic understanding of how our economic system works, of having an awareness of our problems, and of wanting to help solve our problems.

INCREASING YOUR BUSINESS VOCABULARY

The following terms should become part of your business vocabulary. For each numbered statement, find the term that has the same meaning.

gross national product or GNP   *output per worker-hour or*
life-style   *productivity*
                                                                 per capita output

1. The figure that results from dividing the GNP of a country by the population of that country.
2. A person's way of living, judged in part by the goods and services used and by what the person likes to do for self-improvement, recreation, and entertainment.
3. The total value of all goods and services produced in a country during a year.
4. The amount of goods that one worker, on the average, can produce in one hour.

UNDERSTANDING YOUR READING

1. How does the United States compare with the rest of the world in land size, population, and output of goods and services?
2. "One way of finding out how well our economy is doing is to compare output from year to year." What does this statement mean? Do you agree with it?
3. GNP includes the spending of what three groups?
4. If prices of goods and services remain exactly the same over a long period of time, would it be fair and accurate to compare a country's GNP from year to year at current prices?
5. What is the difference between "current prices" and "adjusted prices" of goods and services?
6. What is the difference between per capita output and output per worker-hour?
7. If the GNP remains the same from one year to another but the population increases by about 10 percent, has there been economic growth? Explain.
8. How has increased productivity affected the well-being of workers?
9. Name three things which have contributed to our high output.
10. Life-style is partly measured by the quality and quantity of the goods and services a person enjoys. What other factors determine a person's life-style?
11. Is there room for improvement in our economic system? What are some economic problems that need solving?

USING YOUR BUSINESS KNOWLEDGE

1. The GNP of a small island in the Caribbean increased 10 percent in one year — from $100,000 to $110,000. Does this mean that this little economic unit had a 10 percent increase in the amount of goods and services produced?
2. Make a list of some things that you and your family have contributed to the GNP during the past few months.
3. The GNP of Country A is $200 million. The GNP of Country B is $400 million. Does this mean that the per capita output of Country B is about twice that of Country A? Explain.
4. In a recent year the GNP of the United States was over $2 trillion in current dollars. Ten years before, it was less than $1 trillion. In the next ten years the GNP is expected to reach the $2.5 trillion mark. What differences does it make to you and to

other people in your community whether the GNP is increasing or decreasing?

5. Various products, services, and conditions contribute to your life-style. List at least ten things that you consider important to reach and maintain the life-style you want.

6. Explain how two families of the same size and the same incomes might have different life-styles.

7. List three things that you and your classmates can do to prevent or reduce pollution at your school.

SOLVING PROBLEMS IN BUSINESS

1. The 1980 production schedule of tiny Posterland listed on page 38 shows its GNP at current prices of $4,500 and at constant 1960 prices of $1,500. If Posterland's population in 1980 was 500, what was its per capita output?
   (a) at current prices?
   (b) at constant prices?

2. Some very simple machines such as the wheelbarrow and the hand truck have increased productivity or output per worker-hour. Frank Mellinger, who works in a warehouse, can move one 60-pound box at a time by hand. Using a hand truck, he can move four 60-pound boxes at once in the same length of time.
   (a) Frank can move 15 boxes in one hour without using a hand truck. What is his productivity in boxes?
   (b) If he uses a hand truck, what is Frank's productivity?
   (c) How many workers without hand trucks would it take to do the work Frank does with a hand truck?

3. There is a small island in the Caribbean that produces shell jewelry to sell to tourists from cruise ships. The island's production record is shown below:

Year	No. of items produced	Current price per item
1970	1,000	$ .25
1975	2,000	$ .50
1980	4,000	$1.00

   (a) What is the island's GNP at current prices for each year?
   (b) What is the amount of increase in number of items produced in 1975 over 1970?

(c) What is the rate of increase in number of items produced in 1980 over 1975?

(d) If the island expects to maintain the same rate of increase for 1985, how many shell items will it produce?

EXPANDING YOUR UNDERSTANDING OF BUSINESS

1. The GNP does not include the services of homemakers and other things we do without pay for ourselves and others. Aren't these services as important as the ones we pay for? Why do you think that they are not included in the gross national product?

2. Look through some recent newspapers and news magazines for items which mention the gross national product. Select two or three clippings and mount them on a piece of paper. What do these articles tell you about the GNP?

3. In determining our gross national product, only *final* goods and services are included. This avoids having some items counted more than once. For example, a mining company sells iron ore to a company that makes steel. The steel company sells the steel to an automobile manufacturer who produces finished cars. The iron ore is not counted at each step. Its value is included only once: in the price paid for the final product, the car.

   Below is a list of things produced in our economy. Tell whether you think each item should be counted as part of our GNP. If you do not think it should be counted, tell why.

   (a) An electric toaster bought as a gift for newlyweds.
   (b) Telephone service installed in your home.
   (c) Telephone service installed in a government office.
   (d) Tires sold to a company to install on motorcycles it produces.
   (e) Grooming services for a poodle.
   (f) Paper sold to the publisher of this book.
   (g) Flowers sold to a florist.
   (h) Flowers sold by a florist.
   (i) A computer paid for by a city government.
   (j) Automobile for your family's use.
   (k) Automobile for the state highway patrol's use.
   (l) Peaches sold to a cannery.

4. Using the telephone directory and other sources of information, find out whether any agency in your area recycles materials. Prepare a brief report showing what materials are recycled, how the recycling is done, and for what the recycled materials are

used. Include in your report a statement of the benefits you think come from recycling.

5. The Environmental Protection Agency was established by the federal government to help in cleaning up and maintaining the environment. Write a brief report on what the EPA does to carry out this responsibility. Your school library probably has government publications and other resources to help you find the information.

UNIT 2

The Economic Role Of Business

UNIT OBJECTIVES

After studying the parts in this unit, you will be able to:

1. Describe the four basic types of businesses.

2. Tell the main features of the various forms of business ownership.

3. Explain the effect of power-driven machinery and automated equipment on our capacity to produce goods and services.

4. Give examples to illustrate how the interdependence of nations makes world trade necessary.

47

WHAT BUSINESSES DO

PART OBJECTIVES

After studying this part and completing the end-of-part activities, you will be able to:

1. Name the four basic kinds of businesses.
2. Explain how marketing activities add value to products.
3. Describe six different kinds of activities that are performed by most businesses.
4. Explain the difference between gross profit and net profit.
5. Give the average percent of profit made by manufacturers.
6. Describe two benefits that come to a community as a result of new or expanded business activity.

If you are like most young people, you probably like to wear cotton T-shirts. Did you ever think about how many businesses are involved in getting a T-shirt to you? First, the cotton is planted and harvested; then it is made into cloth from which the T-shirt is made. The shirt has to be marked for size, boxed, and then stored until it is sold to the store from which you buy it. Several businesses are involved in this process. These businesses are different in many ways, but all are alike in one way — they are helping put a product that you want on the market. There are over 14 million business firms in the United States. While there are some differences among them, they all supply or help to supply goods and services to satisfy your wants and needs. Basically, there are four different kinds of businesses: extractors, manufacturers, marketers, and service businesses.

EXTRACTING PRODUCTS
FROM NATURE

Businesses that grow products or take raw materials from nature are called **extractors**. The farmer who grew and sold the cotton for your T-shirt is one. Silver and coal miners are also important extractors. So are those who dig copper in Montana, pump oil in Texas, and run lumber camps in Washington. Sometimes the extractor's products are ready to be sold just as they come from the earth or the sea, like the crabs sold on Fisherman's Wharf in San Francisco. But most food products and raw materials need some processing or change in form before the consumer can use them.

MANUFACTURING NEW PRODUCTS

The **manufacturer** takes the extractor's products or raw materials and changes them into a form that consumers can use. The manufacturer might make a product, such as a toaster, or process a product, such as packaging and freezing vegetables. Some manufacturers are only a part of the total activity of producing goods from the extractor's products. Your T-shirt is an example. The process might be something like this: A textile mill in North Carolina takes cotton grown on an Alabama farm, spins

Illus. 5-1

Manufacturers produce goods that are ready for consumers to use.

it into yarn, and makes the yarn into cloth. Another plant in New England takes the cloth and dyes or prints it. A clothing factory in New York buys the cloth and makes it into shirts. Together, extractors and manufacturers change the form of resources from their natural states into products for consumers.

MOVING GOODS FROM PRODUCERS TO CONSUMERS

Our advanced technology and our skilled labor force enable producers to make thousands of different products at a reasonable cost. But if these products are not available when and where consumers want to buy them, they are of no use to consumers.

If all the goods you use had to be bought directly from their producers, it would be very hard and very expensive for you to buy things. You might have to travel to South America to buy a banana. What an expensive banana that would be!

Bridging the gap between producers and consumers can be very complicated. The services of many businesses are often needed before goods actually reach consumers. All the activities that are involved in moving goods from producers to consumers are performed by marketers; the activities themselves are called **marketing** or **distribution**.

Marketing includes more than transporting and selling products. Marketers design store windows to attract your attention and arrange displays in supermarkets to feature certain new products. They test new products to see whether consumers will like them and buy them. They advertise to let the consumer know that a product is available and to persuade him or her to buy it. They package goods to protect the products and to present them in attractive and convenient sizes. And they store goods until they are needed by other marketers or consumers. All these marketing activities add value to products by bringing them where the consumer is, at the time they are wanted, in the assortment wanted, and at prices the consumer is willing to pay.

RAPID GROWTH IN SERVICE BUSINESSES

Firms that do things for you instead of making or marketing products are called **service businesses**. These businesses are perhaps the fastest growing part of our business world. In a recent 10-year period, the number of people employed in service industries increased over 40 percent. Before the end of the 80's, it is expected that about 20 million people will be working in businesses that provide service to others.

As people come to have more leisure time and more money to spend, they want more and more businesses to do things for them. Also, as more women enter the labor force, they tend to pay someone to perform many services that they once did for themselves and their families. This, too, has increased the size of the service industry.

Illus. 5-2

Many consumers enjoy recreation activities provided by service businesses.

Some service businesses serve individual consumers. Some serve other businesses. And some serve both individual consumers and other businesses. Today you can find a service business to move you from Maine to Oklahoma, cut your hair, wash your car, figure your income tax, board your dog, give you guitar lessons, clean your clothes, rent you a pair of skis, pull a tooth, take you on a tour, and almost any other thing you can think of.

ACTIVITIES MOST BUSINESSES PERFORM

There are many different types and sizes of businesses. A business may be as small as a newspaper stand on a neighborhood corner, or as large and complex as an oil company which has wells, refineries, and service stations in many different countries. Although individual businesses may be very different in the way they operate, most of them perform basically the same kinds of activities. Some of these important activities are: (1) buying goods and services; (2) selling goods and services; (3) storing goods; (4) handling money and keeping records; (5) extending credit to customers; (6) providing services to customers; and (7) packaging and dividing goods.

1. Businesses buy goods and services both for resale and for their own use. The owner of a men's clothing store, for instance, must buy slacks, jackets, suits, coats, and other items to sell. The store owner also needs sales tickets, a cash register, display cases, and other supplies. He or she needs services offered by other businesses, such as advertising space in a newspaper or a window cleaner to wash the display windows.

2. Businesses must sell goods and services if they expect to stay in operation. Some businesses — grocery stores, hardware stores, jewelry stores, and others — sell goods. Other businesses — telephone companies, airlines, hospitals, law firms, and so on — sell services.

3. Goods must be stored until they are sold or until the customer wants them delivered. For example, toys are produced the year round, but most of them are stored until merchants order for Christmas. Manufacturers need storage yards and warehouses to store raw materials, supplies, and finished products.

4. All businesses must handle money and keep records. Business owners need to know how much they have sold, how much of what they sold was returned by customers, and how much they owe to others. They need to know the amount they are spending for building repairs, rent, salaries, and other expenses. Their records show whether their business is making or losing money and give them information they need for government reports.

5. Most businesses extend credit to their customers. Many businesses would not be able to operate if manufacturers and other businesses did not allow them to buy on credit. And merchants find that most customers today expect credit at stores where they shop.

6. Almost all businesses give certain services with the goods they sell to customers. Often a customer will buy from the business that offers the most service. A store may provide parking space, lounges, a coffee shop, telephones, and delivery service.

7. Many businesses package and divide goods to meet customer needs. For example, marketers design packages to protect goods and make them more attractive. Marketers also package goods to protect them while they are being delivered or to make them attractive as gifts. Businesses that sell goods may buy them in large quantities and divide them into small quantities for resale to customers. A supermarket might buy tomatoes by the bushel and package them into trays of three tomatoes each, which is a convenient size for the customer.

REWARDING BUSINESS OWNERS WITH PROFITS

As you learned in Unit 1, business owners are entitled to profits because of the risks they take in investing their money and because of the extra work and responsibilities that go with ownership and management. But most businesses do not make the huge profits that some people suppose. The average profit on sales for manufacturing businesses is about 5 percent a year. As you know, competition with other businesses helps keep prices and profits down to reasonable figures. Then, too, some people don't understand the difference between gross and net profit. **Gross profit** or **margin** is the difference between the selling price and the cost price of an article. **Net profit** is what is left after all expenses have been paid. Suppose Jan Irwin, the owner of a camera shop, sells a camera for $20. She bought the camera for $12, so she has a gross profit of $8. But out of this $8 she must pay for rent, supplies, advertising, taxes, and many other expenses. Her records show that all expenses related to the sale of the camera amount to $7. She has therefore made a net profit of $1 on the camera — or a net profit of 5 percent ($1 ÷ $20) on the selling price.

Industry	Profits as Percent of Sales
All manufacturing corporations	5.4%
Selected industries	
Aircraft, guided missiles and parts	4.9
Drugs and medicines	12.5
Electrical and electronic equipment	5.7
Food and kindred products	3.2
Iron and steel	3.3
Motor vehicles and equipment	4.9
Paper and allied products	5.3
Petroleum and coal products	7.1
Printing and publishing	6.1
Textile mill products	3.1

Illus. 5-3

Most businesses do not make the huge profits sometimes supposed. This chart shows profits, after taxes, of large corporations in various industries in a recent year.

BUSINESSES HELPING COMMUNITIES

Almost everyone is pleased when a new business opens in a community. A new business benefits the community in many ways. Perhaps the most important benefit is that a new business creates jobs. This means that the people who work directly for it have incomes to support themselves and their families. As they spend their incomes for goods and services, there is a multiplier effect.

Let's see how this multiplier effect works. The money that workers spend is in turn spent by those who receive it. This creates more jobs and income in the community. For example, part of each worker's income is spent for food. The food store manager pays out part of this money for stock. The manager also pays part of it to employees, who in turn spend their money somewhere else for goods and services. If new people come to the community to work, more houses will probably be needed. This means that local builders will hire more workers and buy more materials. As each dollar is spent, each business is likely to buy more goods and hire more people to meet its customers' demands. So when a new job is created in a community, each dollar paid to workers is said to multiply itself.

THE MULTIPLIER EFFECT—
HOW BUSINESS CREATES JOBS AND INCOME

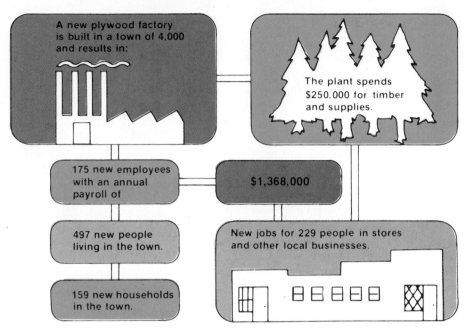

A new plywood factory is built in a town of 4,000 and results in:

The plant spends $250,000 for timber and supplies.

175 new employees with an annual payroll of

$1,368,000

497 new people living in the town.

New jobs for 229 people in stores and other local businesses.

159 new households in the town.

Illus. 5-4

A new business can benefit a whole community. Here is how the multiplier effect works.

Another benefit from a new or expanded business is that it pays taxes to the community. This means that the community has more money to build new schools, repair its streets, provide better police and fire protection, and improve other services such as parks.

When a new business comes to a community, it buys such things as electricity, office furniture and supplies, equipment, and tools. Some of these things will be bought from firms in other towns, but much will be bought locally. This gives income to local businesses and, in turn, paychecks to their employees.

Businesses also tend to attract other businesses. When one business settles in a community, other businesses often come to supply it. For example, small businesses may spring up to supply a large factory with such things as small parts, office supplies, cleaning services, and advertising services. Each of these smaller firms hires people and buys goods and services. So more jobs and more income are created in the community.

SOCIAL RESPONSIBILITIES
OF BUSINESSES

Business owners and managers today must do more than just provide a worthwhile product or service at a reasonable price in order to make a profit and stay in business. They must hire workers without discrimination; they must pay good wages and provide other benefits, such as insurance and holidays. They must provide a safe working environment; and they must show concern for the general welfare of their workers. These are economic benefits that workers in any community expect.

In addition, businesses today assume social responsibilities to the community. Many firms participate in training programs for unskilled workers. The firms provide advice and managerial assistance to members of minority groups in setting up and operating their own businesses. They cooperate with schools in many ways — by providing speakers, by employing students in part-time jobs, and by sponsoring such programs as Junior Achievement. Many business firms contribute generously to education, to charities, and to civic and cultural projects. In fact,

Illus. 5-5

Forestry engineers are visiting this school to teach students how to plant and care for trees.

leaders from business are often also the leaders of these projects.

The social responsibility of business is also seen in the efforts of many firms to avoid polluting the air, the water, or the natural beauty of the countryside. Helping to keep a clean environment is an important part of business planning today. Before they allow a new business to locate in their area, most communities require the firm to show that its operation will not cause pollution. There are still many problems to be worked out to improve the environment and keep it clean, but progress is being made by cooperation between businesses and the communities in which they are located.

Adding the economic and social benefits together, you can see why most communities welcome new businesses.

INCREASING YOUR BUSINESS VOCABULARY

The following terms should become part of your business vocabulary. For each numbered statement, find the term that has the same meaning.

extractor   *marketing or distribution*
gross profit or margin   *net profit*
manufacturer   *service business*

1. The activities that are involved in moving goods from producers to consumers.
2. The difference between the selling price and the cost price of an article.
3. A business that takes an extractor's products or raw materials and changes them into a form that consumers can use.
4. The amount left over after expenses are deducted from the gross profit.
5. A business that grows products or takes raw materials from nature.
6. A business that does things for you instead of making or marketing products.

1. What are the four basic types of businesses?
2. What is meant by the statement that some extractors' products are ready to be sold to the consumer in their natural state?
3. How does a manufacturer differ from an extractor?
4. Name several marketing activities other than transporting and selling goods.
5. How does marketing add value to a product?
6. Why are service businesses among the fastest growing of the basic types of businesses?
7. What similar activities are performed by most businesses? Give at least six.
8. What is the average percent of profit made by manufacturers?
9. What is the difference between gross profit and net profit?
10. How does the multiplier effect of new businesses result in more jobs and income in the community?
11. In what ways other than economic do businesses contribute to the community?

1. List four marketing activities that might be involved in getting a bar of soap from the manufacturer to the supermarket.
2. If two firms make the same percentage of profit on sales, will they also make the same amount of dollar profit from their business operations?
3. Daniel Mathews is a dairy farmer. Explain under what conditions he might be considered as (a) an extractor only; (b) an extractor and a marketer; (c) an extractor and a manufacturer (or processor); and (d) an extractor, manufacturer, and marketer.
4. If a business has a large gross profit, is it sure to have a net profit? Explain your answer.
5. Lani Kokua owns and operates the Islands Gift Shop, where she sells arrangements of fresh flowers and shell jewelry. Give two examples of each of the following:
   (a) goods which she would buy for resale
   (b) goods she would buy for use in her store
   (c) services she might offer to her customers
   (d) services she might buy from other businesses
6. The Chamber of Commerce and the Economic Development Council of Metro City have persuaded the Plastics Processing Company to open a plant in the city's industrial park. The company expects to employ 250 people there. Name at least five ways in which the city would probably benefit from the new business.

1. The Julio Telini Company is considering building a cannery in Santa Rosa. The company's accountants estimate the monthly income and expenses for the new plant to be:

Income from sales	$120,000
Expenses:	
Salaries...	$ 60,000
Raw materials purchased	$ 36,000
Rent on equipment..............................	$ 4,000
Miscellaneous expenses	$ 3,000
Taxes..	$ 4,800

(a) What is the total amount of the cannery's estimated monthly expenses, including taxes?

(b) What will be the cannery's net profit if the estimates are accurate? (Calculate net profit by subtracting the total estimated expenses and taxes from estimated income.)

2. Joe Raintree, a sophomore at Butte Valley High School, decides to go into the lawn business to earn money. He buys the following equipment for this personal business venture:

1 power lawn mower	$120.00
1 rake	8.00
1 hoe	7.00
1 pair of electric trimming shears	40.00
1 hand edger	10.00
1 light wheelbarrow	20.00
1 pair of work gloves	5.00

(a) How much does Joe have invested in equipment?

(b) If he mows lawns for an average price of $7 each, how many does he have to mow to pay for his equipment, assuming that he has no other expenses?

3. The fish catch and the value of the catch along the Atlantic coast for a recent year are shown below:

Area	Catch (million pounds)	Value (million dollars)
New England states	581	$203
Mid-Atlantic states	214	70
Chesapeake Bay states	669	86
South Atlantic states	345	72

(a) What was the total weight of the catch for the South Atlantic states, expressed in full (including the zeros)?

(b) What was the dollar value of the catch from the area where the catch was largest, expressed in full?

(c) How many pounds of fish were caught along the entire Atlantic coast?

4. The cost price and the percent of gross profit (based on cost price) for a number of items are given below:

	Cost Price	Percent of Gross Profit (based on cost)
Radio	$ 40	30%
Record album	6	25
Motorcycle	500	20
Watch	27	33⅓
Television set	250	23

(a) What is the amount of gross profit on each item?
(b) What is the selling price of each item?

5. Andrew Meekins, Edward Grover, and Grace Carney grow peanuts on their farms. They sell all they grow to the Radnor Hog Farm. The peanut-fed hogs are then sold to a meat processor to be made into a special kind of ham. The farmers receive 25¢ per pound for the peanuts. In a recent year, the crops for each farmer were:

Meekins	8,000 pounds
Grover	32,000 pounds
Carney	61,000 pounds

(a) How much did each farmer receive for his or her peanut crop?
(b) What percent of the peanuts did Radnor buy from each farmer?

EXPANDING YOUR UNDERSTANDING OF BUSINESS

1. Communities often advertise in newspapers and business magazines to encourage new businesses to locate in their towns. In their lists of advantages, they include such things as these:

low taxes
good schools
good supply of skilled workers
transportation facilities
water and power available
recreation facilities
other firms of the same type nearby

(a) Which of the factors do you think are the most important? Why?

(b) Would some factors be more important to some kinds of businesses than others?

(c) Does your city advertise for new businesses? You can find out by calling the Chamber of Commerce.

2. Read question 6 of "Using Your Business Knowledge" on page 59. Some citizens prefer that businesses not locate in their communities. What are some of the arguments you think they might list opposing the locating of new businesses such as the Plastics Processing Company in their towns? Do you think that the advantages are more important than the disadvantages?

3. Be prepared to give an oral report about an interview with the owner of a local business firm. Plan carefully in advance for your interview. Ask the business owner questions such as these:

(a) Why did you choose to go into this particular kind of business?

(b) What risks do you take in operating your own business?

(c) What methods do you use to compete with similar businesses for customers?

(d) What training and experience should a person have before attempting to start his or her own business?

4. What social and economic changes are taking place in our country to cause more and more people to want to buy services rather than perform them for themselves? What changes will this likely cause in our business system?

5. When businesses leave a community, the multiplier effect can work in reverse. If several businesses in your community fail during the year, how might the welfare of individual consumers, workers, other businesses, and the local government be affected?

HOW BUSINESSES ARE ORGANIZED

PART OBJECTIVES

After studying this part and completing the end-of-part activities, you will be able to:
1. Tell how ownership differs among sole proprietorships, partnerships, corporations, and cooperatives.
2. State the advantages and disadvantages of the three major types of business ownership.
3. Tell the difference between a consumers' cooperative and a producers' cooperative.
4. Explain how municipal corporations and business corporations are different.

Before the football team at your school starts its season, it must organize. Some players will be assigned to the offensive team while others will play defense. On both offense and defense, some players will be chosen to play the line and others will be in the backfield. The players are placed in the way that will benefit the team most and make it easier to reach its goal of winning games.

In a similar way, a business also must organize to produce goods and services for the consumer. Many questions must be answered in the organizing process. Who will make the decisions? Who will buy the goods to sell? Who will keep the records on what is bought and sold? Who will get the profits? If there is a loss, who must bear it? Most of the answers to these questions are found in the way a business is owned and organized.

THREE MAJOR TYPES OF BUSINESS OWNERSHIP

The three major types of business ownership are the sole proprietorship, the partnership, and the corporation. Later in the part, you will learn about another type of business ownership, the cooperative.

A **sole proprietorship** is a business owned by one person. Most sole proprietorships are small firms such as grocery stores, restaurants, gas stations, barber shops, and drugstores.

A **partnership** is owned and managed by a small group, often not more than two or three people, who become "partners." By written agreement, these partners share the profits or losses and the responsibilities of their business.

A **corporation** is a business owned by a number of people and operated under written permission from the state in which it is located. The written permission is called a **certificate of incorporation**. The corporation acts as a single individual in behalf of its owners. By buying shares of stock, people become owners of corporations. They are then known as **stockholders** or **shareholders**. A corporation may have very few owners, but most corporations have many owners. The American Telephone and Telegraph Company, for example, has more than 3 million owners. Even if you own just one share of stock in this giant

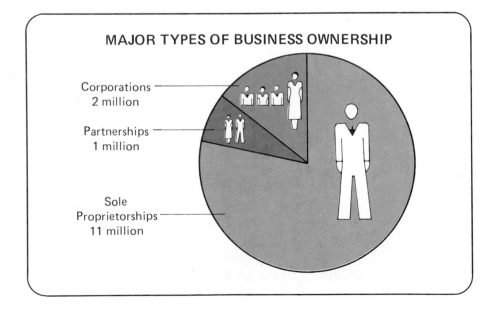

MAJOR TYPES OF BUSINESS OWNERSHIP

Corporations
2 million

Partnerships
1 million

Sole
Proprietorships
11 million

Illus. 6-1

As this chart shows, the majority of businesses in our country are operated as sole proprietorships.

company, you are still one of its owners. Most mining, manufacturing, and transporting of goods is done by corporations. And many of our consumer goods are supplied by supermarkets, department stores, and other businesses organized as corporations.

The size and the nature of a business are key factors in choosing the best type of ownership and organization for it. To help you understand each type of ownership, the next few pages tell a story of how a young man started a business and worked to make it grow.

THOMAS MAHONEY'S BUSINESS

During his first years in high school, Thomas Mahoney held a number of different part-time jobs after school and on Saturdays. He thought about retailing as a career and took business courses in school. In his senior year, he became a part-time sales trainee in the sporting goods department of a large department store. After graduation, he accepted a full-time job with the store.

In the next few years, Tom worked hard and was successful as a salesperson. He prepared for advancement by taking several evening school courses. Soon he was promoted to assistant manager of the sporting goods department. By this time he was married, earning a good salary, and saving some money. But he wanted to own his own business. He liked the idea of earning profits for himself and of being his own boss. So in his spare time he began planning his own business. Before too long, he resigned his job in the department store and was on his own.

Because of his experience and his interest in selling sporting goods, Tom decided to open a sporting goods store. He chose the name Sportsworld. He rented a small store in a shopping center and bought showcases and other equipment. With the help of a bank loan, he bought his stock of merchandise.

Tom had learned a lot about selling sporting goods in the department store, but he found that owning his own business required long hours and much decision making. He ordered merchandise, built window displays, and did most of the selling and the stock work. His wife helped him keep his business and tax records. A student was employed part-time. Tom owned the business by himself, so it was a sole proprietorship. All the profits — or losses — were his.

Illus. 6-2

Thomas Mahoney is the sole proprietor or owner of this store. Many of the businesses in your community are sole proprietorships.

THE PARTNERSHIP OF MAHONEY AND RUBIN

Sportsworld was a success. Tom paid his bills on time and paid himself a fair salary. Each month he made payments on his bank loan until it was paid off. Profits were put aside in a savings account.

Soon Tom felt that it was time to expand the business, but he needed more money than he had saved. He also needed the help of someone who knew more about advertising and bookkeeping than he did. A friend, Alex Rubin, was a salesperson in another store and had studied advertising and other business subjects in junior college. Tom invited Alex to become a part owner of Sportsworld.

With their combined skills, experience, money, and other property, they could afford to offer a larger variety of sporting goods. They could also afford to add new lines of merchandise — camping supplies and sportswear. Offering a greater variety of items would attract more people to the store and increase sales.

They consulted an attorney, Linda Vernon, about setting up the partnership. With her help, Tom and Alex drew up a written agreement called the **articles of partnership**. Among other things, this agreement provided that:

1. The name of the firm will be Sportsworld.
2. Mahoney will invest $40,000 in cash and property. Rubin will invest $20,000 in cash.
3. Each partner will draw a salary of $1,500 a month.
4. Profits and losses after salaries are paid will be shared in proportion to each partner's investment: two thirds to Mahoney and one third to Rubin.
5. Mahoney will have main responsibility for sales, selection and purchase of merchandise, and customer and community relations. Rubin will handle financial records, payroll, store maintenance, advertising and sales promotion, and other details of operating the business.
6. In the event of the death or the necessary withdrawal of one partner, the remaining partner will have the right to purchase the departing partner's share of the business.

Before Mahoney and Rubin signed the articles of partnership, their lawyer pointed out some of the legal responsibilities of partners. For example, each partner could be held personally responsible for all the debts of the business. This would even include debts incurred by the other partner without the first partner's consent. Each partner was also bound by the agreements made for the business by the other partner. To avoid problems, the partners agreed to talk over all important business matters, such as hiring people or buying new equipment.

Illus. 6-3

Mahoney and Rubin remodeled and enlarged Sportsworld by taking over the store next door. They added sportswear and a camping supplies section.

Under Mahoney's and Rubin's joint management, the partnership was very successful. At the end of the first year, there was a profit of $12,000 after the partners' salaries had been paid. Since they had agreed to share profits in proportion to their investment in the business, Tom received two thirds or $8,000 and Alex received one third or $4,000.

SPORTSWORLD AS A CORPORATION

Sportsworld continued to grow under the Mahoney and Rubin partnership, and the partners considered the possibility of expanding the business even more. A new shopping center was being built on the other side of town. Should they open a branch store there? Should they also enlarge the present store? Should they add new sales and storage space and also lines of outdoor furniture and boats? To do these things, they needed more money, so they thought about adding more partners. However, they decided against this. They reasoned that they did not need partners to help them manage the business since they could hire qualified assistant managers. Also, there would be personal risks in being responsible for the actions of other partners.

Linda Vernon, their lawyer, advised them that if they formed a corporation, each member would not be personally responsible for the debts of the business. In case of a business failure, each member could lose only the amount he or she had invested. Again with Linda Vernon's help, Tom and Alex dissolved the partnership and drew up a plan for a corporation, Sportsworld, Incorporated. The corporation was to represent a total investment of $120,000. Their financial records showed that the partnership was worth $90,000, so they needed to raise another $30,000.

Tom and Alex decided to divide the $120,000 into 12,000 shares, each with a value of $10. Based on the partnership agreement and the corporation plans, they divided the 12,000 shares this way: (1) Tom received 6,000 shares worth $60,000; (2) Alex received 3,000 shares worth $30,000; and (3) they offered for sale 3,000 shares valued at $30,000.

The information about the division of shares of stock and other information about the corporation was put in an application submitted to the state government. The application asked permission to operate as a corporation. After approving the application, the state issued a certificate of incorporation authorizing the formation of Sportsworld, Inc.

Illus. 6-4

A stock certificate is evidence of ownership in a corporation. The corporation attorney, Linda Vernon, has invested $5,000 in Sportsworld, Inc., for 500 shares.

Tom and Alex were no longer owners of the partnership. They had sold their partnership to the new corporation. In return they had received 9,000 shares of stock, or a part ownership amounting to $90,000. These 9,000 shares were divided in proportion to the investment in the former partnership. The 3,000 shares offered for sale were sold to 30 people who had confidence in the new corporation. The corporation, then, had 32 different stockholders.

Tom and Alex called a meeting of the stockholders to elect officers, to make plans for operating a branch store, and to transact other business. Each stockholder had one vote for each share of stock that she or he owned. Since Tom and Alex together owned 9,000 of the 12,000 shares, they had enough votes to control the operation of the business.

At the stockholders' meeting, these people were elected as directors of the corporation: Greg Snyder, Constantine Raboli, Kenneth Voss, JoAnn McCline, Thomas Mahoney, Paulette McKenna, and Alex Rubin. These seven people made up the **board of directors**. The board's responsibility was to guide the corporation properly. The board's first act was to elect the executive officers of the corporation. The directors elected Tom

Mahoney as president, JoAnn McCline as vice-president, Kenneth Voss as secretary, and Alex Rubin as treasurer. As full-time employees, the officers receive regular salaries for managing the business.

Illus. 6-5

If any stockholder of Sportsworld, Inc. wants to withdraw his or her investment, he or she can sell the shares of stock to anyone without affecting the organization and life of the business.

At the end of a year, after all taxes were paid, the corporation had a net profit of $15,800. The board of directors voted to keep $5,000 of this in the business for expansion and to divide the other $10,800 among the stockholders. Since the corporation had issued 12,000 shares, each of the 32 stockholders received 90 cents for each share of stock that he or she owned ($10,800 ÷ 12,000 = $.90). The part of the profits that each stockholder receives is called a **dividend**. In addition to their salaries, Mahoney received $5,400 ($.90 × 6,000 shares), and Rubin received $2,700 ($.90 × 3,000 shares).

COMPARING TYPES OF OWNERSHIP

You have read about Tom Mahoney as a sole proprietor, as a partner with Alex Rubin, and as a major stockholder in a corporation. As you have seen, Tom Mahoney found some good features and some not-so-good features about each experience. Illus. 6-6 shows a summary of the main advantages and disadvantages of the three types of ownership.

TYPE OF OWNERSHIP	ADVANTAGES	DISADVANTAGES
Sole Proprietorship	It is easy to start the business. The owner makes all the decisions and is his or her own boss. The owner receives all the profits.	Capital is limited to what the owner can supply or borrow. The owner is liable (responsible) for all debts, even to losing personal property if the business fails. Long hours and hard work are often necessary. The life of the business depends upon the owner; it ends if the owner quits or dies.
Partnership	It is fairly easy to start the business. More sources of capital are available. More business skills are available.	Each partner is liable for business debts made by all partners, even to losing personal property if the business fails. Each partner can make decisions; there is more than one boss. The partnership ends if a partner quits or dies. Each partner shares the profits.
Corporation	More sources of capital are available. Specialized managerial skills are available. The owners are liable only up to the amount of their investments. The ownership can be easily transferred through sale of stock; the business is not affected by this change of ownership.	It is difficult and expensive to start the corporation. The owners do not have control of the decisions made each day, unless they are officers of the company. The business activities of the corporation are limited to those stated in the certificate of incorporation.

Illus. 6-6

Each type of business ownership has advantages and disadvantages.

FORMING COOPERATIVES FOR
CONSUMERS AND PRODUCERS

Sometimes people join together to operate a business known as a cooperative. A **cooperative** is a kind of corporation, but it operates under a separate set of laws. There are two main types of cooperatives. One type is a **consumers' cooperative**, an organization of consumers who buy goods and services more cheaply together than each person could individually. For example, farmers and members of labor unions may form cooperatives to buy such products as groceries and gasoline and such services as insurance and electricity. Farmers also form cooperatives from which they buy products needed to run their farms.

A second type of cooperative is a **producers' cooperative**. It is usually a farmers' organization that markets such products as fruits, vegetables, milk, and grains. Sometimes the cooperative operates processing plants such as canneries. A producers' cooperative lets small farmers band together for greater bargaining power in selling their products.

A cooperative is much like a regular corporation. Its formation must be approved by the state. It may sell one or more shares of stock to each of its members. A board of directors may be chosen by the members to guide the cooperative. But a cooperative differs from other corporations in the way it is controlled. In a regular corporation, a person usually has one vote for each share she or he owns. A cooperative may be controlled in two ways: each owner-member may have one vote; or, each

Illus. 6-7

By joining together to sell their products, farmers can get better prices.

member's vote may be based on the amount of service he or she has received from the cooperative.

Most consumers' cooperatives sell to nonmembers as well as members. Prices in cooperative stores that sell to nonmembers are set at about the same level found in other local stores. Most of the profits a cooperative earns may be refunded directly to members at the end of the business year; part may be kept for expansion of the business.

ORGANIZING CORPORATIONS FOR SERVICE

When driving into towns, you have probably seen signs like "Bluefield — Incorporated." An incorporated town is called a **municipal corporation**. Unlike a business corporation, it is organized not to make a profit but rather to provide services for its citizens with money from their taxes. It does not issue stock representing ownership. It has its own officials, its own schools, and its own police and fire departments. It repairs its own streets; and it provides its own water supply, street lighting system, and other services for its citizens. It levies taxes and passes rules and regulations to operate effectively.

Certain other groups are organized as nonprofit corporations. Like the municipal corporation, nonprofit organizations are those which operate to provide a service but not for profit. Among these are churches, private colleges and universities, the American Red Cross, Boy Scouts of America, Future Business Leaders of America, and Distributive Education Clubs of America. Both community governments and nonprofit agencies find that the corporate form of organization provides the most effective way for them to deliver their services to the public.

The following terms should become part of your business vocabulary. For each numbered statement, find the term that has the same meaning.

INCREASING YOUR BUSINESS VOCABULARY

articles of partnership	dividend
board of directors	municipal corporation
certificate of incorporation	partnership
consumers' cooperative	producers' cooperative
cooperative	sole proprietorship
corporation	stockholder or shareholder

1. A group of people elected by stockholders to guide a corporation.
2. An organization which farmers form to market their products.
3. A business owned by one person.
4. A written agreement made by partners in forming their business.
5. An association of two or more people operating a business as co-owners and sharing profits or losses according to a written agreement.
6. An incorporated town or city.
7. An organization of consumers who buy goods and services together.
8. A business made up of a number of owners but authorized by law to act as a single person.
9. A document, generally issued by a state government, giving permission to start a corporation.
10. The part of the profits of a corporation that each stockholder receives.
11. A person who owns stock in a corporation.
12. A business that is owned by the members it serves and is managed in their interest.

UNDERSTANDING YOUR READING

1. What are the key factors to be considered in choosing the best type of ownership and organization of a business?
2. What personal satisfaction did Tom Mahoney expect to enjoy by owning his own business? What other advantages did he find in starting his own firm?
3. What disadvantages did Tom Mahoney find as the operator of a sole proprietorship?
4. What advantages over his original organization did Tom Mahoney have in going into partnership with Alex Rubin?
5. What are some of the points that should be agreed upon and recorded in the articles of partnership?
6. What are two advantages that a corporation has over a partnership?
7. Name two disadvantages of a corporation.
8. What evidence of ownership did Mahoney and Rubin receive when they changed from a partnership to a corporation?
9. In a corporation, who elects the board of directors?
10. Who actually manages a corporation?
11. For what reason did the corporation's board of directors keep part of the profit before dividing the remainder among the stockholders?

12. What is the purpose of a consumers' cooperative?
13. In what ways does a producers' cooperative serve its members?
14. How does a cooperative differ from a regular corporation?
15. What is the difference between a municipal corporation and a business corporation?

USING YOUR BUSINESS KNOWLEDGE

1. The table below shows the number of sole proprietorships, partnerships, and corporations in various kinds of businesses for a recent year. Study the table and answer the questions which follow it.

Industry	Number (thousands)		
	Proprietorships	Partnerships	Corporations
Total	11,358	1,096	2,105
Percent distribution	78	8	14
Agriculture, forestry, and fishing	3,470	121	62
Mining	60	18	15
Construction	963	60	198
Manufacturing	223	31	214
Transportation and public utilities	346	17	81
Trade	2,282	195	646
Finance, insurance, and real estate	827	447	414
Services	3,153	207	473

(a) What industry has the greatest number of businesses?
(b) In which type of business is there the greatest number of sole proprietorships?
(c) In which type of business is there the greatest number of partnerships?
(d) In which type of business is there the greatest number of corporations?
(e) Which type of ownership do most service businesses have?

2. Some of the features of the four types of business organizations which you read about in this part are given in the following statements. Name the type of organization to which each statement applies. (Some may apply to two types.)

(a) The owner is his or her own boss.

(b) If one of the owners makes a large, unwise purchase and the business can't pay the bill, another owner might have to pay it even if she or he has to use personal funds to do so.

(c) The business can sell stock to raise more money.

(d) If a profit is made, the owner gets it all.

(e) Owners agree on how they will divide profits and share losses.

(f) Owners allow a board of directors to make decisions about the business.

(g) Farmers join together to transport, store, and sell their crops.

(h) Owners must get written permission from the state in which the business is located before it can operate.

(i) An owner may be added to help make business decisions.

(j) The amount of control a person has in the business may depend upon the value of the products and services bought from the business during the year.

3. Could the policies and the management of a corporation with more than 10,000 stockholders be controlled by just one stockholder? Give reasons for your answer.

4. The community of River Valley has petitioned its state government for a certificate of incorporation so that it can become a town. When River Valley becomes a corporation, can it sell stock and issue dividends to stockholders? Explain.

5. Shari Reid and her partner, James Bailey, fail in business. The debts are about $8,000 greater than the value of the business. Ms. Reid has personal property worth more than $10,000, but her partner has nothing. How much of the debt of the business will Ms. Reid probably have to pay?

SOLVING PROBLEMS IN BUSINESS

1. As an art major at the university, Louis Sabu specializes in hand-tooled leather. To make extra money, Louis rented a stall in a mall near the university to sell leather items. Louis's income and expenses for the month of December were as follows:

Income from sales	$850
Expenses	
Rent for stall, including utilities	125
Cutting tools	45
Leather and supplies	110
Advertisement in university paper	20

  (a) What was the total of Louis's expenses for December?

  (b) How much profit did Louis make in December?

2. John Simons, Aretha Mullins, and Carla Ott formed a corporation with a beginning investment of $300,000.

  (a) How many shares of stock with a value of $25 would have to be sold to provide this amount?

  (b) How many shares could John buy for $160,000?

  (c) How much would Aretha have to pay for 500 shares?

3. Refer to the discussion of the Mahoney and Rubin partnership on pages 67 and 68.

  (a) If, at the end of the second year of operation, this partnership had made a net profit of only $4,200 after payment of the partners' salaries, how much would be each partner's share of the profit?

  (b) If the business had instead incurred a loss of $1,800, what would have been each partner's share of the loss?

4. Ginny and Robert Sayler own stock in four corporations. Below is a record of their stock holdings and the dividend they received for each share at the end of the first quarter of a recent year.

Company	Number of Shares Owned	Quarterly Dividend Per Share
American Telephone And Telegraph	100	$1.25
Avon Products	20	.70
William Wrigley, Jr.	50	.60
Levi Strauss	100	.55

  (a) How much dividend income did the Saylers receive from each of their stocks for the quarter?

  (b) What was their total dividend income for the quarter?

  (c) If each corporation paid the same amount per share for the remaining three quarters, how much dividend income would the Saylers receive from each for the year?

  (d) What total dividend income would the Saylers receive for the year?

5. After all expenses were paid, Hillsdale Consumer Cooperative had $13,000 left over. Of this amount, $3,000 was set aside for expansion of the business. According to its policy, Hillsdale would refund to each member an amount in proportion to the amount he or she bought during the year. Since total sales for the year were $500,000, the refund would be 2 percent, or 2¢ for every dollar each member had spent at the co-op during the

year. The following were among the members; their total purchases are shown in even dollars:

G. T. Frazier	$1,000
A. G. Whitbeck	650
J. Fantoni	750
R. Perlin	100
H. S. Anson	1,250

(a) How much refund did each of these members receive?
(b) What was the total amount refunded to these five members?

EXPANDING YOUR UNDERSTANDING OF BUSINESS

1. Visit a local shopping center; take a pad and pencil with you. Write down the names of at least 10 businesses located in the center. Beside each firm name, write down whether you believe the firm to be a proprietorship, a partnership, or a corporation. Be able to explain to the class what part of the firm name led you to identify it as you did. If you could not identify the type of organization by the name, be able to explain why.

2. Corporations are required to issue an annual report to their stockholders each year. Several ways in which you might get such a report to review are: (a) borrow one from a member of your family or a friend who owns stock; (b) ask your school or community librarian if the library has corporation annual reports; (c) visit a corporation in your community and ask for a copy of its report; or (d) write to a corporation and ask for a copy of its report. Using one of these suggestions, try to obtain annual reports from two corporations. Write a brief report showing the types of information contained in both reports.

3. There are several types of stock. Using a text in business principles, accounting, or business law, try to find definitions of the following types: common stock, preferred stock, cumulative preferred stock, participating preferred stock.

4. Some cooperatives sell to members and nonmembers. If anyone is permitted to buy, why would people wish to join as members?

5. In most partnerships the partners are general partners, but sometimes there are limited partners and silent partners. Explain the difference between each of these types. (Refer to business law and business principles textbooks in your library.)

6. Franchising is becoming a popular way of going into business. Franchise businesses are being established in all sorts of fields, but they are particularly common in the motel, restaurant, and prepared-food fields.

    (a) Explain what franchises are.

    (b) List the names of four or five franchise businesses in your area and describe the services rendered by two of the firms on your list.

    (c) What are the advantages and disadvantages of this way of going into business?

7. What is Junior Achievement, Inc.? Look into the nearest Junior Achievement program in your area. If possible, visit some of the Junior Achievement "companies" that are in operation. Be prepared to report orally to the class on the results of your investigation.

7 IMPROVING METHODS OF WORK

PART OBJECTIVES

After studying this part and completing the end-of-part activities, you will be able to:
1. Explain how the use of machines has improved the way people live.
2. Show the advantage of interchangeable parts by giving an example of their use.
3. Give an example to show that automation has improved our ability to produce goods, services, and information.
4. State five things a computer does with data.
5. List four uses of computers in business and government.
6. Explain what word processing is.

If you had toast for breakfast this morning, it was probably made with an automatic toaster. Almost every home in the United States has a toaster. Nearly all homes also have electric coffee makers, steam irons, refrigerators, and vacuum cleaners. We depend on many devices to help us to do housework faster, more easily, and with better results than was possible for our grandparents. Having these items in our stores in large quantities and at reasonable prices has been made possible only through the use of modern machines and efficient production methods. And this is true for most of the goods you buy today.

USING MACHINES:
THE INDUSTRIAL REVOLUTION

There was a time when each family provided for most of its own needs and wants. Most of the goods a family produced met basic needs; there were few luxuries. But as our economy developed, the demand for more and better products also grew. Faster, less costly methods of making goods were needed to keep up with the demand for goods.

Around the middle of the 18th century, imaginative people started inventing machines to do much of the work of producing goods. Gradually many more goods were produced by machine than by hand. This period was known as the Industrial Revolution.

People invented — and are still inventing — machines to keep up with the demand for goods and services. In many ways, the Industrial Revolution is still going on. Businesses are always looking for newer, faster, and better ways of producing goods.

Today's worker can produce many times more goods than a worker could produce at the beginning of this century. This great increase in productivity is due mainly to the use of machines and to advancements in business management, science, and technology. **Technology** is the use of scientific and technical knowledge to produce goods, services, and information. For example, today's industries use modern tools and power-driven equipment to produce goods and services for us. Very little human effort is required in much of our production.

USING MASS PRODUCTION
AND DIVIDING THE LABOR

Power-driven machinery makes it possible for industry to engage in **mass production**. This is the production by machine of great numbers of the same kind of article. With mass production, many more items can be produced at a lower cost than if they were made by hand. In the 1800's, for example, tin cans were made by hand at the rate of about six an hour. The cans were so expensive that they were saved and used over and over again. Today mass production enables one worker operating one machine to produce more than 20,000 tin cans an hour.

In mass production, no one person does all the work needed to make any one product. Instead, many workers are involved in

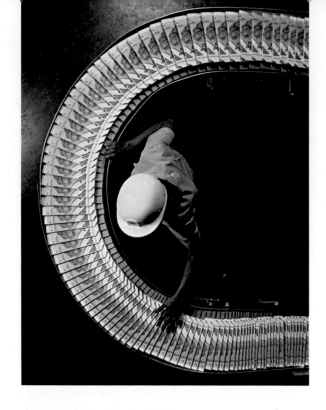

Illus. 7-1
Machinery has made it
possible to mass
produce many items
quickly and efficiently.

making a single product such as a stereo, watch, or car. Each worker is highly skilled in operating a machine that makes one part or is skilled in fitting parts together. This specialization of work is called **division of labor**.

Businesses also specialize in their production. One business may make only motors for automatic washers. Another may make only automobile mufflers. Larger businesses may divide production among several plants that they own. For example, one plant may make only automobile transmissions. Another may make only automobile bodies. Parts produced in one plant are then shipped to another plant and assembled into an automobile.

With mass production, products are standardized. Whether a machine turns out five or five thousand items in a day, each of those items will be just like all the others. Suppose one day the water refuses to drain out of your family's Model 700 Cleanmore washing machine. Your mother calls the Cleanmore store and asks for the person who repairs washers. The appliance repair specialist comes to your home, looks over the washer, and tells your mother that the pump is broken. With your mother's permission, a new pump is installed and the machine is usable again in an hour or so. Your mother didn't have to buy a new washer. Why? Because all Cleanmore Model 700's are made alike, and if a part breaks you don't have to throw the washer away. You just order a new part.

Parts that are made exactly alike so that one can replace another that is worn out are called **interchangeable parts**. You can see how important interchangeable parts are every time you need to replace a battery in your portable radio or the spark plugs in the family car.

PRODUCING MORE GOODS WITH AUTOMATIC MACHINES

Standardized products have another advantage — they can be made in large quantities by automatic machines. Many increases in productivity are the result of automation. **Automation** is the use of electronic or mechanical equipment to produce goods, services, and information with a minimum of human effort. A great deal of physical effort is reduced in factories through the use of automated machinery. In automobile plants, for example, huge presses automatically form the tops of cars in one operation. In making ball-point pens, machines automatically perform 36 different operations in assembling the ball and tip.

Automatic machines can do more than just reduce the amount of physical work needed to produce goods. They can also reduce the amount of mental work needed. Businesses today use automatic machines to produce information and prepare reports.

THE SPECIAL LANGUAGE OF AUTOMATION

Many inventions have introduced new words to our language. Automation is one of these. People who work with automated machines often use specialized terms. Some of them look familiar, but have a special meaning. For example, **data** means facts or information of all kinds. In computer language, it usually means facts to be processed. Business data includes such things as customer names and addresses, stock numbers, prices, and account balances. To **process** means to change the form of the data in some way. For example, you might put names in alphabetical order; you might add a column of figures to get a total; or you might subtract a payment from a customer's account to find the new balance. In each case, you would be processing data. Processing data by using automatic machines that require little human attention is called **automated data processing**. You will learn more of these specialized terms later in this part.

USING PUNCHED CARDS TO PROCESS DATA

The invention of automated data processing machines, like many inventions, was the result of an inventor's meeting a need. To speed up the processing of the 1890 census, the Bureau of the Census called on Dr. Herman Hollerith, a noted statistician, for help. He developed a card on which data could be recorded in the form of punched holes. By 1890 when the census was to begin, he had invented a series of machines that could sort the punched cards and summarize the data they contained. Using Dr. Hollerith's invention, the 1890 census took only two and a half years to complete, five years less than the 1880 census took.

The punched card is still used for recording data for automated data processing. You have probably noticed that bills for gas and electricity or bills for credit purchases are often in punched-card form. A department store statement on a punched card is shown in Illus. 7-2. Each hole punched in the card represents a certain kind of information. Notice that the customer is asked to return the stub of the card with the payment. These stubs are then fed into the machine, which reads the holes so that the correct amount will be credited to the customer's account.

Illus. 7-2

Punched cards are often used for business forms such as checks, invoices, tax bills, and statements from stores.

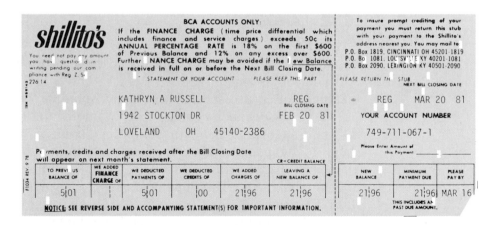

Automated data processing using punched cards is summarized in Illus. 7-3. In the illustration you will find three more specialized terms: input, source document, and output.

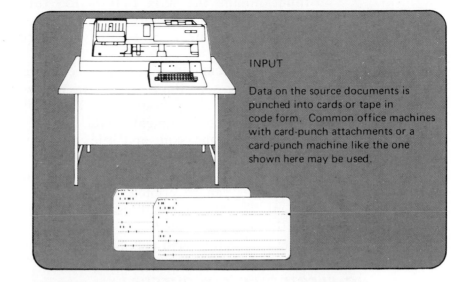

INPUT

Data on the source documents is punched into cards or tape in code form. Common office machines with card-punch attachments or a card-punch machine like the one shown here may be used.

Illus. 7-3

A summary of the procedures involved in automated data processing.

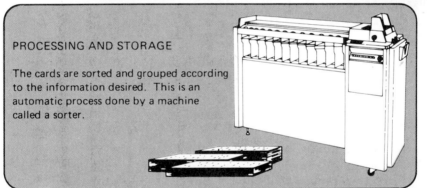

PROCESSING AND STORAGE

The cards are sorted and grouped according to the information desired. This is an automatic process done by a machine called a sorter.

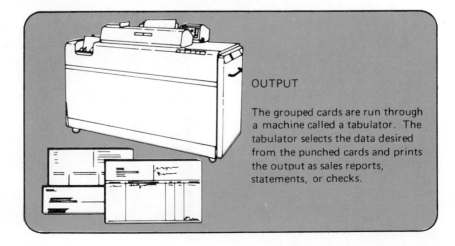

OUTPUT

The grouped cards are run through a machine called a tabulator. The tabulator selects the data desired from the punched cards and prints the output as sales reports, statements, or checks.

Input means the data that is fed into a machine to be processed. If you have a charge account, your name and address will be punched into a card with your account number. These items are input.

A **source document** is the first record made of a transaction. When you buy something, the clerk makes out a sales ticket, gives you a copy, and keeps one. The copy that is kept is the company's source document. Data from it — such as the item sold, amount of the sale, and sales tax — will be punched into cards as input.

Output is the processed data put in a requested form. Output for businesses can be printed and punched out in the form of a statement like the one in Illus. 7-2. It can be a printed list of names. It can be a printed check. Or it can be one of a variety of other forms, even printed pages of a report or book.

USING ELECTRONIC COMPUTERS FOR FASTER PROCESSING

Automated data processing using punched cards is not fast enough for businesses that must process a great deal of data. The electronic computer was developed to meet the need for a faster method. It is a machine that receives data; stores it; "remembers" it; adds, subtracts, multiplies, and divides; and produces the desired output. Based on the data fed into the computer, problems are solved and reports are prepared. The processing of data by electronic computers is called **electronic data processing** or simply EDP.

Illus. 7-4

When data has been processed by an electronic computer, the output can be read on a computer terminal screen.

While the punched card is a basic means of input for automated data processing, other means are more often used for the electronic computer. For example, you may have seen a bank number printed on the bottom of a check in magnetic ink. Magnetic ink is used because it can be read by computers. Data is also recorded on tapes and disks made of magnetic material. Paper tape into which holes are punched is another means of input. Ever since computers were invented, scientists have continued looking for newer, faster means of input.

TELLING THE COMPUTER WHAT TO DO

The first workable computer went into operation in 1946. However, it was not used in business until 1953. Since then, computers have changed very much. The computer's features have astonished many people and have caused them to refer to the computer as an ''electronic brain.'' But a computer is basically an arrangement of wires, switches, and magnets. It can do only what a person has planned for it to do. It cannot think. A computer can store data, recall it instantly, and combine it with other data to produce a report or give the answer to a problem. But it can do this only if a person has given it step-by-step instructions to follow. This set of instructions is called a **program**. The program is written in a code which can be read by the computer. The person who writes these instructions is called a **programmer**.

One of the first steps in writing the program is to plan in diagram form the order in which the job is to be done. This diagram is called a **flowchart**. It shows how each step leads, or flows, into the next step. If you wanted to, you could make a flowchart of any task, even making a pizza. Of course, you don't need a flowchart to make a pizza; but if you did, it would look something like the one in Illus. 7-5. The chart shows a step at which you decide whether you want to make a plain or pepperoni pizza. It also directs you to the next step for either one you choose. You can see how important the order of the steps is. For example, if you put the sauce in the pan first, you not only wouldn't have a pizza, but you would have a mess to clean up.

In a similar way, if incorrect data or an incorrect plan for processing data is given to a computer, the computer will give out incorrect answers.

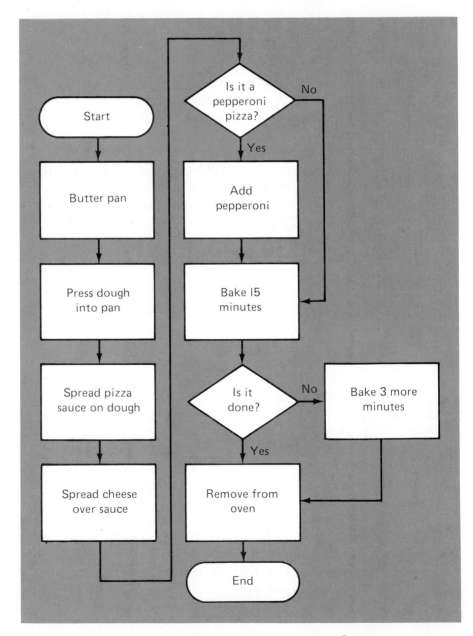

Illus. 7-5

A flowchart for making a pizza. The shapes of the figures have special meanings to the programmer. For example, the rectangle means do a task and the diamond means make a decision. Other figures are also used in business flowcharts.

USING COMPUTERS IN BUSINESS AND GOVERNMENT

Computers are programmed to handle many business data processing problems. Because they must keep many records and prepare many reports, businesses have a great amount of paperwork. Since computers work so fast, they have helped businesses with many of their recording and reporting tasks. A computer can prepare payrolls and can even write paychecks. It can keep a daily record of the goods a business has sold or has on hand. Airline and hotel reservations can be made or confirmed in a few seconds with a computer. Computers can help insurance companies keep track of when premiums are due for millions of insured people. Computers help the government figure taxes and social security payments. They can help banks keep records and can prepare monthly checking account statements for a bank's customers. Some computers can even read words printed in a foreign language and translate them into English. And they can help a physician diagnose the illnesses of patients.

Illus. 7-6

Computer terminals are a convenient way to provide information needed for business meetings.

AUTOMATING TYPEWRITTEN COMMUNICATIONS

Automation has been so successful in speeding up data processing that business has applied it to other office tasks. In the mid-1960's, the electric typewriter was changed to give it the ability to store information that is typed into it (input) and to later type out the information automatically (output). As information is typed into an automated typewriter, it is recorded on a special device such as a magnetic card or disk. The magnetic card or disk stores the information that will later be used to make the final copies. With automated typewriters if the typist finds an error or wants to add or take something out, special keys allow changes to be made without having to erase. When the typist is satisfied with the material, the typewriter will automatically type one or more copies in correct form at very fast speeds. The automated typewriter thus makes the typist's job much easier and increases his or her productivity.

Business has found it profitable to use automated typewriters to handle communications such as routine letters and reports. By using specially trained people, a procedure can be set up to complete routine tasks much faster and at less cost. The procedure includes dividing the office work so that managers, secretaries, and typists perform the tasks that they can do best. Using automated equipment, the typist specializes in doing most of the typewritten communications. This frees the secretary to assist the manager in looking up information for reports, helping to write reports, and composing some of the routine letters. The manager can then devote more time to operating the business. This method, called word processing, has been adopted by many businesses. Today, **word processing** means using specially trained people, automated equipment, and organized procedures to handle business communications. Word processing speeds up the processing of words in much the same way that the computer speeds up the processing of numbers.

INCREASING YOUR BUSINESS VOCABULARY

The following terms should become part of your business vocabulary. For each numbered statement, find the term that has the same meaning.

automated data processing	mass production
automation	output
data	process
division of labor	program
electronic data processing	programmer
flowchart	source document
input	technology
interchangeable parts	word processing

1. The data that is fed into a machine for processing.
2. The first record made of a transaction.
3. To change the form of data in some way.
4. The processing of data by electronic computers.
5. Parts that are made exactly alike so that one can be used to replace another that is worn out or broken.
6. The production by machine of great numbers of the same kind of article.
7. The use of specially trained people, automated equipment, and organized procedures to handle business communications.
8. Processing data by using automatic machines that require little human attention.
9. Data that has been processed and put into some requested form.
10. A first step in planning a computer program, written in diagram form.
11. A set of step-by-step instructions, written in code, telling the computer what to do.
12. A person who writes computer programs.
13. The use of scientific and technical knowledge to produce goods, services, and information.
14. Using electronic or mechanical equipment to produce goods, services, and information with a minimum of human effort.
15. Facts or information of all kinds.
16. Specialization by workers in performing certain portions of a total job.

UNDERSTANDING YOUR READING

1. How has the use of machines improved the way people live?
2. What made possible the increase in worker productivity during this century?
3. What made mass production possible?
4. What is the advantage of interchangeable parts?
5. How has automation increased our ability to produce goods, services, and information?
6. For what business forms are punched cards sometimes used?
7. State five things a computer does with data.
8. What does a programmer do?
9. What is the purpose of a flowchart?
10. Give four examples of ways computers are used by government and business.
11. How does word processing speed up business communications?

USING YOUR BUSINESS KNOWLEDGE

1. Many devices in the home are designed to operate automatically. Examples are an automatic dishwasher and an automatic record player. List in order the steps one such machine follows as it operates through one complete cycle.

2. Give some specific examples to show why the concept of interchangeable parts is of great benefit to: (a) a homemaker; (b) a farmer; (c) an automobile manufacturer; (d) an automobile owner; and (e) a proprietor of a hardware store.

3. Examine the flowchart in Illus. 7-5. If the answer to the question "Is it a pepperoni pizza?" is no, what is the next step? What is the total possible baking time provided for in the flowchart? Can this flowchart be used for making a mushroom or sausage pizza?

4. An important characteristic of automation is that electronic or mechanical equipment is used to operate or control other equipment. The thermostat that turns a furnace off and on is one example. Give several other examples of automation that exist in your home or the homes of people you know.

SOLVING PROBLEMS IN BUSINESS

1. After studying the legal forms typed daily by personnel in the office, Decker and Whalen Legal Services, Inc., decided to install a word processing system. The firm planned to start with one word processing station and add others as needed. The cost of the first word processing station was broken down as follows:

1	Automated typewriter	$11,000
1 dz.	Magnetic disks	36
1 dz.	Carbon ribbons	60
1	Work station desk	400
1	Typist's chair	110

(a) What was the cost of the first word processing station?

(b) If another station of the same type is added, what will the total cost of the two stations be?

2. Sharon Vogan's old refrigerator needs to be repaired again. She is trying to decide whether to buy a new one for $640 or have a new motor installed in her present one for $185. With the cost of the new repair, she wonders if she will be spending more for repairs than a new one would cost. A check of her records shows that she has already spent the following for replacement parts and labor:

1 Automatic defrost fan $60
1 Motor belt   40
3 Light bulbs   5

(a) What is the total cost of repairs to date?

(b) What will be the total cost of repairs if Ms. Vogan has the new motor installed?

(c) What is the difference between the cost of the new refrigerator and the total cost of repairs?

3. The president of the Seaboard Corporation realized that installing new equipment would be very expensive. Before making a decision on whether or not to buy the machinery, the president asked the accounting department to make a cost study. The following information was presented:

Cost of new equipment $125,750
Necessary remodeling and
   installation costs......................... 32,150
Trade-in value of old equipment....... 12,500
Estimated life of new equipment...... 8 years

If the cost of buying and installing the equipment is to be spread over its estimated life, what will be the estimated annual cost of putting in the new equipment?

4. The minicomputer is recommended for firms whose data processing needs are too large for a desk calculator and too small for a full-scale computer system. The owners of Daniels Distributors found that to purchase a minicomputer adapted to their needs would cost $30,000. But they could rent the equipment for $1,200 per month. If they purchased the equipment later, they could apply half of the rental fees up to six months toward the purchase price.

(a) What is the total rental for six months?

(b) What amount could Daniels apply toward the purchase price after six months?

(c) What would be the remaining cost of the minicomputer?

EXPANDING YOUR UNDERSTANDING OF BUSINESS

1. Because of modern mass production methods, Americans buy an almost countless number of products at a reasonable cost. Most of these products are satisfactorily made in great quantities by machine. Why, then, do some people prefer to buy hand-tailored suits, custom-made furniture, and other individually made items?

2. Many businesses, such as large department stores and chain stores, have installed cash registers which are directly linked to

a computer. What advantage does this offer the company? Find out whether a local store has such a cash register and, if so, try to identify each item on a customer's receipt.

3. Automated, or word processing, typewriters are widely used in businesses which require large quantities of repetitive typing, such as form letters. One of these is called the Magnetic Card Selectric Typewriter, or MCST. Prepare a brief report of the MCST or a similar automated typewriter. Your school's typewriting teacher might help you with your research. Some points you might include are: a description of the machine, some operating advantages, how corrections are made, and several uses of the machine in business.

4. In recent years, energy shortages have caused nationwide concern. With so many automatic devices in the home, consumers must plan for reduced power and power failures. Make a list of all the power-operated items in your home. Beside each, write an item or a method which you could use as a substitute in case of a power failure. Are there any items for which there are no substitutes? If so, in what way would you be inconvenienced without them?

8

FOREIGN TRADE AND YOUR ECONOMY

PART OBJECTIVES

After studying this part and completing the end-of-part activities, you will be able to:
1. Explain how people, communities, and nations throughout the world depend on each other.
2. Give an example to show the difference between foreign trade and domestic trade.
3. Tell how we depend upon world trade for many goods and services.
4. Describe how tariffs and import quotas affect world trade.
5. Explain why the metric system can make it easier to trade with other countries.

Imagine how difficult life would be if you had to make everything you wanted. Just providing enough clothes to wear would keep you very busy. You probably would have only one pair of shoes, and they would have to last a very long time. And making such things as a radio, a watch, or a motorbike would be almost impossible, so you would probably do without those.

Fortunately, you are able to buy things you want from people who have goods and services to sell. This buying and selling is called **trade**. Trading is an important part of your economy. It helps individuals, communities, and nations get the things they want and need. In your own community, for example, you find many things to buy which were not made there. Because your community, like you, cannot produce all the things it needs, it must trade with other communities and nations for most of the needs and wants of its citizens.

For example, suppose a person in Omaha, Nebraska, buys a car from a local dealer. The car was probably manufactured in Detroit. The heater, battery, tires, and other parts may have been produced in communities in other states. But at least 30 raw materials used to make these parts came from other nations.

You can see that the automobile customer in Omaha would not have gotten a car if it were not for trade among communities in the United States and trade between the United States and other countries. Trade among people and businesses in the same country is called **domestic trade**. Trade among different countries may be called **world trade, foreign trade**, or **international trade**.

TAKING ADVANTAGE OF ADVANTAGES

What did your family have for breakfast this morning? Coffee, cereal, and sliced bananas, perhaps? If it were not for trading with Brazil for the coffee and with Honduras for the bananas, you might have had only cereal. The sugar on your table may have come from the Philippines. Even the paper your morning newspaper was printed on may have come from Canada.

Our country has many natural resources, a skilled labor force, and modern machines and methods of production. Yet we cannot provide ourselves with all of the things we want. We go beyond our borders to get many things we need and want. We carry on trade with as many as 150 foreign countries in one year. Why do we trade with other countries? To answer this, let's first look at why there is trade among different sections of our own country.

The various sections of our country have certain special advantages. These advantages may be such things as climate, deposits of minerals, rich soil, a favorable location, or many workers with special abilities and skills. These kinds of advantages make it possible for a state or region to produce a certain good or service of higher quality or at a lower cost than another state or region. Thus, Florida has an advantage over Wisconsin for growing oranges. Minnesota has an advantage over Florida for producing iron ore. Georgia has an advantage over Wyoming in growing peanuts. And Michigan has an advantage over Maine in making cars.

Trade allows each state or region to specialize — to devote most of its resources to producing the kind of goods it produces best. And each state exchanges its special products for the special products of other states. What is the result for you as a consumer? You benefit by having many different kinds of products that are generally better in quality and lower in price than if each state or region tried to supply most of the things its people need.

Most nations of the world have some special advantages also. Brazil, for example, has an advantage over the United States in producing coffee. Saudi Arabia has an advantage over most other countries in crude oil. Australia has an advantage in wool. Korea and Taiwan have an advantage in the number of skilled laborers who can assemble radios and make textiles. And, compared with these and many other countries, the United States has advantages for the production of airplanes, tractors, computers, office machines, and many varieties of food and other agricultural products. Because of trade and modern means of transportation, nations everywhere can specialize in kinds of production they can do best.

IMPORTING GOODS FROM OTHER COUNTRIES

Consumers want many goods that are not produced in this country. Also, many products in our country are not produced in large enough quantity to satisfy our needs and wants. But, thanks to world trade, we can still have these products.

Those things we buy from other countries are called **imports**. Imports account for our total supply of bananas, coffee, cocoa,

Illus. 8-1

The U.S. buys services as well as goods from foreign countries. This Swiss bank in San Francisco is one foreign business that offers services to Americans.

spices, tea, silk, and crude rubber. About half the crude oil and fish we buy come from other countries. Imports also account for 20 to 50 percent of our supply of carpets, sugar, leather gloves, dishes, and sewing machines. To keep making industrial and consumer goods, we depend on importing tin, chrome, manganese, nickel, copper, zinc, and several other metals.

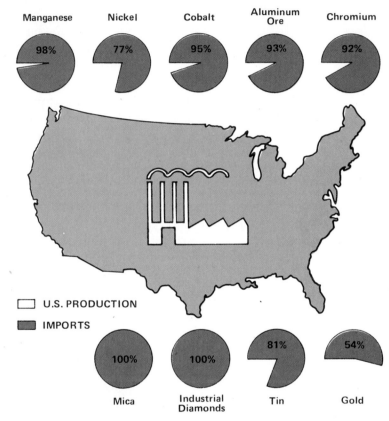

Illus. 8-2

The United States produces only small amounts of many materials that are needed in industries. The illustration shows the percentage of import of various materials we used in a recent year.

If no raw materials were imported, you would have to do without many of the products you use today. Without world trade, many of the things you want and need would cost more than they do now. This is because other countries' advantages allow them to produce goods and services at less cost.

Many people prefer to buy certain imported goods — even at higher prices — because of their difference or quality. For example, you may like imported Japanese cameras better than American brands. So you may buy a Japanese camera even though it costs more. Or perhaps you are willing to pay more for a pair of German binoculars, a Swiss watch, or an imported cashmere sweater because you have confidence in the quality and workmanship of these products.

EXPORTING PRODUCTS TO OTHER COUNTRIES

The goods and services we sell to other countries are called **exports**. Just as imports benefit you, exports benefit the people of other countries. People in nations throughout the world run their factories with machinery made in the United States. They work their land and harvest their crops with American-made tools. They eat food made from many of our agricultural products. They use our chemicals, fertilizers, medicines, and plastics. They see our movies and read a good deal of our printed matter.

Two segments of the American economy — machinery and agriculture — are especially dependent on selling in foreign markets. Our exports in the machinery and transport equipment fields include diesel engines, buses, tractors, oil-drilling rigs, earth-moving equipment, jet planes, computers, and air conditioning and refrigeration equipment. Large amounts of farm

Illus. 8-3

Through world trade, these Japanese and American engineers combine their skills in a building project.

products are also sold abroad each year. Farmers who grow such crops as cotton, wheat, soy beans, and rice depend on selling in foreign markets.

The jobs and incomes of millions of American workers depend directly on success in exporting. And the profits of many businesses depend in part on the demands of other countries for American products.

U.S. TRADE, 1978

EXPORTS TO (MILLIONS)	COUNTRY	IMPORTS FROM (MILLIONS)
$143,660	All countries	$172,026
	Selected countries:	
28,372	Canada	33,529
12,885	Japan	24,458
6,681	Mexico	6,093
7,119	United Kingdom	6,513
2,978	Brazil	2,881
4,166	France	4,054
3,360	Italy	4,103
2,910	Australia	1,659
3,727	Venezuela	3,545
1,925	Israel	719
948	India	980
1,040	Philippines	1,207
2,252	Soviet Union	540
680	Poland	434
91	Liberia	133
39	Iceland	174

Illus. 8-4

Some of the trading partners of the United States.

PAYING FOR FOREIGN GOODS

Suppose that each of the 50 states had a different kind of money, each with a different value. Imagine the trouble you would have in traveling through New England if you had to change your "Massachusetts Money" into "Rhode Island Money" and then into "Connecticut Money." If you lived in Chicago and were ordering products from Oregon, you would need to convert your "Illinois Money" into "Oregon Money" to make payment. This is what we must do when we travel in or trade with other countries. It is one reason why world trade is so much more complicated than domestic trade.

Each nation has its own type of money and its own banking system. In the United States, we use dollars; Mexico uses pesos; France, francs; Japan, yen; and so on. When American businesses buy olive oil from Italy, for example, arrangements are made to change American dollars into liras, the Italian money. If you were to visit Spain, you would need to have pesetas to pay for meals and other expenses. When Spanish people come to this country, they need to change their pesetas into dollars.

Because of the differences in value of the monies of the world, rates of exchange are established among countries. The **rate of exchange** is the value of the money of one country expressed in terms of the money of another country. If the Mexican peso is listed as .04, this means that the peso is worth 4¢ in our money and that an American dollar could be changed into 25 pesos. The approximate values of the currencies of several foreign countries on a recent date are given in Illus. 8-5.

Illus. 8-5

This table shows approximate values of some foreign currencies. However, these values change frequently due to many conditions.

COUNTRY	MONEY UNIT	VALUE IN U.S. MONEY
Canada	Dollar	86¢
England	Pound	$2.26
India	Rupee	12.5¢
Japan	Yen	42/100 of a cent
Portugal	Escudo	2¢
Sweden	Krona	24¢
Venezuela	Bolivar	23¢
West Germany	Deutsche mark	58¢

The problem of foreign currency exchange is solved by the "foreign exchange market," which is composed mainly of banks around the world. The banks are willing to buy and sell the currencies of the various countries. They provide the needed — and often very complex — services which allow traders to make and receive payments.

USING TARIFFS TO LIMIT TRADE

In the United States, people are free to trade among the 50 states. Almost no barriers are placed in the way of trade from one state to another, but this is not true among different countries. The most important restriction on trade among nations is the tariff. A **tariff** is a tax which a government places on imported products. Suppose you wanted to buy a bicycle made in England. The English bike producer sets a price of $60. Our government places a 20 percent tariff ($12) on the bike when it is imported. If the shipping charges are $10, you must pay $82 for a bike which would cost only $60 in England.

The $12 tariff which you would pay on the bike would go to our government. Some governments use the tariff as a means of raising revenue. But in most industrialized countries, tariffs bring in only a very small part of total government revenue. Tariffs are generally used as a means of protection from foreign competition. Tariffs are included in the price consumers pay for imported goods. This can mean that the price of the imported goods will be higher than the price of goods of domestic producers. Imposing tariffs can thus reduce the amount of imported goods that consumers will buy. In our bicycle example, if a bike of comparable quality is made and sold in this country for $75, you will probably buy it rather than the $82 English bike. But what if there were no $12 tariff on the English bike? You might well prefer to buy it at the $70 price.

There are several reasons why protection from imports is desired. If a country depends heavily on imports for its supply of certain products, such as steel, that supply might be cut off in wartime. Therefore, the government may wish to protect with tariffs an industry which is important to national defense, even though the industry may not produce as cheaply as the same industry in other countries.

Another reason for imposing tariffs may be to protect new industries. When new industries get started, they usually cannot produce as efficiently as established ones. So they may have trouble competing against more efficient producers in other countries. Nations often set up tariff barriers to give "infant industries" the protection they need to get started.

Many people believe our tariffs protect American workers. They argue that without tariffs on imports from countries where wage rates are low, our producers might have to reduce wages in order to compete in price. Thus, it is said, our workers would either get lower incomes or perhaps lose their jobs. However, the important point is not how high the hourly or weekly wages are but how productive the workers are. Low wages usually mean low efficiency, and this may actually cause high prices. In fact, workers in Japan have complained in recent years that they cannot compete with the highly efficient American workers despite the fact that their wages are still quite a bit below those in the United States.

OTHER TRADE BARRIERS

Today there are other barriers to foreign trade which may be more important than tariffs. One example is the **import quota**. This is a limit on the amount of a given type of product that may be imported within a given period of time. Our government has placed quotas on such goods as sugar, cattle, dairy products, and textiles. Most countries also have other restrictions such as buying regulations, licensing requirements, and complicated customs procedures that are designed to limit imports.

CHANGING TO THE METRIC SYSTEM

Over 90 percent of the countries of the world use the metric system of measuring. The **metric system** is a decimal system; that is, it is based on the number 10. It uses just one basic unit for each type of measurement (weight, distance, volume, and temperature). For example, we use many terms to measure distance, such as inch, foot, yard, and mile. The metric system replaces these terms with meter, a basic unit which is a little longer than a yard. Units to measure very large or very small

Illus. 8-6

The distance from home plate to the wall of this stadium is given in meters as well as in feet.

amounts are defined by multiplying or dividing the basic units by 10, 100, or 1,000. For example, since the meter is the basic measure of distance, to measure long distances you use kilometers (1,000 meters = 1 kilometer). That way you can say that Chicago is about 460 kilometers from St. Louis, rather than 462 000 meters. (As you can see here, in the metric system a space is used instead of a comma to show thousands when grouping five or more digits.) If you are not very familiar with the metric system, you should study Appendix D of this book, which will explain it to you.

The United States is one of the few countries which does not use the metric system. Our system of measurement becomes a barrier to foreign trade when we sell to or buy from countries which use the metric system. For example, an American who buys a foreign car may find that a special set of metric-sized tools is necessary to make repairs on the car. In the same way, a foreign buyer of an American tractor may find it necessary to have a special set of U.S.-sized tools. Foreign trade would be much simpler if everyone used the same system of measurement. In some cases foreign buyers will not even accept goods measured according to the U.S. system.

The United States is making changes that will gradually convert us to the metric system. You may have seen some food packages which show the amount in grams or liters, which are metric measures, in addition to ounces or quarts. And we are getting used to hearing the temperature quoted on television in metric degrees Celsius as well as in our familiar degrees Fahrenheit. Americans are slow to accept the change. But eventually the United States will join the rest of the world in using only the metric system. Removing this barrier will help to improve our trade with other nations.

INCREASING YOUR BUSINESS VOCABULARY

The following terms should become part of your business vocabulary. For each numbered statement, find the term that has the same meaning.

domestic trade	rate of exchange
exports	tariff
import quota	trade
imports	world, foreign, or
metric system	international trade

1. Goods and services sold to another country.
2. A limit on the amount of a given type of product that may be imported within a given period of time.
3. The buying and selling of goods and services among people and businesses within the same country.
4. The value of the money of one country expressed in terms of the money of another country.
5. Trade among different countries.
6. Goods and services bought from another country.
7. A decimal measuring system used by most countries of the world.
8. The buying and selling of goods and services.
9. A tax which a government places on imported products.

UNDERSTANDING YOUR READING

1. What is the difference between foreign and domestic trade?
2. Give some examples of regional advantages in production in the world and in the United States.
3. Give an example of a food, a raw material, and a manufactured good which we would not have without world trade.
4. What percent of our supply of aluminum ore is imported?
5. What is one reason why you might prefer to buy an imported product, even at a higher cost?
6. What two segments of the American economy particularly depend on international trade?
7. Why are rates of exchange established?
8. State three reasons that are given by countries for placing tariffs on imports.
9. How does an import quota limit trade?
10. How does the U.S. system of measurement act as a barrier to foreign trade?

USING YOUR BUSINESS KNOWLEDGE

1. It is said that no community or nation today can be completely independent. Do you agree or disagree? Explain.
2. How does world trade contribute to a better life-style for many people in various countries?
3. Suppose the United States were completely self-sufficient. Would it make sense for the U.S., as a highly productive nation, to follow a policy of exporting many goods and not importing any?

4. An American manufacturer of electric toasters wants to sell its products to the people of India. Can you think of some difficulties that this business might have in entering the Indian market?

5. What are "infant industries"? Give a few examples of such industries, either in the United States or in other countries. Should infant industries be protected by high tariffs? If so, for how long?

6. Some people feel that the United States should place a high tariff on compact cars that are imported. Give arguments for and against such a tariff.

SOLVING PROBLEMS IN BUSINESS

1. Bill Gonzalez had a summer job inspecting tomatoes and packing them in shipping boxes. He worked eight hours a day, five days a week, for $3.25 an hour.
   (a) How much did Bill make per day?
   (b) How much did he make per week?
   (c) If he worked 11 weeks during the summer, what were his wages for the summer?

2. The table below shows the approximate value of some imported foods for 1977 and 1978. The value is stated in millions of dollars:

Food	1977	1978
Meat and meat products	$1,300	$1,900
Fruits, nuts, vegetables	1,500	1,800
Coffee	3,900	3,700
Sugar	1,100	700
Fish	2,100	2,200

   (a) What is the total value of the foods imported by the U.S. in 1977?
   (b) What is the total value of the foods imported in 1978?
   (c) Was there an increase or a decrease from 1977 to 1978?
   (d) What was the amount of increase or decrease?

3. Using the information in Illus. 8-5, tell what the equal amount in U.S. dollars would be for these amounts in foreign currency:
   (a) in Portugal, 100 escudos.
   (b) in Japan, 136 yen.
   (c) one Canadian dollar.
   (d) in India, 6 rupees.

4. To make their exports suitable for use in other countries, U.S. manufacturers must produce goods that are measured in the

metric system. As you know by now, many of our measures do not convert exactly into a standard measure of the metric system. To what sizes would the items listed below be converted for export to countries using the metric system? For example, if a manufacturer wanted to export paint, which is sold in gallon cans in this country, it would probably export the paint in 4-liter (about 1¼ gallons) cans. (Refer to Appendix D.)

(a) a quart bottle of liquid detergent
(b) a 50-yard bolt of polyester fabric
(c) an automobile engine measured in cubic inches
(d) a 12-inch ruler
(e) a bathroom scale that measures in pounds

5. The table below shows the approximate values of the exports and imports going through nine large ports in a recent year.

Port City	Exports (million $)	Imports (million $)
Boston	$ 9,600	$14,700
New York	19,900	26,200
Baltimore	12,300	15,300
Miami	8,700	9,200
New Orleans	12,800	12,900
Houston	12,200	17,300
Los Angeles	7,300	13,800
San Francisco	13,400	16,000
Chicago	18,800	21,400

(a) What is the total value of the exports for the year? the imports?
(b) Which port city reported the largest business in terms of value? What is the value?
(c) Which port imported and exported the least amount? What was the value?

EXPANDING YOUR UNDERSTANDING OF BUSINESS

1. What does the term "balance of trade" mean? Using a reference which gives governmental statistics, such as the *Statistical Abstract of the United States* or *The World Almanac*, prepare a brief table showing the U.S. balance of trade position for the past four years.
2. Look through the stock of food supplies that your family presently has on hand. Make a list of the ingredients that you think were probably imported. Indicate where some of these items may have come from.

3. What is the European Economic Community or, as it is usually called, the Common Market? What countries are members? What is the purpose of the Common Market? Prepare an oral or written report on the subject. An encyclopedia or a world almanac will help you.

4. Join with three or four of your classmates to form a committee. Arrange to talk with local business people who have knowledge of the kinds of goods imported for sale in your community. These people may be owners of small stores or department managers or buyers in large firms. Make a list of products that are imported by businesses such as these: drugstore, gift shop, music store, delicatessen, sporting goods store, women's clothing department, and grocery store.

5. Agencies are often called by a word made up of their initials. These words are called acronyms. OPEC is an acronym relating to world trade. Find out what it means and list the nations which are involved.

UNIT 3
Finding Your Career

UNIT OBJECTIVES

After studying the parts in this unit, you will be able to:

1. Describe several industry groups and worker categories that help us understand our nation's work force.

2. Explain how learning about people, data, and things is useful in looking at the kinds of work that people do.

3. Give several reasons why it is important to plan ahead for your future work.

THE WORLD OF WORK

PART OBJECTIVES

After studying this part and completing the end-of-part activities, you will be able to:

1. Explain what is meant by the term "work force."
2. Give examples of firms which are in the service-producing industries.
3. Give examples of firms which are in the goods-producing industries.
4. Tell what the difference is between blue-collar and white-collar workers.
5. Discuss three things which affect the demand for workers.
6. Give two sources of information about the work force.

You have learned how important human resources are to our economy. The production of goods and services could not be accomplished without millions of people who are in the world of work.

The work that each individual does is important. Ted Mitchell works as a salesperson in a large shopping center. He helps provide an important service to people who buy things in the store where he works. Betty Bond works in a pottery shop and makes vases and bowls. She is providing goods that many people desire. Ted and Betty both got started on their careers by taking courses in school that helped prepare them for the work they would do later.

111

It might seem as though it is too early for you to begin planning for the work you will do in your future. Many people in the world of work, however, have found that early career planning helped them get into the right careers. Learning about our work force, the kinds of jobs that are available, and sources of information about careers will help you in your career planning.

INDUSTRY GROUPS

Our work force is made up of men and women working on many different kinds of jobs. The **work force** is the total of all the persons 16 years of age and older who are either employed or who are looking for employment. When you seek your first full-time job, you will become part of the work force. There are over 100 million persons in our work force today.

Illus. 9-1

Our work force has grown steadily over the past 20 years and will continue to increase as men and women seek employment. The 1985 bar shows the projected growth for that year.

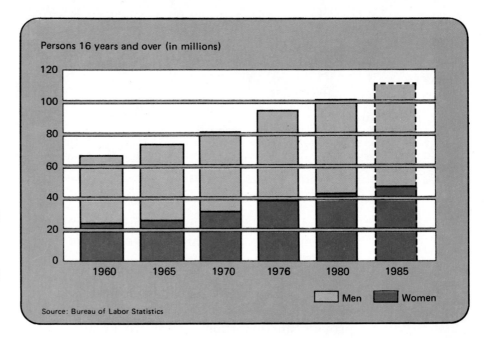

Persons 16 years and over (in millions)

Source: Bureau of Labor Statistics

☐ Men   ◼ Women

The jobs that all workers hold are found in nine groups of businesses. These groups are called industries and are shown in Illus. 9-2. In thinking about jobs that may be of interest to you, it is helpful to know something about the industries in which jobs are found.

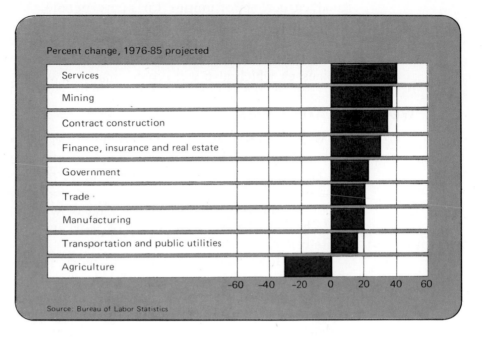

Percent change, 1976-85 projected

	-60	-40	-20	0	20	40	60
Services							
Mining							
Contract construction							
Finance, insurance and real estate							
Government							
Trade							
Manufacturing							
Transportation and public utilities							
Agriculture							

Source: Bureau of Labor Statistics

Illus. 9-2

Employment growth will vary widely by industry through the mid-1980's.

Each of the nine industries is primarily concerned with providing either goods or services. Four of the industries mainly produce goods and five of the industries mainly provide services. Most of the people in the nation's work force are employed in the industries providing services. These services include education, health care, government, transportation, banking, and insurance. Those industries which produce goods, such as raising crops, building homes, and manufacturing equipment, require less than one half of the work force.

In general, more jobs will become available in the service-providing industries than in the goods-producing industries throughout the next decade. This will be true in part because more people are moving to cities and demanding increasing amounts of city services. Also, our rising income and living standards increase the demand for improved services, such as health care and police and fire protection. Other service-industry businesses which will have good job growth include retail stores, shopping centers, and wholesale companies. Good jobs will also be available in banks, insurance companies, truck companies, telephone companies, and government offices.

Goods-producing industries will not have as many jobs available as will service industries, but they still will offer some good career opportunities for many people. Mining companies, especially those dealing in coal and oil, appear to have a bright future. Automobile manufacturers, clothing firms, highway builders, and medical supply companies are among those businesses which also will require many new employees.

WORKER CATEGORIES

Within each of the industry groups, workers are employed in a variety of jobs. These jobs are divided into categories based on the kind of work that is done. In addition to considering types of businesses or industries in which you may like to work, it is important for you to consider the kind of work you would like to do. The two largest categories of workers are blue-collar and white-collar.

Blue-collar workers tend to do work that requires physical skills and the operation of equipment. These workers are important to our economy because they produce and service goods that we need. Blue-collar workers build houses, work on assembly lines, repair TV sets and highways, and produce many other goods and services.

Illus. 9-3

Blue-collar workers like this welder help to produce many of the goods that you use.

White-collar workers do work that emphasizes mental skill and the ability to deal with people. This group includes salespersons, secretaries, business managers, teachers, lawyers, and accountants. Over one half of our work force is employed in white-collar jobs.

There are several groups of workers within the white-collar category which are of special interest to business students. These groups are clerical workers, sales workers, professional and technical workers, and managers and administrators. You may find your specific interest to be within one of these groups. Each group requires different kinds of skills, abilities, and education.

Clerical workers include secretaries, typists, accounting workers, cashiers, and receptionists. These workers do a variety of work within an office. You will find that a high school diploma and some special training, such as shorthand and typewriting, are required for most clerical work.

Illus. 9-4
Typing and filing are office skills that many clerical jobs require.

Sales workers include salespersons in retail stores, insurance agents, real estate brokers, and warehouse workers. Some training beyond your high school education will usually be required if you decide to join workers in this group.

Professional and technical workers include accountants, bank loan officers, teachers, airline pilots, lawyers, and engineers. You will need a college education, such as in accounting and finance, to get one of these jobs.

Managers and administrators include sales managers, store managers, school administrators, and executives of corporations. Both education and experience are important in these jobs.

Illus. 9-5

Most technical workers need college degrees for the work that they do.

FUTURE NEED FOR WORKERS

In looking ahead to your future work life, you may want to consider those jobs which will likely be in greatest demand. Predicting the future of any job or career area, however, is quite difficult. Nevertheless, there are some things which have an effect on the future demand for workers.

Naturally, the way a business is expected to grow affects the demand for certain types of workers. For example, it is expected that banks and loan companies will grow in the next ten years as people save and borrow more money. You can be sure that those businesses will need more workers. Retail trade is expected to continue to increase as consumers want more goods and services, so more workers will be needed in that area, too.

Another thing that affects future demand for workers is

turnover. Turnover is the number of jobs that have to be filled because people leave their jobs. One reason for leaving a job may be promotion to a higher level job. Other reasons include moving to another city, retirement, or dismissal. Whatever the reason, the turnover rate in a given job area has an important effect on the future demand for workers in that area.

New technology also influences the need for workers. As businesses use more and more equipment and electronic devices to produce goods, services, and information, fewer workers are needed to do certain kinds of work. The use of computers in business is an example of how modern technology affects workers. A business which once employed several clerk-typists to type statements showing how much customers owed today uses a high-speed computer to print these statements in only a few minutes. New kinds of workers are now needed by that company, however, to operate the computers and to work with information that the computers produce.

In Illus. 9-6 you will see categories of workers which will likely have the greatest number of openings in the 1980's. You can see that the demand for white-collar workers, in general, will have the greatest future growth. This growth will be largely due to the trend among consumers to demand more services that are provided by white-collar workers.

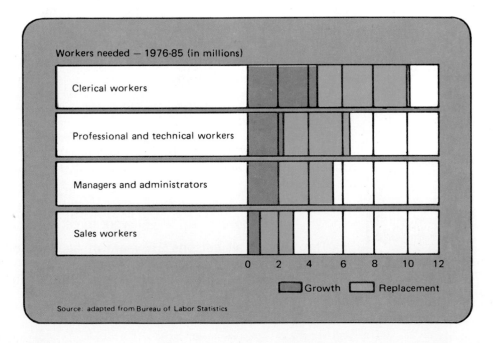

Illus. 9-6

Job openings are determined by replacement plus growth.

WORK FORCE INFORMATION

There is a lot of information available for you regarding the work force of our nation. The U.S. Government, through the Department of Labor, gathers and analyzes information about the work force. Many businesses print booklets which tell about careers in their industry. In addition, there are career magazines and books that can provide you with information to help you explore careers.

The division of the Department of Labor which provides most of the information useful in career planning is the Bureau of Labor Statistics (BLS). As you look for more information about jobs and the work force, you will find information from this source to be quite helpful and available in most libraries. Two of the BLS publications which are useful in career planning are the *Occupational Outlook Handbook* and the *Occupational Outlook Quarterly*. The *Handbook* is published each year and has up-to-date information for you. It tells about changes taking place in the world of work and discusses careers that seem to have good futures. The nine industries and the worker categories are used in the *Handbook*, and a lot of helpful charts and graphs are shown. This *Handbook* is written for use by students who are doing some serious career planning.

The *Occupational Outlook Quarterly* is published four times a year. The *Quarterly* is a magazine that tells about changes taking place in various occupations. It also gives helpful hints about planning for careers. It is a source of information that can be useful to you as you look for additional information to help you in your own career planning.

INCREASING
YOUR
BUSINESS
VOCABULARY

The following terms should become part of your business vocabulary. For each numbered statement, find the term that has the same meaning.

blue-collar workers	white-collar workers
turnover	work force

1. The total of all persons 16 years of age and older who either are employed or are looking for employment.
2. The number of jobs that have to be filled because people leave their jobs.

3. Workers who perform work that requires physical skills and the operation of equipment.
4. Workers who perform work that emphasizes mental skill and the ability to deal with people.

1. Who makes up our work force?
2. What are the nine industry groups in the world of work?
3. Why will future career opportunities be better in the service-producing industries than in goods-producing industries?
4. What kind of work do blue-collar workers tend to do?
5. What kind of work do white-collar workers tend to do?
6. How does the growth of a business affect the demand for workers?
7. In what ways does new technology affect the need for workers?
8. As you go about your career planning, what are some sources of information that will be helpful to you?
9. What kind of information is found in the *Occupational Outlook Quarterly*?

1. What are some of the ways in which our rising standards of living increase the demand for services?
2. What are some businesses in your community which would be included in each of the nine industries? With which of these do you tend to have the most contact?
3. Why are both blue-collar jobs and white-collar jobs important to our economy?
4. If an industry has a lot of older workers, how would that affect future career opportunities in that industry?
5. What are some examples of how new technology affects the demand for workers?

1. The need for clerical workers is expected to increase by 5 million workers in 10 years. If there now are 16 million clerical workers, how many will there be in 10 years? How many clerical workers will there be if the same number of new workers is added in a second 10-year period?
2. A business employs 100 white-collar workers and 50 blue-collar workers. If they hire 25 new white-collar workers and 20 new blue-collar workers, how many workers will they have in all? If 45 workers then retire, how many workers will they have?

3. The following is the percent of white-collar and blue-collar workers employed in each of four industries. Services, 95% white-collar; Trade; 85% white-collar; Manufacturing, 75% blue-collar; Contract Construction, 80% blue-collar. If Services employs 20 million total workers, Trade 5 million, Manufacturing 20 million, and Contract Construction 5 million, how many white-collar workers and how many blue-collar workers are employed in each of these industries?

4. One of the large stores in a shopping center employs 48 salespersons, 6 department managers, 2 credit clerks, 2 secretaries, 1 accountant, and 1 store manager.
   (a) How many employees, including the store manager, are there in this store?
   (b) If the credit clerks, secretaries, and the accountant make up the office staff, what percent of all employees is the office staff?
   (c) If two thirds of the salespersons work part-time, how many part-time salespersons are there? How many salespersons are full-time workers?

5. Look at the chart below. If a community has 2,000 persons employed and they are distributed in the same proportion as shown below, how many people are employed in government? in services? in wholesale and retail trade? in manufacturing? What is the total number of people employed in those four industries? How many people are there employed in the remaining five industries?

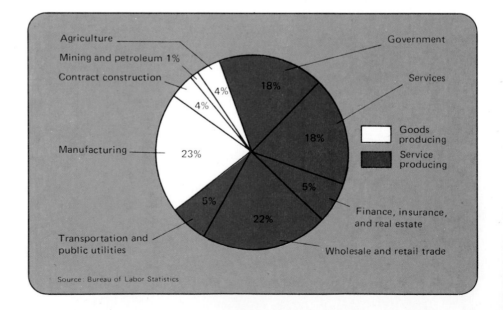

6. One group of blue-collar workers laid 160 miles of railroad track; how many kilometers did they lay? One group of white-collar workers drove 550 kilometers in making sales of a new product; how many miles did they travel?

EXPANDING YOUR UNDERSTANDING OF BUSINESS

1. One of the *Occupational Outlook Handbooks* contains the following statement: "The demand for workers in any occupation depends ultimately on the tastes and desires of consumers." Make a list of ways in which consumer demands can affect certain jobs.
2. The percentage of women entering the work force has been increasing while the percentage of men in the work force has been decreasing. What are some of the reasons for this change? What effect does this change have on employment opportunities for both men and women?
3. What factors are causing the mining industry to now have a bright prediction for future employment prospects?
4. Find out about the impact of new technology on businesses in your community. Talk with business owners or employees about their experiences with it.

10 WORKERS IN YOUR ECONOMY

PART OBJECTIVES

After studying this part and completing the end-of-part activities, you will be able to:

1. Explain how jobs can be classified according to data, people, and things.
2. Tell how levels of education affect employment and wages.
3. State at least five job titles that are common in business.
4. Give at least two reasons why people work.
5. Discuss three trends affecting workers.

You know that in a free enterprise system you have the right to select the work you will do to earn a living. Since there are so many kinds of jobs from which to choose, making a selection is not easy. Knowing about the work people do on various jobs and the benefits they receive is important in making your selection.

Before he went into sales work, Ted Mitchell worked part-time in a gas station. He did minor service and repair work on cars, pumped gas, and sold items such as batteries and seat cushions to customers. Ted found that selling items to customers was the part of the job he liked the best. To learn more about sales work, he took special courses and talked with several people who had sales careers. His decision to become a salesperson proved to be a good one for him.

Betty Bond always enjoyed working with her hands and creating things. For a while she considered becoming a hair stylist, but one day she visited a pottery shop with her art class. After watching people working there, she knew she would enjoy doing that kind of work. She got her job in pottery making after graduation from high school. Someday Betty hopes to have her own pottery shop.

WORKING WITH DATA, PEOPLE, AND THINGS

There are several ways that you can look at the kinds of work people do. One of the ways that has been helpful to many people is to consider how much work is done with data, people, and things.

Most jobs require some work with data (information), some contact with people, and some work with things (equipment). Most jobs, however, emphasize one of these three over the others. When you are planning your future, you need to consider which you would like to do most.

Jobs which emphasize working with data require persons who like to work with numbers, facts, and ideas. Accountants, computer programmers, and file clerks have jobs that deal mostly with data. Courses in accounting, data processing, and office procedures will help you determine whether or not you prefer working with data.

Illus. 10-1

Working with data involves organizing numbers, facts, or ideas.

Workers who have a lot of contact with people must enjoy dealing with people's needs and problems. Just liking to be around people is not the same; in this kind of work, you often need a lot of patience. For instance, when a salesclerk talks with a customer who cannot make up his or her mind and keeps the salesclerk from helping others who want to buy something, the salesclerk must remain calm and not become upset. When a receptionist must deal with a caller who is angry about not having an appointment which he or she thought had been made, some solution must be found without getting into an argument about who is right or wrong. Workers who have a lot of contact with people also include insurance agents, secretaries, and loan application clerks.

Some workers spend most of their time operating machines and equipment — that is, working with things. These workers must be skilled in the use of their equipment and have pride in the work that is produced. Jobs which involve a lot of work with things include typists, duplicating machine operators, and mail clerks.

Illus. 10-2

The workers on this housing rehabilitation project are skilled in repairing old buildings.

JOB TITLES

The jobs that people work on are given titles. A **job title** is the name that is given to the work that someone does. Job titles tell you a little about some tasks that are performed on a job. For instance, a data entry operator is the job title for someone who enters data into a computer system. A duplicating machine operator works with machines which duplicate or reproduce information. A statistical typist spends a lot of time typing reports which contain numbers. Common job titles used by businesses include the following:

Adding Machine Operator	Assistant Loan Officer
Audit Clerk	Buyer
Clerk-Typist	Mail Order Clerk
Coding Clerk	Accountant
Computer Operator	Internal Auditor
Systems Analyst	Payroll Clerk
Administrative Assistant	Advertising Manager
Executive Secretary	Hotel Desk Clerk
Transcribing Machine Operator	Loan Clerk

Illus. 10-3

An Administrative Assistant performs a variety of office duties.

In looking for information about jobs, you can use job titles to look up information about the kind of work that is done on those jobs. The *Dictionary of Occupational Titles*, another publication of the Department of Labor, gives job descriptions for thousands of job titles. The descriptions tell something about the work that is done with data, people, and things on each job. The following example from the *Dictionary of Occupational Titles* is a job description for one of the above titles:

> Clerk-Typist. Compiles data and operates a typewriter in performance of routine clerical duties to maintain business records and reports. Types reports, business correspondence, application forms, shipping tickets, and other matter. Files records and reports, posts information to records, sorts and distributes mail, answers telephone, and performs similar duties.

BENEFITS FROM WORKING

There are a lot of reasons why people work. At one time, work was a means to survival. Today work for most people is more than that. People still work to earn money to take care of basic needs, such as food, clothing, shelter, and transportation. But there is also a real satisfaction that comes from working on a job that you are good at and that you really like to do. Getting personal satisfaction from the work that you do is one important benefit.

The wage you are paid for the work you do is also important. You should be able to earn enough at least to take care of your basic needs and wants. In selecting a job, you need to know how much money you will be able to earn on that job.

The amount of wages you are paid for a certain job depends on many factors. Two of the important ones are the amount of experience you have and how much education and training are required. In general, jobs requiring education beyond high school and those requiring specialized training, such as in electronics, pay more than those which require only a high school diploma.

In considering benefits from work, you should also take into account the employee benefits offered. An **employee benefit** is something that you receive free or at very low cost from your employer. For instance, some employers pay for health insurance for their workers. Retirement plans, life insurance programs, low-cost meals in the company cafeteria, and special recreation programs are often included among employee benefits. Each of these costs the employer money. By having these provided for you, you can then use your earnings for other needs and wants.

TRENDS AFFECTING WORKERS

In addition to knowing about the work performed and the job benefits, you should keep in mind certain trends that will affect the work you may do in your future. You may be wondering if the world of work will be similar to the one in which your parents and other adults are working right now. It probably will not be the same. Some of the changes will be small and will affect few jobs; others will be big and will affect a lot of workers. There are five trends for you to consider at this time:

1. Employers are looking for more skill and more education in their workers. Staying in school, getting the best education you can, and getting the right kind of training are important now and will be even more important in the future.

2. More and different jobs are open to women. Many women are filling positions in careers formerly open only to men. There are many women who now have managerial positions in offices, retail stores, and large corporations. Employment laws will continue to help give both women and men better opportunities to choose occupations they really want.

Illus. 10-4

Many women like this architect are choosing careers that used to be filled by men.

3. Workers must be mobile. You might be qualified for a good job but find that it is not located in or near your community. To have the job you want, it might be necessary for you to move from one community to another. The willingness to move from one community to another is called **mobility**. Mobility may also be important if your employer wants to promote you to a better job in a different plant or store. Not everyone wants to move from a community and friends, but some work opportunities demand it.

4. Advancement in jobs will depend more and more on skills and abilities developed through education, training, and work experience. You often have to prove yourself on your first job to get an advancement. Men and women, regardless of age or race, will have good chances to move ahead when they are prepared for advancement.

5. More supervisory and managerial people will be needed. Offices, stores, factories, and other firms are growing in size and need more supervisory personnel. For the person who is skilled at scheduling work, giving leadership to others, and making decisions, these jobs hold good opportunities for advancement.

MAKING A WISE CHOICE

There are a lot of steps to be taken as you move toward making a wise choice concerning your future work. Getting information about the world of work and the job opportunities it has is one important step. The growth in the work force in the 1980's is estimated to be about 17 million people. Which job will you be in? Will it be the right job for you? To help get good answers to such questions, Part 11 has some ideas about exploring careers and making career decisions.

INCREASING
YOUR
BUSINESS
VOCABULARY

The following terms should become part of your business vocabulary. For each numbered statement, find the term that has the same meaning.

employee benefits   mobility
job title

1. The willingness of a worker to move from one community to another.

2. The name that is given to a job.
3. Things of value which workers receive free or at very low cost from their companies.

1. Give an example of what it means to work with data, with people, and with things.
2. What are some of the common job titles found in business?
3. What are some benefits people get from their work?
4. In what ways are education and training related to the kinds of jobs people get?
5. What are some important trends in terms of what employers are looking for in future workers?
6. Why is it necessary for some people to be mobile if they are to find the jobs that they really want?

1. What are some problems you may face when working on a job that has a lot of people contact?
2. What are some ways in which you can determine whether or not you would enjoy working on a job that has a lot to do with data?
3. What are some of the job titles that are used for workers in your school?
4. Give several reasons why earnings often increase as the amount of schooling a worker has completed increases.
5. Why is it important to take the right courses in high school and to have a regular attendance record if you want to get a good job later?

1. There are 85 full-time workers in Turner's Toys and Games Store. If 45 are men, how many women are employed there? If 10 additional women workers and 5 additional men workers are hired, what will the total number of workers be? How many women and how many men workers will there be employed in that store?
2. In one midwest community, there are 6,000 people working in various businesses. Only 1 percent of these people are self-employed. What is the number of people who are self-employed? Another 20 percent are in sales work. How many people work in sales?

3. In one town there will be 550 high school seniors graduating this year. Suppose that 40 percent of the graduates go on to college, 5 percent go into the armed forces, 15 percent work as homemakers and do not seek jobs, and the remainder go directly into the work force. How many of the graduates will go on to college and how many will go directly into the work force?

4. Teresa Calvo has been offered a job that is in a town 150 kilometers from where she now lives. Her state has just recently started converting miles to kilometers. If it costs her 10 cents a mile to drive to that town, how much will the round trip cost Teresa?

5. One company showed the following production figures for a four-year period:

1st year	107
2nd year	118
3rd year	125
4th year	130

   (a) By how much did production increase from the first year to the fourth year?
   (b) In which year was the production increase the greatest?
   (c) What was the percent of increase from the third year to the fourth year?

6. In 1970, 14.2% of our nation's workers had completed at least four years of college; by 1980 the figure reached 18%. By 1985, the figure is projected to be 20%. If a community's work force has 200,000 workers and has the same proportions as the nation's work force, how many college graduates were in the community's work force in 1970? in 1980? How many will there be in 1985?

EXPANDING YOUR UNDERSTANDING OF BUSINESS

1. The introduction of word processing equipment and procedures into many businesses has caused changes in jobs. Find out about some of the specific jobs that have been affected by word processing. What new jobs have been created?

2. Visit a local business and find out what you can about the different kinds of job titles that are used in that business. Also find out what the business expects in terms of education and training when new workers are hired.

3. Some workers today are called a "new breed of workers." These workers are said to demand good pay, sensitive bosses, meaningful work, and good working conditions. What are some

of the reasons why workers today are interested in these benefits? Do you think that the higher levels of education of workers affect some of these demands? If so, in what ways?

4. What you are doing now in school is part of your preparation for your future work role. The courses you are taking, the work habits you are developing, and the attendance pattern you are establishing will all be important to future employers who consider you for a job. Why are these things of interest to a future employer? What are some of the courses that you feel will be especially helpful in preparing you for your future work role?

5. Invite one or more business persons to talk with your class about job trends in your community. Ask the speaker what new job titles are being used in businesses today and why those job titles have come into being. Also find out about the training and experience that is desired for some of those jobs.

11 EXPLORING BUSINESS CAREERS

PART OBJECTIVES

After studying this part and completing the end-of-part activities, you will be able to:

1. Explain what career exploration is and why it is important.
2. Give at least two sources of information about careers in a local community.
3. Conduct a career interview based on a planned approach.
4. Describe ways you can find out about your interests and abilities.
5. Give at least six questions that you can ask when considering your values.
6. Describe four steps to follow in making a career decision.

Charlie Brown and some of his friends were on a class trip. "Where are we going now?" asked Lucy. "To look at a car wash," explained Linus. "Well," responded Lucy, "that barber we just saw worked hard, didn't he? He had to stand there all day cutting hair." "That's why we have field trips," explained Charlie Brown, "to show us what jobs to avoid."

Finding out about jobs and the work people do teaches us several things, including what jobs we might not want. Not everyone enjoys doing the same thing. What one person likes another may dislike.

What you have learned about the work force and careers in business will help you think about your future work role. There is additional information you will need; career exploration is a good way to get it.

EXPLORING CAREERS

Career exploration is an important process. It involves learning things about yourself and about jobs in the world of work. When you explore careers, you find out where various jobs are located, what training they require, and what some of their advantages and disadvantages are.

Career exploration is not just something you do today in class and get it over with. It should go on until you make a career choice. Here are some ideas that can help you in your career exploration.

You can explore careers in school or out of school. One good way to explore a career is to get a part-time or summer job in a career area in which you are interested. You can learn a lot from each job. You will learn which job tasks you enjoy and which ones you dislike. You will learn whether or not you like to work with people, or data, or equipment. Also, the people with whom you work can give you helpful information about career planning.

Illus. 11-1

These students in Hawaii are exploring careers in hotel management through on-the-job experience.

You might be interested in several career areas right now. Time might not permit you to get part-time work in each of those areas, so you need other ways to explore careers too.

One way, if you have not already done this, is to observe the occupations that are all around you. For instance, how many different kinds of workers are employed in your school? There are teachers, administrators, office workers, maintenance people, business managers, and others. What can you find out about the work they do? When you go to a supermarket or drugstore, look around at the various kinds of people who work in those kinds of businesses. In almost every business, there are "behind-the-scenes" jobs that you might not see unless you look for them. Examples are the stock clerk in a department store and the shipping clerk in a manufacturing firm.

CAREERS IN YOUR COMMUNITY

The information you have read in Parts 9 and 10 about the work force, number of workers, and the different kinds of jobs is based on national information. The area in which you live and in which you plan to work might or might not be like the national picture. There are various ways that you can get information on your local labor market. Here are some suggestions.

One good way is to read newspaper want ads which tell you about jobs that are now in demand. You also can talk with your school counselors or business teachers to see what kinds of local information they have.

Many cities have **government employment offices** that help people find jobs and give out information about careers. Employers who need workers contact these offices for help. A government employment office can help you get information about your local labor market and can help you look for part-time or full-time work.

SOURCES TO READ AND STUDY

There is a lot of information available about various jobs and career fields. Many industries, educational publishers, and professional business organizations, such as the Administrative Management Society, have developed information about occupations. Your library or counseling office will very likely have publications for you to look at.

Illus. 11-2

Counseling offices are good sources of information about various career fields.

Some books can help you explore certain business career fields, such as data processing, accounting, and retailing and wholesaling. There are also some magazines that are written especially to help young people who want to explore the career world.

You probably like to watch films and filmstrips. You will find quite a few on careers. Some companies have cassette tapes and pictures telling about various careers; these can be used to supplement your reading. As you read, look, and listen, try to imagine working conditions and tasks done on various jobs. You will find that some jobs just seem to appeal to you while others have no appeal. Your personal feelings about a job are important. Try to understand your likes and dislikes for certain types of work; they will help you select the right career.

USING MATERIALS ON CAREERS

As you use the various sources of information, here are some tips for you to keep in mind.

1. As you view films and listen to tapes, keep in mind that they tend to be quite general in describing jobs. A film on careers in advertising may introduce you to jobs in that industry, but you will want to get additional information about specific duties and requirements of the jobs.

2. Since films and tapes are often designed to attract people to a particular field, they may make the field they are discussing look more glamorous than it actually is. They often fail to tell anything about the disadvantages of the jobs or careers.

3. Information should be up to date. Find out the date of publication. If you base your entire idea about a job or career on a source of information that is out of date, you may fail to get the preparation you need.

4. Use a variety of sources. Let each one tell you something about the subject. You can come to your conclusion with the help of your counselors, teachers, and parents.

CAREER INTERVIEWS

Career interviews are also a good way to get information about careers. A **career interview** is a planned discussion with a worker to find out about the work that person does, the preparation that is necessary for that career, and the person's feelings about his or her career. Interviews will help you get an insight into what really goes on in jobs in a career area.

Through interviews you will often find out what is good and what is bad about a job. Most workers are willing to share their experiences and ideas with you. Interviews show how important it is to select the right career and prepare for it.

Before you begin an interview, think about the questions you want to ask. Here are some questions that are often asked by career explorers when they interview workers:

1. How did you get into your present job?
2. What other jobs have you had? Why did you leave your other jobs to take this one?
3. In what ways do you find your job to be satisfying? In what ways is it not satisfying?
4. What are some things you do in performing your job?
5. In what ways do you think your job is better than other jobs? In what ways is it not as good?
6. What do you believe are some of the most important qualifications for the work you are doing? What training and education are needed?
7. What advice would you give a young person who is considering this line of work?

It is important that you ask the right questions. Get the information that is important to you. Encourage the person you are interviewing to talk freely. Be a good listener.

YOUR ABILITIES, GOALS, AND VALUES

After you have learned facts about the world of work and have developed a feeling for some jobs, there is at least one more very important thing to think about before making a career decision: YOU. What are your strengths and weaknesses? What special abilities do you have? What are your goals in your career? What is important to you in life? The answers to each of these questions will affect your career choice.

There are a number of ways you can learn about your own abilities. You can begin by reviewing the courses you take in school and the grades you get. Your courses and grades tell you something about your likes and abilities. You can also discuss these things with counselors, teachers, and friends.

Other sources of help are interest and ability tests. These tests can give you some information on your interests and abilities related to career opportunities. Getting to know yourself is an important part of career exploration.

Illus. 11-3

Special abilities and interests can be helpful clues in choosing the right career.

Your own values, the things that are important to you in life, must be considered too. You can check out some of your values by answering questions such as these:

1. Is it important to you to earn a lot of money?
2. Are you mainly interested in being of service to others?
3. Do you do your best work in the morning? at night? When do you do your clearest thinking?
4. Are you happier working indoors or outdoors?
5. Can you work under pressure? Do you enjoy routine work?
6. Are you even-tempered? What causes you to become angry or frustrated?
7. Is it important for you to have a job that others think is important even if you don't really care for it?

Eventually you will make a career decision. That career decision will help you plan the courses you take in school. It can help you decide what kind of part-time work to try to get and which career area to follow closely.

MAKING A CAREER DECISION

It is usually not possible to be certain whether or not any decision you make will turn out just the way you expect it to. Good decisions, though, generally are made if you follow the right steps. If you follow these steps, they will help you make the best decision that can be made:

1. Get as much information as you can.
2. Sort out and think about the facts you have gathered.
3. Think about different plans of action and what might happen if you follow them.
4. Select what seems to be the best plan of action and follow it.

Your search for the right career could go on for a long time. Over the years ahead, some of your values and likes will change. New jobs and careers will come along for you to learn about. You should be ready to make job changes and career-decision changes whenever they seem to be right. Exploring careers should be something you do throughout your life.

LOOKING AHEAD

If you tried to sum up what you have learned about exploring careers and making career decisions, you probably would include the following:

Learn as much as you can about the work force and job opportunities.

Learn about a variety of careers.

Work on part-time jobs in career areas in which you are interested.

Read about jobs and listen to workers talk about their careers.

Find out what requirements there are for getting into certain jobs and for achieving success in a career.

Know something about which jobs have opportunities for employment in the future.

Get to know yourself and your values.

Choose a career goal and let it guide you in selecting courses and in making decisions about preparing for your career.

This book will be of real help to you as you continue to think about your future. You will learn additional facts about the economic world and how business functions. At the end of each unit, there will be a Career Focus section which will add to your knowledge about careers. Learn all you can; your future and your career are important.

INCREASING YOUR BUSINESS VOCABULARY

The following terms should become part of your business vocabulary. For each numbered statement, find the term that has the same meaning.

*career exploration   government employment office
career interview*

1. An important process that involves learning about yourself and about jobs in the world of work.
2. A planned discussion with a worker to find out about the work that is done, preparation necessary, and feelings about that career.
3. A government agency that helps persons find jobs and has information available about careers.

UNDERSTANDING YOUR READING

1. What are some of the ways to become involved in the process of exploring careers?
2. Why are some jobs said to be "behind the scenes"?
3. What are some of the things that you should keep in mind when you use materials on careers?
4. List at least five questions that can be used when interviewing someone about the job he or she has.
5. What are some ways in which you can find out about your own strengths and weaknesses?
6. What questions can you ask yourself that will help you understand what you consider to be most important in life?
7. There are certain steps that should be followed in arriving at a decision; what are they?
8. Exploring careers is something that people do throughout their lives; what are some of the reasons why this is so?

USING YOUR BUSINESS KNOWLEDGE

1. What are some of the things that can be learned from working on a part-time job that will help you in exploring careers?
2. What would you look for in want ads that will help you learn about jobs and which ones are in demand? What other sources of information are important?
3. Why is it important to write out questions before you interview a worker?
4. How can the grades you get in a course tell you something about your abilities (your strengths and weaknesses)?

SOLVING PROBLEMS IN BUSINESS

1. Laura Romano was trying to decide whether to become a nurse. A nursing education would require her to go to school for three more years after high school. The tuition at the school for nurses would cost $600 each year. Her room and board would cost $800 a year. And her books and uniforms would be about $500 for the three-year period.
   (a) What would it cost Laura for the above items for the three-year course?
   (b) If she got a part-time job to pay for her schooling and earned $5.00 per hour, how many hours would she have to work to pay for all of the above costs?
2. Steve Rupp got a job in a hospital as a medical secretary. He had to take extra courses at a community college for this job. These courses cost him $570. He earns $190 a week.
   (a) How many weeks will it take for him to pay for his community college work?
   (b) If he works 40 hours a week, what is his hourly rate of pay?

3. George McCoy went to the library and found 16 filmstrips dealing with careers in business. Ten filmstrips lasted for 15 minutes and six lasted for 25 minutes. If George watches all of them, how many hours will he spend in viewing the filmstrips?

4. Dora DeTellem wants to save $1,200. Her job pays $200 per week. Taxes take 25 percent of her salary, and living expenses take another 60 percent.
   (a) If she saves the balance of her salary, how many weeks will it take her to save $1,200?
   (b) If she brings her living expenses down to 50 percent, how much sooner will she achieve her savings goal?

5. Bill Rolfsen's job as a receiving clerk involves working with figures. In just a few hours he received the following shipments:
   (a) One order that came in said that the shipment was 4 meters long and 2 meters wide. Approximately how many feet long and how many feet wide was the shipment?
   (b) Another sheet listed an order for 10 bottles which held 1 liter each of a new cleaning fluid. Approximately how many quarts of cleaning fluid are there in that order?
   (c) A box that was delivered was marked to show that it weighed 2 kilograms. That seemed very heavy to Bill. Do you think that he should be able to lift that box without much difficulty? Why or why not?

EXPANDING YOUR UNDERSTANDING OF BUSINESS

1. Make a list of all of the career resources in your school that could be of help to someone looking into careers. Be sure to check reference shelves, the card catalog, and periodicals in the library or resource center. Your counselor's office and the business education department are also places to look for materials to be included on your list.

2. Interview a worker on a job that you think would be of interest to you. Develop an interview outline to help you ask the right questions. Write a report of the interview after you have completed it.

3. Write a report on a part-time job that you have now or one that you had and can still remember. Describe the job in general and then tell about some of the specific things that you had to do on the job. Write some comments about what you liked best and what you liked least about the work, the people with whom you worked, and the working conditions. End your report by writing a one-paragraph summary of how this part-time job has helped or could help you plan for your future.

4. Interview a job counselor (sometimes called a placement counselor) from a government employment agency or from your

school district. Ask about jobs that are available today and those that are expected to be available in the future. You might include questions about some of the changes that have taken place in the job market in the past few years. An interview form will help you here. After you have completed your interview, write a report which outlines the information you gained.

5. From the list of library sources you compiled in question 1, select two or three pamphlets that describe a job about which you know nothing or very little. Read those pamphlets and write a report on why you feel that career could be a good one for you or for someone else. Find out as many good things as you can about the job. Then list at least three things that you feel would be disadvantages of that job. Give a report to the class on what you find out.

As you know, there are thousands of business firms in this country. Each one of those businesses must have competent workers in order to continue operating. There is probably a place for you in business, if you want it. But before you can choose a job you must first know what jobs are available. You need to know what kinds of work are done on different jobs. It is also important to know what education and training you need to succeed and what kind of a future there is for the career you are thinking about.

You are already familiar with many kinds of businesses. All businesses need workers to meet customers, to sell goods and services, to answer telephones, to type reports and letters, to file business papers, to run business machines, and to do many other tasks.

Workers who do similar tasks are considered to be in the same job family. The job families that are found in almost all businesses are clerical, secretarial, accounting, data processing, and distributive. You will find workers from these job families in clothing stores, banks, grocery stores, restaurants, movie theaters, record companies, and automobile manufacturing plants.

CLERICAL WORKERS

The clerical job family is one of the largest and fastest growing. It is estimated that there are about 5 million clerical workers and that almost 300,000 new clerical workers are needed each year.

Clerical workers include those who keep records, answer

telephones, operate adding and calculating machines, file papers, ship and receive packages, greet office visitors, and act as messengers. Most clerical workers have at least a high school education. In addition to general business, special business courses such as typing, office procedures, and business communications will help you prepare for clerical work.

The need for clerical workers will continue to increase. Naturally, those with higher degrees of clerical skill will have the best chances for the better jobs and for promotions.

SECRETARIAL WORKERS

Secretaries are important to every organization. They are particularly important to the communications of their firms. Secretaries usually know shorthand or know how to use dictation recording machines. In addition to their communication functions, secretarial workers assume important responsibilities. They often serve as special assistants to the executives. Some secretaries specialize in areas such as legal or medical work. Word processing installations have made new career opportunities available to many secretaries.

Secretaries often begin their training in high school business education classes. Additional post-high school training is needed for the higher level secretarial positions. In addition to regular clerical and shorthand skills, secretarial workers must have an excellent knowledge of the English language. They must also be able to make decisions.

There are over 3,500,000 workers in this job family already, and there is a need for almost 300,000 new secretarial workers each year. There are great secretarial career opportunities for both women and men.

ACCOUNTING WORKERS

No business can continue to operate unless it knows whether or not it is making a profit. Accounting workers record the business transactions as they occur so that the amount of profit or loss can be determined. Accountants analyze the records and help make important decisions for their companies.

Some accounting workers get beginning jobs with only a high school education, but most complete post-high school work in accounting. The best accounting jobs require a college degree. Being good in arithmetic and liking to work with figures are important to success in this job family.

There are over 2,500,000 bookkeeping workers and accountants. There are openings for about 150,000 new accounting workers every year.

DATA PROCESSING WORKERS

Business has much more information now than it had 20, or even 10, years ago. Because of the great growth in the amount of information available, more businesses have come to depend on machines to process that information. This has called for more people to operate those machines. Some typical data processing workers are: data entry operators, who prepare information for the machines; programmers, who tell the computers the steps to take in order to do a certain job; and computer operators, who actually run the machines. Many of the routine record-keeping tasks once done by clerical and bookkeeping workers are now done on electronic data processing equipment.

Data processing workers must be specially trained. Some of this training is available in most high schools, but often post-high school work is needed for the more important jobs and for those who want to be promoted to better positions. To be a successful data processing worker you must have good technical knowledge and skills, be able to concentrate, and enjoy working with details.

There are over 1,000,000 persons employed in this job family. Over 25,000 new workers are needed each year.

DISTRIBUTIVE WORKERS

Persons employed in the distributive job family work on jobs in businesses such as retail stores, shopping centers, loan companies, wholesale houses, insurance companies, and real estate agencies. There is a large demand for both full-time and part-time workers in sales jobs.

Distributive workers must like to work with people and provide services which are needed by customers and clients. The expanding needs and wants of our population will cause growth in retailing, where almost half of the distributive workers are employed. Most distributive workers have completed a high school education and have received some special training by the store or firm for which they work.

There are over 5 million persons employed in this job family, and there is a need for 300,000 new workers each year.

UNIT 4
Your Role As A Consumer

UNIT OBJECTIVES

After studying the parts in this unit, you will be able to:

1. Explain how you become an informed consumer.

2. Identify nine general rules a consumer should follow in buying.

3. Describe four rights and four responsibilities that consumers have.

PART 12   Being an Informed Consumer
PART 13   Shopping for the Best Buy
PART 14   Your Consumer Rights and Responsibilities

BEING AN INFORMED CONSUMER

PART OBJECTIVES

After studying this part and completing the end-of-part activities, you will be able to:

1. List seven buying decisions you should make whenever you plan to purchase anything.
2. Give an example of product information you can find on a label.
3. Describe how you can use advertisements to gather information about products and services.
4. Tell how private product testing agencies aid you as a consumer.
5. Explain how Better Business Bureaus can provide you with consumer information.

The gross national product of the United States is well over two trillion dollars a year. Of that amount, almost two thirds represents products and services sold to individual consumers like you. Stop for a minute and think about how many different things you buy and consume in a year. Just consider all the different items of clothing you have. And what about all the books, pens, records, tapes, combs, and many other products you use? In addition to consuming goods, you also use numerous services. You talk on the telephone; go to dances, movies, and sporting events; and receive treatment from doctors, dentists, and orthodontists.

This all means that as a consumer, you are very important to business and the economy. The buying decisions that you and other consumers make spell the difference between success and failure for many businesses. But the quality of your decisions also means the difference between your living well or living poorly on the money that you have available. Your goal should be to make the most effective use of every dollar you have to spend.

USING GOOD JUDGMENT IN BUYING

While it probably isn't possible to carefully plan every single purchase you make, you can develop the habit of using good judgment for most of the things you buy. Whenever you plan to buy anything, you must make a number of important decisions. Among these decisions are:

1. Would you rather buy this item than another item which you could buy for the same money?
2. Which dealer should you go to?
3. What quality of merchandise do you want to buy?
4. What price are you willing to pay?
5. Should you pay cash or buy now and pay later?
6. Do you really need this item now, or can you wait awhile?
7. If you make this purchase, what other important item may you have to do without?

Each purchase should be judged according to whether it will give you more pleasure than something else you might have bought instead. Purchases must be guided by the relationship between the need or want for one article and the possible needs or wants for others.

SOURCES OF CONSUMER INFORMATION

To make wise buying decisions, you need to know certain kinds of information about the products you want to purchase. There are numerous sources you can turn to in order to get the information you need. Some of the most helpful sources are labels on products, advertisements, product testing agencies, newspapers, magazines, radio, television, experts or specialists, Better Business Bureaus, and government organizations. While you won't use every one of these sources for each purchase you make, the more information you get, the better your purchase decisions will probably be.

USING PRODUCT LABELS

A **label** provides written information about a product. The label may tell you what the product is made of, what the size is, how to care for it, and when and where it was produced. As an example, if you want to buy a pair of slacks, you should know whether they are washable or will have to be dry-cleaned. The label on the slacks will give you this information. The label may be printed on the carton, can, or wrapper, or on a tag attached to the product. It may also be stamped or sewn onto the product. Whatever the form, a label should give you useful information about the product. Study it carefully.

Illus. 12-1

Reading the label on a product can tell you what you need to know before buying.

Labels often show the grade of a product. A **grade** indicates the quality or size of a product. For example, beef may be stamped "prime," "choice," "good," or some other grade. Foods are often graded by companies or by government agencies. Look at the label in Illus. 12-2. The USDA (United States Department of Agriculture) shield means that the product has been inspected and approved by that government agency.

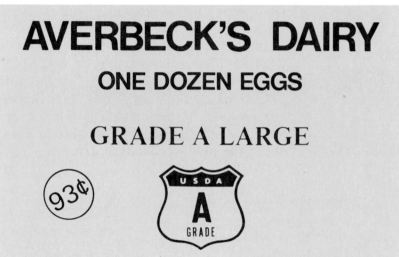

Illus. 12-2

Many foods are dated to show freshness. The date on this label means that freshness of the eggs is not guaranteed after March 2.

USING ADVERTISING

Use advertisements as a source of information to learn about products and services. Look for advertisements that tell you what the product is, how it is made, and what it will do. Ask yourself if advertising statements give facts which you can use to compare the product with other products. Or are vague and general claims made that really tell you nothing about the product? If an advertisement states, "Buy Zappos — they're better!" you should ask, "Better than what? And on what basis are comparisons made?" Compare the advertisements in Illus. 12-3. Which one would be more helpful to you in buying a tennis racket?

Illus. 12-3

Some advertisements appeal to feelings such as a desire to
have friends, to be healthy, or to be like famous people.
The advertisement on the left really tells you nothing about
the racket but the price. Some advertisements appeal to our
reasoning ability. The advertisement on the right gives
specific information that can be used to compare the tennis
racket with other brands.

LOOKING AT REPORTS
OF PRODUCT TESTING AGENCIES

There are a number of private organizations which can help
you become a more completely informed consumer. Two such
organizations are Consumers' Research, Inc., and Consumers
Union of the United States, Inc. They test consumer goods and
report on their quality. Consumers' Research publishes its
findings in *Consumers' Research Magazine*. Consumers Union
publishes its findings in a magazine called *Consumer Reports*.

Another testing organization is Underwriters' Laboratories, Inc. It tests electrical and other products for safety. Look at the UL seal in Illus. 12-4.

Illus. 12-4

The UL seal appears on electrical goods that have been tested and have met the safety standards set up by Underwriters' Laboratories, Inc.

CHECKING MAGAZINES AND NEWSPAPERS FOR CONSUMER INFORMATION

In addition to special testing and reporting agencies, some magazines also test and rate products. *Good Housekeeping* and *Parents' Magazine* are examples. When a product has been tested by one of these publications and found to meet standards of performance or quality, the product can display the magazine's seal of approval on the label. There are other magazines devoted to information on special products, such as stereo equipment and cars.

Magazines and newspapers often carry articles of help to consumers. Most newspapers run weekly columns written by home economists on "best food buys." Another regular feature in many newspapers is the "Plentiful Foods List" prepared by the Department of Agriculture. Other articles may deal with such things as what to look for in a used car and how to cut home heating costs.

Illus. 12-5

Checking the newspaper for helpful buying tips is one way to be an informed consumer.

GETTING INFORMATION FROM
RADIO AND TELEVISION

Like magazines and newspapers, radio and television are sources of consumer information. Many stations carry regular programs which inform the public about product safety, care and use of products, and shopping tips.

BUSINESSES PROVIDING
CONSUMER SERVICES

Many businesses have special departments devoted to consumer service. Some firms provide their customers with booklets on a variety of consumer topics. Household Finance Corporation, a personal loan company, publishes a series of booklets to help consumers manage their money. Banks and insurance companies also publish this type of material. Some large retail firms provide printed materials to help consumers with their buying problems. J.C. Penney and Sears, Roebuck both publish series of pamphlets to help their customers improve their buying abilities.

GETTING ADVICE
FROM A SPECIALIST

Sometimes it is wise to get an expert's advice on what to look for in a product. This is especially true when you have never before bought an item, or when the item is complicated. For example, most of us could not judge whether a used car's transmission is worn or its brakes need to be replaced. But an automobile mechanic could give expert advice about the condition of the car.

CONSULTING THE
BETTER BUSINESS BUREAU

Almost every community has a Better Business Bureau. Better Business Bureaus are chiefly concerned with problems which arise from false advertising or misrepresented products and services. They can provide you with some very helpful information. For example, suppose you were considering buying a used car from a dealer. You could call the Better Business Bureau to find out what experiences others have had in buying from that dealer. If consumers have reported the firm as being unreliable, you can find out about these complaints. Better Business Bureaus give facts only; they do not recommend products or firms. They will give you the information, but you are free to interpret it in your own way and to make your own decision.

CONSUMER INFORMATION PROVIDED BY THE GOVERNMENT

The federal government formed the Consumer Product Information Center to serve as a headquarters for consumer information. In addition to making government publications easier for consumers to get, the Center publishes information resulting from the research programs and the testing of products by the government. The agency has distribution centers in several major cities.

The Department of Agriculture is another source of consumer information. USDA publications specialize in information about food — judging quality, buying wisely, improving marketing practices, planning meals, and improving nutrition. Other farm- and home-related topics are also covered.

The U.S. Office of Consumer Affairs is an agency of the federal government that coordinates consumer programs. It also produces consumer information publications on various subjects.

You should not overlook sources of information in your own city or state. Most states and many cities and counties have some type of consumer agency from which you can get information. Labor unions, civic clubs, and even some churches provide materials, sponsor programs and fairs, and hold meetings on topics of consumer interest. Look around you. You will be surprised to find that with just a little effort you can find sources that will help you become an informed consumer.

INCREASING YOUR BUSINESS VOCABULARY

The following terms should become part of your business vocabulary. For each numbered statement, find the term that has the same meaning.

grade   label

1. A statement attached to a product giving information about its nature or contents.
2. An indication of the quality or size of a product.

UNDERSTANDING YOUR READING

1. What are seven important buying decisions you should make every time you plan to purchase a product or service?
2. What kinds of information can you find on labels?
3. What is meant by the grade of a product?
4. What does it mean if you find the USDA shield on a product?
5. How can advertising help you in making decisions?
6. How do private testing agencies aid you?
7. In what ways do magazines and newspapers help consumers become better informed consumers?
8. What does it mean if a product displays the *Good Housekeeping* seal?
9. In what ways do radio and television provide information for consumers?
10. What services can a Better Business Bureau provide for you?
11. What are some of the major government sources of consumer information?

USING YOUR BUSINESS KNOWLEDGE

1. How can your buying decisions affect the economy?
2. Suppose that you were given the money to buy a portable stereo. From what sources could you get information about quality features to look for in stereo sets?
3. If you were to purchase the following items, for which would the advice of a specialist likely be needed? Give your reason for each answer.

   (a) used car   (c) portable radio
   (b) new motorcycle   (d) used water skis

4. If you were shopping in a supermarket, on which of the following items would you look for dated labels? Explain your answer for each item.
   (a) fresh milk
   (b) a pencil
   (c) medicine
   (d) sugarless gum
   (e) lettuce
5. Andy Colberg answered the door to find a man who said that he is in the roof-repair business. He said that he had walked around Mr. Colberg's house and found some serious defects in the roof and around the chimney. If Mr. Colberg will let him do the job within the week, he will give a reduced rate. Mr. Colberg was aware that he needed some roof repairs, but had just not gotten around to getting it done. He notices the name on the

caller's truck is Ready Roof Repair Company. From what source could Mr. Colberg find out whether the firm is reliable? How can he find out whether the price is really a reduced rate?

SOLVING PROBLEMS IN BUSINESS

1. The advertisement below appeared in a newspaper during the month of March:

> **CLEARANCE SALE**
>
> SAVE, yes SAVE ½ and more!
> Buy NOW! Buy for NEXT YEAR!
> A small deposit will hold your
>   selection!
> Don't miss these fine values!
>
> | | Regular Price | Sale Price |
> |---|---|---|
> | Fur-Trimmed Coats. . | $159.95 | $74.95 |
> | Finer Winter Coats . . | $ 99.95 | $49.95 |
> | | | |
> | Raincoats . . . . | $ 34.95 | $16.95 |

   (a) How much were the fur-trimmed coats reduced?
   (b) How much were the finer winter coats reduced?
   (c) How much were the raincoats reduced?

2. An advertisement for Tunney's Men's Shop read, "Buy two pairs of stretch socks for $3.99 and get a third pair free." The Gentlemen's Shop ran an advertisement the same day which read, "Stretch socks, $1.50 a pair. Buy three pairs and get a fourth pair for $.74."
   (a) Assuming the socks are of equal quality, at which store are the socks priced lower?
   (b) How much will be saved on the price of each pair of socks at the store where the price will be lower?

3. Gus and Sherry Nadick have four liters of milk delivered to their home every Monday and Thursday. The cost is 54¢ a liter. The home delivery cost is 2¢ per liter higher than the supermarket cost.
   (a) How many liters of milk are delivered in a four-week period?
   (b) What is the cost of the milk for the four-week period?

    (c) How much would the Nadicks save in four weeks by buying their milk at the supermarket?

4. In a recent year, about $44 billion was spent on advertising. The approximate percent of the total that was spent on each of the different media is shown below. Calculate the amount spent on each medium.

Medium	Percent
Newspapers	29
Magazines	6
Television	20
Radio	7
Direct mail	14
Outdoor	1
Business and farm publications	4
Other	19

5. Near the end of the summer, Wheeler's Garden Store marked down a number of items for quick sale. The regular selling price, marked-down price, and cost of each item to the store are shown below. Each item was sold at the marked-down price.

Item	Regular Price	Marked-Down Price	Cost
21-inch power mower	$129.99	$119.50	$101.00
Riding lawn mower	450.00	399.95	375.00
Electric hedge trimmer	36.00	32.88	27.00
Deluxe barbeque grill	64.95	49.68	54.50
Lawn furniture set	149.99	112.88	90.00

   (a) By what amount was each item marked down?
   (b) How much profit or loss was realized on each item?
   (c) What was the total profit realized on the five items?

EXPANDING
YOUR
UNDERSTANDING
OF
BUSINESS

1. If two thirds of the gross national product represents products and services sold to individual consumers, what does the remaining one third represent?

2. Examine the permanent-care labels on three articles of clothing which you or your family have bought recently. The law requires that most clothing bear labels showing both what should be done and what should not be done in cleaning the garment. Write a statement from each label which you believe follows this regulation.

3. Collect advertisements from newspapers and magazines that represent each of the following appeals: (a) desire for comfort, (b) pride of ownership, (c) desire to be healthy, (d) desire to be famous, (e) desire for security. Write a short statement explaining how each advertisement makes the appeal.

4. The government requires that labels on some processed foods show the ingredients that are used in the product and the nutritional value of the product. Examine food packages in your home and find an ingredient label and a nutritional label. Do you think this information should be provided to the consumer? Why or why not?

5. Find out which of the following consumer agencies are located in your area. List the address of each one you find. Give an example of the kind of information available from each.

cooperative   federal information center
cooperative extension service   municipal consumer agency
Better Business Bureau   state consumer agency

6. Newspapers carry both news stories about consumer events and columns which provide consumer information. Examine one issue of your local newspaper, and make a list of all articles which are about consumers. Indicate which articles are published as a consumer information service.

SHOPPING FOR THE BEST BUY

PART OBJECTIVES

After studying this part and completing the end-of-part activities, you will be able to:
1. Explain why it is important to take your time before you buy.
2. Tell why you should not always buy the item with the lowest price.
3. Describe how a promotional sale is different from a clearance sale.
4. Tell how brand names can help you as a shopper.
5. Describe how unit pricing can benefit you.

Millie Vance and Blanche Scott went shopping one day because Millie was looking for a new electric toaster. Only two weeks before, Blanche had purchased a Toast-Rite for $22.95, and she was very pleased with her purchase. As they walked through the stores, Blanche praised the features of the Toast-Rite. She was also quite happy with the price she had paid. Then as they passed a counter of toasters in one store, Millie saw a Most-Toast model for $18.95 that seemed to have all of the features of the toaster that Blanche had bought. Millie and Blanche read the label and inspected the Most-Toast model very carefully. They came to the conclusion that it really was a good buy. Millie was quite pleased to purchase one, but you can imagine how Blanche felt.

She was disappointed that she had paid $4 more than she should have. Blanche realized that she had not shopped properly when she was looking for her toaster.

How do you decide what to buy? How can you use your money wisely and shop so that you receive good value and get your money's worth? The competition in our economic system helps you. Most merchants try to give good values and honest service to attract your patronage and to hold your buying loyalty. You can buy wisely and avoid costly mistakes by following some general rules for buying.

SOME GENERAL RULES FOR BUYING

1. Take your time.
2. Buy at the right time.
3. Compare prices and services.
4. Look for genuine sales.
5. Avoid impulse buying.
6. Examine what you buy.
7. Buy from merchants whom you trust.
8. Know brand names.
9. Look for unit pricing.

Illus. 13-1

When you have learned to follow these buying rules, you will be a smart shopper.

TAKING YOUR TIME

Time is precious to you; but if you are a smart shopper, you will be willing to take your time when making purchases. Sometimes consumers get impatient. They want to buy right now, and often this costs them money. Being willing to wait might mean postponing a purchase until you have saved enough money to pay cash, until you can afford to make a larger down payment, or until you know a special sales event is coming.

Waiting to buy also means slowing down and giving yourself a chance to look for the best values. If you learn to pace yourself sensibly, you will probably find that your money goes farther toward buying the things you need and want. As a smart shopper you will plan your purchases carefully and refuse to be hurried into buying anything. In this way, you avoid buying merchandise that you really do not need and that will not serve your purposes.

BUYING AT THE RIGHT TIME

In order to buy at the right time, you will need to know something about timing from the business point of view. You should be aware of some of the conditions under which products are often sold at reduced prices.

One of these conditions is the season in which products are most in demand. When fresh fruits and vegetables are at their peak, they are usually lower in price. Manufactured products, such as clothing, are usually more expensive in season than out.

Grocery stores may reduce prices on canned corn in July because low-priced fresh corn is available. Department stores may feature sales of winter coats in August, and the sports shops may put bathing suits on sale the day after Labor Day when the summer beach season ends. Bakeries sometimes have "day-old" counters from which they sell baked goods which were not sold at the peak of their freshness. There are many conditions under which merchandise is sold at reduced prices.

COMPARING PRICES AND SERVICES

Except for utilities, such as water and electricity, or for very specialized goods, there are few things that are not produced or sold by more than one business. Competition and a desire to gain a larger share of the market see to that. Therefore, you have a choice of where to buy, and you can compare prices and services.

Illus. 13-2

To be sure you are getting the best buy, compare prices of most products you shop for.

Whenever and whatever you buy, you will want to get your money's worth. Quality merchandise generally costs more, but buying low quality merchandise can sometimes turn out to be expensive. For example, if you buy for a very low price a blank stereo tape on which you want to record music, it may break or not give you the quality of sound you really want. A good quality tape may cost you more but may last twice as long as the other and will probably give you more pleasure.

Smart shoppers are also careful of advertisements that use such phrases as "normally sells for" or "sold elsewhere for." Sometimes these are honest ads of marked-down items. But sometimes the prices mentioned in them are really made up. The smart shopper follows the rule of comparing prices to find out if what is being offered is a true reduction in price.

The smart shopper also compares services from store to store. Reputable merchants try to give good service, but the types of service differ. Some merchants sell for cash only; others extend credit. Some merchants deliver goods; others do not. Some may have a very large stock from which a selection may be made; others have smaller stocks.

Service is important, but you should not pay for more service than you actually need, just as you should not pay for more quality than you actually need. As a good buyer you should know what you want, seek out what you want, and buy what you want at the best prices.

LOOKING FOR GENUINE SALES

You have probably seen "Sale" signs a thousand times. They are used so much as gimmicks to try to sell more goods that many shoppers no longer know when a real sale is going on. Many so-called sales are not really sales at all, and you should check them carefully. Sometimes they consist of regular goods at regular prices being heavily advertised with the word "sale." When an item is really on sale, it is offered at a price lower than its normal selling price.

Retailers run three main types of sales. With **promotional sales**, the merchants try to promote the sale of their regular merchandise by making temporary price reductions. They may do this to open a new store or to publicize a new location for an established store. Merchants may have promotional sales to build acceptance for new products by offering them at low introductory prices. The retailers hope that customers will buy the products at the reduced prices, like them, and then buy at the regular prices in the future. Retailers also use promotional sales to draw customers into their stores. They hope that the customers who buy the sale merchandise will buy other products at the regular prices.

Clearance sales are used to "clear" merchandise that retailers no longer want. This may be shopworn stock, leftovers such as odd sizes and models, or a line of merchandise that the store is no longer going to carry. Clearance sales usually offer some real bargains, but it is important to be sure that you can really use a sale item before you buy it. Also, you should be sure that the merchant did not buy low-quality merchandise especially for the sale.

Illus. 13-3

For this end-of-summer clearance sale, the merchant reduced prices on leftover merchandise.

There are sales, however, which feature **special-purchase merchandise**. This is merchandise bought for a special sale rather than marked down from the regular stock. Special-purchase merchandise may include goods purchased from a manufacturer who is overstocked, goods that are no longer to be made, or stock of a company that is going out of business.

To be able to take advantage of sales, you have to look for sales which are genuine and which are truthfully advertised. Even then you must know the regular price of the product so that you can buy only those things which represent a real saving.

AVOIDING IMPULSE BUYING

You can keep from making costly buying mistakes partly by avoiding impulse buying. **Impulse buying** happens when you see an item attractively displayed and suddenly decide to buy it. Occasionally buying something on impulse, such as a school pep pin, is a nice part of life. The cost is small and the item is usually worth the price. But buying other items like clothing, records, or cosmetics just on impulse can be costly. You may not really need the item, for one thing. Or it might not be the best value for the price, as you would have discovered if you had shopped around.

Making a shopping list and sticking to it can help you stop impulsive buying. Research firms often study customers to find out why they buy. Such firms found out that in supermarkets people without shopping lists buy many more items and also buy more luxury items than do people with shopping lists. Most consumers are open to suggestion. An attractive display of products, for example, can tempt you to buy something that you had not planned to buy. But you can save money if you buy from a shopping list whether it is for groceries, hardware, or clothing.

EXAMINING WHAT YOU BUY

Always try to examine what you buy. Even if you are not an expert, you can often tell whether one item is better than another or whether it is exactly what you want. As you continue to study and examine goods, you will learn to recognize differences in quality.

Illus. 13-4

Examining goods before you buy is an important part of being a smart shopper.

As you examine the quality of merchandise, you should remember an important rule of buying: "Don't buy quality you don't need." This means that the intended use of the product determines how high a quality you need. For example, you wouldn't need to buy expensive finished walnut if you were building a doghouse. Rough lumber would do just as well. But if you were building a bookshelf for your room, you might want the walnut rather than the rough lumber.

BUYING FROM MERCHANTS WHOM YOU TRUST

You should make every effort to judge quality for yourself. But sometimes you may have no way of proving for yourself exactly what you are getting. One of the best guarantees you can have that the things you buy are of good quality is to buy from merchants of established reputation. The wise merchant knows that a satisfied customer is likely to return. The merchant knows the uses and the quality of the goods being offered for sale. The seller is also concerned about matching the proper goods with customers' needs. If you buy from merchants of established reputation, you can usually rely on them and their salespeople to help you make your selections.

KNOWING BRAND NAMES

Many goods are advertised nationally and are sold in almost every community. Among these goods are clothing, shoes, tools, canned foods, toothpaste, cosmetics, furniture, and appliances. Manufacturers of such goods often place brand names on the items they make. A **brand name** is a special name given to a product by a manufacturer to distinguish it as being made by that particular firm. "Levi's," for example, is the brand name of a world-famous line of clothing.

Learning to recognize brand names can help you in several ways. First, you can usually expect uniform quality even when brand name goods are bought in different stores. This is especially helpful in buying goods that are difficult to inspect for quality, such as canned goods. Second, brand names make it possible for you to do comparison shopping at several stores to find the best price and service. Third, brand name items often have better guarantees behind them. It is true, of course, that some unbranded items are comparable in quality to brand name items and are less expensive. They can be good buys if you know how to examine goods for quality.

Some stores have their own brand names. These are called **house brands**. Examples are the "Ann Page" brand of the A & P Company and "Kenmore" as the house brand for appliances sold by Sears, Roebuck and Company. House brands are usually sold for less than nationally advertised brands. Buying house brands, therefore, may often save you money and offer you good quality at the same time.

LOOKING FOR UNIT PRICES

Some products, particularly in supermarkets, are offered under so many brands and in so many sizes that it is difficult to compare values. For example, Great Growers Catsup may come in 44-ounce bottles, while Land of Plenty Catsup is in 14-ounce bottles. A single price stamped on the top of each bottle doesn't help you very much in determining the best buy — unless you are a wizard at math. And most of us are not.

To help shoppers compare value among various brands and sizes of the same product, many stores show the total price and the price of one standard measure, or unit, of the product. In the case of the catsup, a standard unit would be one ounce. If you knew how much one ounce of each brand of catsup cost, you could easily tell whether Great Growers Catsup was a better buy than Land of Plenty Catsup, regardless of the size of the containers. Listing the cost of one standard measure of a product is called **unit pricing**.

To give you an idea of how unit pricing helps you compare values, suppose you need to buy catsup. In the supermarket you see that a 44-ounce bottle of Great Growers Catsup costs 99 cents. On another shelf are offered three 14-ounce bottles of Land of Plenty Catsup for $1.00. Which is the better buy? With the total prices only, it is hard for you to figure. But if each bottle also showed the cost per ounce — the unit price — you could quickly compare the prices. In this case, the 44-ounce bottle would show a unit price of 2.25 cents an ounce. The three 14-ounce bottles would cost 2.38 cents per ounce. Unit pricing would quickly tell you that the 44-ounce bottle is the better buy.

Illus. 13-5
Stores which feature unit pricing often use labels like these. You can easily see which product is the better buy.

Larger sizes do not always mean better value, though. And you often are not aware of this if the label does not show the unit price. The smart shopper, then, will look for the store which features unit pricing. Or it might be a good idea to take a small pocket calculator with you to the supermarket. When you are armed with this inexpensive tool, the unit price is easy to determine.

INCREASING YOUR BUSINESS VOCABULARY

The following terms should become part of your business vocabulary. For each numbered statement, find the term that has the same meaning.

brand name   promotional sale
clearance sale   special-purchase merchandise
house brand   unit pricing
impulse buying

1. A special name used for products sold by one particular store or chain of stores.
2. Goods bought especially for a sale rather than marked down from regular stock.
3. A special name given to a product by a manufacturer to distinguish it as being made by that particular firm.
4. Selling items below regular price to increase the sales of regular merchandise or to draw customers into the store.
5. Unplanned purchases you make when you see an item attractively displayed and suddenly decide to buy it.
6. Showing the cost of one standard measure of a product for comparison of brands and sizes.

7. Using a price reduction to sell items that a merchant no longer wishes to carry in stock.

UNDERSTANDING YOUR READING

1. What are two possible advantages of being willing to postpone a purchase rather than buying at the first opportunity?
2. What is one reason why a merchant might reduce the price of fresh strawberries?
3. Why is it not always wise to buy the lowest priced item?
4. What is meant by a genuine sale?
5. What is the difference between a promotional sale and a clearance sale?
6. What is special-purchase merchandise?
7. Why should you avoid impulse buying?
8. How can recognizing brand names help you as a shopper?
9. What are house brands?
10. How can unit pricing help you?

USING YOUR BUSINESS KNOWLEDGE

1. If you know exactly what merchandise you are looking for, why is it still important to buy from a merchant whom you trust?
2. "Don't buy quality you don't need." Give an example other than the one given on page 165 of a time when you would be unwise to buy the best quality of a product that is available.
3. A discount store advertises for sale certain well-known products at less than regular prices.
   (a) Does this mean that the prices of all products in the store are less than the regular prices in other stores?
   (b) Do you recommend buying at discount stores? Why?
   (c) If you do purchase at discount stores, what are some precautions that you might take?
4. The Greenhills Coffee Shop sells a full-course roast beef dinner for $4.75. Directly across the street, the Hearthside Restaurant sells a similar dinner for $7.75. Both have a fair share of business.
   (a) Why doesn't the Greenhills Coffee Shop get all the business?
   (b) What services might customers get in the Hearthside Restaurant that they couldn't get in the Greenhills Coffee Shop?
   (c) Are those who buy the more expensive dinner poor money managers? Why or why not?

SOLVING PROBLEMS IN BUSINESS

1. Darlene Kempo was planning to buy a new winter coat. In December she saw a coat she liked. It was priced at $95.50. Darlene realized that often prices are reduced after Christmas, so she decided to wait. In January she bought the coat for $79.95.
   (a) How much did Darlene save by waiting one month?
   (b) If the merchant had paid $65.00 for the coat, how much profit was made on the sale?

2. If bread is not sold on the day it is baked, the Village Pastry Shop sells it at 60 percent of its original price the next day. White bread normally sells for 50 cents a loaf.
   (a) At what price does day-old white bread sell?
   (b) One day the Village Pastry Shop had 9 loaves of bread left over. If they sold all the loaves the following day, how much did they make from the sale of day-old bread?

3. Stacey's Appliances is moving to a new store. To avoid having to move a lot of merchandise, they are having a pre-moving clearance sale. Stacey's has advertised that they will reduce the price of all merchandise in their old store by 25 percent for one day.
   (a) What would the sale price of a $512 refrigerator be?
   (b) A customer paid $27.60 for a clock radio during the sale. What was the original price of the radio?

4. Carl Riley is at the supermarket and wants to buy some ground beef. He can buy 1½ pounds of ground beef for $2.25. The supermarket is also having a special on the same ground beef of 4 pounds for $5.60.
   (a) If Mr. Riley buys 1½ pounds, how much is he paying per pound?
   (b) How much is he paying per pound if he buys 4 pounds?

5. Bud and Ellen Carr are a young couple living in a small apartment. They try to save money on purchases, but buying food in large quantities sometimes results in spoilage. They can buy potatoes in different quantities at the prices listed below. The estimated spoilage for each quantity is also shown.

Quantity	Price	Estimated Spoilage
2 kilograms	$ .99	None
4 kilograms	1.89	1 kilogram
12 kilograms	3.99	4 kilograms

   (a) Calculate the cost per kilogram for the purchase of each different quantity, before spoilage. Have your answer correct to the nearest tenth of a cent.
   (b) Calculate the cost per kilogram of each quantity, after subtracting spoilage.

EXPANDING YOUR UNDERSTANDING OF BUSINESS

1. Are there supermarkets in your area which display unit pricing? If you do not know, check the newspaper ads. If a store uses unit pricing, it will usually advertise this fact. Visit a supermarket that uses unit pricing to see how the prices are displayed for the customers. You might also ask the store manager how customers reacted when the store began using unit pricing.

2. For each article listed below, tell whether you would choose to buy a higher quality item or whether you would choose a lower but acceptable quality item. Give reasons for each choice.
   (a) Outdoor paint for your two-story frame home.
   (b) Tires for the car your brother drives a few miles into town to work each day.
   (c) A sweater you wear often.
   (d) A wallet to give to your father, who is a salesperson.
   (e) A ballpoint pen for school use.

3. Almost every department store and supermarket and many discount stores carry house brand merchandise. Many also carry comparable brand name items. Visit one of these stores to make price and size or quantity comparisons between the two. Do you find any important differences? Be prepared to share your information with the class.

14 YOUR CONSUMER RIGHTS AND RESPONSIBILITIES

PART OBJECTIVES

After studying this part and completing the end-of-part activities, you will be able to:

1. List four basic rights and four responsibilities that consumers have.
2. Give three examples of consumer dishonesty.
3. Explain why you should report a business for following unethical practices.
4. Tell how the Federal Trade Commission aids consumers.
5. Explain how trade associations help consumers.

Marie Stanley was very proud of her new digital watch. It not only told the time and date but also had a light for reading the watch at night. Unfortunately, after about five weeks the watch began to show the incorrect time and the light would not work. She took the watch back to the store where she had bought it but was informed that the watch would have to be returned to the manufacturer to be repaired.

The papers that came with the watch gave the manufacturer's address and said that the watch would be repaired free of charge within the first year after purchase, unless it had been misused.

Three weeks after sending the watch to the manufacturer, Marie received a letter stating that an inspector had checked her watch and had found signs of improper use. The letter said that

Marie would, therefore, be charged $15 if the repairs were made. Marie knew she had not abused the watch. She did not believe she should pay $15 for repairs for damage she had not caused, yet the watch was of no use to her unless it was repaired.

Clearly, either the manufacturer or the retailer was not being fair with Marie. But such abuse happens sometimes. There was a time when unfair actions by businesses were much more common. To combat those abuses, consumers began joining together to demand just treatment from business. This banding together became known as the consumer movement.

President John F. Kennedy, recognizing the growing consumer movement, declared that every consumer has four basic rights. They are:

1. The right to be informed — to be given the correct information needed to make an informed choice.
2. The right to safety — to be protected from goods and services that are hazardous to health or life.
3. The right to choose — to be assured of the availability of a variety of goods and services at competitive prices.
4. The right to be heard — to be assured that consumer interests will be fully considered by government when laws are being developed and enforced.

A great deal of action by government, private groups, and individuals has taken place to see that these rights are protected.

Rights are only one aspect of the consumer movement. You also need to consider the responsibilities that consumers have. As a consumer, you should be aware that rights and responsibilities are equally important if you are to get the best value for your money. Among your consumer responsibilities are these:

1. The responsibility to be informed.
2. The responsibility to be honest.
3. The responsibility to be reasonable in complaining when your rights are violated.
4. The responsibility to report unethical business practices to protect other consumers.

BE INFORMED

Probably the most important responsibility you have as a consumer is to be informed. Just having the right to be informed will not make you an informed consumer; you must obtain and use the information available to you. A producer might put a complete label on a product, but it is up to you to read and use the information given you. To be an informed consumer, you should continually learn about the many goods and services available. From among these, you should learn how to make choices that will best suit your needs, your wants, and your ability to pay. You should keep informed about your rights as a consumer, and you should know something of the laws and the agencies that protect these rights. You should also know how and to whom to report a violation of these rights.

Being an informed consumer is hard work. But the extra effort spent in making your dollars go as far as possible will be worth it.

BE HONEST

Most people are honest, but those who are not cause the rest of us to pay higher prices. The things that shoplifters take from stores result in losses to businesses that must be made up, usually in higher prices to everyone. In a recent year, shoplifting losses for the nation were about $31 billion.

Some people who would not think of shoplifting may be dishonest in other ways. Merchants report many dishonest acts by customers. For example, a person might use a dress once for a formal occasion and then return it, or a customer might buy a stereo from a discount house and take it for servicing to a retail store which has a generous repair plan on the same brand of stereos that it sells. Also, customers have been seen taking a low price tag from an article and putting it on a more expensive item which they buy. And there have been many complaints about customers who turn in at the cash register discount coupons for merchandise that the shoppers have not purchased.

As a responsible consumer, you must be as honest with business as you want business to be with you. You must be as quick to tell the cashier that you have received too much change at the checkout counter as you are to say that you received too little. You have to be aware that dishonesty, in addition to the moral issue, usually results in higher prices which all consumers must pay.

COMPLAIN REASONABLY

As a buyer, you are usually responsible for what you buy, if the merchant has been honest with you. If you are dissatisfied, however, and wish to complain, you should do so in a reasonable way.

Your goal in complaining about an unsatisfactory product or service is getting your problem solved. But you should first be sure that you have real cause for complaint. Be sure that you have followed the directions for using the product. One consumer angrily returned a record player because he could not make it work; he was embarrassed to learn that he had failed to remove a piece of plastic placed under the turntable for safe shipping.

When you have the details of your complaint firmly set, you should calmly explain the problem to an employee of the firm from which you bought the item. In most cases, the firms will be glad to correct the problem, for they want you to continue to buy from them. But if you act in an angry or threatening manner, you risk getting the same kind of response. And this will at least delay your getting the problem solved.

If you feel that your complaint is not handled fairly by the salesperson or the complaint department, you should take the

Illus. 14-1

Complaining about a product in a reasonable way will usually bring results.

matter up with the owner or an official of the firm. If that fails, and the firm is a part of a national company, a letter to the customer relations department at the main office often gets results. If you do not get a response within a reasonable time, a second letter with copies sent to several consumer agencies will often bring a quick reply. If your complaint is about your charge account, the firm is required to answer your letter within 30 days. If you fail to get what you think is a fair adjustment, you may contact one of the following:

1. The Better Business Bureau.
2. The local or state Bureau of Consumer Affairs or the state Attorney General's office.
3. Your social welfare agency, if you or your family are receiving financial aid from the government.
4. A lawyer or the Legal Aid Society, if the problem is quite serious.
5. In larger cities, the Small Claims Court. This court is operated for filing of small claims only.

REPORT UNETHICAL PRACTICES

As a responsible consumer, you should report unethical business practices to protect other consumers from also becoming victims. Suppose the hand brake on your two-week-old bicycle fails to work, and the new cycle shop from which you bought the bike refuses to live up to its guarantee to replace all parts that break under normal use within 90 days. After several unsuccessful attempts to get the bicycle fixed, you might be tempted to give up, pay someone else to fix your bike, and mark it off as a bad experience. This might solve your problem, but it won't prevent other people from losing money in the same way you did. You should report the matter to some agency, such as those discussed in this part, which could use persuasive or legal means to get the shop to live up to its word both to you and to future customers.

KNOW YOUR CONSUMER RIGHTS

As mentioned earlier, if you are an alert, responsible consumer you have certain rights. Most of your rights are satisfied by just plain honest and fair dealings. Few businesses are ever dishonest on purpose. However, being a skillful consumer means that you know what your rights are and how to protect them.

GET A PRODUCT DESCRIPTION

Most items that you buy should be described in ads, on labels, or by a salesperson. You are entitled to know what the product is and what it will do. But sometimes we buy carelessly. We may not weigh the facts given in advertising or by a salesperson, and we blame the seller for our poor purchases. There are times, though, when false information is given to a customer in an effort to make a sale. This misrepresentation is known as **fraud**.

To be defrauded, you must actually be deceived. Suppose that you are looking at a used car. If the salesperson tells you that it is a late '75 model when you know that it is a '74 model, there is no fraud. You were not deceived even though the salesperson was not telling the truth. When a salesperson puffs up the product — says "it's the best" or "it's a great value" — there is no fraud. If, however, the salesperson tells you that the car has just had a complete engine overhaul when, in fact, the engine is almost worn out, this is fraud.

CHECK THE GUARANTEE

A **guarantee** or **warranty** is a promise by the manufacturer or dealer, usually in writing, that a product is of certain quality or that defective parts will be replaced. Statements like these are guarantees: "This garment is guaranteed not to shrink more than 1 percent." "Contains 50 percent new wool." "Defective parts will be replaced within 30 days without charge." Written guarantees provide useful evidence if you need to seek replacement of a faulty product.

You should insist on seeing a copy of the guarantee when you buy an item. And you can require the store to put in writing any other guarantees that have been offered. Guarantees are sometimes spelled out in ads for the product. You should keep a copy of the ad as evidence of the guarantee. Read the guarantee carefully to find out just what is covered and for what period of time. The guarantee may apply to the entire item or only to some parts of it. No guarantee will cover damages caused by misuse. You should also find out who will service the product during the guarantee period.

USE THE FEDERAL TRADE COMMISSION

One of the many government agencies which help to protect your rights as a consumer is the Federal Trade Commission (FTC). It tries to prevent one firm from using unfair practices to run competing firms out of business so that it will have all the market for itself. When a business has control of the market for a product or service, it is said to have a **monopoly**. Competing firms try to get your business by offering a variety of products and services at various prices. By driving out this competition, monopolies limit your right to choose.

The Federal Trade Commission also protects other consumer rights. It regulates advertising and encourages informative and truthful advertising. Among other things, it requires textile firms to label wool and other fabrics so that you will know what the material is made of and how to care for it. In these and other activities, the Federal Trade Commission guards your right to be informed. As a consumer, you can report directly to the Federal Trade Commission if you feel that any of your rights which come under its protection have been violated.

GET HELP FROM OTHER GOVERNMENT AGENCIES

Federal, state, and local governments are very much concerned that the products available to the consumer are safe to buy and use and that the buyer's rights are protected. The federal government has set up various agencies to protect the consumer. The National Bureau of Standards, for example, tests goods, sets up standards, and controls weights and measures. The Department of Agriculture sets up standards for grading farm products sold in interstate commerce. It also controls the processing of meat, inspects it, and stamps meat and meat products with grades according to their quality. State and local governments have agencies which protect the consumer's interest through such activities as inspecting food processing plants and checking the accuracy of weights and measures in stores.

Illus. 14-2

Consumers can safely buy meat of good quality because of inspections made by the Department of Agriculture.

In addition to the Federal Trade Commission, the Food and Drug Administration, among other things, makes sure that food, drug, and cosmetic products are not harmful to consumers and that labels of these products do not mislead the consumer.

The U.S. Postal Service also protects consumers by investigating and stopping fraudulent use of the mails. Postal inspectors guard against such schemes as the sale of worthless stock and the fraudulent sale of land.

States and cities often require that merchants obtain licenses to sell products such as drugs or to operate such businesses as restaurants and barber shops. Businesses that handle food must meet cleanliness requirements. New plumbing and electrical installations must be approved by the proper officials.

JOIN WITH OTHER CONSUMERS

Sometimes trying alone to exercise your right to be heard can be frustrating and costly. It may be fairly easy to take your complaint to a local store or agency for help. In some states, consumers might also get help without too much difficulty from a state agency. But making a complaint to a firm in another part of the country can be troublesome.

Suppose that your family bought a television set which caught fire and damaged the walls in your TV room. You learned that the wiring was faulty and the product was not like its advertised claims. As you looked for help from various sources, you learned that other consumers have had the same trouble with the product. But the manufacturer is located in Texas and you live in Vermont. What can you do? You and other consumers can join together to sue the manufacturer in a federal court. When a group of citizens join together to sue a business for deceptive or dishonest practices, the process is called a **class-action suit**.

AID FROM BETTER BUSINESS BUREAUS

In Part 12 you learned about the Better Business Bureau as a source of consumer information. It is also a source of help when you are exercising other rights and responsibilities.

Better Business Bureaus are chiefly concerned with problems which arise from false advertising or misrepresented products and services. If you feel that your rights have been violated by such practices, and there is a Better Business Bureau in your community, it can often help you. The bureau will usually ask you to report your problem in writing so that it can get all the details straight. It will then contact the firm and try to persuade the firm to correct the practice or make good on its claim for the product or service in question. Most businesses do so willingly. But one of the bureau's most powerful tools of persuasion is publicity in local news media about the unfair practices of firms that deliberately deceive their customers. Also, because all bureaus have access to the information of other Better Business Bureaus, the report would follow the firm all over the country. Such bad publicity would cause the firm to lose customers, and most firms will change their practices to avoid loss of customers.

PRIVATE GROUPS CAN SERVE

There are a number of other private organizations which help to protect your rights as a buyer. Sometimes businesses form **trade associations**. These are organizations of firms engaged in one line of business. Many trade associations establish standards of quality for the products that their members manufacture. These standards of quality help assure you that you are getting a good buy for your money when you buy that type of product. For example, the American Institute of Laundering sets up standards of washability for fabrics. If a fabric's tag shows the seal of this association, the fabric has met the association's standards. Some trade associations also publish codes of ethics that members are urged to follow. Several trade associations now serve as central complaint departments to resolve consumer problems which may have been mishandled on the retail or manufacturer levels.

Local businesses also often work together to help protect themselves and their customers from unethical or dishonest business practices.

The following terms should become part of your business vocabulary. For each numbered statement, find the term which has the same meaning.

class-action suit	monopoly
fraud	trade association
guarantee or warranty	

1. A firm which has control of the market for a product or service.
2. An organization of firms engaged in one line of business.
3. A promise that a product is of a certain quality or that defective parts will be replaced.
4. When false information is given to a customer in an effort to make a sale.
5. Legal action brought against a business by a group of consumers with a similar complaint about deceptive or dishonest practices.

1. What are four basic rights that every consumer has?
2. What are four responsibilities that every consumer has?
3. What is the most important responsibility that you have as a consumer?
4. Give at least three examples of consumer dishonesty.
5. What is meant by complaining in a reasonable way?
6. Why should you report businesses that are following unethical practices?

7. Why should you get a good description of a product or service before you buy it?
8. What are some of the precautions you should take when you buy an item that has a guarantee?
9. How does the Federal Trade Commission aid consumers?
10. Give examples of ways in which the following government agencies help the consumer: (a) the National Bureau of Standards, (b) the Department of Agriculture, (c) the Food and Drug Administration, and (d) the U.S. Postal Service.
11. How do trade associations help consumers?

USING YOUR BUSINESS KNOWLEDGE

1. Why do merchants often accept merchandise returned by dissatisfied customers, even though the law might not require it?
2. Suppose that the first time you wash a new wool sweater it shrinks so much that it no longer fits you. You washed the sweater in hot water, but you notice that the label in the sweater says to use cold water. Would you have a fair complaint against the business that sold you the sweater? Why?
3. Which of the following would be considered fraud? Give the reasons for your decisions.
   (a) A salesperson says the quadraphonic sound system you are looking at is the best brand made. After you buy it, you find it rated in a consumer magazine as the second best.
   (b) The label in a shirt says the colors will not fade. After washing it, you find that instead of a bright red shirt you now have a pale pink one.
   (c) The person who sells an electric popcorn popper says it is completely washable. Before using it, you put it in a sink filled with water to wash it. The first time you try to make popcorn, there is a flash and the popper's electrical unit catches fire. When you return the popper to the store, the salesperson tells you that she did not mean the popper could be put under water. She says you should have known that electrical appliances should not be put in water. She refuses to give you either a refund or an exchange.
4. Why do state and city governments require that some individuals and businesses have licenses in order to sell certain goods and services? Mention several different goods or services for which sale licenses are required.

SOLVING PROBLEMS IN BUSINESS

1. Barney Owens is thinking about subscribing to a weekly consumer magazine so that he can be better informed. The magazine is offering a special trial subscription of 26 weeks for $14.30. The normal subscription rate for 26 weeks is $15.60.
   (a) What is the cost per issue normally?
   (b) What is the cost per issue under the special subscription rate?
   (c) How much would Barney save per issue by taking advantage of the special subscription rate?

2. The Direct Nursery Sales Company guarantees that its products will satisfy the customer or that the purchase price plus postage will be refunded. Last year's sales and returns were:

Total sales	$120,000
Products returned for refund	5,400
Cost of postage on returned goods	600

   (a) What was the total cost to the nursery of the products that were returned, including postage?
   (b) What was the total amount of sales, deducting the cost of refunds and postage?

3. If shoplifting losses by businesses are $31 billion a year and there are 57 million families in this nation, how much does shoplifting cost each family a year? This figure represents an amount your family spends but receives nothing for.

4. Elaine Lee bought a new thermometer so she could tell what the outdoor temperature was in degrees Celsius. The thermometer came with a written guarantee that it was accurate within two degrees. Elaine wants to try out the thermometer by comparing it with her old but reliable Fahrenheit thermometer. If the temperature on her Fahrenheit thermometer reads 68 degrees, what should her new Celsius thermometer read?

EXPANDING YOUR UNDERSTANDING OF BUSINESS

1. Because business losses to shoplifters have been growing so rapidly, more and more businesses are prosecuting offenders who are caught. Through your library and interviews with local business people and the Chamber of Commerce, prepare a report on this problem. Consider these questions:
   (a) What is the extent of the problem in your area?
   (b) What is the estimated amount of loss by all local businesses in a year?
   (c) What are businesses doing to prevent shoplifting?
   (d) What are the penalties for those found guilty of shoplifting?

2. From your home or from friends, gather five written guarantees. Read them very carefully. Make two lists from the guarantees. First, list all statements that give you specific information or instructions. Second, list all statements that are vague or general. Finally, evaluate each guarantee and rate it as either acceptable or unacceptable.

3. The Fair Packaging and Labeling Act was passed to encourage businesses to package and label their products in such a way that the consumer would be better informed. In your library, find out what the provisions of this law are. Then find some packages or labels that illustrate how businesses are cooperating with the law.

4. Find out if there is a Bureau of Consumer Affairs in your city or state. If there is, what is it attempting to do to help consumers?

5. From such sources as a local consumer agency, post office, or library, try to find out what your rights and responsibilities are in each of the following cases. Write a paragraph or two summarizing your findings.

(a) You receive unordered merchandise through the mail.

(b) After seeing it advertised in the newspaper, you go to a store to buy a pocket-size calculator at the advertised price of $19.95. The salesperson tells you that the advertised model is sold out and then tries to sell you a higher priced model.

(c) You agree to buy an encyclopedia set for $85 from a door-to-door salesperson. The next day, you feel that you had not given the purchase enough thought and had signed the contract too early.

CAREER FOCUS

Since the consumer movement began, opportunities for careers in providing consumer services have been increasing. Hundreds of businesses have established consumer affairs departments. Departments and agencies handling consumer matters at all levels of government employ large numbers of people in a variety of consumer service jobs. Many states have established separate departments to protect consumer interests. And nearly every county in the 50 states employs Cooperative Extension Agents and home economists who advise consumers.

WORKERS IN CONSUMER SERVICES

People who work in consumer services hold many different types of jobs. Workers might be grouped according to their major duties. The inspectors and sanitarians would be one group of consumer-related workers.

Another group works in research and testing. Some of these workers perform tests to determine the safety and durability of products. A merchandise evaluator, for example, may be employed by a large department store to see that the toys the store sells are safe. One private laboratory employs over 2,000 people to test the safety of electrical products. Among other workers in this group are those who conduct research to find out what consumers plan to buy or what television shows they watch most.

Information processing and communication are major functions of some consumer service workers. This group includes people who gather, write, broadcast, or publish information for consumers. For example, consumer reporters may do comparative shopping for certain groceries in several supermarkets. Or they may gather data on the effects of inflation on the family's nutrition. Their findings may be published in a consumer column in a newspaper or broadcast on a consumer-interest radio or TV show. Consumer education teachers, extension agents, and consumer counselors who provide information to help you become a better consumer are also among this group.

An increasing number of jobs are becoming available to handle consumer complaints. A federal consumer agency installed a "Hotline" telephone for consumer complaints and inquiries. In the first year, almost 60,000 Hotline calls were received. Think of the number of people needed to receive and follow up these complaints. Consumer affairs directors in businesses, complaint clerks in private consumer agencies, and directors of state and local consumer protection offices are examples of jobs in this category.

Another group of consumer service workers devote their time to protecting consumer rights. Consumer protection specialists, for example, may work in regional offices of the Federal Trade Commission. They investigate complaints of violations of laws relating to consumer rights. Consumer protection lawyers are also included in this group.

The largest group of workers in consumer services includes those in office services. These are the secretarial, clerical, accounting, and data processing workers who perform the information processing upon which all other workers in the field depend.

Most consumer-related jobs involve dealing with the public. Workers must be tactful and pleasant. Often workers will have to listen to the complaints of people who are angry about unsatisfactory products or services. It is important that the workers listen patiently and show an honest desire to help. Through their attitude and voice, they should serve as a calming influence on customers. Ability to handle details and to record them accurately is needed. Workers must also be able to communicate well.

EDUCATION AND TRAINING
FOR CONSUMER SERVICE

Consumer services offer opportunities for people from a variety of educational backgrounds. High school graduation, including such courses as typing, filing, and office machines, is usually adequate for the beginning office jobs. Courses such as general business and consumer economics will give the beginning worker a basic understanding of consumer problems.

Professional jobs usually require a college degree. A study of consumer affairs directors shows that most studied business administration or home economics. They had job experience in marketing, sales, customer service, and public relations. College courses that would be helpful include consumer economics, consumer law, consumer behavior, public policy, and consumer education. More specialized careers, such as consumer law, require additional preparation beyond the four-year degree.

LOOKING AT THE FUTURE
IN THE FIELD OF CONSUMER SERVICE

It is expected that the consumer movement will continue and that career opportunities in consumer services will grow. As consumers increasingly hold producers responsible for providing good, safe, and durable products and efficient services within a safe and clean environment, businesses will probably need more consumer specialists to help them meet these responsibilities.

Government and other agencies will also probably employ people in a variety of consumer-related jobs to see that consumer rights are protected. And as consumers themselves become more aware that being informed is the best way to be effective consumers, additional jobs in information processing and communication will be available.

If these trends continue, employment prospects in consumer services are good for those who are adequately prepared.

UNIT 5
Managing Your Money

UNIT OBJECTIVES

After studying the parts in this unit, you will be able to:

1. Give several reasons why it is important for individuals and families to develop money management goals.

2. List the steps that should be followed in preparing an individual's or family's budget.

3. Keep records of income and expenditures for an individual or a family.

4. Explain why it is difficult to compare prices of goods and services from one year to the next.

15 USING YOUR INCOME WISELY

PART OBJECTIVES

After studying this part and completing the end-of-part activities, you will be able to:
1. Explain why you need to plan how you spend your money.
2. Identify the basic steps to good money management.
3. Explain why everyone does not have the same money management goals.
4. Discuss how proper use of your possessions is related to good money management.
5. List the five items on which the average family spends the largest part of its income.

How would you feel if someone gave you $500,000? You probably would be very happy, and you could probably think of many things to buy with the money.

Would you still be willing to accept the money if it were to be given to you over a period of 45 years instead of in one lump sum? You would then be receiving over $11,000 a year.

Well, as an average high school graduate, you will earn at least $500,000 in your lifetime. That is a lot of money, but there will be many demands on it. You will have to pay for food, shelter, clothing, transportation, and many other expenses. Your problem when you get a steady job will be the same one you face

189

now — you have only so much money to pay for all the possible goods and services you need and want. The solution to the problem is learning to manage your money carefully and wisely.

WHAT IS MONEY MANAGEMENT?

Many people have the wrong idea about money management. They think it means pinching pennies, doing without things, and not having any fun. They are wrong. If you learn to manage your money well, you may be able to buy things you really want but have not been able to buy before. Planning ahead and deciding what is really important will help you to have money to spend on those things you enjoy.

Money management means getting the most for your money. It means careful planning, saving, and spending. You will have to decide what you want and what you can afford.

There are six basic steps involved in good money management:

1. Setting goals based on what is important to you.
2. Providing for basic needs.
3. Saving money for future expenses.
4. Making wise decisions when you buy.
5. Using properly the things that you buy so that you will get the most good from them.
6. Living within your income.

Illus. 15-1

By carefully planning how you spend your money, you can get more of the things you need and want.

SETTING GOALS

The first step in good money management is setting goals. **Goals** are simply things you want to achieve. Goals may be short-term or long-term. A family's short-term goal, for example, might be paying its debts, taking a vacation trip, or buying new carpeting. As a student, your short-term goal might be to buy an electronic calculator. Long-range goals often involve large amounts of money. A family might have a long-range goal of buying a new house or a college education for one of the children. Your long-range goal might be to buy a car.

Goals are personal. They are not the same for all people, or even for everyone within a given age group. Your goals will be affected by such factors as your age, where you live, and your interests and values. A family's goals will be affected by similar factors, plus its size.

Goals also change from time to time. A family's goals will change as its needs change. For example, an apartment or a small house might best suit the needs of a newly married couple. A young, growing family might set the goal of buying a larger house. Stop and think about how your goals may have changed in the last few years and what your goals may be at age 20 or 30.

No matter how much goals change, they are important to good money management. Working to achieve a certain goal probably gives an individual or a family the best reason for practicing good money management.

MEETING BASIC NEEDS

The second step in money management, after setting goals, is to meet basic needs. Basic needs are essential things you must have to live. But everyone's needs are a little different. Needs depend on where you live and what life-style you follow. If you live in a southern city, for example, you have different transportation and clothing needs from those you would have if you lived on a large ranch in the Northwest. For some people, an apartment is ideal; others feel they need a house.

Basic needs must be met, and they cost money. In planning the use of your money, you must decide how much to set aside for those basic needs. After you have met basic needs, you can decide what to buy with the money you have left.

SAVING FOR FUTURE EXPENSES

In addition to providing for your basic needs, you must prepare for large expenses in the future. You do this by developing a savings program. You will learn about saving in Unit 8.

Everyone has a special reason for saving. Maybe you want to buy a car or pay for a vacation trip. Perhaps you want to be a beautician or an auto mechanic and will need equipment. Unless you manage your money wisely and plan your savings, you may not be able to do or get the things you want.

BUYING WISELY

All of us have so many needs and wants that we could never manage to meet all of them. What we must do is to stretch our limited incomes as far as possible. An important part of this stretching is buying wisely.

To buy wisely, you must gather information carefully before making your purchases. You must plan your purchases so that you buy the right item or service at the right time and at the right price. Unplanned buying often leads to disappointment and wasted money. Planned buying leads to better use of money and greater satisfaction from the things you buy.

USING POSSESSIONS PROPERLY

After careful planning and buying, you should use your possessions properly. Use your possessions carelessly, and you lose money. A radio in an unlocked locker can be stolen. Clothing must be cleaned and repaired or it will soon be unwearable. Cars and motorcycles need regular tune-ups and oil changes. Things you own will give you greater satisfaction and last longer when properly cared for. Taking care of your possessions is an important part of money management.

LIVING WITHIN YOUR INCOME

Do you ever run out of money before the end of the week? A lot of people have that problem. They have not learned to live within their incomes.

It isn't always easy to live within your income. But if you don't, you will probably have to borrow money. Borrowing money isn't bad, but you have to pay to borrow money. And if you don't have to pay to borrow money, you will have more money to satisfy other needs and wants.

Illus. 15-2

By performing some services yourself, you can stretch your income. This car owner is saving money by changing his car's oil himself.

A FAMILY'S SPENDING

Illus. 15-3 shows the average spending of a city family of four in the United States. As you can see from this typical plan for spending, basic needs take a large share of a family's income. The biggest expense for the average family is food. The second largest expense is housing, which includes rent or payments on a house, heating, electricity, water, repairs, and furnishings. A third large expense is income taxes. Clothing and transportation are important basic expenses too. Almost 80 percent of a typical family's income is spent for the five items listed first in Illus. 15-3.

SPENDING FOR A TYPICAL CITY FAMILY OF FOUR

Expense Category	Amount	Percent of Total
Food	$ 4,610	25
Housing	4,180	22
Income taxes	2,740	15
Clothing and personal care	1,610	9
Transportation	1,570	8
Social security and disability taxes	1,075	6
Medical care	1,070	6
Other (savings, gifts, contributions, recreation)	1,765	9
TOTAL SPENDING	$18,620	100

Source: U.S. Department of Labor

Illus. 15-3

Basic needs and taxes account for a major portion of the average family's spending.

INCREASING YOUR BUSINESS VOCABULARY

The following terms should become part of your business vocabulary. For each numbered statement, find the term that has the same meaning.

goal   money management

1. Getting the most for your money.
2. Something that a person or family wants to achieve.

UNDERSTANDING YOUR READING

1. Why is it important to plan how you are going to spend your money?
2. What six steps are involved in good money management?
3. What is the first step in money management?
4. What are some of the factors that affect a person's goals?
5. How is proper use of your possessions part of good money management?
6. What are the five items on which the average family spends the largest part of its income?

1. Suppose that the Bergman family and the Mandrake family both have incomes of $15,800 a year. The Bergmans live in a large city; the Mandrakes live in a rural area. The Bergmans have no children; the Mandrakes have two. What might account for the differences in the ways the two families spend their incomes?
2. The first cost of an item may be only a part of the total cost. For each of the items listed, name some expenses in using the item:
   (a) television set
   (b) camera
   (c) sewing machine
   (d) stereo tape player
3. The income of the Ortega family is well above the national average. Therefore, the Ortegas feel it is not necessary to plan the use of their income. They find, though, that they are having difficulty making ends meet. Suggest some reasons why the Ortega family may be having financial difficulty.
4. What is the difference between short-term and long-term goals of an individual or a family? Give several examples of each of these two types of goals.

1. Stanley Simmonds repaired a leaky faucet and patched a hole in a window screen. He spent $2.50 for the parts for the faucet and $1.50 for the screen patch.
   (a) How much did his repair jobs cost?
   (b) If Stanley's parents had paid $25 to a household repairer to have the same jobs done, how much more would the repairs have cost?
2. The members of the Lavely family have the following jobs and regular monthly income:

Mr. Lavely, store worker and part-time house painter $1,000
Mrs. Lavely, salesperson   500
Linda Lavely, part-time receptionist   150
Jim Lavely, newspaper carrier   80

   (a) What is the Lavely family's total monthly income?
   (b) What is the family's total yearly income?
3. Look back at Illus. 15-3, which shows average spending for a city family of four members. Using the percent figures shown in the illustration, draw a pie chart showing how the average family spends its income.

4. Four years ago in a certain city, milk sold for $1.49 a gallon. Today, a local store priced it at 50¢ a liter. How much has milk gone up in price per liter over the four-year period?

5. The Malora family has some lawn furniture that is falling apart. Rebuilding and painting the old furniture would take about 10 hours of work; lumber and nails would cost about $12; and the paint and brush would cost about $7.50. If the Maloras rebuild the furniture, they estimate that it will last another 3 years. They are undecided whether to rebuild the old furniture or to buy new furniture for $97.50.

   (a) If the new furniture will last for about 10 years, what is the yearly cost of wear and tear?

   (b) What will be the yearly cost of the rebuilt furniture (not including a charge for labor)?

EXPANDING YOUR UNDERSTANDING OF BUSINESS

1. "The more you earn, the more you spend." Do you agree or disagree with this statement? Why? How does a person's life-style relate to this statement?

2. Ask your grandparents or someone their age what kinds of money management problems they had when they were your age. What differences between now and then can they tell you about?

3. It has been said that you could be wealthy if you saved all the raises in pay you received during your lifetime. Do you think this idea is practical?

4. Find out approximately how much your family spends for some of the categories of spending in Illus. 15-3. What are some of the reasons why differences exist between the figures in the illustration and your family's spending?

5. The costs of food and housing have gone up rapidly in the past few years. Find out why these two areas increased so much. What proportion of a family's income do they require today as compared with three years ago or five years ago?

KEEPING PERSONAL MONEY RECORDS

PART OBJECTIVES

After studying this part and completing the end-of-part activities, you will be able to:

1. Explain why you need to know your goals before you can prepare a budget.
2. Prepare an Income and Expenditures Record.
3. Prepare a Comparison of Savings and Expenditures with Budget Allowances Record.
4. Explain why budgets have to be changed from time to time.

Brian Houston has a job delivering the evening newspaper for which he earns $15 a week. He also helps an elderly neighbor by running errands and doing odd jobs around the neighbor's house. The neighbor pays Brian $5 a week for his help. Brian tries to be careful with his money, because he wants to save enough money to buy a motorbike. However, by the end of the week he never seems to have any money left for savings. In fact, many times his money is gone before the end of the week.

Brian told his parents about his money problems, hoping that they might offer to give him an allowance. Instead, they suggested that he try to manage his money more wisely. So Brian decided to set up a plan for saving and spending. Such a plan is called a **budget**.

A good budget may be just a simple record of how much money you make, how much you want to save, and how much you plan to spend. A good budget should take very little of your time, and it can aid you in several ways. In the first place, it is a basic step toward better money management. Also, a budget will help you set goals for yourself. Further, putting your plans in writing will help you to follow them.

DECIDING ON YOUR GOALS

Before making up your budget you will need to decide what your goals are. Do you want to save money for a special occasion? Do you want to buy a record album or a new sweater? You must decide which of the things you want are most important. Then you can budget your money so that you can meet your goals.

Brian's goal is to save enough money to buy a motorbike. He decided to try to save $6 each week. To do this he needed to plan how he will use all the money he has available. This means Brian has to plan his **expenditures** — amounts actually spent for food, clothing, and other items. By thinking back to what he normally spent for different things, Brian developed the budget shown in Illus. 16-1.

Illus. 16-1

Brian Houston's budget of income and expenditures for a week.

Brian Houston
Weekly Budget

Estimated Income			Estimated Expenditures		
Newspaper route	15	00	Savings	6	00
Helping neighbor	5	00	Entertainment & Recreation	7	50
			Clothes & Personal items	5	00
			School supplies	1	50
Total income	20	00	Total Savings & Expenditures	20	00

After Brian prepared his budget he tried to follow it, but he kept no records to show how he was actually spending his money. At the end of a few weeks he found that he hadn't saved anything, but he couldn't remember where his money had gone. So Brian decided that he needed not only a budget but also records to show exactly how his money was being spent.

RECORDING INCOME AND EXPENDITURES

A budget shows how money should be spent; records show how money has actually been spent. Both are necessary, but records can become burdensome if they are too detailed. They should be kept as simple as possible and yet show the information that is needed. Brian decided to keep his record of income and expenditures in the form shown in Illus. 16-2 on page 200. Study this illustration carefully, and follow along with the steps Brian went through in filling out this record.

1. Brian wrote down the total amount budgeted and the amount budgeted for each item. These amounts were to remind him at all times of how much he was allowing for each item. He then drew a line across the whole page so that he would not confuse the budget amounts with the amounts he received and spent.

2. On March 3, the day he started the record, Brian had $2.50 in cash. To distinguish between the beginning balance and the amounts to be received during the week, he wrote the word "Balance" in the Explanation column. Notice how the year, month, and day are entered in the Date column.

3. Also on March 3, Brian received his pay of $15 for delivering papers and spent $2.50 for a ticket to the school band's spring concert. He also put aside the $6 he wanted to save. Notice how these entries are made.

4. A similar entry is made for each day of the week. When amounts were spent for two or more purposes, the total was entered in the Payments column and the individual amounts were entered in their own columns. For example, look at the entries for March 5.

5. Brian proved, or balanced, his record at the end of each week to be sure that he was keeping it accurately. After his last entry, he drew a single line across all the money columns to indicate addition.

6. Next he found the totals of the Receipts and Payments columns. He wrote these totals directly under the last line on which he had recorded an entry. At any time, the difference between the total of the Receipts column and the total of the Payments column should be the same as his cash on hand. The difference between Total Receipts

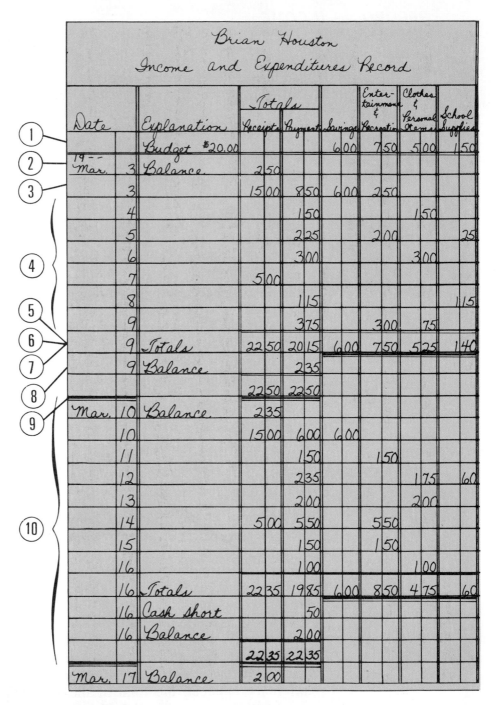

	Date		Explanation	Totals Receipts	Totals Payments	Savings	Entertainment & Recreation	Clothes & Personal Items	School Supplies
①			Budget $20.00			6 00	7 50	5 00	1 50
②	19-- Mar.	3	Balance	2 50					
③		3		15 00	8 50	6 00	2 50		
④		4			1 50			1 50	
		5			2 25		2 00		25
		6			3 00			3 00	
		7		5 00					
⑤		8			1 15				1 15
		9			3 75		3 00	75	
⑥		9	Totals	22 50	20 15	6 00	7 50	5 25	1 40
⑦		9	Balance		2 35				
⑧				22 50	22 50				
⑨	Mar.	10	Balance	2 35					
⑩		10		15 00	6 00	6 00			
		11			1 50		1 50		
		12			2 35			1 75	60
		13			2 00			2 00	
		14		5 00	5 50		5 50		
		15			1 50		1 50		
		16			1 00			1 00	
		16	Totals	22 35	19 85	6 00	8 50	4 75	60
		16	Cash short		50				
		16	Balance		2 00				
				22 35	22 35				
	Mar.	17	Balance	2 00					

Illus. 16-2

Brian Houston's record of income and expenditures.

and Total Payments was $2.35. Brian counted his money and found that he had exactly $2.35, in addition to the $6.00 he had saved. So he knew that his record was correct.

7. Brian found the totals of each of the special columns. He then added these totals and compared the sum with the total of the Payments column. The two amounts were the same. This gave him further proof that he had recorded everything he had spent.

8. He added the cash balance ($2.35) to the total of the payments and then brought down to the next line the totals of the Receipts and Payments columns. This showed that the Receipts equaled the sum of the Payments and the Balance.

9. Brian then drew a double line across the Date column and all the money columns to show that his record book had been balanced. To show the amount of money on hand at the beginning of the second week, he brought down the balance of $2.35 in the Receipts column.

10. Brian recorded receipts and payments during the second week as he did during the first. When he totaled the Receipts and Payments columns at the end of the second week, he found the cash balance to be $2.50 (plus the $12.00 he had saved). But when Brian counted his money, he found that he had only $2.00. He probably had lost 50 cents or had forgotten to record a payment. So he entered 50 cents in the Payments column. He usually did not write an explanation of an entry, but in this case he did write "Cash Short" in the Explanation column. He thought that he might be interested in how much his cash was short from week to week. After making an entry for the cash shortage, Brian ruled and balanced his record as he had done at the end of the first week.

COMPARING SAVINGS AND EXPENDITURES WITH YOUR BUDGET

As a reminder of how much to save and spend, on the first line of the record Brian had written his budget **allowances** — amounts of money budgeted for savings and for each expenditure. But at the end of each week he wanted to know exactly how his savings and spending compared with his budget allowances. To get this information he used the form shown in Illus. 16-3. Study it to see how Brian prepared this record.

1. Brian entered his budget allowances for the week of March 3 to 9.

2. He entered the amounts that he had actually saved and spent during the first week, getting this information from the income and expenditures record.

3. The differences between his budget allowances and the amounts he actually saved and spent told him how well he had kept within his budget. For example, he saved exactly $6 as he had planned. He had allowed $1.50 for school supplies but spent only $1.40, thus having 10 cents to carry over to the next week. He spent 25 cents more for clothes and personal items than he had planned. To show that he spent more than his budget allowance for this item, he circled the 25 cents.

4. Brian again entered the amounts that he had budgeted for the week.

5. He added the amounts carried forward and the budget allowances to find the amounts available for the second week. For example, the amount available for school supplies was $1.60; but the amount available for clothes and personal items was only $4.75 since during the first week he had gone over his budget on this item by 25 cents.

Illus. 16-3

Comparison of Brian Houston's savings and expenditures with his budget allowances over a two-week period.

Date 19--	Explanation	Savings	Entertain + Recreation	Clothes + Personal Items	School Supplies	Totals
Mar. 3-9	Budget	6 00	7 50	5 00	1 50	20 00
	Saved & Spent	6 00	7 50	5 25	1 40	20 15
	Carried Forward	—	—	(25)	10	(15)
Mar. 10-16	Budget	6 00	7 50	5 00	1 50	20 00
	Available	6 00	7 50	4 75	1 60	19 85
	Saved & Spent	6 00	8 50	4 75	60	19 85
	Carried Forward	—	(1 00)	—	1 00	—
Mar. 17-23	Budget	8 00	8 50	6 00	1 50	24 00
	Available	8 00	7 50	6 00	2 50	24 00

Brian Houston
Comparison of Savings and Expenditures
with Budget Allowances

CHANGING YOUR BUDGET

Budget allowances are estimates, and sometimes they have to be changed. Maybe the first estimate was not very accurate. Then too, every person's requirements change from time to time. At the end of the second week, Brian decided that he should make some changes in his budget allowances. For one thing, another of his neighbors wanted him to babysit a few hours a week, so this meant he could earn an extra $4.00 a week. Also, Brian knew that several school parties were coming up and that he would probably be spending more for recreation, clothes, and personal expenses. And he wanted to put aside another $2.00 a week in savings.

After considering all these things, Brian revised his budget estimates as follows:

Savings	$ 8.00
Entertainment and recreation	8.50
Clothes and personal items	6.00
School supplies	1.50
Total estimated savings and expenditures	$24.00

Brian recorded these new budget allowances in his comparison form (Illus. 16-3) and added them to the amounts carried forward to show the budget amounts available for the third week.

If your budget is carefully planned, estimates will not need to be changed very often. If the amount allowed for a particular item is too small, it may be due to one of several reasons: (1) an unusual expense may have occurred; (2) the cost of the item may have increased; or (3) you may have been careless in spending. It should be remembered that increasing an allowance for one item usually requires a decrease in the allowance for one or several other items, unless your income has also increased.

INCREASING YOUR BUSINESS VOCABULARY

The following terms should become part of your business vocabulary. For each numbered statement, find the term that has the same meaning.

allowance   budget   expenditure

1. An amount of money budgeted for savings or expenditures.
2. A plan for saving and spending income.
3. An amount actually spent for food, clothing, or other items.

UNDERSTANDING YOUR READING

1. Why is it important to know your goals before trying to prepare a budget?
2. Why did Brian Houston decide the amount of savings as his first step in preparing his budget?
3. How did Brian decide what amount to budget for each purpose?
4. Why did Brian's first try at budgeting his money fail?
5. Why did Brian write the budgeted amounts in his income and expenditures record before he recorded any transactions?
6. What types of amounts did Brian write in the Receipts column of his income and expenditures record?
7. Why did Brian total the individual expenditures columns at the end of each week?
8. Why might you have a cash shortage at the end of the budget week?
9. What was the purpose of Brian's comparison of savings and expenditures with budget allowances?
10. What are some of the reasons why budgets have to be changed from time to time?

USING YOUR BUSINESS KNOWLEDGE

1. At the end of his second budget week, Brian Houston found that his income would be $4 a week more in the future. How did Brian budget this additional $4? Do you think his decision about what to do with this extra money was a good one?
2. Donna Evans says she can't possibly keep a budget because she never knows exactly how much her income will be or how much she will spend. What advice can you give her to convince her that a budget can work for her?
3. Every week Pat Hagan puts into savings any amount he has not spent during the week. If he needs more money than he has budgeted, he withdraws from his savings to meet expenses. Is Pat following a good money management plan? Explain.
4. Many teenagers have a goal of owning a car. If you should become the owner of a car, what major changes would you expect to make in a budget like Brian Houston's?

SOLVING PROBLEMS IN BUSINESS

1. On March 17, Brian Houston revised his budget estimates as shown on page 203. His new total of estimated savings and expenditures was $24 a week. In this problem you will keep Brian's record for the next week, from March 17 to March 23. Draw up a form like the one shown in Illus. 16-2 or use the form included in your *Activities and Projects.*
   (a) On the first line write Brian's revised budget allowances. Then draw a line across the entire page.

(b) On the second line write the balance of cash on hand as of March 17. Obtain this information from Illus. 16-2.

(c) Enter the following financial activities that Brian completed:

March 17 Received $15.00 pay for newspaper route; placed $8.00 in savings.

18 Expenditures: container of shoe polish, 75 cents; movie ticket, $3.75.

19 Received $5.00 for helping neighbor; expenditure: notebook paper, 75 cents.

20 None.

21 Expenditure: hairbrush, $1.75.

22 Received $4.00 for babysitting; expenditures: stereo tape, $8.00; ball-point pen, 55 cents.

23 Expenditures: ticket to basketball game, $2.00.

(d) Rule and balance the record in the same way that Brian did at the end of the first and second weeks. Refer to Illus. 16-2. Brian's cash on hand at the end of the third week was $.45.

(e) Now prepare a comparison form similar to Illus. 16-3. Draw a form similar to this one or use the form given in your *Activities and Projects*.

(f) On the first line of the comparison form, record the amounts available for the week of March 17 to 23. Obtain this information from Illus. 16-3.

(g) On the second line of the form, enter the amounts saved and spent. Then determine the amounts carried forward and enter them on the third line.

2. Complete the instructions given below for Brian Houston's budget for the week of March 24 to 30.

(a) On the next line of the comparison form, enter the budget allowances. Calculate the amounts available for the week of March 24 to 30 and record them on the following line.

(b) Prepare a second page for the income and expenditures record or use the form in your *Activities and Projects*. On the first line, write Brian's budget allowances and draw a line across the entire form. On the second line, write the balance of the cash on hand of $.45.

(c) Record the following transactions that Brian completed during the week:

March 24 Received $15.00 pay for newspaper route; placed $8.00 in savings.

25 Expenditures: magazine for English class, 50 cents; ticket to dance, $3.00.

26 Received $5.00 for helping neighbor.

28 Received $3.00 for babysitting; expenditure: school newspaper, 15 cents (charge to entertainment).

29 Expenditure: watchband, $2.50.

30 Expenditure: ticket to basketball game, $2.00.

(d) Rule and balance the record. Brian's cash on hand is $7.30.

(e) Complete the comparison for the week.

3. Brian's paper route is 6 kilometers long. On foot, it takes him an hour and a half to complete the route.

(a) What is his speed in kilometers per hour?

(b) Brian thinks that when he gets his motorbike he will be able to complete the route twice as fast. What will be his speed in kilometers per hour when he delivers the papers by motorbike? How long per day will it take him?

(c) The newspaper is delivered 6 days per week. How many miles per week does Brian travel delivering papers?

EXPANDING YOUR UNDERSTANDING OF BUSINESS

1. A recent study showed that American teenagers buy 20 percent of all cars sold, 20 percent of all clothes, half of all movie tickets, 55 percent of the soft drinks, 90 percent of the records, 44 percent of the cameras, and 27 percent of the cosmetics. Based on these facts, what do you think would happen to our business world if all people under 18 were suddenly to quit spending money?

2. Do you have a budget? Whether you have a job or not, you probably receive and spend some money each week. Using the budget set up by Brian Houston in this part as a model, prepare an estimate of your weekly income and expenditures. Then make up an income and expenditures record for yourself similar to the one shown in Illus. 16-2. Keep an exact record for one week. How does your record compare with your estimate?

3. Besides the money they spend themselves, teenagers have another important effect on the American economy. This is in what they have to say about how their family's money is spent. How do you think that having a teenager in the family influences the family's spending?

17 KEEPING FAMILY MONEY RECORDS

PART OBJECTIVES

After studying this part and completing the end-of-part activities, you will be able to:

1. Explain why savings should be decided first in the preparation of a budget.
2. Discuss the difference between fixed expenses and variable expenses.
3. Name the eight divisions of items a family usually includes in a budget.
4. Explain how to use a filing system for keeping track of bills.
5. Tell why a statement of net worth should be prepared every few years.

When Brian Houston went to his parents with his money problems and they suggested that he manage his money more wisely, they were actually hinting that he should do as they do. It is even more important for a family to manage its money wisely than it is for an individual. In a family when more than one person is earning and spending money, it is quite easy to lose track of finances unless care is taken. The family with a good money management plan will usually live better than it could without a plan.

PREPARING THE FAMILY BUDGET

When a family budget is being prepared, just as when a personal budget is being prepared, the amount to be saved should be decided first. If this amount is not considered first, the allowances for other expenditures may take up all the income and leave nothing for savings. It is fairly easy to decide on allowances for **fixed expenses**, those bills such as house payments and insurance payments that regularly occur and are for the same amount each time. **Variable expenses** occur less frequently, are for widely differing amounts, and are much more difficult to estimate. For example, medical and dental expenses may not occur very often, but they may be large when they do occur. Such expenses should be provided for somewhere in the budget. If allowances are not made for them, variable expenses may use up a large part of savings.

MAKING A BUDGET
FOR THE HOUSTONS

Brian Houston's father, Roy Houston, has a **net income** or **take-home pay** of $14,400 a year, or $1,200 a month. This is the amount Mr. Houston receives after taxes and other deductions have been taken from his earnings. Brian's mother, Julie, has a part-time accounting job which gives her a net income of $3,600 a year, or $300 a month.

To gather information on which to base their budget, the Houstons read several booklets on family income planning. They learned that family savings and expense items are often classified under eight main divisions:

1. **Savings.** Included are savings accounts, government bonds, and stocks.
2. **Food.** Included are food eaten at home and meals eaten away from home.
3. **Clothing.** Included are clothing, dry cleaning, sewing appliances, and shoe repairs.
4. **Household.** Included are rent, mortgage payments, taxes, insurance, gas and electricity, coal or fuel oil, telephone, water, household furnishings, household supplies, and painting and repairs.
5. **Transportation.** Included are payments on the automobile, automobile upkeep and operation, fares for public transportation, and auto and drivers' licenses.
6. **Health and personal care.** Included are medical and dental expenses, drugs, eyeglasses, hospital and nursing ex-

penses, accident and health insurance, barber and beauty shop, and children's allowances.

7. **Recreation and education.** Included are books, magazines, newspapers, theaters, movies, concerts, vacations, school expenses, hobbies, radio and TV, musical instruments, and club dues.

8. **Gifts and contributions.** Included are church, Community Chest or United Appeal, charitable organizations, and personal gifts.

The Houstons decided they wanted to save $200 a month and then made an estimate of their past expenditures based mainly on their checkbook record. After that they prepared the budget shown in Illus. 17-1.

Illus. 17-1

The Houston family's budget of income and expenditures for a month.

The Houston Family Monthly Budget January, 19--					
Estimated Income			Estimated Expenditures		
Roy's net income	1,200	00	Savings	200	00
Julie's net income	300	00	Food	350	00
			Clothing	120	00
			Household	325	00
			Transportation	170	00
			Health & Personal Care	90	00
			Recreation & Education	95	00
			Gifts & Contributions	150	00
Total income	1,500	00	Total Savings & Expenditures	1,500	00

KEEPING INCOME AND EXPENDITURES RECORDS

After planning their budget, the Houstons set up an income and expenditures record which would show them whether their plan was working. This record is shown in Illus. 17-2. Notice that this record is similar to the one kept by Brian in Part 16.

The Houstons' first entry at the beginning of the month was

for money put in their savings account. By setting aside that amount first, they could be sure of saving part of their income. Entries for expenditures were recorded each Saturday and at the end of the month, except for especially large payments which were recorded immediately. Incomes were entered on the days they were received. The Houstons ruled and closed their record as Brian did, except that their record was ruled and balanced at the end of the month.

The Houston Family
Income and Expenditures Record

Date	Explanation	Totals		Distribution of Savings and Expenditures							
		Receipts	Payments	Savings	Food	Clothing	House-hold	Trans-portation	Health & Personal Care	Rec. & Ed.	Gifts & Contrib.
	Budget $1,500			200 00	350 00	120 00	325 00	170 00	90 00	95 00	150 00
19-- Jan. 1	Balance	300 00									
2			200 00	200 00							
7			191 50		84 50	9 00	17 50	20 00	2 00	23 50	35 00
10	Mortgage payment		200 00				200 00				
14	Roy's salary	600 00	217 00		87 50	33 00	4 50	15 00	23 00	19 00	35 00
15	Julie's salary	150 00									
17	Car payment		90 00					90 00			
21			219 00		97 00		43 00	15 00	5 00	22 00	37 00
28	Roy's salary	600 00	172 75		86 50	15 00	2 00	15 00	3 50	15 75	35 00
29	Julie's salary	150 00									
31	Totals	1,800 00	1,290 25	200 00	355 50	57 00	267 00	155 00	33 50	80 25	142 00
31	Balance		509 75								
		1,800 00	1,800 00								
Feb. 1	Balance	509 75									

Illus. 17-2

The Houstons' income and expenditures record for January.

COMPARING THE RECORD
WITH THE BUDGET

At the end of each month, totals of the columns in the income and expenditures record were entered on the comparison form shown in Illus. 17-3. Mr. Houston circled those amounts that represented expenditures greater than the budget allowed.

Month 19--	Explanation	Savings	Food	Clothing	House-hold	Trans-portation	Health + Personal Care	Rec. + Ed.	Gifts + Contrib.	Totals
January	Budget	200 00	350 00	120 00	325 00	170 00	90 00	95 00	150 00	1,500 00
	Saved & Spent	200 00	355 50	57 00	267 00	155 00	33 50	80 25	142 00	1,290 25
	Carried Forward	—	(5 50)	63 00	58 00	15 00	56 50	14 75	8 00	209 75
February	Budget	200 00	350 00	120 00	325 00	170 00	90 00	95 00	150 00	1,500 00
	Available	200 00	344 50	183 00	383 00	185 00	146 50	109 75	158 00	1,709 75

The Houston Family
Comparison of Savings and Expenditures
with Budget Allowances

Illus. 17-3

The Houstons' comparison of savings and expenditures with budget allowances for a one-month period.

When the Houstons set up their budget, they had $300 in cash on hand and in their checking account. They decided to keep about this amount in reserve to meet any unusual expenses. So this amount was not budgeted for current expenses. That is why the $300 is shown in the income and expenditures record but not in the comparison form.

As far as the Houstons could tell from their records, they were following the budget satisfactorily. At the end of January, the clothing category had a fairly large balance. However, the Houstons planned to take advantage of end-of-winter sales to buy some clothing, so this would reduce the clothing balance considerably by the end of February. Some of the other categories had large balances at the end of January, but these balances will be needed to take care of large expenditures in future months. For example, auto insurance will come from the transportation account, and doctor and dental bills will come from the health and personal care category. Generally speaking, the Houstons' budget seems to be working rather well.

KEEPING A RECORD OF UNPAID BILLS

The Houstons receive monthly bills for such expenses as utilities and also make a monthly payment on their house. Since these payments are made regularly each month, there is little chance that the Houstons will forget about them. But other bills need to be paid at less regular intervals. For example, life insurance premiums are due twice a year, in March and September. Property taxes must be paid in June and December. If there is no record to remind the Houstons when such bills will be due, they may fail to budget for them.

The Houstons bought a file box similar to the one shown in Illus. 17-4. The box contains a folder for each month of the year. As bills are received, they are placed in the folder for the month in which they are to be paid. There is also an extra folder marked "Next Year" in which the Houstons keep all bills and papers, plus reminders about such things as property taxes and insurance premiums, to be taken care of in the following year.

Illus. 17-4

A file for reminders and unpaid bills. Bills that have been paid are removed from this box and filed in another container.

FILING BUSINESS PAPERS

Current bills, receipts, income and property tax records, wills, insurance policies, deeds to property — all are important in a family's business affairs. Records such as these must be kept in an orderly manner so that the information they contain can be located easily when it is needed. Stationery and office supply stores sell a wide variety of filing equipment for home use. A family should select the type of equipment which is best suited to its needs.

Some business and personal papers should be filed for long periods of time. An insurance policy, for example, should be kept until the contract has been fulfilled or canceled. Records involving the transfer of property should be held for as long as the property is owned. Copies of tax returns must be retained for at least three years from the deadline date for filing the returns.

Receipts for payment of bills, especially those involving large sums of money, should be kept until there is no possibility that payment will be demanded a second time.

DETERMINING FINANCIAL NET WORTH

Sometimes a family or individual wants to know what they are worth financially. This can be done by listing everything that is owned (**assets**) and what is owed (**liabilities**). The value of some assets is determined by estimating their present resale value. Information helpful in preparing a statement of financial worth is available from the expenditure records of previous years.

The Houstons' statement of **net worth** is shown in Illus. 17-5. As you can see, net worth is determined by subtracting liabilities from assets (Total Assets $58,335 − Total Liabilities $26,420 = Family Net Worth $31,915). If a family or individual prepares

Illus. 17-5

The Houston family's statement of net worth.

THE HOUSTON FAMILY
STATEMENT OF NET WORTH
DECEMBER 31, 19--

Assets		Liabilities and Net Worth	
Cash (checking account)	$ 375.00	First National Bank	$ 320.00
Cash (savings account)	750.00	G. Wilcox & Co.	400.00
U. S. Savings Bonds	210.00	Mutual Savings & Loan	25,700.00
Clothing	800.00	Total Liabilities	26,420.00
House and Lot	47,300.00		
Household Furnishings	4,200.00	Family Net Worth	31,915.00
Automobile	4,700.00		
Total Assets	$58,335.00	Total Liabilities and Net Worth	$58,335.00

such a statement every two or three years, they can obtain a fairly good idea of how well they are doing with their money management. A net worth that increases from year to year usually indicates that a family or individual is making financial progress and is practicing good money management.

INCREASING YOUR BUSINESS VOCABULARY

The following terms should become part of your business vocabulary. For each numbered statement, find the term that has the same meaning.

assets	*net income or take-home pay*
fixed expenses	*net worth*
liabilities	*variable expenses*

1. Everything of value that a person, family, or business owns.
2. Expenses which occur infrequently, are for widely differing amounts, and are difficult to estimate.
3. The difference between the assets and the liabilities of a person, family, or business.
4. Expenses such as house payments and insurance payments that regularly occur and are for the same amount each time.
5. The amount a person receives after taxes and other deductions are withheld from his or her earnings.
6. Debts that a person, family, or business owes.

UNDERSTANDING YOUR READING

1. What is the first thing to decide in preparing a family budget?
2. What is the difference between fixed and variable expenses?
3. Into what eight divisions are family savings and expense items usually classified?
4. How did the Houstons decide how much money to allow for each item in their budget?
5. Why did the Houstons not include the $300 they had in reserve as part of their budget?
6. Why did some categories of the Houstons' budget seem to have large balances at the end of January?
7. Why did the Houstons need a file box?

8. How can a filing system be used to keep track of when bills are due?
9. Is the furniture that is owned an asset or a liability?
10. Why should a statement of net worth be prepared every few years?

USING YOUR BUSINESS KNOWLEDGE

1. Some people have trouble keeping a budget because they spend impulsively. They see something in a store they would like to have and they buy it without thinking. Then they find that they have spent money planned for other expenses, and they end up taking money from their savings or trying to cut corners in their other spending. What advice can you give to impulsive spenders?

2. Consider a family of five people: the father, working as a salesperson for a furniture store; the mother, working as a supermarket manager; and three children, ages 14, 9, and 7.
   (a) What are some fixed expenses that this family is required to meet weekly or monthly?
   (b) What are some variable expenses that they might have to meet?

3. Look at the Houstons' comparison record on page 211 and answer these questions.
   (a) At the end of January, for which items had the Houstons spent more money than the budget allowed?
   (b) At the end of January, for which items had they spent less money than the budget allowed?
   (c) Why do you think that the amount saved and spent rarely exactly equals the budgeted amount?

4. Phillip Martinez estimates that the expenses for medical and dental services for his family will average about $200 a year. In the first year after he began keeping records, these expenses amounted to $85. In the second year they were $79. Should Mr. Martinez change his budget allowance for medical and dental expenses for the following year? Why or why not?

5. Some people keep their business papers in a drawer in their desks. Each time a bill or receipt is received, they stack it in the drawer. What drawbacks can you see in that system of storing records?

6. Do you agree or disagree with these statements? Why?
   (a) A large income is necessary to have security and happiness.
   (b) Budgets take the fun out of spending.
   (c) Every member of the family should have a part in deciding how the family income should be used.

SOLVING PROBLEMS IN BUSINESS

1. In this problem you will continue the Houston family's record of income and expenditures for the next month, February. Draw a form similar to the one shown in Illus. 17-2 or use the form included in your *Activities and Projects*.

    (a) Write on the first line of the record the Houstons' budget allowances for February, obtaining the information from Illus. 17-1. Draw a line across the entire form.

    (b) On the second line write the balance of cash on hand as of February 1, $509.75.

    (c) Enter in the record form the following activities that the Houstons completed during February. Use Illus. 17-2 as a guide.

    Feb. 2 Payments: food, $79.50; clothes, $46.00; gasoline and oil, $17.00; cosmetics and drugs, $16.25; household, $15.75; church, $35.00; deposited in savings, $200.00.

    13 Income: Roy, $600.00. Payments: food, $82.50; clothes, $57.00; car maintenance and two new tires, $153.00; dental bill, $22.50; movie tickets, $14.00; church, $35.00.

    14 Mortgage payment: $200.00.

    15 Car payment: $90.00.

    18 Income: Julie, $150.00. Payments: food, $90.50; electric and telephone bills, $62.25; gasoline, $15.50; church, $35.00.

    22 Payments: stereo record, $9.00; doctor bill, $20.00; prescription drugs, $7.75; children's allowances, $6.00; shoes, $32.00; church, $35.00.

    28 Income: Roy, $600.00; Julie, $150.00. Payments: food, $89.00; gasoline, $15.00; school supplies, $4.00; sports equipment, $10.00; birthday present for grandmother, $12.00.

    (d) Rule and balance the Houston family's record for February. Cash on hand was $503.25.

    (e) Now prepare a comparison form similar to that on page 211. Draw a form similar to this one or use the form given in your *Activities and Projects*.

    (f) On the first line of the comparison form, record the amounts available for February, obtaining this information from Illus. 17-3.

    (g) On the second line enter the amounts saved and spent as shown in the income and expenditures record.

    (h) Calculate and record the amounts carried forward at the end of the month.

2. In this problem you will continue the Houston family's record of income and expenditures for the next month, March.
   (a) On the comparison form, enter the budget allowances for March.
   (b) Calculate and record the amounts available for March.
   (c) Enter on the income and expenditures record the following transactions that the Houstons completed during March.

   March 1 Deposited in savings, $200.00.
          4 Payments: food, $66.00; dinner at restaurant, $22.50; towels and linens, $15.00; gasoline, $16.75; phonograph record, $9.00; church, $35.00.
          8 Paid premium on life insurance, $75.00.
         10 Mortgage payment, $200.00.
         11 Payments: food, $72.00; shoes, $25.00; refrigerator repairs, $28.50; gasoline, $15.00; subscription to magazine, $6.00; wedding present, $10.00; church, $35.00.
         15 Income: Roy, $600.00.
         18 Income: Julie, $150.00. Payments: food, $75.00; automobile and driver's licenses, $32.50; prescription drugs, $8.25; children's allowances, $6.00; newspaper bill, $4.50; church, $35.00.
         25 Payments: food, $87.00; suit, $75.00; paint for house, $18.00; payment on car, $90; gasoline and oil, $15.00; tickets to high school play, $6.00; school expenses, $12.00; birthday present, $10.00; church, $35.00.
         31 Income: Roy, $600.00; Julie, $150.00. Payments: food, $73.50; gasoline, $15.00; doctor's bill, $12.00; medicine, $8.50; dental bill, $13.00; newspaper, $6.00; phonograph record, $8.00; contribution to orphanage, $10.00; deposited $60.00 in savings account.

   (d) Rule and balance the Houston family's record for March. Cash on hand was $457.25.
   (e) On the next available line of the comparison form, enter the amounts saved and spent.
   (f) Calculate and record the amounts carried forward at the end of the month.
   (g) Enter the budget allowances for April.
   (h) Calculate and record the amounts available for April.
3. The Houstons try to keep careful records so that they can plan their expenses for the future. On a recent weekend trip, the

Houstons traveled 552.5 kilometers. They spent $25.50 for gasoline for the trip.

(a) If gas was selling for 30 cents a liter, how many liters of gas did they use?

(b) How many kilometers per liter of gas did their car average for the trip?

EXPANDING YOUR UNDERSTANDING OF BUSINESS

1. Explain how each of the following might require a change in a family's budget. Be as specific as possible.
   (a) A daughter enters college.
   (b) The family income increases by one fourth.
   (c) The family moves to the suburbs.
   (d) The family buys a second car.
   (e) An aged parent moves in with the family.
   (f) Two teenagers start driving the family car.
   (g) A family which had been renting buys a home.
2. From newspapers and other sources, try to find out how much money was budgeted for the following items by your town, county, or district.
   (a) School needs.
   (b) Streets or highways.
   (c) Police department.
   (d) Fire department.
   (e) Public welfare.
   (f) Mayor's office.
   (g) Public library.
   (h) Parks.
3. Every family has the problem of arranging certain records in an orderly way. Suggest a plan for filing and organizing each of the following materials so that a particular item can be located quickly when it is needed.
   (a) Children's health records.
   (b) Christmas card list.
   (c) Family birth certificates.
   (d) Manufacturer's instructions for care and use of appliances.
   (e) Telephone numbers.
   (f) Product guarantees.

18 THE CHANGING VALUE OF MONEY

PART OBJECTIVES

After studying this part and completing the end-of-part activities, you will be able to:
1. Discuss how the value of a dollar has changed over the years.
2. Explain what happens to prices during periods of inflation and deflation.
3. Explain the three actions that government can take to control inflation or deflation.
4. Discuss why quick action is usually taken against deflation but not against inflation.

You probably have heard people talk about the good old days when prices of goods and services were much lower. A pair of shoes that cost $45 in 1980 cost only $20 in 1970. The average price of a house in 1950 was less than $10,000; today it is over $60,000. But what do these startling changes in prices mean to you? Are you getting less for each dollar you spend, or is the quality of goods increasing so that you are getting true value for your money?

Unfortunately, a dollar is not a fixed measure like a quart or a meter. The value of a dollar does not stay the same. We know that a quart is always 32 ounces and a meter will always be about 40 inches long. But although $15 will buy a shirt today we do not know what $15 will buy three or five years from now. Prices change, even though the quality of the goods or services we buy stays the same. The value of the dollar, as measured by what it can buy, changes from year to year.

THE CHANGING DOLLAR

A common problem for all consumers is that the value of the dollar has changed steadily through the years. The prices of goods and services have risen so rapidly that a dollar buys less now than it did a few years ago. Suppose that a school lunch cost 50 cents a few years ago and that now it costs 70 cents. The price of lunches in that case has risen 40 percent. If the average price of all goods and services has risen 40 percent, the consumer will need $1.40 to buy what $1.00 used to buy. At times prices for some items have doubled or even tripled in just a few months. Such price increases make it difficult for many consumers to live within their budgets.

USING THE CONSUMER PRICE INDEX

To make information about price changes available to everyone, the federal government publishes price indexes. A **price index** is a series of numbers showing how prices have changed over a number of years. The **consumer price index** shows the changes in the average prices of goods and services bought by consumers.

Illus. 18-1 gives the consumer price index for the period of 1967 to 1979. In compiling the chart, the average prices of some 300 goods and services in 1967 were taken to represent 100 percent. The figure given for each year is a percentage of this average. For example, the amount 110 for the year 1969 means that an item that cost $1.00 in 1967 would have increased in cost to $1.10 by 1969.

Changes in prices may not seem important from day to day. But over a number of years the changes may be very important. In the twelve-year period from 1967 to 1979, prices rose an average of 10 percent per year. A 10 percent increase may not seem to be too burdensome, but it is significant when you consider the total increase over the twelve-year period.

The consumer price index was 100 in 1967; in 1979, it had climbed to 225. That means that the prices of goods and services increased by 125 percent in 12 years (225 − 100 = 125 increase). A person with a take-home pay of $500 a month in 1967 would have needed, in 1979, take-home pay of about $1,130 to be equally well off.

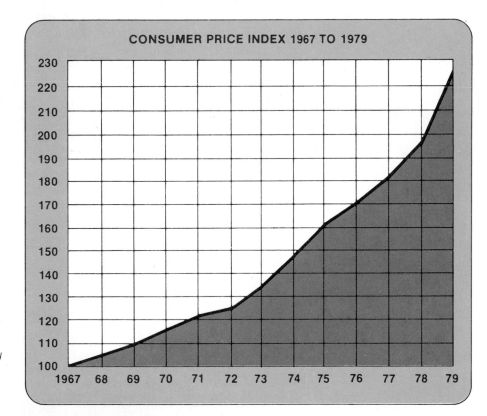

Illus. 18-1

This graph shows how the consumer price index changed from 1967 to 1979.

LESS BUYING POWER WITH INFLATION

An increase in the general price level is called **inflation**. With inflation there is a decrease in the purchasing power of a dollar. Inflation occurs whenever the demand for goods and services tends to be greater than the supply. In a period of prosperity when almost everyone has a job, many people spend their earnings freely and greatly increase their credit purchases, especially those made on the installment plan. As a result, the demand for goods and services of all kinds tends to increase rapidly. This causes prices to rise.

As prices rise, wages and salaries also tend to rise. If increases in wages and salaries are offset by increased production, there is no effect on prices. But if increases in wages and salaries are greater than increases in production, there are more dollars to be spent for a limited amount of goods. That gives prices another push upward. To meet the demand or the expected demand for more goods and services, businesses expand. They build new stores and factories and spend large amounts for equipment. All this spending in turn increases demand and tends to add to the upward movement of prices.

Local and federal governments may also contribute much to inflation. Governments spend enormous amounts of money for defense, education, welfare, roads, and many other kinds of goods and services. If governments raise enough in taxes to match all their payments, their expenditures do not increase demand. For each dollar they spend, the public has one dollar less to spend. But if governments borrow large amounts from banks and then spend those amounts, they increase demand. Governments spend their borrowed funds, but the amount that the public has to spend is not decreased.

Illus. 18-2

Rising prices make it difficult for consumers to buy many of the things they want.

MORE BUYING POWER
WITH DEFLATION

A decrease in the general price level is called **deflation**. With deflation there is an increase in the purchasing power of a dollar. Deflation tends to occur when the supply of goods and services is greater than the demand. When prices become high because of inflation, consumers may cut down on their purchases. This may happen either because they think that prices are too high or because they have already bought to the limit of their money and credit.

Because of the decreased buying by consumers, businesses have less demand for their products. They may decrease the number of their employees or have employees work fewer hours. Then the employees have less money to spend, and they decrease their buying. The decreased buying by employees still further decreases demand and makes deflation even more serious. As business becomes less active, stores and factories may delay expansion. This again decreases demand and helps to push prices down.

Deflation is also encouraged when government increases taxes more than it increases spending. When it does this, it takes money away from consumers that they might otherwise spend, and does not make an offsetting increase in its spending. This decreases the total demand for goods and services and tends to cause prices to decrease. Although prices are lower, unemployment is higher. While the dollar's buying power is increased, consumers have less money to spend.

ACTING AGAINST INFLATION

As individuals, we cannot do very much to affect either inflation or deflation. When prices seem to be too high, we may postpone making some purchases. If many consumers do this, the demand for goods may fall off, and prices may decrease as a result. But most of us are not able to postpone many of our purchases. We must spend regularly for food, clothing, and shelter. And if we need or want something like a new car or a refrigerator, we probably want it now and not three or four years from now when prices may be lower. Also, we have no way of knowing that prices will be lower in the future; they are more likely to be higher.

Government, acting for all of us, can help to fight inflation. Among other things, it can:

1. Increase taxes. An increase in taxes takes money away from consumers and thus reduces their purchases of goods and services.
2. Reduce government spending. A reduction in spending, especially when accompanied by higher taxes, decreases demand and thus decreases prices.
3. Encourage higher interest rates. Higher interest rates make it cost more to borrow money to buy such things as a car or a house. Higher interest rates also increase what a business must pay if it wants to borrow to expand its facilities. Some buying may therefore be postponed or avoided entirely. Decreases in purchases may result in a decrease in the demand for goods. A smaller demand for goods may help bring down prices.

ACTING AGAINST DEFLATION

To combat deflation, government can follow policies just the opposite of those used to combat inflation. Among other things, it can:

1. Decrease taxes. A decrease in taxes leaves more money in the hands of consumers. Consumers then can increase their purchases of goods and services. An increase in spending by the general public will help to increase prices.
2. Increase government spending. An increase in spending that is not offset by an increase in taxes increases demand and, thus, prices.
3. Encourage lower interest rates. Lower interest rates tend to encourage individuals and businesses to borrow in order to buy. With increased borrowing, consumers have more money to spend. This helps to increase the demand for goods and eventually will provide a support for prices.

WHY MORE IS DONE ABOUT DEFLATION THAN INFLATION

When deflation threatens, quick action is usually taken. Everyone notices the slowing down of business and the loss of jobs that deflation brings. Public officials do whatever they can to avoid the hardships that deflation causes. Furthermore, the actions taken to combat deflation are usually well received. Almost everyone likes to have taxes reduced. Few object to increased spending for public works or services that benefit them. Also, few object to lower interest rates, especially if they want to borrow to buy a home or some other major item.

But when inflation threatens, such prompt action is not likely to be taken. The strong demand for goods and services that usually occurs during inflation makes businesses prosperous and jobs plentiful. Wages and salaries increase. Prices also may be increasing, but the increases are not so noticeable at first. So before inflation becomes really serious, most people do not want anything done that will affect what seems to be a good condition. Often nothing is done to control inflation until it has gone so far that it cannot be completely avoided. Then it can only be slowed down or kept from increasing.

Usually the means of fighting inflation are unpopular. Few people like to pay higher taxes or higher interest rates. The idea of reduced government spending is approved by many people, but few favor reductions in the public works or services that affect them and their jobs.

INCREASING YOUR BUSINESS VOCABULARY

The following terms should become part of your business vocabulary. For each numbered statement, find the term that has the same meaning.

consumer price index   inflation
deflation   price index

1. A series of numbers showing how prices have changed over a period of years.
2. A decrease in the general price level.
3. A price index that shows the changes in the average prices of goods and services.
4. An increase in the general price level.

UNDERSTANDING YOUR READING

1. Why can dollars not be used to compare the value of goods over several years?
2. Who prepares price indexes?
3. What is the consumer price index?
4. How much did the consumer price index increase from 1967 to 1979?
5. According to Illus. 18-1, what was the consumer price index for 1969? for 1972?
6. What are some of the causes of inflation?
7. What usually happens to prices when the demand for goods increases rapidly?
8. How can governments help cause inflation?
9. What are some of the causes of deflation?
10. What are some effects on businesses of decreased demand for goods?
11. Name three things that the government can do to act against inflation and three things it can do to act against deflation.
12. Why is quick action usually taken against deflation but not against inflation?

USING YOUR BUSINESS KNOWLEDGE

1. If Michael Rodowski puts $1,000 away in a safe place in his house, can he expect that at the end of five years the money will buy more than, the same as, or less than it would have when he put it away? Explain why.
2. What are some of the ways in which credit purchases affect inflation or deflation?
3. Which is more likely to increase inflation: (a) an increase in government spending with no increase in taxes; (b) an increase in government spending with an equal increase in taxes; (c) a decrease in government spending with an increase in taxes?
4. The average family spends from 18 to 25 percent of its take-home pay for food. If prices for food increase very rapidly, what effects can you see that such increases would have on a family's life-style?

SOLVING PROBLEMS IN BUSINESS

1. J. J. Nees bought a pair of shoes that cost $45. Just one year ago, the same pair of shoes sold for $42. Two years ago, they cost $38.
   (a) How much did the cost of the shoes increase in the last year? In the last two years?
   (b) Was the increase in cost greater last year or the year before? What was the difference in the amount of the increase?

2. Robert Holihan eats lunch at the school cafeteria. The lunches cost 70¢ each.
   (a) How much does he pay for 5 lunches each week?
   (b) How much does he spend for lunches in 4 weeks?
3. The consumer price index rose by 13.9 percent in one year. How much would a person who earned $12,000 in the first year have to earn in the second year to have the same purchasing power?
4. The chart below shows the costs of nine consumer items over a 20-year period. Figure the approximate percent of increase or decrease in price in the 20-year period for each item. Which item had the largest percent of increase? Of decrease?

	Original Cost	Final Cost
White bread	$ .15	$ .85
Hamburger (1 pound)	.39	1.49
Milk (½ gallon)	.40	.95
Bananas (1 pound)	.12	.33
Eggs (1 dozen)	.52	.80
Refrigerator	491.00	330.00
Man's suit	71.00	132.00
19-inch black-and-white TV	187.00	145.00

5. At a certain dairy store a liter of milk cost 50¢ two years ago. If the price has increased by 15 percent, what would you expect to pay for a liter today?

EXPANDING YOUR UNDERSTANDING OF BUSINESS

1. Your text lists several things that the government can do to act against inflation. What are some things that families can do? That individual consumers can do? Check current articles in magazines and newspapers for ideas.
2. In 1980 the average American worked 3½ hours out of every working day in order to pay his or her taxes. In what ways are taxes good and in what ways are they bad for our economy?
3. Possible trends toward inflation and deflation in our economy are important to consumers. Look through newspapers and magazines for the past month. Clip any stories that you find which deal with economic problems. Do they indicate that the country is in good or bad economic shape? Are we in a period of inflation, deflation, or neither?
4. Several price indexes are used as indicators of business activity in the United States. Besides the consumer price index, which you learned about in this part, indexes are prepared for

wholesale prices and industrial goods, industrial production, and retail store sales. You can find information about these indexes in the *Statistical Abstract of the United States, The Wall Street Journal*, or in almanacs. What effects do you think a drastic change in one of these indexes would have on our economy?

5. Two problems which our economy has had to face at some time are recession and depression. A **recession** is a slump, a time when the economy slows down, prices drop, unemployment rises, and production drops. A **depression** is a very severe slump with high unemployment, low production, and scarcity of money among consumers. You may have read about the depression that the United States experienced during the 1930's. Do some library research about depressions. What usually causes them? What brought the U.S. out of the 1930's depression?

A growing field of career opportunities is the money management area. Individuals and families are generally earning more and more money, and there are also increasing opportunities to spend that money. As you know, great care must be taken to manage your money properly. You are also probably aware that many people find it difficult to handle their money in such a way that they can provide for all their needs and some of their wants. There are thousands of jobs available for those who are willing and able to advise and assist others in money management matters. These career opportunities exist in government at all levels, banks, insurance companies, consumer finance agencies, and privately owned financial advisory services.

WORKERS IN MONEY MANAGEMENT

Individuals who work in careers in money management might best be recognized by the businesses in which they serve. For example, banks often have financial advisors on their staffs. These advisors will help you make financial decisions and plan budgets. If you are thinking about borrowing money to buy a car or a home, the advisors will help you look at your present income and expenses to see what would be your best decision.

Insurance companies frequently have counselors who will aid you in planning for the better use of your income. They will help you look at your present and future financial needs. Naturally, they hope you will buy insurance from their companies, but their main purpose is to help you look realistically at your own financial standing. They know that if you are pleased with their services and advice you will probably buy insurance from them sometime in the future.

Many financial institutions and the U.S. Department of Agriculture hire home economists who are specialists in individual and family financial matters. Often these home economists spend much of their time talking to groups about methods of proper budgeting.

A growing number of private businesses specialize in helping people who are in financial trouble. Sometimes when families or individuals start buying on credit, they commit themselves to pay more in monthly payments than they actually earn. In those cases they might go to a debt adjusting firm for help. A debt adjuster gets a list of all a family's creditors and the amount owed to each. The adjuster will then work out a budget for the family or individual. Part of the budget will be a plan for paying off the creditors. The debt adjuster also checks with the creditors to see if they will go along with the plan for repayment. The creditor firms usually agree to the plan because they know that they are more likely to get their money with the help of a debt adjuster. And the debtor usually agrees to take on no new debts until the present debts are paid. The debt adjuster's final task is to advise the individual concerning how to avoid financial problems in the future.

There is a trend among many large businesses to offer financial counseling to their employees. It is believed that if workers do not have financial worries they will be happier and more productive. If this trend continues, it may create many new job opportunities for those who are trained in money management matters.

If you are interested in money management on a larger scale, there are thousands of opportunities in business and government for working on budgets. In these jobs you usually work with much larger amounts of money and much more complicated spending and saving categories.

EDUCATION AND TRAINING
FOR MONEY MANAGEMENT

Most people working as money managers or counselors have some college training. In fact, most of them are college graduates and many have advanced degrees. Courses important for success in this field include accounting, economics, finance, home economics, consumer law, and psychology. In addition to the formal education money managers need, those working in the field must be able to work easily with people. Also, they must be able to keep confidential the information they get about individuals and businesses.

LOOKING AT THE FUTURE
IN THE FIELD OF MONEY MANAGEMENT

It seems quite likely that there will be an increasing need for individuals who are trained in money management matters. The need is more apparent when there is decline in the nation's economy, but money management workers are always needed. As more businesses offer financial counseling to employees, larger numbers of money management personnel will be needed.

UNIT 6
Using Banking Services

UNIT OBJECTIVES

After studying the parts in this unit, you will be able to:

1. List eight services provided by banks.

2. Explain how to open and maintain a checking account.

3. Reconcile a bank statement.

4. Identify the methods used to cash and deposit checks.

5. Name five means of payment other than cash or checks and tell when each should be used.

SERVICES OFFERED BY BANKS

PART OBJECTIVES

After studying this part and completing the end-of-part activities, you will be able to:
1. Give two reasons for putting your money in the bank.
2. List eight services provided by banks.
3. Tell the difference between checking and savings accounts.
4. Give an example of an electronic transfer of funds.
5. Tell how a full-service bank differs from a special-purpose bank.
6. Explain how banks earn most of their income.
7. Give two examples of ways the Federal Reserve System serves its member banks.

Banks serve you and the community in so many ways that it is hard to imagine what life would be like without them. Yet sometimes people forget that banks are businesses just as are stores and factories. And like many other businesses, banks perform services for their customers. The many services that banks provide are important to you and your community in carrying out daily business activities.

One of the ways that banks serve you is by providing a safe place for you to keep your money until you need it. Banks can also help your money grow by putting it to work in the community through loans. And banks offer advice on how to manage money so that it will be used in the best way. In all, there are over 150 ways in which banks serve their customers.

Right now, you may be earning some money from a part-time job. When you complete your education and get a full-time job, you will earn a lot more money. Learning what services banks offer and how these services can help you is important in getting the most out of the money you earn.

ACCEPTING DEPOSITS

One of the main services that banks provide is accepting money from their customers for safekeeping. Mike Adamson, a student who works part-time and summers, is an example of a customer who uses this service. Mike gets $90 a week take-home pay from his summer job. He wants to save most of this for a down payment on a car. Mike knows that if he carries the money with him or keeps it at home, he may be tempted to spend it or it may be lost or stolen.

To protect his money, Mike may put most of his weekly pay in the bank. The money he puts in the bank is called a **deposit**. When he makes a deposit, Mike becomes a depositor. The record that a bank keeps of a customer's deposits is called an **account**.

Illus. 19-1

When you deposit money in your account, a bank teller will handle the transaction.

CHECKING ACCOUNT SERVICES

After Mike Adamson has deposited his money in the bank, he may want to use part of it to pay bills. He can do this by telling the bank to pay out or transfer his money. This makes it unnecessary for him to go to the bank in person to take out the amount he needs. The bank provides different ways through which Mike can transfer his money. One of the most common of these transfer methods is by check. A **check** is a depositor's written order directing a bank to pay out money. The check gives the bank a record to show that it was ordered by the depositor to pay out a certain amount of money. A bank account against which checks can be written is a **checking account**.

PROVIDING SAVINGS ACCOUNT SERVICES

Mike may put the money he does not need to pay his immediate bills in a **savings account**; that is, an account in which the money is to be "saved" or left for a period of time. Since the bank will have Mike's money for a longer period of time than if it were in his checking account, it will pay him for the use of it. The amount paid for the use of money is called **interest**. If the bank pays 6 percent interest on savings and Mike is able to deposit $500 of his summer pay in the savings account and leave it there for a year, he will earn $30 interest — a nice addition to his car fund.

STORING VALUABLES IN SAFE-DEPOSIT BOXES

Besides offering a place to deposit money, banks offer **safe-deposit boxes** where you can store your valuables. Since these boxes are in well-guarded vaults, they are the safest place to keep such things as jewelry, bonds, birth records, insurance policies, and copies of wills. Not even the bank has the right to open your safe-deposit box unless it is ordered to do so by a court of law. The box can be opened only by you or by someone who has been given the right to open it for you. Safe-deposit boxes are rented by the year. You can choose from a variety of sizes to suit your needs.

LENDING MONEY

Many people, businesses, and government units need to borrow money at some time. For example, a business may want to borrow money to expand, to build a new warehouse, or to buy merchandise for resale. Or a family may borrow to buy a car or pay college tuition for a son or daughter. Banks are glad to lend money to those who need to borrow, if it seems likely that the loans will be repaid when due. In fact, a bank needs to make loans. It receives most of its income from the interest that it charges to borrowers. Even when you buy items like clothes or sports equipment and pay for them with a bank charge card (such as MasterCard or VISA) you are borrowing money from the bank.

FINANCIAL ADVICE AND PLANNING SERVICES

Many banks help their customers by offering financial advice and planning services. Officers of a bank can advise customers about such things as whether it is wise to buy a certain house, how to manage money better, or how to exchange United States money for foreign money. Customers can get help from their bank on almost any financial problem.

Illus. 19-2

In many banks, customers can find a variety of information on financial planning.

PROVIDING INVESTMENT SERVICES

Most banks will give advice on investments that customers can make. **Investments** are savings that are put to work to earn more money. For example, money in a savings account is an investment because the savings account earns interest. Federal government bonds are another kind of investment that can be bought through a bank. If a depositor wants to buy bonds regularly — such as once a month — the bank will automatically deduct from the depositor's account the cost of each bond. A bank will also cash government bonds for its customers and pay them whatever interest has been earned. There is no charge for these services.

Banks also will buy for their customers bonds issued by businesses and by state and local governments, including school districts. Banks will give advice and help their depositors buy or sell other kinds of investments. A fee is usually charged for these services.

Illus. 19-3
This bank officer helps customers decide how to invest their money.

TRUST SERVICES

Many banks manage investments for their customers. When they do this, the money or other property that is turned over to the banks for investment is said to be held in trust. Banks that perform only this kind of service are called **trust companies**. Many banks have trust departments that perform the same services as trust companies.

Trust departments are used by people of all ages, but they are especially useful for very young people and for elderly people. A young person who inherits money may not have the skill and experience to manage it wisely. The bank will take care of the money and will make proper investments with it.

An elderly person may have the trust department of a bank manage her or his money because that person no longer wants to do it. The bank will make investments and will keep the customer informed about what is happening to his or her money.

TRANSFERRING FUNDS ELECTRONICALLY

Each year Americans use more and more banking services. With checking accounts alone, Americans write more than 110 million checks each day. That is almost 1,300 every second! You can imagine how many people, machines, and hours of work it takes to process all those pieces of paper. Add to that the resources it takes to handle all the activities for savings accounts, bank loans, and the many other banking services. Banks, indeed, are very busy places.

In order to serve their customers faster, better, and at less cost, banks have come to depend on computers. With the use of computers, money can be moved from one account to another electronically; that is, without the need for a written form such as a check. This transfer of money electronically is called **electronic funds transfer**, or EFT. EFT gives faster and less costly service than has been possible in the past.

Here are some of the EFT services now available:

1. Businesses can eliminate the need for payroll checks by directing the bank to pay their employees through EFT. The bank will subtract the total amount of the payroll from the account of each business and add the amount earned to each employee's account, even if the employees' accounts are in several different banks.

2. Individuals can direct their banks to pay automatically such monthly bills as utility and telephone charges. Each month when the electric bill is due, for example, the bank subtracts the amount of the bill from the customer's

account and adds the same amount to the utility company's account.

3. Automatic computerized "tellers" — actually computer terminals — allow customers to make deposits and withdrawals, transfer money from one account to another, or make loan or bill payments at any hour of the day or night. Automatic tellers are placed in convenient locations outside of the bank, such as in shopping malls, airports, and on street corners.

4. Many businesses hesitate to accept a check as payment without proof that the customer's account contains at least the amount of the check. With EFT, however, customers can have their checks approved at a terminal located in the store. The information from the terminal tells the merchant that the amount of the check is covered by the customer's account.

Other EFT services are available and more are being developed all the time. EFT has helped banks eliminate a lot of their paperwork. Although it has sped up the transferring of funds, EFT is not expected to replace traditional banking methods.

BANKS FOR SPECIAL PURPOSES

Some banks offer all the services discussed in this part. Other banks are organized for special purposes. **Savings banks**, for example, may provide a variety of services, but they are organized mainly to handle savings accounts and to make loans to home buyers. Trust companies, as you have learned, serve mostly by managing people's money and property for them. **Investment banks** help large corporations get money for new buildings, machinery, and other long-term needs.

Most banks are organized as **commercial banks**. These are often called **full-service banks** because they offer the full range of banking services. Commercial or full-service banks handle checking accounts, make loans to individuals and businesses, and provide other banking services such as those you have been reading about. Often a commercial bank will perform services similar to those of banks organized for special purposes. These services may be handled in different departments of a commercial bank, such as a savings department, a trust department, a real estate department, a personal loan department, or an investment department. Because commercial banks have so many different departments, they have been called "financial department stores." There are over 14,000 commercial banks in the United States, and in one recent year they accepted over a billion dollars in deposits. Most likely you will have your accounts in a commercial bank.

EARNING A PROFIT

Banks expect to earn a profit for their owners just as other businesses do. Some banking services, such as selling government bonds, are free; but banks earn part of their income by charging for their services. For example, fees are charged for checking account services, for managing trust accounts, and for the use of safe-deposit boxes. However, banks earn most of their income by charging interest on loans to individuals, businesses, and governments and by investing part of the money that depositors put in their savings accounts. From their income, the banks must pay their expenses (such as employees' salaries and interest on savings accounts) and what remains is profit for the owners.

SAFEGUARDING DEPOSITS
THROUGH THE FEDERAL RESERVE SYSTEM

A bank's operations are regulated more strictly than the operations of most businesses. If another kind of business fails, possibly only a few people will lose money. But banks handle other people's money, and if a bank fails thousands of people will be affected. Government regulation is necessary to assure the safety of depositors' money. State banks operate under the banking laws of the state in which they are located. National banks operate under the banking laws passed by the federal government as well as those of the state in which they are located.

The federal government set up the **Federal Reserve System** to help banks serve the public most efficiently. All national banks are required to join the Federal Reserve System, and state banks may become members. Banks that join the system are known as member banks.

As an individual, you cannot open a savings account in a Federal Reserve bank or borrow money from it. A Federal Reserve bank is a banker's bank. Its relationship to member

BOUNDARIES OF FEDERAL RESERVE DISTRICTS

BOUNDARIES OF BRANCH TERRITORIES

■ FEDERAL RESERVE BANKS

● BRANCH BANKS

⑫ DISTRICT NUMBER

SOURCE: *Federal Reserve Bulletin.*

Organization of the Federal Reserve System

Illus. 19-4

Under the Federal Reserve System, the United States is divided into 12 Federal Reserve districts. A Federal Reserve bank is located in each district.

banks is similar to that of your bank to you. You may go to your bank to deposit money or to get a loan. The Federal Reserve bank serves its members in the same way — by receiving their deposits, lending them money, and providing them with other banking services.

HELPING COMMUNITIES GROW

There is a great deal more to banking than what you have read in this part. But from what you have learned so far, you can see that banks are important to all of us. Over a million people work in America's 47,000 banking establishments. Banking services help build homes, start new businesses, plant crops, finance educations, buy goods, pave streets, build hospitals, and buy new equipment. These services are made possible because of the savings of many people.

Bank deposits do not remain idle in bank vaults. They are put to work. When you make a deposit in your bank, you are making your money work for you and for your community.

INCREASING YOUR BUSINESS VOCABULARY

The following terms should become part of your business vocabulary. For each numbered statement, find the term that has the same meaning.

account
check
checking account
commercial bank or
   full-service bank
deposit
electronic funds
   transfer

Federal Reserve System
interest
investment bank
investments
safe-deposit box
savings account
savings bank
trust company

1. A bank that handles the transactions of businesses that need to obtain large amounts of money.
2. A bank that mainly handles savings accounts and makes loans to home buyers.
3. A bank account on which interest is paid.
4. A bank that handles checking accounts, makes loans to individuals and businesses, and provides other banking services.
5. Money that is placed in a bank account by a customer.
6. A nationwide banking plan set up by our federal government to assist banks in serving the public more efficiently.
7. The record that a bank keeps of a customer's deposits.
8. A bank account against which a depositor may write checks.
9. An amount paid for the use of money.
10. An order written by a depositor directing a bank to pay out money.
11. A bank that manages the money and property of others.

12. A box in a bank vault for storing valuables.
13. The transfer of money electronically from one account to another.
14. Savings that are put to work to earn more money.

UNDERSTANDING YOUR READING

1. Give at least two reasons for putting money in a bank.
2. List eight services that are provided by banks.
3. How are checking accounts different from savings accounts?
4. Why might you someday want to borrow from a bank?
5. Give three examples of the kinds of financial advice a customer might seek from a bank.
6. What two age groups find trust departments of banks especially helpful?
7. Give an example of an electronic funds transfer.
8. How is a full-service bank different from a special-purpose bank?
9. How do banks earn most of their income? Name two other ways in which banks earn income.
10. Why is government regulation of banks thought to be necessary?
11. Give two examples of the ways the Federal Reserve System serves its member banks.
12. Give three examples to show the importance of banks to the economy of a community.

USING YOUR BUSINESS KNOWLEDGE

1. Suppose you have an uncle who says, "I don't trust banks. The safest place for my money is in my house; only I know where it is hidden." What are some arguments that you could use to encourage him to put his money in a bank?
2. Jane Yavner and Sara Newcomb operate a small antique shop. At the end of the day they deposit in the bank all the cash they received except a small amount of change and a few bills which they keep in their safe. Explain why they are wise to follow this method of handling their money.
3. For each of the following, list the types of banking services that the group or individual would be most likely to use and tell why:
   (a) a rock band
   (b) a retired person
   (c) a service station operator

(d) a car buyer

(e) the school ecology club

4. Suppose your community had no bank. How might the citizens solve the following money problems?

(a) What might they do with the money they saved?

(b) How might an employer pay the employees?

(c) How might a home buyer get funds to buy a house?

(d) How might a farmer pay for some machinery that he or she wants to buy?

(e) How might citizens pay their taxes?

SOLVING PROBLEMS IN BUSINESS

1. Mike Adamson, as you remember, is saving for a car. He worked 12 weeks during the summer on a road construction crew. His take-home pay was $90 a week.

(a) If he deposited all his paychecks in the bank, what was the total amount he deposited during the summer?

(b) If he put $50 each week in his savings account, how much did he have saved at the end of the summer?

2. Marsha Drummer deposited her paycheck in the bank every two weeks. She instructed the bank to buy for her each payday a $50 government savings bond and to deduct the cost of the bond, $25, from her account.

(a) At the end of the year, how many bonds had she bought?

(b) What was the total cost of one year's investment in bonds?

(c) If she held the bonds long enough for them to be worth their printed value, $50 each, what would be the total value of her investment?

3. Because of a shortage of coins, the government asked all citizens to turn in their collections of pennies, nickels, and dimes. George and Sara Herron suggested that their four children empty their piggy banks and deposit the money in savings accounts. Not only would they be helping with the coin shortage, but their money would be earning interest as well. Mr. Herron picked up coin wrappers from the bank and the children counted their coins and put them in rolls. One roll held 50 pennies, 40 nickels, or 50 dimes. When they had finished, they had these quantities:

12 rolls of pennies
9 rolls of nickels
2 rolls of dimes

(a) What was the value of the pennies?

(b) What was the value of the nickels?

(c) What was the value of the dimes?

(d) What was the total amount the Herrons deposited?

4. Christine Prado has a checking account balance of $120. She has her paychecks automatically deposited in her account. Her earnings for October were $920. During the month she wrote checks for $75, $125, $25, and $250. She also had $100 automatically transferred from her checking to her savings account. In addition, she used her EFT card at an automatic teller terminal to withdraw $50 in cash. Find Christine's bank balance after these transactions.

5. Nat Conte operated a small but busy record shop. He hoped to enlarge it soon and sell stereo equipment. To do this he would need a loan, and he had been advised by his bank to keep detailed records of his volume of business. The form he used to show the daily deposits of his cash receipts is shown below, with the deposits for four weeks.

Days	1st Week	2d Week	3d Week	4th Week
Monday	$167.06	$176.14	$143.50	$159.63
Tuesday	179.78	191.29	163.57	171.58
Wednesday	89.68	96.14	79.70	81.57
Thursday	163.69	159.78	144.83	164.52
Friday	203.45	222.97	191.46	197.54
Saturday	280.94	296.93	264.27	287.34

(a) Find the total of Nat's deposits for each of the four weeks.

(b) Find the total deposited on each day of the week for the four-week period.

6. To raise money for a class outing at the end of the semester, the general business class of Booker T. Washington High School sold cans of dry-roasted nuts. The 0.5-kilogram cans sold for $1.25 each. The students deposited the total amount of their sales each week in a special account in the school's accounting office. During one month, the records of the three students with the highest sales showed the following:

Date	Addie Smith	Jack Heinz	Rosa Ramirez
October 5	8 cans	3 cans	5 cans
October 12	6	5	5
October 19	5	4	1
October 26	11	7	4

(a) How many cans did each student sell?

(b) How much did each student deposit during October?

(c) How many kilograms of nuts did each student sell?

(d) Suppose a student in the class had not had any instruction in the metric system and wanted to know how many pounds each student sold. Find the number of pounds sold by each of the three students.

EXPANDING YOUR UNDERSTANDING OF BUSINESS

1. Many changes have taken place in banking during the last 25 years. Talk with your parents and neighbors and see how many changes in banking you can list which have taken place during that time. As a start, you might list night banking hours.

2. Secure the following information from at least one bank in your community:

(a) The name and address of the bank.

(b) Is it a state bank or a national bank?

(c) Does it belong to the Federal Reserve System?

(d) Is it a commercial bank, or has it been organized for a special purpose?

(e) Does it provide safe-deposit facilities for its customers?

(f) Does the bank offer services other than those presented in this part? If so, give a brief explanation of each.

3. Five examples of items which might be kept in a safe-deposit box were given in this part. Talk with several adults and try to find out at least five other items which are stored in safe-deposit boxes. Ask also if there are items which should not be kept in safe-deposit boxes, and tell why they should be kept elsewhere.

4. "Anyone can start a bank. All you need is money and a desk to operate from." Do you agree with this statement? Write a brief paper explaining why you think the statement is or is not true.

5. A bank's advertisement reads: "All major employees bonded for your protection."

(a) What does "bonded" mean?

(b) How does it protect the bank's customers?

(c) Why is bonding important to the bank?

6. Write a brief report about the purposes of the Federal Reserve System other than what was discussed in this part. A high school economics textbook should be a good source of such information.

7. Some people prefer to continue the use of checks rather than switch to the EFT system. Talk with several people who have bank accounts and find out their opinions about EFT. Report your findings by listing several advantages and disadvantages of the EFT system.

20 OPENING YOUR CHECKING ACCOUNT

PART OBJECTIVES

After studying this part and completing the end-of-part activities, you will be able to:
1. Give two reasons for having a checking account.
2. Explain why it is important to find out whether a bank is a member of the Federal Deposit Insurance Corporation before depositing money in that bank.
3. Tell why the bank requires you to sign a signature card when you open a checking account.
4. Prepare a deposit slip.
5. Tell the difference between checkbooks with registers and those with stubs.
6. Explain why account numbers are printed in magnetic ink on checks.
7. Show how to record your first deposit on a check stub or register.

As Steve Kowalsky wrote the last of several checks to pay his monthly bills, he realized how important his checking account was in handling his business affairs. He looked at the distances his checks must travel to reach the firms to which he was sending money. The first, a deposit in a nearby savings and loan association, would travel about three miles. The checks for the rent and the electric bill for his apartment would go about nine miles. His gasoline credit card payment would travel to another city three hundred miles away.

If Steve had made these payments in person he would have had to spend many days traveling several hundred miles to the various offices and would have added expenses of gasoline and wear and tear on his car. Traveling to pay bills once a month would be very expensive indeed. But thanks to his checking account, he could make all the payments within a few minutes in the comfort of his home and would have added expenses of only a few postage stamps.

A CHECKING ACCOUNT FOR SAFETY AND CONVENIENCE

When you open a checking account you will find, as Steve did, that it will be a convenient way to handle your business affairs. Checking accounts also offer many safety features. People who keep a lot of money on hand risk losing it by fire or theft. And when money is readily available at home, there may be a great temptation to spend it needlessly. While you will need to keep pocket money on hand for small purchases, you will want to keep most of your money safe by putting it in the bank.

With a checking account, you can write checks at home and pay your bills by mail as Steve did. This will save time and energy. You can safely send a check through the mail because it can be cashed only by the person or the business to which it is made payable. If it is lost, it can be replaced at very little or no cost. Also, after a check is paid by a bank, it is returned to the person who wrote it. The paid check is evidence that the payment was made.

At one time there was a real risk in depositing money in banks. There was the chance that banks might fail and that depositors would lose the money they had on deposit. In 1933, however, the federal government greatly reduced this danger by establishing the **Federal Deposit Insurance Corporation (FDIC)**. This is a government agency, but the money for its operation is provided by banks rather than by the government.

The FDIC guarantees each account in an insured bank up to $100,000. All member banks of the Federal Reserve System are required to join the FDIC. Banks that are not members of the Federal Reserve System may become members of the FDIC by meeting certain requirements. Almost 99 percent of all banks are members of the FDIC.

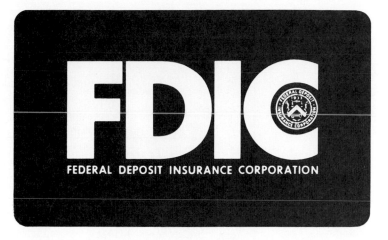

FEDERAL DEPOSIT INSURANCE CORPORATION

Illus. 20-1

Look for this sign when you deposit money in a bank. It means your funds are safe up to $100,000.

SIGNING THE SIGNATURE CARD

It's easy to open a checking account. Just take your paycheck or cash to a clerk or teller in any bank and say that you want to open an account. The bank employee will help you to sign a signature card, make your deposit, and select your checks.

With a regular checking account, a bank will take money from a customer's account only if the customer signs a check telling the bank to pay out a certain sum of money. Therefore, the bank must keep each depositor's signature on record to compare with the signature on his or her checks. For this reason, you will be asked to sign your name on a card when you open your account. This card is the bank's official record of your signature and is called a **signature card**.

A bank account used by two or more people is called a **joint account**. Each person who will write checks on a joint account must sign the signature card. A joint account is often used by husband and wife. Illus. 20-2 shows a signature card which has been signed by Robert W. and Mary C. Larkin for a joint account. Either of the Larkins can write checks on the account just as if there were only one owner. The signature card for a business would be similar to the one shown, but it would show the name of the business and the signatures of all people authorized to sign checks for the business.

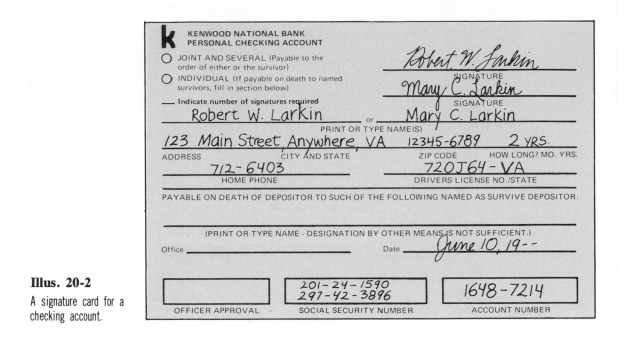

k KENWOOD NATIONAL BANK
PERSONAL CHECKING ACCOUNT

○ JOINT AND SEVERAL (Payable to the order of either or the survivor)
○ INDIVIDUAL (If payable on death to named survivors, fill in section below)

Robert W. Larkin
SIGNATURE

Mary C. Larkin
SIGNATURE

— Indicate number of signatures required

Robert W. Larkin   or   Mary C. Larkin
PRINT OR TYPE NAME(S)

123 Main Street, Anywhere, VA   12345-6789   2 YRS.
ADDRESS   CITY AND STATE   ZIP CODE   HOW LONG? MO. YRS.

712-6403   720J64-VA
HOME PHONE   DRIVERS LICENSE NO./STATE

PAYABLE ON DEATH OF DEPOSITOR TO SUCH OF THE FOLLOWING NAMED AS SURVIVE DEPOSITOR:

(PRINT OR TYPE NAME - DESIGNATION BY OTHER MEANS IS NOT SUFFICIENT.)
Office _____   Date *June 10, 19--*

OFFICER APPROVAL

201-24-1590
297-42-3896
SOCIAL SECURITY NUMBER

1648-7214
ACCOUNT NUMBER

Illus. 20-2

A signature card for a checking account.

FILLING OUT A DEPOSIT SLIP

When you deposit money in your checking account, you will fill out a **deposit slip** or **deposit ticket**. This is a form on which you list the items which you are depositing — coins, paper money, or checks. The items and the deposit slip are given to the bank clerk or teller.

The deposit slip should show the depositor's name and account number, the date, the items deposited, and the total amount of the deposit. Most banks print the depositor's name and account number on the deposit slips which they furnish. Some banks provide deposit slips with blank spaces for this information. Illus. 20-3 shows a deposit slip made out by Janet L. Perry, a depositor in the Riverview National Bank. Her deposit consisted of $46.25 in cash and four checks.

Each check is identified by the number of the bank on which it is drawn. This number is assigned to each commercial bank in the country by the American Bankers Association. You can see the three parts of this number in Illus. 20-4. The first part of the number above the line indicates the city or state in which the bank is located. The second part is the number assigned to the individual bank. The number below the line is a Federal Reserve number that banks use in sorting checks. Only the two top numbers are listed on the deposit slip, as shown in Illus. 20-3.

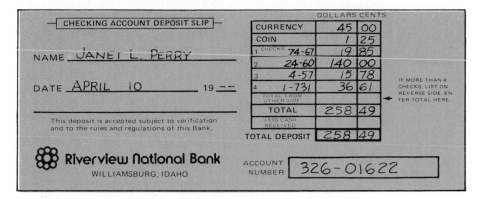

CHECKING ACCOUNT DEPOSIT SLIP		DOLLARS	CENTS
	CURRENCY	45	00
	COIN	1	25
NAME JANET L. PERRY	1 CHECKS 74-67	19	85
	2 24-60	140	00
	3 4-57	15	78
DATE APRIL 10 19--	4 1-731	36	61
	TOTAL FROM OTHER SIDE		
	TOTAL	258	49
This deposit is accepted subject to verification and to the rules and regulations of this Bank.	LESS CASH RECEIVED		
	TOTAL DEPOSIT	258	49

IF MORE THAN 4 CHECKS, LIST ON REVERSE SIDE. ENTER TOTAL HERE.

Riverview National Bank
WILLIAMSBURG, IDAHO

ACCOUNT NUMBER **326-01622**

Illus. 20-3

Janet L. Perry's completed deposit slip.

Sometimes checks are identified on the deposit slip by the name of the person from whom the check was received or by the name of the bank on which it was drawn. You should use the method your bank prefers.

Suppose Miss Perry wants to deposit only her payroll check of $155.20 and needs $25 for spending money. She will list the check the same way checks are listed in Illus. 20-3. The "Total" line will show $155.20. On the line "Less Cash Received" she will enter $25 and subtract to show the "Total Deposit" of $130.20. The cashier will record her deposit of $130.20 and give her $25 in cash.

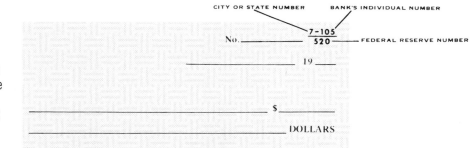

CITY OR STATE NUMBER   BANK'S INDIVIDUAL NUMBER

No. _____ 7-105
                      520 ——— FEDERAL RESERVE NUMBER
_____ 19 ___

_____ $ _____
                          DOLLARS

Illus. 20-4

Each commercial bank in this country can be identified by the number assigned to it by the American Bankers Association.

GETTING A RECEIPT FOR YOUR DEPOSIT

When you make a deposit in your checking account, the teller gives you a receipt. The receipt may be printed by a machine at the same time that it registers the deposit in the bank's records. This type of receipt is shown in Illus. 20-5. As an alternate method, an acknowledgment of the deposit may be written or stamped on a duplicate copy of the deposit slip. Deposits may also be made at automatic teller computer terminals located away from the bank building. Illus. 20-6 shows a receipt for a deposit made at an automatic teller station.

FIRST NATIONAL BANK OF DAWSON

MEMBER
FEDERAL DEPOSIT INSURANCE CORPORATION   DAWSON, ALASKA

ALL ITEMS ARE CREDITED SUBJECT TO PAYMENT
THIS IS YOUR RECEIPT
THE BANK SYMBOL, TRANSACTION NUMBER, DATE, AND AMOUNT OF YOUR DEPOSIT ARE SHOWN BELOW

FNB425∞JUN 1   50.00 D44

ALWAYS OBTAIN OFFICAL RECEIPT WHEN MAKING DEPOSIT

Illus. 20-5

When this receipt was printed, the amount of the deposit was also registered in the bank's records.

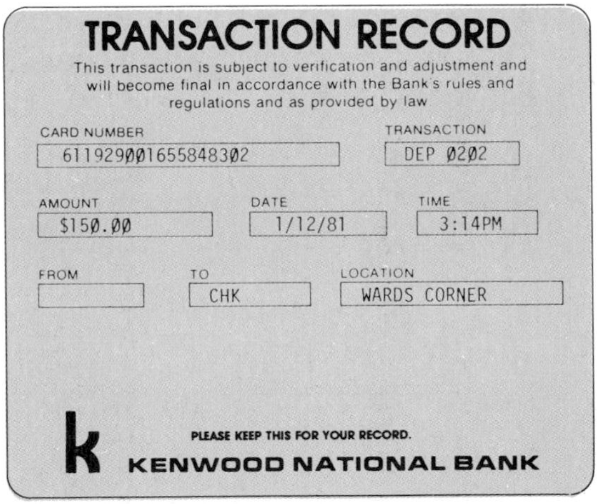

TRANSACTION RECORD

This transaction is subject to verification and adjustment and will become final in accordance with the Bank's rules and regulations and as provided by law

CARD NUMBER	TRANSACTION
6119290016558483302	DEP 0202

AMOUNT	DATE	TIME
$150.00	1/12/81	3:14PM

FROM	TO	LOCATION
	CHK	WARDS CORNER

PLEASE KEEP THIS FOR YOUR RECORD.
k KENWOOD NATIONAL BANK

Illus. 20-6

This receipt was printed at an automatic teller computer terminal located away from the bank and available to the customer 24 hours a day. Note the kinds of information recorded.

Deposits may be sent through the mail. Mail deposits should not include cash because it may be lost. Include only checks and similar forms, to be discussed later, that can be replaced if they are lost.

SELECTING YOUR CHECKBOOK

When you become a depositor, your bank will supply you with blank checks bound in a **checkbook**. Checkbooks are often given to depositors without charge, but many banks charge when a depositor's name and address are printed on each check. Today checks may be personalized in ways other than just printing the depositor's name. You may choose from a variety of colors and designs; an example is shown in Illus. 20-7.

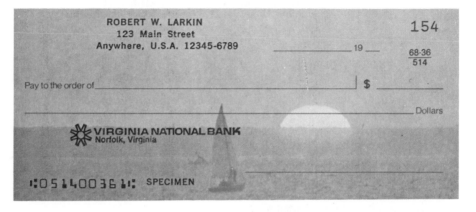

Illus. 20-7

Depositors may choose check designs showing sports, local landmarks, flowers, military emblems, or even photos of themselves.

Besides blank checks, a checkbook contains forms on which a depositor writes a record of deposits made or checks written. In some checkbooks, this record is kept on the **check stub** for each check. The stub is bound in the checkbook and is separated from the check by a perforated line (see Illus. 20-9). Another type of checkbook provides a **check register** which is a separate form for

Illus. 20-8

When you open your checking account, a bank employee will help you select your checks.

recording deposits and checks. Often checkbooks also contain deposit slips.

When checks are printed, the bank number and the account number are usually printed in magnetic ink. These magnetic ink numbers enable banks to sort checks quickly with machines that "read" the numbers. Illus. 20-9 shows magnetic ink numbers in the lower left corner of the check.

101 $ ______
______ 19 ___
TO ______
FOR ______
DOLLARS | CENTS
BAL. FOR'D
DEPOSITS
TOTAL
THIS CHECK
OTHER DEDUCTIONS
BAL. FOR'D

JANET L. PERRY
702 JAMESTOWN DRIVE
WILLIAMSBURG, IDAHO 83290-5549
101
______ 19 ___
92-403
1241
PAY TO THE ORDER OF ______ $ ______
______ DOLLARS
Riverview National Bank
WILLIAMSBURG, IDAHO
FOR ______ ______
⑆124104035⑆ 326⑈01622⑈

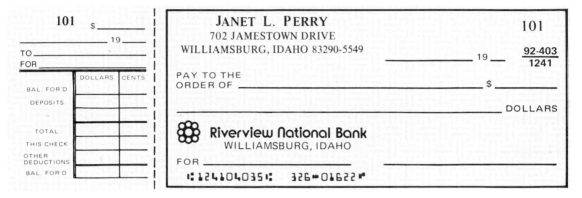

Illus. 20-9

A check and stub. The magnetic ink numbers at the lower left can be read by a computer. These numbers contain the bank's number and the customer's account number.

RECORDING YOUR DEPOSITS

When you make a deposit in your checking account, you should enter the amount on the check stub or check register. Illus. 20-10 shows the deposit information entered on a check

101 $ ______
______ 19 ___
TO ______
FOR ______

	DOLLARS	CENTS
BAL. FOR'D		
DEPOSITS	258	49
TOTAL	258	49
THIS CHECK		
OTHER DEDUCTIONS		
BAL. FOR'D		

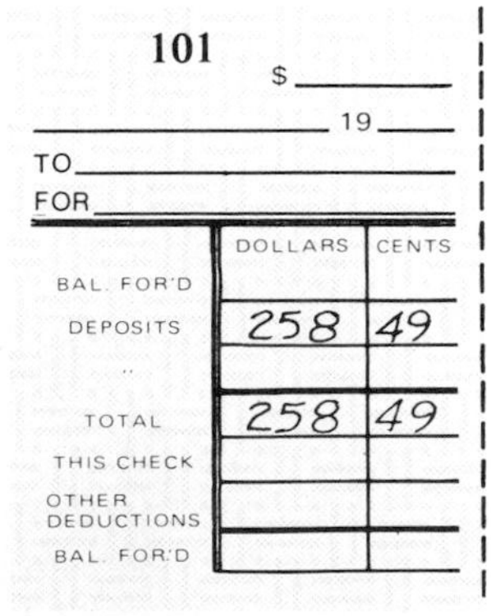

Illus. 20-10

Janet Perry's check stub with her first deposit recorded.

stub. On April 10, Janet Perry deposited $258.49. (See the deposit slip in Illus. 20-3). This amount is now entered on her check stub on the line opposite "Deposits." Since Janet is opening a new account, there is no balance to be entered on the "Bal. For'd" line. The amount $258.49 is entered on the "Total" line.

Janet Perry is now ready to write checks up to the amount she has deposited in her account. In the next part, you will learn how this is done.

INCREASING YOUR BUSINESS VOCABULARY

The following terms should become part of your business vocabulary. For each numbered statement, find the term that has the same meaning.

checkbook
check register
check stub
deposit slip or deposit ticket

Federal Deposit Insurance
   Corporation
joint account
signature card

1. A form that accompanies a deposit and shows the items deposited.
2. The perforated end of a check on which a depositor keeps a record of deposits and checks.
3. A federal agency that guarantees bank deposits up to $100,000 for each account.
4. A separate form on which the depositor keeps a record of deposits and checks.
5. A card, kept by a bank, that shows the signatures of persons authorized to draw checks against an account.
6. A bank account that is used by two or more people.
7. A bound book containing blank checks and check stubs or a check register.

UNDERSTANDING YOUR READING

1. What are two reasons for having a checking account?
2. Why should a person who wishes to deposit money in a checking account be interested in knowing whether the bank is a member of the Federal Deposit Insurance Corporation?
3. Why does the bank require you to sign a signature card when you open a checking account?
4. Who should sign a signature card for a joint account? Why?
5. How is cash listed on a deposit ticket?

6. How many parts are included in the number assigned to each bank by the American Bankers Association? What does each part mean?
7. How may checks be listed on a deposit ticket?
8. If a depositor wished to deposit part of a check and receive part of the amount of the check in cash, how would this be shown on the deposit ticket?
9. If you have both cash and checks to deposit, should you send your deposit by mail? Why?
10. Explain the difference between a checkbook with a register and one with check stubs.
11. Why are account numbers printed in magnetic ink on checks and deposit tickets?
12. Explain the procedure followed by a new depositor in entering the first deposit on the check stub.

USING YOUR BUSINESS KNOWLEDGE

1. If you sign your full name on the signature card when you open your account and then sign your nickname on a check, do you think the bank should pay the check? Give a reason for your answer.
2. Some organizations require that, in addition to the name of the organization, the signatures of two officials appear on the organization's checks. Why might more than one signature be required?
3. Kim and Stephen Wong have a joint bank account and both have signed the signature card. Must they both sign each check? Why?
4. "I want a checkbook that really fits me," Margie Jones told the bank clerk when she opened her checking account. If you were the bank clerk, how would you explain to Margie the different ways in which checks can be personalized?

SOLVING PROBLEMS IN BUSINESS

1. At the beginning of this part, you read that Steve Kowalsky wrote a check for a deposit to his savings account and three checks to pay his monthly bills. Here are the amounts:

Savings	$100.00
Rent	225.00
Electric bill	62.50
Gasoline bill	52.25

(a) What is the total amount of Steve's payments on his monthly bills?

(b) What is the total amount of Steve's four checks?

2. When Patty Tennison received her monthly paycheck for $810, she decided to keep $50 in cash and deposit the rest in her checking account. Before making her deposit, Patty had a balance of $127.50.

(a) How much did Patty deposit?

(b) What was the new balance in her checking account?

3. On August 30, Coralee Sanchez deposited the following items in her checking account, No. 250-136-6, in the Mercantile National Bank:

Paper money: $50.00
Coins: 2.38
Checks:

From whom received	Drawn on	Amount
Carson's Drug Co.	Mercantile National Bank, 13-94	$10.05
Joan R. Bonville	City Bank of Commerce, 35-71	16.00
Sheila J. Padget	Citizens State Bank, 79-228	6.50
John S. Sanchez	Western Park Bank, 71-225	14.30
Acme Foods, Inc.	Union National Bank, 56-61	135.95

From the information given, prepare a deposit slip for Ms. Sanchez.

4. Carl and Darlene Kirnberg have a joint bank account numbered 6-624-0642. They want to deposit their paychecks and get $25 each in pocket money for the week. Their paychecks for two weeks show the following:

$\frac{7-28}{520}$ $378.40

$\frac{7-742}{520}$ $247.62

Complete a deposit slip for their account showing the deposit total, cash returned, and net deposit. Use the current date.

5. Jack Gretakis has to drive 3.2 kilometers from his home to his bank. He pays 40¢ a liter for gasoline, and his car averages 6.4 kilometers per liter. Jack's father says that he should mail his check to the bank for deposit and save money. Jack says his gasoline isn't really costing him more than postage would each week.

(a) How many kilometers does Jack drive in one round trip?

(b) How much does the gasoline for one round trip cost?

(c) Which costs less, to mail the check or to drive to the bank?

EXPANDING
YOUR
UNDERSTANDING
OF
BUSINESS

1. The odd-looking numbers printed in magnetic ink in the lower left corner of a check are written in a kind of computer language called *Magnetic Ink Character Recognition* or *MICR*. In Illus. 20-9 you read that the two groups of numbers represent the bank's number and the customer's number. When the bank pays a check you write, the check is returned to you with another number in MICR printed in the lower right corner of the check. Ask your parent or another adult to let you examine a returned check and find out what the added MICR number is.

2. Some banks advertise as "24-hour banks" or "anytime banks." Do any banks in your community offer after-hours services? If so, write a brief description of how a customer would use the services. Give one reason why after-hours service might be needed.

3. Many banks today do not have a minimum age requirement for a person who wants to open a checking account. Visit a local bank or talk with a bank employee to find out if there is an age requirement at the bank. Write a brief report on the reasons given for having or not having an age requirement.

4. Here are four newspaper headlines telling about the loss of money by people who had not kept their money in a bank:

   Robbers Take Merchant's Cash Stashed in Milk Can
   Fire Destroys Widow's Home and Life Savings
   Worker Loses Billfold and $800
   Senior Citizen Loses Cash to Con Man

   What arguments would you use to try to convince each of the four people involved — before their losses occurred — to deposit his or her money in a bank?

5. Below is a list of terms that relate to joint bank accounts. Write a short definition of each term. You might refer to a high school business law textbook or ask a bank employee to help you with your definitions.
   (a) Joint and several (See Illus. 20-2 showing the joint and several account of the Larkins.)
   (b) Tenants in common
   (c) Joint tenants with right of survivorship
   (d) Tenants by entirety

21 WRITING PERSONAL CHECKS

PART OBJECTIVES

After studying this part and completing the end-of-part activities, you will be able to:

1. Show that you can correctly maintain a check stub or register.
2. Write checks that are free from errors.
3. Explain the risks involved in making a check out to "Cash."
4. Explain how and when you would stop payment on a check.

Checks are very important and very busy pieces of paper. Over 40 billion of these little "orders to pay" are written every year by the over 100 million owners of checking accounts. If all the checks written in one year were laid end to end, they would wrap around the earth over 150 times. But checks are too busy traveling for business purposes to wrap around the earth.

Checks scurry about the country riding in wallets, handbags, envelopes, and mail pouches and on trains, planes, and in trucks. They crisscross the nation's cities and towns and travel to farms, to ships at sea, and to foreign countries. They go in and out of houses, businesses, government offices, and banks of all shapes and sizes. They are written on, typed on, stamped on, and imprinted with magnetic ink. They are shuffled by hand, stored temporarily under money drawers of cash registers, and stacked and bound with rubber bands. They are sped through machines which read and sort them by the thousands a minute. Finally, they find their way back to the mailbox of the person who wrote them and are still in good shape, ready to serve as proof that they paid certain bills.

You will probably add thousands of checks to this stream of traveling paper after you open your checking account. How well your checks travel to their destinations and back to you will depend largely on whether you follow the simple procedure for writing your checks correctly. If you do, you will find that using your checking account will be easy and enjoyable.

FILLING OUT THE CHECK STUB OR REGISTER

Whether you are using a check stub or register, you should always fill out the stub or register before writing the check. Otherwise, you may forget to record the information about the check. Later on you may not remember the amount of the check or to whom it was written. In that case, you will not know how much money you have in your checking account.

Study Illus. 21-1. It shows that Janet Perry has written a check for $15.95 to The Slax and Jax Shop. The left portion of the illustration shows the stub for this check. Note carefully the information recorded on the upper and lower portions of the stub. The upper portion contains the amount, date, name of the person or business to whom the check is written, and the purpose of the

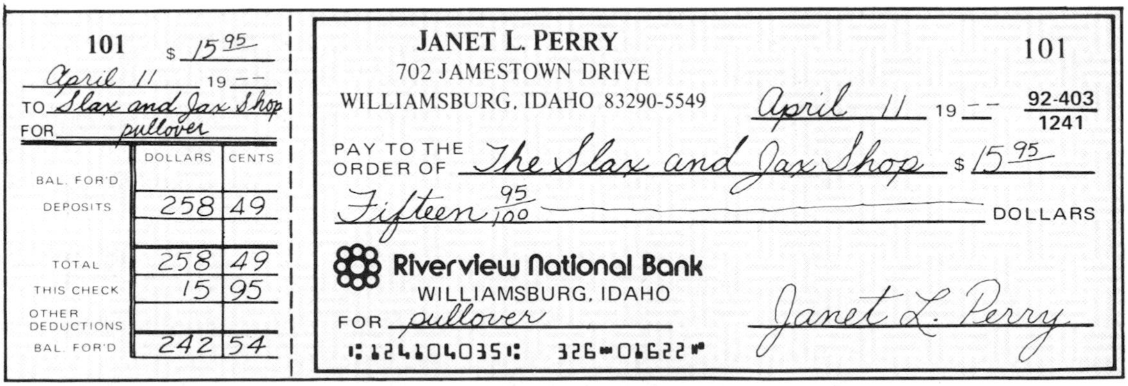

Illus. 21-1

A properly filled out check and check stub.

check. The lower portion of the stub shows how much is in the account both before and after the check is written. The balance at the bottom of the stub is carried forward to the stub of the next check and is entered opposite the heading "Bal. For'd." It is entered on the stub for check No. 102 in Illus. 21-2.

If Janet used a check register instead of stubs, her transactions would be recorded as shown in Illus. 21-3. The information recorded is about the same, but the arrangement is different.

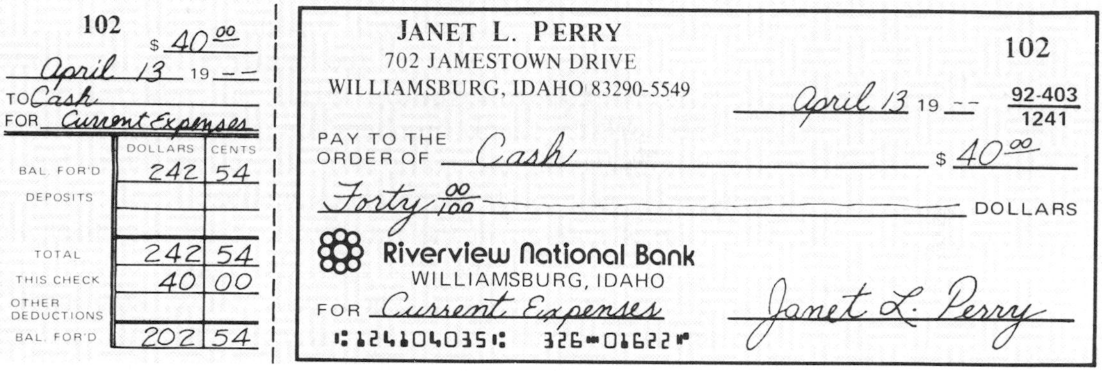

Illus. 21-2

A check made payable to "Cash."

PLEASE BE SURE TO DEDUCT ANY PER CHECK CHARGES OR MAINTENANCE CHARGES THAT AFFECT YOUR ACCOUNT

CHECK NO.	DATE	CHECKS DRAWN OR DEPOSITS MADE	BALANCE FORWARD →	✓		
D	4/10	TO Deposited paycheck	DEDUCT CHECK − ADD DEPOSIT +		258	49
		FOR for 3/16–3/31	BALANCE →		258	49
101	4/11	TO The Slax and Jax Shop	DEDUCT CHECK − ADD DEPOSIT +		15	95
		FOR pullover	BALANCE →		242	54
102	4/13	TO Cash	DEDUCT CHECK − ADD DEPOSIT +		40	00
		FOR Current Expenses	BALANCE →		202	54
D	4/16	TO Deposit	DEDUCT CHECK − ADD DEPOSIT +		20	50
		FOR	BALANCE →		223	04
103	4/22	TO Spangler Gifts, Inc.	DEDUCT CHECK − ADD DEPOSIT +			88
		FOR postage due on 4/8 order	BALANCE →		222	16
AT	4/29	TO Cash from automatic teller	DEDUCT CHECK − ADD DEPOSIT +		30	00
		FOR game tickets and dinner	BALANCE →		192	16

Illus. 21-3

This page from a check register shows correctly recorded transactions.

WRITING THE CHECK

After you have filled out the check stub or register, you are ready to write the check. Remember that a check is an order to the bank to pay out your money, so fill out the check completely and carefully.

Your check should contain these six items: the check number, the date, the name of the person or business to whom the check is written, the amount, the purpose for which the check is written, and your signature. Let's look at each of these items.

1. Checks are numbered consecutively. These numbers help you compare your records with the checks that have been paid and returned to you. If the numbers are not printed on the checks, you should write them in the space provided. When check numbers are printed, the numbers usually appear on the stubs also. Check registers have a column for you to fill in the check numbers.

2. The date is entered in the proper space on the check just as it was entered on the stub or in the register.

3. The person or business to whom payment is being made is the **payee**. In Illus. 21-1, the payee is The Slax and Jax Shop. This name is written on the line following "Pay to the order of." A check may also be made payable to "Cash" or to "Bearer." But if such a check is lost, it can be cashed by whoever finds it. For this reason, you should never make a check payable to "Cash" or "Bearer" unless you are going to cash it at the time it is written.

4. The amount of a check is written twice. It is first written in figures after the printed dollar sign following the payee's name. Write the amount close to the dollar sign so that a dishonest person cannot insert another figure between the amount and the dollar sign. A check on which the amount has been dishonestly increased is called a **raised check**. Cents are usually written somewhat smaller so that the amount in dollars and the amount in cents can easily be distinguished. Write the cents figures close to the dollar figures so that no additional numbers can be inserted.

   The amount is written a second time on the line below the payee's name. Spell out the amount in dollars. Write

103	$ (88¢)		JANET L. PERRY		103

103	$ (88¢)
april 22 19--	
TO *Spangler Gifts, Inc.*	
FOR *Invr. 4/19*	

	DOLLARS	CENTS
BAL. FOR'D	202	54
DEPOSITS	20	50
TOTAL	223	04
THIS CHECK		88
OTHER DEDUCTIONS		
BAL. FOR'D	222	16

JANET L. PERRY
702 JAMESTOWN DRIVE
WILLIAMSBURG, IDAHO 83290-5549

103

April 22 19 --   92-403 / 1241

PAY TO THE ORDER OF *Spangler Gifts, Inc.* $ (88¢)

Only eighty-eight cents —————— DOLLARS

Riverview National Bank
WILLIAMSBURG, IDAHO

FOR *Invoice of April 19*   *Janet L. Perry*

⑆124104035⑆ 326⊫01622⊪

Illus. 21-4

A check is not often written for an amount less than $1. But if such a check is written, this form should be used.

the cents in figures as a fraction of a dollar. Begin writing at the far left end of the line so that the amount cannot be changed by adding a word at the beginning of the line. Draw a line from the fraction to the printed word "Dollars" to fill all unused space.

If the amount written in figures does not agree with the amount written in words, the bank may pay the amount written in words. But if there is a serious difference between the two amounts, the bank may call the customer and ask for instructions concerning payment. The bank may also return the check to you and ask you to replace it. There is usually a charge when a check is returned for any reason. If a firm receives your check on which the amounts disagree, the firm will probably return it to you and ask you to write another check.

5. It is a good idea to write the purpose for which each check is written on the line labeled "For" at the bottom of the check. Writing the purpose will later help you remember why you wrote each check. For example, in Illus. 21-1 Janet Perry wrote "pullover" so that at a future time she would know that Check 101 was used to buy a sweater.

6. The person who signs a check is called the **drawer**. In the checks you have just studied, Janet L. Perry is the drawer. As drawer, you should sign your checks with the

same signature that you wrote on your signature card. A married woman should use her given name in signing checks. For example, she should sign Jean S. Harmon, not Mrs. William Harmon.

On checks issued by a business or other organization, the firm's name may appear as a printed signature and is often followed by the word "By." The person who signs the check writes his or her name after "By." This shows that the check should be charged to the firm and not to the person who signs the check. Examples of such signatures are shown in Illus. 21-5 and 21-6.

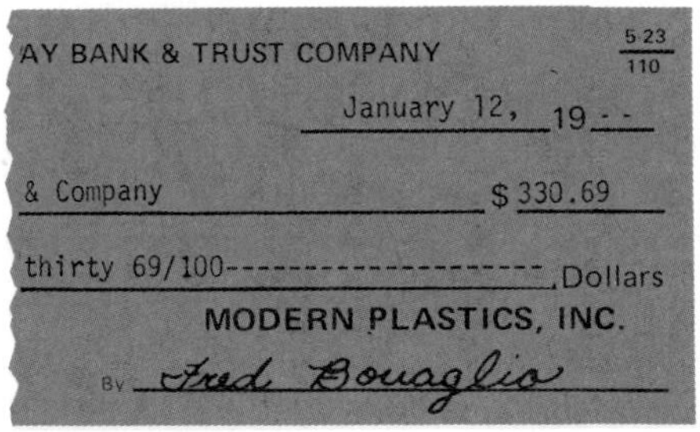

Illus. 21-5
Signature for a business.

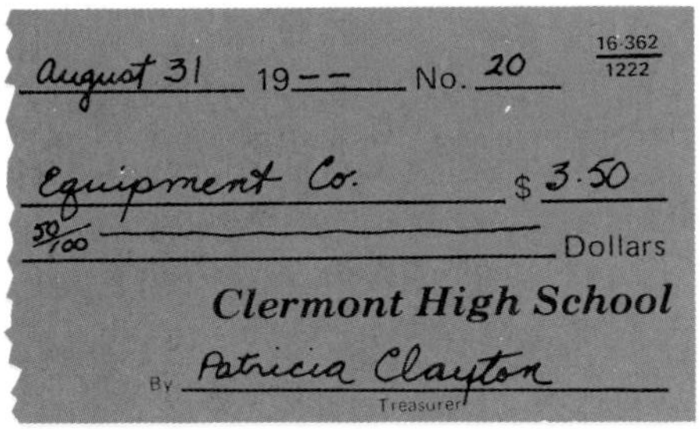

Illus. 21-6
Signature for a school organization.

The bank may subtract from the depositor's balance only the amounts of EFT transactions and checks that the depositor has actually signed. If the bank cashes a check signed by someone who had no right to use the depositor's signature, the bank may be held responsible. Writing another person's signature on a check without his or her authority is a crime called **forgery**. A check with such a signature is a forged check.

FOLLOWING GOOD CHECK-WRITING PROCEDURES

Anyone who writes checks has a great deal of responsibility. But if you remember the following eight precautions, there is little chance of your losing money because of poorly written checks.

1. Write checks only on the forms your bank gives you. It is possible to write a check on just about anything — even a shingle. But millions of checks are written every day. Sorting these checks and exchanging them among banks is a tremendous job. This job can be completed at a reasonable cost only by the use of machines that sort the checks according to numbers printed in magnetic ink. If the check does not have these numbers, the sorting will be interrupted, the check may be delayed, and a charge for handling the check may be made.

3. Tear up all checks on which you make errors. Don't try to erase an error or retrace your writing. No one who handles a check after you write it can be sure whether the changes were made by you or by someone who had no right to make them. Before destroying the check, record its number and write "void" on the check stub or in the register to show that the check was not used.

3. Always sign the same way you signed your signature card. Otherwise, the bank may refuse to pay your checks.

4. Always fill in the amount. If you leave it blank, you may be held responsible for amounts filled in by others.

5. Write a check only if you have enough money in your account to cover it. A bank is not expected to cash checks for more than the amount that is in your account. Writing checks for more money than you have on deposit is called **overdrawing**. When an account is overdrawn, the bank may not pay the check. In addition, most banks charge the depositor a fee for the extra handling costs. Special arrangements can be made with the bank to give you an automatic loan if you overdraw your account. Otherwise, intentionally overdrawing is against the law.

6. Record every check. Some people carry a few blank checks in their wallets instead of carrying their checkbooks. When one of these checks is used, the drawer should make a note of it and as soon as possible record it on the check stub or in the register. Otherwise, she or he may completely forget about the check and write other checks for more than is on deposit. It is also important to promptly record all transactions made at the automatic teller. Since no check is written, it is easy to forget to record withdrawals. But a receipt is given for each transaction. Note the last entry in the check register shown in Illus. 21-3.

7. Use the current date. A **postdated check** is one which is dated later than the day on which it is written. For example, a check written on October 1 but dated October 15 is postdated. You might postdate a check because you do not have enough money on deposit on October 1 to cover the check but plan to deposit money by October 15. This is a bad business practice because you may not be able to make the deposit or may forget to make it as you planned. As a result, your account may be overdrawn.
8. Write all checks in ink. Someone may be able to raise the amount of a check written in pencil without making any erasures that you can see. In that case, the bank may charge the drawer's account for the larger amount because the drawer cannot prove that the check was written for the smaller amount. Businesses often use **check protectors** or check writers to guard against possible changes in the amount of a check. These machines stamp the amount on the proper line of the check so that the amount cannot be changed.

STOPPING PAYMENT ON A CHECK

In certain situations you may want to tell your bank not to pay a check you have written. Suppose Janet Perry's check for $45.67 to Joseph Fields was lost. Before she writes a new check, she should ask the bank not to pay the first one. This is called **stopping payment**. The bank will ask Janet to fill out a stop-payment form such as the one shown in Illus. 21-7. This

RIVERVIEW NATIONAL BANK

June 5, 19--

Received: Office ________ Date ________ 19____ Time ________

☒ Please STOP PAYMENT on the following described check, issued by the undersigned

Amt.	Date	Ck. No.	Payee
$45.67	6/1/--	130	Joseph Fields

It is understood that you agree to indemnify us for said amount and losses, expenses and costs incurred by us arising from our compliance with the above order.

Account Number 326-01622

Account Name and Address: Janet L. Perry, 702 Jamestown Drive, Williamsburg, ID 83290-5549

☐ Please cancel the above stop payment.

Date ________ 19____

Signature ________

Signature *Janet L. Perry*

AUTHORIZATION

Illus. 21-7
A form for stopping payment on a check.

form is a written notice from the drawer telling the bank not to pay a certain check. The notice includes the date, the check number, and the amount of the check. It also shows the name of the payee and the signature of the drawer. Most banks charge a fee for stopping payment on a check.

Stopping payment is a privilege that should be used only for good reasons. Once you have issued a check, it may be passed from one person to another. You can be held responsible for damages that your stopping payment on a check may cause to rightful holders of the check.

INCREASING YOUR BUSINESS VOCABULARY

The following terms should become part of your business vocabulary. For each numbered statement, find the term that has the same meaning.

check protector   *payee*
drawer   *postdated check*
forgery   *raised check*
overdrawing   *stopping payment*

1. The person who signs a check.
2. A machine that prints the amount of the check on the check form.
3. The crime of signing another person's name to a check without the authority to do so.
4. A check dated later than the date on which it is written.
5. The person to whom a check is made payable.
6. Instructing a bank not to pay a certain check.
7. A check on which the amount was increased by a dishonest person.
8. Writing checks for more money than is in one's account.

UNDERSTANDING YOUR READING

1. Why should the check stub or register be filled in before a check is written?
2. What information is contained on the top part of the check stub?
3. What six important items should you write on a check?
4. Is the payee the person who is paying the amount on the check or the one who is to receive the payment?
5. What risk is involved in making a check payable to "Cash" or "Bearer"? What can you do to avoid the risk?

6. In what places on a check is raising likely to be attempted? What can the drawer of the check do to prevent this?
7. How might a bank or a payee handle a check on which the amount in figures does not agree with the amount in words?
8. What is a forged check?
9. Is it always illegal to overdraw intentionally? Explain.
10. Under what conditions might you stop payment on a check? How would you stop payment?

USING YOUR BUSINESS KNOWLEDGE

1. Compare the information written on a check with the information written on a check stub. What items of information are included:
   (a) on both?
   (b) only on the check?
   (c) only on the check stub?
2. Olivia Moreno likes the convenience of the automatic teller for her banking. She often makes deposits and withdrawals from the automatic teller station which she passes on her way to work. But she frequently forgets to record these banking activities in her check register and seems never to know how much money she has in the bank. Also, twice she has overdrawn her account and has had to pay a fee each time. Can you suggest a plan for Olivia to follow which would allow her to use the automatic teller services and still be sure of having an accurate record?
3. Tina Hobbs feels that it is a waste of time to record information on check stubs. "The bank sends me a statement each month; that's all I need," she says. How could you convince Tina that she should keep records?
4. On October 28, Henry Santee bought for $49.75 a sunshield helmet to wear when he commutes to work on his motorcycle. The merchant agreed to take his personal check, using his driver's license and his company ID card for identification. However, when the merchant saw that Mr. Santee had dated his check November 1, he refused to accept it. Mr. Santee explained that he would deposit his paycheck on October 30, and that by the time the merchant sent the check through the bank, it would be covered. The merchant still refused to take the check. Do you agree with the merchant? Why?
5. Sally Adams, Janet Sheeler, and Margie Altizer agreed to contribute $200 each month to run the apartment they share. They set up a joint checking account at the bank and each

signed the signature card so she could sign checks. From the account they would write checks for rent, food, utilities, and all expenses involved in maintaining the apartment. No personal items could be paid for from the joint-account funds. What suggestions would you offer Sally, Janet, and Margie about handling their joint account to avoid overdrawing?

SOLVING
PROBLEMS
IN BUSINESS

1. Carmen Tillman opened a checking account on June 1 and deposited $94.40, the amount of her first paycheck from her summer job as a daycamp counselor. During the month she deposited three more paychecks of the same amount.
   (a) What was the total of Carmen's deposits?
   (b) During June, Carmen wrote four checks for the following amounts: $25.00, $36.50, $8.75, and $5.45. What was the total amount paid out in checks?
   (c) What was Carmen's balance at the end of June?
2. On July 4, Pete McKenzie was awarded a check for winning a swimming race at his community pool. For this event, the club awarded 20¢ per meter to the person who swam two lengths of the 25-meter pool the fastest. What was the amount of the check Pete won?
3. You are treasurer of the Westchester High School Student Council. Fill out check stubs and write checks for the following transactions of the Student Council. If forms are not available, draw forms similar to that shown in Illus. 21-1. The beginning balance is $167.43. Use the current date. Number the stubs and checks beginning with 28.
   (a) Pay $4.25 to the Ohio Book Store for the book *Parliamentary Procedure*.
   (b) Pay 98 cents to Sandy Geiger for a record book.
   (c) Pay $12.50 to Latimer's Sporting Goods for a basketball trophy.
   (d) Pay $21.92 to Don Schloemer for his traveling expenses to the state convention of Student Councils.
4. On September 1, Jim Lansbury had a balance of $478.25 in his checking account. By special arrangement with the bank, money for his electric bill is withdrawn from his account on the third of each month and transferred to the account of the utility company. During the month he wrote the checks and made the deposits listed on the next page. Record the beginning balance, the checks, and the deposits in a check register similar to the one in Illus. 21-3.

Sept.	Check Number	To	For	Amount
3	AT	Danville Public Utilities	automatic payment Aug. electric	$ 68.95
4	134	Moyer Realty Company	Sept. rent	195.00
6	Deposit			275.24
9	135	J. F. Brunsman, M.D.	Jimmy's sprained ankle	18.90
13	136	Vonderbrink's Clothing Store	balance on suit	64.22
16	137	Bohman Brothers Hardware	paint, wallpaper	42.20
18	Deposit			95.25
20	138	Bushelman Fuel Company	oil contract	62.60
24	139	Vogel's Supermarket	groceries	93.94
28	140	United Appeal	contribution	35.00
30	141	Klein's Drugs	Jimmy's medicine	13.11

5. Each spring the student clubs of Lakeland Valley High School donate money to Valley Hospital for its new equipment fund. This year the Physical Fitness Club raised its part by staging a walkathon around the Municipal Park walking trail, a distance of 5 kilometers. The club invited everyone in the community to participate. It found two sponsors who would pay these awards: The LV Times, $1 for each walker who completed at least one lap; and the Valley Power Company, 10¢ per kilometer. According to the rules, only full laps would be counted. Judges would register one lap for each walker as he or she crossed the finish line. The sponsors agreed to give the club a check for the total amount earned by the walkers. Here are the results:

Number of Walkers	Completed Laps
1	5
3	4
13	3
24	2
27	1

(a) How many people participated in the walkathon?

(b) How many laps did the walkers complete altogether?

(c) What was the total number of kilometers walked?

(d) What was the amount of the award donated by each sponsor?

(e) If the club donated the entire amount received from the walkathon, how much did it donate to the hospital?

(f) How many total miles did the participants walk?

EXPANDING
YOUR
UNDERSTANDING
OF
BUSINESS

1. Listed below are some errors that were made in filling out checks. Explain which errors would probably not affect the use of the checks and which would probably cause the checks to be void.
   (a) The check number was omitted.
   (b) The check stub was not filled out.
   (c) The drawer forgot to sign the check.
   (d) The check was dated January 3, 1980 instead of January 3 of the current year.
   (e) The drawer forgot to fill in the name of the payee.
   (f) The payee's name was misspelled.
   (g) The amount of the check was $54.50. It should have been $45.50.
   (h) The drawer omitted the amount of the check since that information was not available, and in a letter instructed the payee to fill in the correct amount.

2. Payroll checks are often calculated and printed automatically on computers. Try to find a computer-printed check to examine by asking the working members of your family to let you look at their checks; by visiting a bank, a department store, or other large business and asking them to show you a sample of a computer-printed check; or by visiting a local government office and asking to see a sample of their automatically printed checks. When you have seen a computer-printed check, answer the following questions:
   (a) Is the check different in size or appearance from a personal check?
   (b) Are there punched holes in the check?
   (c) What items appear to be printed automatically?
   (d) Are any items printed in magnetic ink?
   (e) Are any of the items different from the six items which you learned should be written in by the drawer of the check?

3. Harvey Graham owed Leonard Saunders $58. He wrote a check to Mr. Saunders and mailed it to him. Later Mr. Graham decided that he did not want to pay all of the debt at once. He therefore asked his bank to stop payment on the check. Do you think it was wise for Mr. Graham to make this request? Why?

4. Interview a local banker and find out the most frequent reasons for which that bank returns checks to the drawer of the check. Based on your interview, list the reasons from the most frequent to the least frequent. Can you suggest ways in which the business skill of writing checks might be improved in your community?

22 HOW YOUR CHECKING ACCOUNT WORKS

PART OBJECTIVES

After studying this part and completing the end-of-part activities, you will be able to:

1. Explain why banks usually charge for checking account services.
2. Name two kinds of personal checking accounts and identify their major differences.
3. Describe a package plan account.
4. Tell why a canceled check is valuable to the drawer.
5. Reconcile a bank statement.

When you open a checking account, the bank you choose and all other banks in the world are at your service. You can sit in your home and write a check to someone who lives in Miami or Kalamazoo or London or Tokyo. Your bank and the banks in the distant cities will serve you by handling your check. This and all the other services the bank performs for you require many employees and some very expensive equipment. As you can see, handling your account is a costly process. Yet, the cost to you is very little compared to the many services available to you. Banks can provide this low-cost service because they put to work part of every dollar you deposit.

If you keep a large balance in your checking account, the bank can lend part of the money to someone else. By doing this, the bank may earn enough money to handle your checking account without any direct charge to you. Some banks today offer such free checking services. But if the account balance is not large, the bank usually charges for checking account services.

The charge that a bank makes for checking account services is known as a **service charge**. A service charge may be made up of (1) a fixed monthly charge for maintaining the account, and (2) a charge for each check written and sometimes for each check deposited. In most banks a separate fee is also charged for special items, such as a stop-payment order or a returned check. Some banks are changing to the fixed monthly service charge for maintaining all personal checking accounts. Free checking account service is offered by many banks to older citizens and other special groups.

USING A REGULAR CHECKING ACCOUNT

If you write a large number of checks each month, you probably should use a regular checking account. With some banks there is no service charge for a regular checking account as long as the account balance does not fall below a certain amount during a month. This minimum balance may be as little as $50 or as high as $300 or more. Sometimes the charges are figured on the average balance of the account during the month. This means that the account may fall below a certain minimum on some days but must average at or above the minimum at the end of the month to avoid a service charge.

Shown below is an example of a bank's service charges based on average monthly balances for personal checking accounts:

Average Monthly Balance of $200 or less $3.00 Charge
Average Monthly Balance of $201 to $400 $2.00 Charge
Average Monthly Balance of $401 or more   No charge

Charges for many regular accounts depend on the number of checks you write as well as your balance. Suppose you write 20 checks on your regular checking account at the Nova State Bank. Under the bank's schedule, shown in Illus. 22-1, your service charge might be $2.60, $2.20, $1.90, or nothing. If your minimum balance at Nova is $176.50, your service charge for the month is $2.20. But if your balance is $372.40, your 20 checks will cost you nothing.

| | Minimum Balance | | | |
Number of Checks	Under $100	$100– 199	$200– 299	$300 or more
0	$ .80	$ .80	$ .50	Free
1	.89	.87	.57	
2	.98	.94	.64	No service
3	1.07	1.01	.71	charge
4	1.16	1.08	.78	
5	1.25	1.15	.85	Unlimited
10	1.70	1.50	1.20	number of
20	2.60	2.20	1.90	checks
30	3.50	2.90	2.60	
Additional Checks	.09 ea.	.07 ea.	.07 ea.	

Illus. 22-1

The Nova State Bank's schedule of service charges.

SPECIAL CHECKING ACCOUNTS FOR LIMITED NUMBERS OF CHECKS

You may need to write only a few checks each month and may wish to keep only a small balance in your checking account. For depositors like you, many banks offer special checking accounts. These accounts may be given names, such as Handi-Check Account, Thrift-Check Account, or Tenplan Checking Account. Charges vary, but the basic charge is for each check written. A typical charge is about 10 or 15 cents per check. There may also be a small monthly fee, often $1 or less. No minimum balance is required by most banks. Suppose you have a special checking account in a bank which charges 10 cents a check and 75 cents a month. If you write 12 checks in a month your service charge would be $12 \times .10 = \$1.20$ plus .75, for a total charge of $1.95.

PACKAGE PLAN ACCOUNTS

Some banks offer a variety of bank services along with the usual checking account services in a package plan account. Like the special account, the package plans often have distinctive names, such as All-in-One Checking Account, BanClub, Gold Account, and United Account. With such an account, you may use a variety of bank services for a flat monthly fee. The fees vary among banks and with the number of services included, but the range is usually from $2 to $4 a month.

Services included in the package plans also vary among banks. These services are typical: no minimum balance, unlimited check writing, personalized checks, safe-deposit box, reduced rates on loans, protection against overdrawing, and bank charge card privileges. The package plan eliminates the separate charges usually made on many of these services.

REVIEWING YOUR BANK STATEMENT

As a depositor, you will need to review the record of your account which the bank keeps. At regular intervals, usually monthly, the bank will send you a report on your account known as a **bank statement**. Statement forms vary, but most show:

1. The balance at the beginning of the month.
2. The deposits made during the month.
3. The checks paid by the bank during the month.
4. Any electronic or automatic teller transactions made during the month.
5. Any special payment the bank has made at your request, such as a transfer of funds from your checking to your savings account, or the automatic payment of a monthly bill such as a car payment.
6. The service charge or other charges for the month, if any.
7. The balance at the end of the month.

See if you can locate examples of each of these items on the bank statement shown in Illus. 22-2.

EXAMINING YOUR RETURNED CHECKS

With the bank statement, the bank will return your checks that it has paid. Before the bank sends you your paid checks, it cancels each one, usually using a machine that stamps or punches holes in the check. The paid checks are called **canceled checks**.

Riverview National Bank

Checking Account Statement

ACCT. 326-01622
DATE 5/1/--
PAGE 1

Janet L. Perry
702 Jamestown Drive
Williamsburg, ID 83290-5549

Please examine at once. If no errors are reported within 10 days, account will be considered correct.

BALANCE FORWARD	NO. OF WITH-DRAWALS	TOTAL AMOUNT	NO. OF DEP.	TOTAL DEPOSIT AMOUNT	SERVICE CHARGE	BALANCE THIS STATEMENT
0.00	14	320.10	4	598.99	1.25	277.64

CHECKS AND OTHER DEBITS		DEPOSITS AND OTHER CREDITS	DATE	BALANCE
		258.49	4/10	258.49
101	15.95		4/14	242.54
102	40.00		4/14	202.54
		20.50	4/16	223.04
103	.88		4/23	222.16
		160.00 ATD	4/23	382.16
104	16.30		4/24	365.86
105	6.22		4/24	359.64
106	25.78		4/26	333.86
107	18.95		4/26	314.91
109	65.33		4/26	249.58
110	33.46		4/27	216.12
111	24.33		4/27	191.79
112	5.80		4/27	185.99
113	12.85		4/27	173.14
		160.00	4/29	333.14
114	4.25		4/30	328.89
	50.00 AP-Valley Power Co.		4/30	278.89
	1.25 SC		4/30	277.64

KEY TO SYMBOLS

AD -	AUTOMATIC DEPOSIT	PC -	PAID OVERDRAFT CHARGE
AP -	AUTOMATIC PAYMENT	PR -	PAYROLL DEPOSIT
ATD -	AUTOMATIC TELLER DEPOSIT	RC -	RETURN CHECK CHARGE
ATW -	AUTOMATIC TELLER WITHDRAWAL	RT -	RETURN ITEM
CC -	CERTIFIED CHECK	SC -	SERVICE CHARGE
EC -	ERROR CORRECTED	ST -	SAVINGS TRANSFER
OD -	OVERDRAFT	TC -	TRANSFER CHARGE

Illus. 22-2

A bank statement.

Be sure to save them. They are valuable records. Your check stub or register is your own record, but the canceled check is evidence that payment was actually received. This is true because the payee must sign his or her name on the back of a check before it can be cashed. Since you receive computer-printed receipts for all transactions made at an automatic teller station, no additional pieces of paper will be returned with your statement for these payments or withdrawals.

COMPARING YOUR RECORD WITH THE BANK'S RECORD

As a depositor, you keep a record of your checking account on check stubs or in a check register. The bank statement gives you a copy of the bank's record of your account. The balances on the two may differ. Bringing the balances into agreement is known as reconciling the bank balance. The statement showing how the two balances were brought into agreement is known as the **bank reconciliation**. Forms for reconciling are often printed on the back of the bank statement.

There are several reasons why the balances shown by your records and the bank statement may be different:

1. Some of the checks that you wrote and subtracted from your balance may not have been presented to the bank for payment before the bank statement was made. These checks, therefore, have not been deducted from the bank statement balance. Such checks are known as **outstanding checks**.
2. You may have forgotten to record a transaction in your check stub or register. This is especially true if you use an automatic teller.
3. A service charge which you have not yet recorded may be shown on the bank statement.
4. You may have mailed a deposit to the bank that had not been received and recorded when the statement was made.
5. An error may have been made by you or your bank. Mistakes made by the depositor probably are the most frequent causes of differences.

Let's see how a bank reconciliation is made. On May 4, Janet Perry received the bank statement shown in Illus. 22-2. The statement balance is $277.64. Janet's checkbook balance is $280.39. She examined her canceled checks which were returned with the statement and found that the checks numbered 108, 115, and 116 were outstanding.

In the bank reconciliation shown in Illus. 22-3, Janet proved the accuracy of the bank statement and her record by (1) subtracting the total of the outstanding checks from the bank statement balance, and (2) subtracting the service charge and the automatic payment of her electric bill from her checkbook balance. In some cases, other additions or subtractions might have to be made in the reconciliation. For example, a charge made for stopping payment on a check should be subtracted from the checkbook balance. Also, a deposit made so late in the month that it did not appear on the bank statement should be added to the balance on the bank statement.

Illus. 22-3

This bank reconciliation helps you bring your records and the bank's record of your account into agreement.

YOU CAN EASILY
BALANCE YOUR CHECKBOOK
BY FOLLOWING THIS PROCEDURE

FILL IN BELOW AMOUNTS FROM YOUR CHECKBOOK AND BANK STATEMENT

BALANCE SHOWN ON BANK STATEMENT $ 277.64	BALANCE SHOWN IN YOUR CHECKBOOK $ 280.39
ADD DEPOSITS NOT ON STATEMENT $	
	ADD ANY DEPOSITS NOT ALREADY ENTERED IN CHECKBOOK $
TOTAL $ 277.64	
SUBTRACT CHECKS ISSUED BUT NOT ON STATEMENT	
108 $ 10.00	TOTAL $ 280.39
115 21.00	
116 17.50	
	SUBTRACT SERVICE CHARGES AND OTHER BANK CHARGES NOT IN CHECKBOOK
	$ 1.25
	Elec. 50.00
TOTAL $ 48.50	TOTAL $ 51.25
BALANCE $ 229.14	BALANCE $ 229.14

THESE TOTALS REPRESENT THE CORRECT AMOUNT OF MONEY YOU HAVE IN THE BANK AND SHOULD AGREE. DIFFERENCES, IF ANY, SHOULD BE REPORTED TO THE BANK WITHIN TEN DAYS AFTER THE RECEIPT OF YOUR STATEMENT.

CENTRAL TRUST

The Owl

Illus. 22-4

When you use an automatic teller, be sure to save the receipt and record the transaction on your check stub or register.

If the balances do not agree, either you or your bank has made a mistake. In that case, you should compare your canceled checks with those listed on the bank statement and with those recorded on your check stubs or check register. Be sure that you have recorded all automatic teller transactions. Then carefully go over the calculations on your check stubs or check register. If you do not find an error in your calculations, take the matter up with the bank right away.

After you have reconciled your bank statement, correct any errors that you made on your stubs or register. Subtract any service charge or automatic payments from the balance so your check stub or register will show the correct balance before you write any more checks.

Illus. 22-5

A page from a check register showing the service charge and an automatic payment subtracted on the date of reconciliation.

PLEASE BE SURE TO DEDUCT ANY PER CHECK CHARGES OR MAINTENANCE CHARGES THAT AFFECT YOUR ACCOUNT

CHECK NO.	DATE	CHECKS DRAWN OR DEPOSITS MADE	BALANCE FORWARD → ✓	3/8	89
115	4/30	TO Madsen's Fashions	DEDUCT CHECK — ADD DEPOSIT +	21	—
		FOR Skirt	BALANCE →	297	87
116	4/30	TO Nelson's Garage	DEDUCT CHECK — ADD DEPOSIT +	17	50
		FOR auto repairs	BALANCE →	280	39
Recon	4/30	TO Service Charge-April	DEDUCT CHECK — ADD DEPOSIT +	1	25
		FOR	BALANCE →	279	14
AP	4/30	TO Valley Power Co.	DEDUCT CHECK — ADD DEPOSIT +	50	00
		FOR automatic payment - electric	BALANCE →	229	14
		TO	DEDUCT CHECK — ADD DEPOSIT +		
		FOR	BALANCE →		
		TO	DEDUCT CHECK — ADD DEPOSIT +		
		FOR	BALANCE →		

INCREASING YOUR BUSINESS VOCABULARY

The following terms should become part of your business vocabulary. For each numbered statement, find the term that has the same meaning.

bank reconciliation   outstanding check
bank statement   service charge
canceled check

1. A statement showing how the checkbook balance and the bank statement balance were brought into agreement.
2. A check given to the payee but not yet returned to the bank for payment.
3. A report given by a bank to a depositor showing the condition of his or her account.
4. A charge made by a bank for checking account services.
5. A check that has been paid by a bank.

UNDERSTANDING YOUR READING

1. Why do banks charge for providing you with checking account services?
2. What are the two charges that may make up the service charge on a checking account?
3. What are the principal differences between a regular checking account and a special checking account?
4. What is a package plan account?
5. What seven items of information are included on a bank statement?
6. How does a depositor know that his or her checks have been paid?
7. Why should you save canceled checks?
8. For what five reasons might your bank statement and your checkbook balance be different?
9. How do you reconcile a bank statement? State the steps briefly.
10. How would you record a service charge on your check stub or register?

USING YOUR BUSINESS KNOWLEDGE

1. Sherry Vilas usually writes about 10 checks a month. Her minimum balance is about $150. Which would be less expensive for Miss Vilas: to have a regular checking account and pay the charges shown in Illus. 22-1 or to have a special account with service charges of 10¢ per check and $2.00 for a book of 20 checks?
2. John and Carla Wirtz are talking about whether to save their canceled checks from their joint account. John says, "Throw

them out; I hate a cluttered house." Carla reminds him, "Remember what happened last year when you tried to use your check register to prove you paid the furniture bill? I think we should save the canceled checks." Do you agree with John or Carla? Why?

3. The Second National Bank of Valleydale offers free checking account services to three groups: persons over 60 years of age, disabled veterans, and churches. Why do you think the bank does not charge these groups while it charges all others for checking services?

4. After getting a part-time job, Jerry Watson wants to open a checking account. He expects to deposit his weekly paycheck of $64.50 and to write about five checks a month. What things should Jerry consider in deciding the type of account to open? Which type of account do you think would likely be best for him? Why?

5. Edward Acosta has received his bank statement for the month of May. The bank statement shows a balance of $401.19, but his checkbook shows a balance of only $364.52.
   (a) What is the most likely reason that the bank balance is larger than Mr. Acosta's balance?
   (b) What steps should Mr. Acosta take to bring the balances into agreement?

6. Look at Janet L. Perry's bank statement in Illus. 22-2 and answer these questions:
   (a) What is her account number?
   (b) How many deposits did she make?
   (c) How many checks were paid?
   (d) Is there a service charge? If so, how much is it?
   (e) Does the statement show any outstanding checks? If not, how would Janet find out if there are any?

SOLVING PROBLEMS IN BUSINESS

1. When Jim O'Leary began to reconcile his bank statement, he found that four checks he had written had not been paid by the bank. The amounts of the checks were: $14.50, $9.25, $10.00, and $26.50.
   (a) What is the total amount of unpaid checks?
   (b) In order to reconcile the statement, should Jim subtract this total from the bank statement balance or from his checking account balance?

2. Service charges for Julie Poynter's regular checking account at Second National Bank are based on the bank's rate schedule, which is:

Minimum Balance	Charge
0–$100	$1.50
$101–$300	.75
over $301	no charge

During a recent six-month period, her minimum balances were: April, $142.71; May, $194.20; June, $97.70; July, $302.43; August, $38.74; and September, $154.36.

(a) How much was Julie's service charge for each month?

(b) What was the total cost for the six-month period?

3. The Northeast State Bank uses the following plan to calculate service charges on checking accounts: monthly fixed charge, 75¢; amount charged for each check written, 7¢; amount charged for each check deposited, 7¢. During the month of July, Eleanor Marshall wrote 12 checks and made 4 deposits which included a total of 8 checks. What was Eleanor's service charge for the month?

4. The rate schedule for regular checking accounts for the Nova State Bank is shown in Illus. 22-1. Walter Grant's account at Nova showed the following minimum balances and number of checks written during the first four months of the year:

Month	Minimum Balance	Number of Checks
January	$ 86.40	21
February	196.84	32
March	316.11	9
April	208.71	13

Using the rate schedule, answer the following questions:

(a) What is the service charge for each month?

(b) What is the total service charge for the four months?

5. Linda and Juan Garza decided to switch to the metric system for gasoline sales at their service station. They found that replacing their six pumps with new ones which compute by liter would cost $270 each. But their old pumps could be converted to metrics for $25 per pump.

(a) How much would the Garzas save by having the old pumps converted?

(b) The old pumps are set to compute gasoline sales at $1 per half gallon. The new pumps will compute by liters. At 3.785 liters per gallon, what will the new pumps show for the cost per liter?

6. In October Leo Kishman received a bank statement that showed a balance of $378.65. The service charge was 85¢. Mr. Kishman

found that the following checks were outstanding: No. 31, $7.16; No. 34, $15.10; and No. 35, $9.95. His checkbook balance at the end of October was $347.29. Reconcile the bank balance.

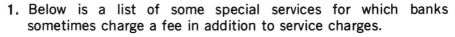

EXPANDING YOUR UNDERSTANDING OF BUSINESS

1. Below is a list of some special services for which banks sometimes charge a fee in addition to service charges.

   (a) overdraft
   (b) insufficient funds
   (c) stop-payment order
   (d) photocopy of a paid check
   (e) extra statement
   (f) dormant account

   (g) postdated check
   (h) omission of account number on a check
   (i) returned deposit item
   (j) counter check used on restricted account

   State briefly the meaning of each item. Find out if a local bank charges for these services and, if so, what amount?

2. Find out whether a bank in your community offers a package plan account. If one does, report the following to your class:
   (a) What services are included?
   (b) What is the name of the account?
   (c) What is the monthly charge?
   (d) How does the charge differ from special and regular account charges?
   (e) Is a charge card plan involved in the package?

3. Some banks figure the service charges and then, to offset part of these charges, give credit for the average balance of the account. Find out whether a local bank uses this service credit feature. Explain how it is used in figuring the customer's service charges.

4. The Sequoia National Bank includes the following statement in its advertising: "If you maintain a minimum balance of $300 or more, or an average balance of $600 or more, there is no service charge for a personal checking account." Why do you think the bank required a higher average balance than minimum balance?

5. Visit a bank in your community that has automatic teller service. Write a brief report on the steps a customer would take to use the automatic teller for the following transactions:
   (a) Obtain $20 in cash.
   (b) Pay a utility bill of $18.92.
   (c) Transfer $100 from a savings to a checking account.

23 CASHING AND DEPOSITING CHECKS

PART OBJECTIVES

After studying this part and completing the end-of-part activities, you will be able to:

1. Explain what an endorsement on a check means.
2. Identify three types of endorsements and tell when each is used.
3. Correctly endorse a check.
4. Discuss your responsibilities in accepting and cashing checks.
5. Explain how a check is cleared.

On her first payday in her part-time job as bagger at the supermarket, Regina Stanford received a check for $52.40. She looked at the check many times, reading her name and the amount. It didn't look like money and it didn't feel like money. But with her name written after "Pay to the order of," it was just as valuable to Regina as if she had received bills and coins from her employer.

You will no doubt receive many checks in your lifetime. You should learn to handle them as carefully as you do cash. As the payee, you can do one of three things with a check: (1) cash it, (2) deposit it in your bank account, or (3) transfer it to another person or business for a payment.

When you are ready to use a check, you should write your name on the back of the check, near the left end. Such a signature is called an **endorsement**. Your endorsement is written evidence that you received payment from the bank or that you transferred your right of receiving payment to someone else.

ENDORSING THE CHECK

In endorsing a check, sign your name in ink exactly as it is written on the face of the check. If Donald F. Scheaffer received a check made payable to D. F. Scheaffer, he should endorse it "D. F. Scheaffer." He should not sign his name "Don Scheaffer" or even "Donald F. Scheaffer."

If your name is not given correctly on a check, first endorse the check exactly as your name is given and then write your name correctly as a second endorsement. If Mr. Scheaffer's check had been made payable to "D. R. Scheaffer," Mr. Scheaffer should endorse it as shown in Illus. 23-1.

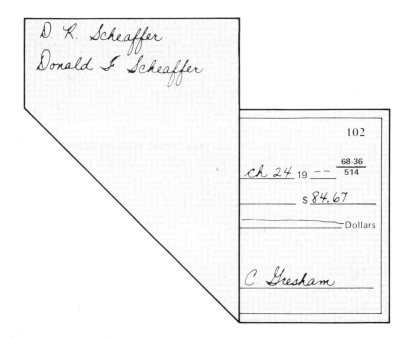

Illus. 23-1

The check is endorsed on the back at the left end.

USING A BLANK ENDORSEMENT

Different endorsements serve different purposes. An endorsement that consists of only the endorser's name is called a **blank endorsement**. The endorsements "Nancy R. Brooks" in Illus. 23-2 and "Donald F. Scheaffer" in Illus. 23-1 are blank endorsements. A blank endorsement makes a check payable to anyone who has the check. A blank endorsement may be used whenever a check is to be transferred, but sometimes another type of endorsement is better.

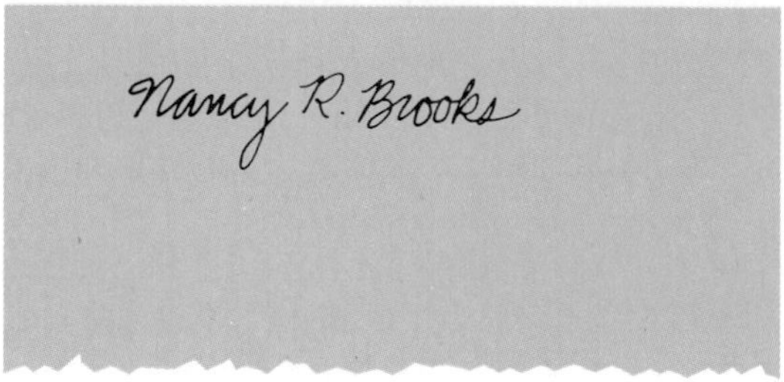

Illus. 23-2
A blank endorsement.

WRITING A SPECIAL ENDORSEMENT

Suppose Nancy R. Brooks receives a check made payable to her. She wants to make it payable to Alan C. Friedman, who operates a service station where she usually buys gas. The check is a payment on the gas bill she owes Mr. Friedman. If she uses a blank endorsement and sends the check to Mr. Friedman, he can cash it when he receives it. But if the check is lost before it reaches him, anyone who finds it may cash it.

To make sure that no one except Mr. Friedman will be able to cash the check, Miss Brooks may use a **special** or **full endorsement**. With this endorsement, she places before her signature the words "Pay to the order of Alan C. Friedman," as shown in Illus. 23-3. Mr. Friedman must sign the check before it can be cashed.

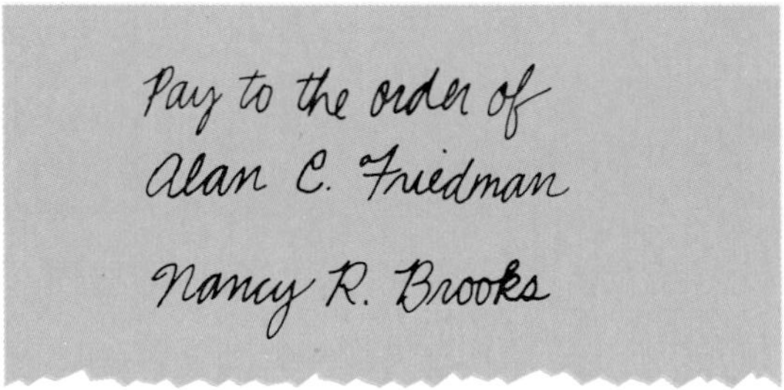

Illus. 23-3

A special endorsement. This is also known as full endorsement.

USING A RESTRICTIVE ENDORSEMENT

A **restrictive endorsement** limits the use of a check to the purpose given in the endorsement. For example, you may have several checks that you want to mail to the bank. If you use a blank endorsement, the checks may be lost and cashed by someone else. But if you place the words "For deposit only" above your signature, you have restricted the use of each check so that it can only be deposited to your account. If a check with such an endorsement is lost, it cannot be cashed by the finder.

Businesses often use rubber stamps for restrictive endorsements that require checks to be deposited only to their accounts. A business thus has no risk of loss if an unauthorized person uses the stamp to endorse a check.

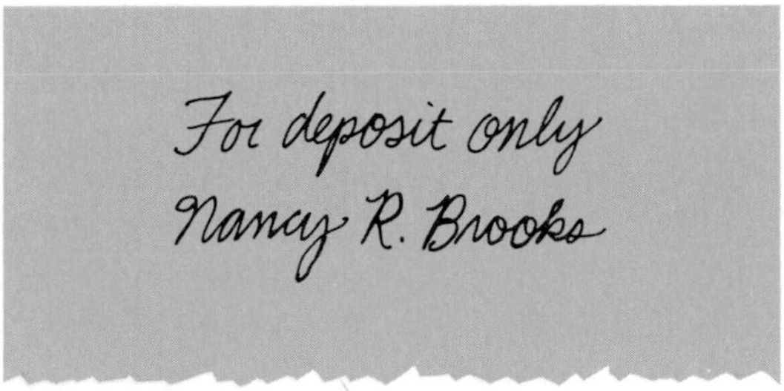

Illus. 23-4
A restrictive endorsement.

For deposit only
Nancy R. Brooks

WHAT AN ENDORSEMENT MEANS

When you endorse a check, your responsibilities are almost as great as if you had written the check yourself. As an endorser, you are actually making this promise: "If this check is not paid, I will pay it." After endorsing a check, the payee usually cashes it or deposits it in a bank. But the payee may transfer the check to another person, who in turn may transfer it to someone else, and so on. Each person who transfers a check should be required to endorse it, for each endorsement is another promise that the check will be paid. In actual use, checks with more than one endorsement are rare.

An endorsement serves as a promise only to those who receive the check after the endorsement is written. It does not apply to persons who held the check before the endorsement. For example, suppose that Jean Whitfield signs a check and gives it to Sam Corbett and that Corbett endorses it and gives it to you. Suppose also that you endorse the check and give it to Harry Paulsen. If the bank later refuses to pay the check for any reason, Paulsen may collect the amount from the drawer (Whitfield) or from either of the two endorsers (Corbett or you). If he collects from you, you have a claim against the drawer

(Whitfield) and against the first endorser (Corbett). But if Paulsen collects from either of them, neither has a claim against you.

ACCEPTING AND CASHING CHECKS CAREFULLY

It is important that you understand your responsibility as a signer and as an endorser of checks. According to law, a check is payable on demand, that is, at the time the holder of the check presents it for payment at the bank on which it is drawn. But a bank may refuse to accept a check if it is presented for payment long after the date on which it was written. So you should present a check for payment within a reasonable time after you receive it.

A check is valuable only when it is drawn on a bank in which the drawer has money on deposit. For this reason you should accept checks only when they are written or endorsed by people whom you know and trust. A check received from a stranger may turn out to be worthless, and it may be impossible for you to find the stranger and collect the money.

Just as you should not cash checks for strangers, you should not expect strangers to cash checks for you. If you must ask a stranger to cash a check, you may have to prove your identity. You may do this by showing your driver's license or some other form of identification. Checks are used so commonly instead of money that you will usually have no trouble cashing them where you are known, but legally no one has to accept your checks.

Illus. 23-5

When you pay for a purchase with a check, you will probably be asked to show identification.

CLEARING CHECKS LOCALLY

A check may be passed from person to person by endorsement. But sooner or later it is returned to the drawer's bank to be paid and charged to his or her checking account. This process is called **clearing a check**. If both the drawer and the payee have accounts in the same bank, clearing is simple. The bank subtracts the amount from the drawer's account and adds it to the payee's account.

When two different banks are involved, clearing is somewhat different, although it is still fairly simple if the two banks are in the same town.

Suppose Ted King's neighborhood rock group feels its new song will really make it big if the group can get more practice time. Ted persuades his father to rent a garage on the outskirts of town (the Kings' neighbor's suggestion) as a rehearsal hall. The rent for one month is $50. Mr. King sends the rental check, written on his account with West Fork National Bank, to Joan Radd Realty. Look at Illus. 23-6 and follow the check on its trip to two banks in the town where the Kings live and back to Mr. King.

Joan Radd Realty endorses the check and deposits it in its account in the Citizens Trust Company. When Citizens Trust receives the check, it adds $50 to the account of Joan Radd Realty, endorses the check, and sends it to the West Fork National Bank for payment. After West Fork National receives the check, it pays Citizens Trust $50 and subtracts that amount from Mr. King's account. The check is then canceled by the West Fork National Bank and returned to Mr. King as his record of payment.

When there are several banks in the same town, the banks usually agree on a certain time of day to clear checks. Each bank makes up one package of its paid checks which were drawn on the other banks — one package for each bank. A messenger may be sent to each bank to exchange packages of checks and pay or collect any difference that might be due. Or, each bank may send a representative to a central place which the banks have selected as an exchange office; here they exchange checks and settle the accounts with each other.

Suppose that when the bank representatives meet, it is found that the Citizens Trust Company has checks totaling $4,000 drawn on the West Fork National Bank and that the West Fork National

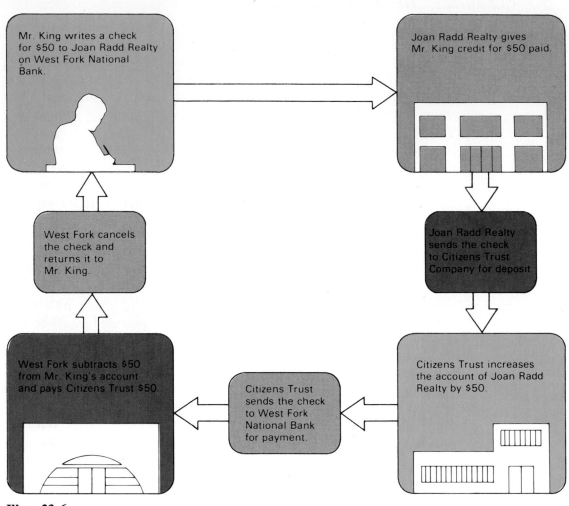

Illus. 23-6

The path traveled by a check.

Bank has checks totaling $4,250 drawn on the Citizens Trust Company. The Citizens Trust Company thus owes the West Fork National Bank $250. It may pay this amount in cash, but usually a method is worked out that makes the handling of cash unnecessary. For example, both banks may maintain accounts with the same bank in a neighboring city. In this case, the bank in the other city may be notified to transfer $250 from the account of the Citizens Trust Company to the account of the West Fork National Bank.

CLEARING CHECKS THROUGH A CLEARINGHOUSE

In large cities where there are many banks, it would not be practical for each bank to send checks for payment to all the banks on which the checks were written. Usually city banks are members of an association which operates a place for members to clear their checks every day. This place is called a **clearinghouse**.

The method of clearing checks through a clearinghouse is similar to the method followed between banks in a small town, except that thousands of checks are handled for many banks. Here, also, cash is not needed to make settlements. Entries may be made in accounts that the banks maintain with the clearinghouse association or with a Federal Reserve bank.

CLEARING CHECKS THROUGH THE FEDERAL RESERVE SYSTEM

One of the services of the Federal Reserve System, which you learned about in Part 19, is clearing checks between banks in different cities. The Federal Reserve System has set up methods so that a check drawn on a bank in another city may be returned quickly to the bank on which it was drawn, and funds are transferred between banks when necessary.

The Federal Reserve System handles millions of checks every day. In a recent year, for example, the Federal Reserve Bank of New York handled almost 6 million checks every business day. Because of the services of the Federal Reserve System, checks can be used to make payments in any part of the country as easily as they can be used locally.

INCREASING YOUR BUSINESS VOCABULARY

The following terms should become part of your business vocabulary. For each numbered statement, find the term that has the same meaning.

blank endorsement   *endorsement*
clearing a check   *restrictive endorsement*
clearinghouse   *special* or *full endorsement*

1. An endorsement including the name of the person to whom the check is transferred.
2. A place where banks exchange checks to clear them.
3. Returning a check to the drawer's bank to be paid and charged to his or her account.

4. An endorsement consisting of a name only.
5. A signature on the back of a check that transfers ownership of the check.
6. An endorsement that limits the use of a check to a specific purpose.

UNDERSTANDING YOUR READING

1. What are three possible ways you may use a check that is made payable to you?
2. What evidence does an endorsement provide?
3. In what place on a check is the endorsement written?
4. If you wish to transfer the ownership of a check from yourself to another person, would you use a blank endorsement, a special endorsement, or a restrictive endorsement? Explain.
5. Which endorsement would you use to limit the use of your payroll check being deposited in your bank account?
6. As an endorser of a check, what promise do you make to other holders of the check?
7. What responsibilities do you have in accepting and cashing checks?
8. Why might you have some difficulty cashing a check in a place where you are not known? What are possible ways that you might use to establish your identity?
9. Does a stranger have the right to refuse to cash your check even if you properly identify yourself? Explain.
10. How are checks cleared (a) in the same bank; (b) between different banks in a small town; (c) between different banks in a large city; and (d) between banks in different cities?

USING YOUR BUSINESS KNOWLEDGE

1. The BestValu Supermarket gives its checkers four rules for accepting checks. These rules must be followed in the order given: (1) Get two IDs (identifications) from the customer. (2) Hand the check and the IDs to the manager for approval. (3) Stamp the check with the store's rubber endorsement stamp. (4) Place the check under the cash tray in the register drawer.
   (a) Why do you think the store requires two IDs?
   (b) Why do you think the check must be approved by the manager?
   (c) What kind of endorsement would most likely be on the rubber stamp?
   (d) What are the advantages of stamping the check immediately after accepting it?
   (e) Why do you think the checks are placed under the cash tray instead of with the cash?

2. For each of the situations below, (a) name the endorsement which should be used, (b) write the endorsement, and (c) give your reason for each.
   (a) Richard R. Holmquist is in the bank and wants to cash his payroll check.
   (b) Doris A. Bishop wants to deposit her payroll check by mail.
   (c) David L. Gilbert uses a check received from Mason B. Zimmer to pay for groceries at Stop & Shop Supermarket.
   (d) Sara A. Cutchens gives two checks to a friend, Leslie Sue Craig, who is to deposit them to Sara's account.
   (e) J. T. Haile deposits a check on which his name has been misspelled as J. T. Hale.
3. Joan Adams has paid you by check for cutting her grass. Since she is your neighbor and you work for her regularly, you accept the check without question. When you try to cash it at a drug store near your school, the owner says he will cash it only if your father endorses it. Why do you think he makes this requirement? Why would he be more willing to accept the check after it is endorsed by your father?
4. A check was endorsed in succession by J. J. Green, M. L. Tinsley, and C. R. Tabb. Mr. Tabb deposited the check in his bank. Later it was found that the check was worthless and that the original drawer could not be located. From whom would Mr. Tabb try to collect? Who would probably lose the amount of the check?
5. Burt Engles maintains a checking account at the Fulton Trust Company. He drew a check on his account for $45.35 and gave it to the Edison Electric Company. The Edison Electric Company deposited the check in the Fifth National Bank, which in turn sent the check to the Fulton Trust Company for payment. Assuming that all parties concerned were located in the same city, draw a chart similar to that in Illus. 23-6 showing the movement of the check from the time it was issued by Mr. Engles until it was returned to him.

SOLVING
PROBLEMS
IN BUSINESS

1. Joan Givens wrote 10 checks during April on her checking account. Her check register shows a balance of $127.60. When her bank statement arrived on May 5, she sorted the canceled checks by number and placed a checkmark by the amount of each in her check register to show that it had cleared the bank. The statement balance was $172.60. On the next page is the list of checks written by Joan and her checkmarks to show the cleared checks:

April	2	26.00 ✓	April 15	7.92 ✓
	2	8.04 ✓	22	15.00 ✓
	7	10.00	27	3.02
	12	5.75 ✓	30	20.98
	15	13.80 ✓	30	11.00

(a) What was the total amount of checks which had not cleared the bank?

(b) Complete the reconciliation of Joan's statement.

2. Paul D. Redford stopped at an automatic teller station to deposit three checks he had received. The amounts were $142.75, $64.50, and $13.80.

(a) What was Paul's total deposit?

(b) Write the correct endorsement that Paul would use.

(c) In order to prepare a correct deposit slip, what other information would Paul need?

3. Agents of Midlands National Bank and Farmers State Bank meet daily at the local clearinghouse to clear checks paid by their banks. Midlands National is located 0.5 kilometer from the clearinghouse; Farmers State is 0.75 kilometer away. The agents set up the following schedule for their meetings:

Monday	10 AM and 4 PM
Tuesday	4 PM
Wednesday	4 PM
Thursday	4 PM
Friday	2 PM and 7 PM

(a) How many kilometers does each agent travel per week to and from the clearinghouse?

(b) What is the total distance that each agent travels expressed in miles?

4. When the four banks in the town of Butler prepared to clear checks one day, they found that they had paid checks on one another as shown in the table below:

Checks Held By	Drawn on			
	First National	Farmers' Trust	Merchants' Mutual	Butler Bank
First National	......	$938.57	$644.63	$1,158.64
Farmers' Trust	$443.74	......	$711.44	$ 208.45
Merchants' Mutual	$304.36	$522.82	......	$ 639.28
Butler Bank	$988.95	$326.31	$783.30	......

Assuming that each bank makes an individual settlement with every other bank, calculate the amount that each bank will either pay to or receive from every other bank.

EXPANDING YOUR UNDERSTANDING OF BUSINESS

1. These establishments can usually be found near any neighborhood: service station, drugstore, grocery store, church, and post office. For each of these, find answers to the following:
   (a) Does the establishment accept personal checks? Why or why not?
   (b) For those which accept personal checks, what kind of identification is required? Is a special endorsement required? Are two-party checks accepted?

2. Some large supermarkets have rules posted about cashing checks. Some of these rules might be: checks in the amount of the purchase only will be accepted; no checks will be accepted unless identification cards are on file in the store; anyone paying by check will be photographed; each person paying by check must record her or his thumbprint on the back of the check. Find out whether these or other rules are posted in a supermarket near you. Ask the manager whether the amount of bad-check loss has gone down since the store began using these methods. Report your findings to the class.

3. Chad Gilbert received a check from a government agency on which these words were printed: "Cash this check promptly. Void after 60 days." Why do you think an agency would print this message on its check? A banker, a lawyer, or a government official are among the people who may be able to help you with your answer.

4. You are a cashier in a supermarket and one of your responsibilities is approving customers' checks. Which of the following checks would you cash and which would you not cash? What additional information might you want in some cases?
   (a) A stranger presents a check made out to him and signed by one of the store's best customers.
   (b) An occasional customer presents a check signed by an unknown person and drawn on an out-of-town bank.
   (c) A 12-year-old boy brings in his father's paycheck to pay the grocery bill. The check was endorsed by his father.
   (d) A customer, unknown to you, presents a check written with a pencil.

(e) A regular customer presents a $35 check dated six months ago.

(f) A stranger offers a $75 check, drawn on a local bank, to pay for a $5.80 grocery bill. The stranger requests change for the difference.

5. Some banks offer special magnetic-printed identification cards to their customers. These cards allow the customer to have checks approved electronically in firms that have credit-check terminals connected to the computers in the customer's bank. Visit a large supermarket, drugstore, or department store and find out if the store has a credit-check terminal. Ask for a demonstration. Write a brief description of the procedure and report to the class.

6. John Claytor resents having to furnish IDs when paying for a purchase by check. He says that he feels the business is questioning his honesty when they demand identification from local residents. "After all," he says, "I've been living in this community for 20 years and I shouldn't have to prove who I am." Do you think John's attitude is justified? Explain.

7. Many stores today have cash registers which are terminals connected to the store's central computer. When the checker keys in the amount of each product purchased, he or she also keys in a code number which will deduct the item from the store's inventory. In this way the store's inventory is kept up to date. In the same way, the checker records information into the register about a check which is given in payment. For example, a customer's social security number or driver's license number may be keyed in. The check is then inserted into the register under a printer head and the information will be printed, along with the store's endorsement, on the back of the check by the register. Visit a large supermarket and ask the manager what that store's procedure is for automatically printing customer information and store endorsement on checks received. Briefly describe the procedure in writing.

24 OTHER WAYS OF MAKING PAYMENTS

PART OBJECTIVES

After studying this part and completing the end-of-part activities, you will be able to:

1. Point out three things to consider in choosing the best method of making a payment or transferring money.
2. Give an example to show under what conditions each of five methods of payment other than cash or checks should be used.
3. Explain why traveler's checks are considered to be the best way for a traveler to make payments.
4. Tell where you could go for advice on the best method of making money payments when you are not sure which one to use.

Until her purse was stolen, Trini Fabian had been enjoying the trip to Pasadena to participate with her school band in the tournament parade. Like most high school students, she does not have a checking account of her own yet. And even if she did have one, she might have trouble cashing a check 2,000 miles from her hometown. She knows a check from her parents will never reach her in time to replace her spending money for the rest of the visit. Even if a check would arrive in time, she would probably have trouble finding someone to cash it. But luckily, there are other ways for Trini's parents to send her money.

As convenient and safe as checks are, there are times, such as in Trini's situation, when personal checks are not the best way to transfer money. But there are other means of making payments. These include: (1) money orders, (2) traveler's checks, (3) certified checks, (4) bank drafts, and (5) cashier's checks. In choosing the best method, you will need to consider where and to whom the money is going, how soon it must get there, and how much you are sending.

USING BANK MONEY ORDERS

A person who does not have a checking account and who wants to send a small payment through the mail may purchase a money order. Money orders are convenient because they can be purchased in so many places. They are sold by banks, post offices, express companies, and telegraph offices. Many retail stores, such as supermarkets and drugstores, also sell money orders.

Tony Guardino has ordered a metric tool set from the Garner Company. The company does not take personal checks on first orders and it would take several weeks for Tony to establish credit with the company. He wants the tool kit right away to work on his car. How should he pay for it?

One way Tony Guardino could pay for his metric tool kit is with a **bank money order**. A bank money order is a form sold by a bank stating that money is to be paid to the person named on the form.

In the bank money order shown in Illus. 24-1, Tony Guardino is sending $22.50 to the Garner Company. He pays the bank $22.50 plus a 50-cent charge for the service. The bank then stamps the amount of the money order on the form and gives it to Tony. He fills in the date, the name of the payee, and his own name and address.

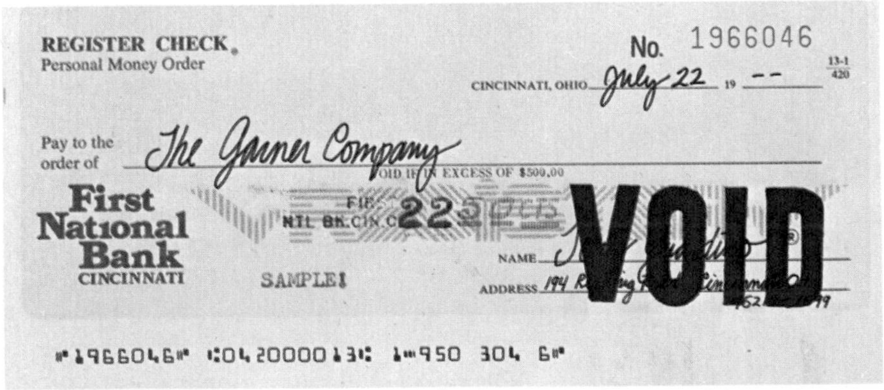

Illus. 24-1

A bank money order.

When this money order has been paid, it will not be returned to Tony as a canceled check would be. It will, however, be returned to the bank that issued it. The money order can then be referred to if Tony wants to prove that payment was made. Since bank practices in issuing money orders vary, you should check with your bank to find out what its practice is before you buy a money order.

PAYING WITH POSTAL MONEY ORDERS

Tony Guardino may also purchase a money order from the post office. A **postal money order** is a form issued by a post office directing that money be paid to a person or business. When you buy a postal money order, the postal clerk registers by machine the amount in figures and words. You then complete the form by filling in the payee's name, your name and address, and the purpose of the money order. Illus. 24-2 shows part of the sample of a $10 postal money order.

You can send a postal money order safely through the mail because it can be cashed only after it is signed by the payee. If a money order is lost or stolen, the receipt copy of the money order may be used in making a claim with the post office. The

Illus. 24-2

When you buy a postal money order, you must fill in the payee's name and your name.

Fill in the name and address of the party you are paying.

Fill in your name and address and the purpose for the money order.

payee of a postal money order may cash it at a post office or a bank or may transfer it to another person by filling in the information called for on the back of the money order.

The largest amount for which a postal money order may be issued is $400. If you want to send a larger amount, you may buy two or more orders. Fees for postal money orders vary with the amounts that are purchased, but the charge is small.

PURCHASING EXPRESS MONEY ORDERS

Money orders issued by express companies are called **express money orders**. Tony Guardino could have used one to pay for his tool kit. Express money orders are sold by offices of the American Express Company, Federal Express Services Corporation, some travel agencies, and many retail stores.

An American Express money order can be written only for amounts up to $200, but you may buy as many orders as you want. Charges are about the same as for postal money orders. If you buy an express money order, you should keep the receipt as long as you may need proof that you bought the money order.

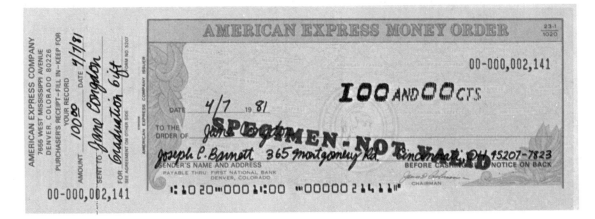

Illus. 24-3

An express money order.

SENDING MONEY WITH TELEGRAPHIC MONEY ORDERS

A **telegraphic money order** is a message directing a telegraph office to pay a sum of money to a certain person. Tony Guardino could have used one. Trini Fabian's parents may have no other choice. Trini, you remember, has had her purse stolen while in Pasadena with her school band. She needs spending money for the rest of her visit. She may either call her father or go to the Pasadena telegraph office and send him a telegram asking for money, say $50. Her father will pay the money plus a handling fee to his Aurora telegraph office. A return telegram will be sent ordering the Pasadena telegraph office to pay Trini $50. The Pasadena company will immediately give Trini the money. If the message is sent promptly, Trini should have the money soon after the call is made or the first telegram is sent. The handling fee will depend upon the amount to be sent.

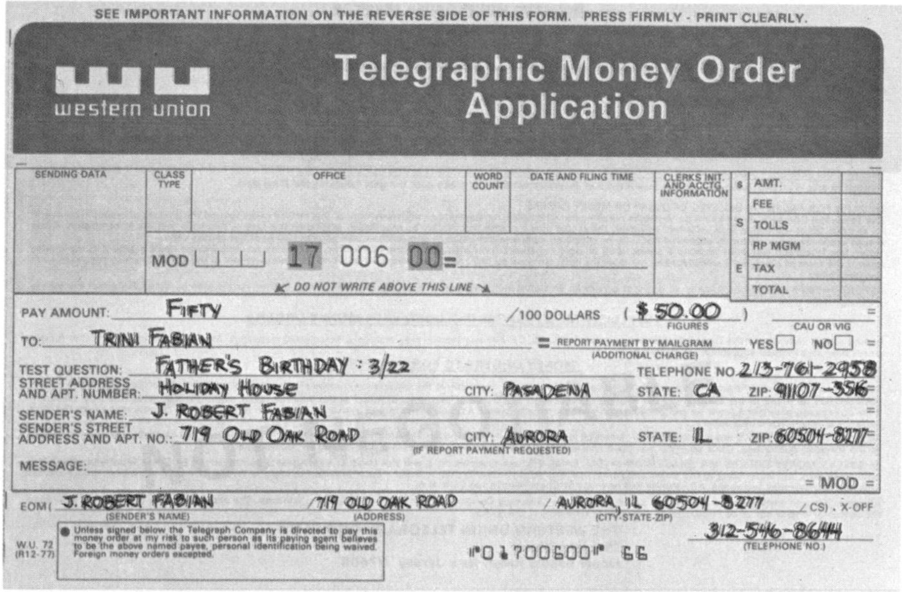
SEE IMPORTANT INFORMATION ON THE REVERSE SIDE OF THIS FORM. PRESS FIRMLY - PRINT CLEARLY.

western union

Telegraphic Money Order Application

SENDING DATA | CLASS TYPE | OFFICE | WORD COUNT | DATE AND FILING TIME | CLERKS INIT. AND ACCTG. INFORMATION | AMT. | FEE | TOLLS | RP MGM | TAX | TOTAL

MOD 17 006 00=

DO NOT WRITE ABOVE THIS LINE

PAY AMOUNT: FIFTY /100 DOLLARS ($ 50.00) FIGURES CAU OR VIG

TO: TRINI FABIAN = REPORT PAYMENT BY MAILGRAM (ADDITIONAL CHARGE) YES ☐ NO ☐ =

TEST QUESTION: FATHER'S BIRTHDAY : 3/22 TELEPHONE NO. 213-761-2958

STREET ADDRESS AND APT. NUMBER: HOLIDAY HOUSE CITY: PASADENA STATE: CA ZIP: 91107-356

SENDER'S NAME: J. ROBERT FABIAN

SENDER'S STREET ADDRESS AND APT. NO.: 719 OLD OAK ROAD CITY: AURORA STATE: IL ZIP: 60504-8277 (IF REPORT PAYMENT REQUESTED)

MESSAGE:

= MOD =

EOM(J. ROBERT FABIAN (SENDER'S NAME) /719 OLD OAK ROAD (ADDRESS) / AURORA, IL 60504-8277 (CITY-STATE-ZIP) / CS) . X-OFF

W.U. 72 (R12-77)

• Unless signed below the Telegraph Company is directed to pay this money order at my risk to such person as its paying agent believes to be the above named payee, personal identification being waived. Foreign money orders excepted.

⑈01700600⑈ 66

312-546-8644 (TELEPHONE NO.)

Illus. 24-4

A telegraphic money order.

To be sure that the right person gets the money, a test question may be sent free. The sender may choose to ask a personal question, such as "What is your father's birthday?" Trini's father would tell the clerk the answer to the question. In order to get the money, Trini would have to give the Pasadena clerk the correct answer. Mr. Fabian could request a report that the money was paid to Trini. For this service, he would pay an additional fee.

A charge is made for any other message sent with the money order. Sending money in this way is somewhat expensive when one considers the cost of the telegrams both ways and the cost of the money order. However, this service is very helpful in an emergency.

USING TRAVELER'S CHECKS

It is risky to carry a large sum of money when you travel, since it can be easily lost or stolen. It is also difficult to pay traveling expenses with personal checks, because you will be dealing mostly with strangers who may not want to take your personal checks. Even money orders may not work out for traveling, as you may not have the identification that is necessary for cashing them.

Special forms designed for the traveler to use in making payment are called **traveler's checks**. You can buy them at banks, offices of express companies, and travel bureaus. They are sold in several denominations, such as $10, $20, $50, and $100. In addition to the value of the checks, there is a charge of 1 percent of the value with a minimum charge of 50¢. This means that $100 worth of traveler's checks will cost $101. However, some banks make no charge for traveler's checks to customers with package plan accounts.

Illus. 24-5
A traveler's check.

The traveler's check has two places for your signature. When you buy the checks, you sign each in the presence of the selling agent. When you cash a check or pay for a purchase with it, you sign again in the presence of the person accepting it. That person

Illus. 24-6

Many travelers prefer to carry traveler's checks because they are a safe and convenient means of payment.

checks to see that the two signatures are alike. At that time you also fill in the date and the name of the payee.

Traveler's checks are commonly accepted throughout the world. Almost any business is willing to accept a traveler's check since there is little chance of its not being signed by the right person.

When you buy traveler's checks, you should immediately record the serial number of each check on a form that is generally given to you by the issuing agency. Then, on the same form record the place and date you cash each check. Keep this record separate from your checks so that you can refer to it if your checks are lost or stolen. If the checks are lost or stolen, report this at once to the nearest bank or office where such checks are sold. The company that issued the checks will replace them.

MAKING PAYMENTS BY CERTIFIED CHECK

Margaret Sandman wants to make a payment to go to someone who does not know her and who doesn't want to accept her personal check. What form of payment can she use? Although there are other means of payment she might use, she may want to have the transaction recorded in her checking account. Miss Sandman may have the bank certify her check as shown in Illus. 24-7. A **certified check** is a personal check on which the bank has written its guarantee that the check will be paid.

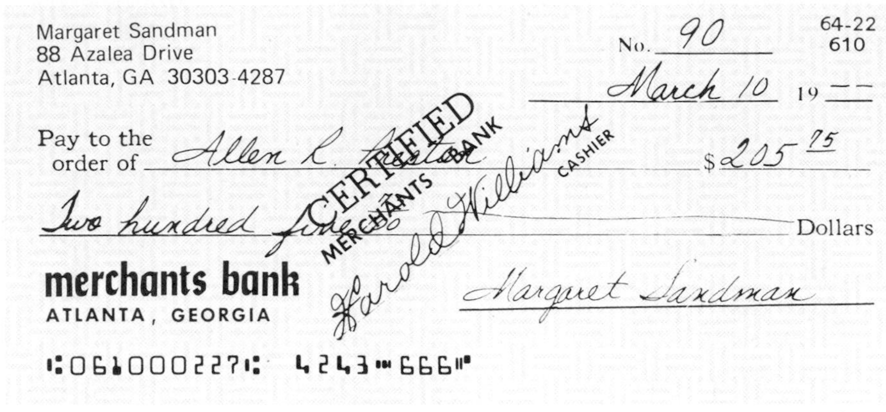

Margaret Sandman
88 Azalea Drive
Atlanta, GA 30303-4287

No. *90*   64-22
                  610

March 10 19 --

Pay to the
order of   *Allen R. _____* $ *205 25*

Two hundred ____ _____ Dollars

merchants bank
ATLANTA, GEORGIA

Margaret Sandman

⑆061000227⑆ 4243⑈666⑈

Illus. 24-7
A certified check.

When the bank writes its guarantee across a check to certify it, the amount of the check is immediately subtracted from the depositor's account. This makes it impossible for the depositor to withdraw the money or to use it for other checks. If the check is not used, it may be returned to the bank and credited to the depositor's account.

PAYING WITH BANK DRAFTS AND CASHIER'S CHECKS

For certain large payments, a bank's own check may be purchased. Banks usually deposit part of their funds in other banks. An employee of a bank may draw checks on these deposits in the same way that you may draw on funds that you have deposited in your bank. A check that a bank official draws on the bank's deposits in another bank is known as a **bank draft**. Banks will sell bank drafts to anyone.

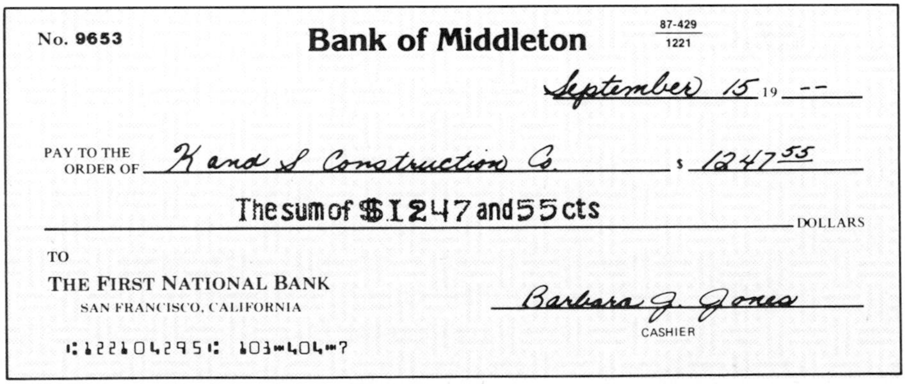

No. 9653   **Bank of Middleton**   87-429
                                                  1221

September 15 19 --

PAY TO THE
ORDER OF   *K and S Construction Co.* $ *1247 55*

The sum of $**1247** and **55** cts _____ DOLLARS

TO
THE FIRST NATIONAL BANK
SAN FRANCISCO, CALIFORNIA

Barbara G. Jones
CASHIER

⑆122104295⑆ 103⑈404⑈7

Illus. 24-8
A bank draft.

Suppose Sam Welton, a builder in Middleton, wanted to make a large payment to the K & S Construction Company in San Francisco. No personal checks will be accepted. Mr. Welton could pay the $1,247.55 with a bank draft. In this case, the draft would be a check which Mr. Welton's Middleton bank wrote on funds it has on deposit in a San Francisco bank. Mr. Welton would pay his bank $1,247.55 plus a small fee for issuing the draft.

A check that a bank draws on its own funds is usually called a **cashier's check**. It has this name because such checks were originally drawn by an employee of the bank known as a cashier. Now such a check is often drawn by another employee. Some banks refer to checks drawn on their own funds as officer's checks, treasurer's checks, or manager's checks, depending on who is authorized to draw them.

Banks commonly use cashier's checks in paying their own expenses. They also sell them to customers just as they sell bank drafts. If the customer has no preference as to whether he or she gets a bank draft or a cashier's check, the bank will recommend one or the other. The choice depends on where the payment is to be sent.

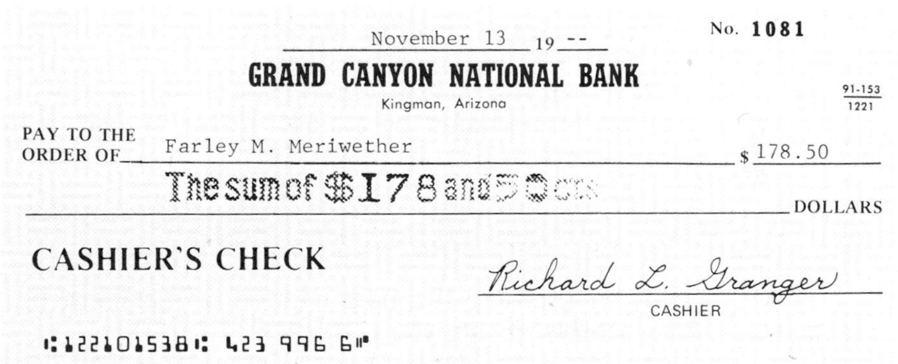

November 13 19 -- No. **1081**

GRAND CANYON NATIONAL BANK
Kingman, Arizona

91-153 / 1221

PAY TO THE ORDER OF___ Farley M. Meriwether ___ $178.50

The sum of $178 and 50 cts ___ DOLLARS

CASHIER'S CHECK

Richard L. Granger
CASHIER

⑈122101538⑈ 423 996 6⑈

Illus. 24-9
A cashier's check.

As with bank drafts, a cashier's check costs the amount of the check plus a service fee. Both bank drafts and cashier's checks are often used to make rather large payments. These banker's checks are more acceptable than the personal checks of an individual whom the payee may not know.

Bank drafts, postal money orders, and express money orders may all be used in sending payments to other countries.

Information about the methods of making foreign payments may be obtained from the bank or from the office where the money order is purchased. Any time you do not know the best means of making a payment, ask your bank for advice.

INCREASING YOUR BUSINESS VOCABULARY

The following terms should become part of your business vocabulary. For each numbered statement, find the term that has the same meaning.

bank draft   express money order
bank money order   postal money order
cashier's check   telegraphic money order
certified check   traveler's check

1. A form purchased from an express company for use in making payments.
2. A check that a bank draws on its deposits in another bank.
3. A form sold by a bank, express company, or other establishment to take care of the financial needs of travelers.
4. A check that a bank employee draws on the bank's own funds.
5. A form often purchased from banks for use in making small payments.
6. A message directing a certain telegraph office to pay an amount of money to a certain person.
7. A personal check that is guaranteed by a bank.
8. A form issued by a post office for use in making small payments.

UNDERSTANDING YOUR READING

1. In choosing the best method of making a payment, what three things should you consider?
2. Give an example to show when you would use (1) money orders, (2) traveler's checks, (3) certified checks, (4) bank drafts, and (5) cashier's checks.
3. What happens to a bank money order after it has been paid?
4. Is it safe to send a postal money order through the mail? Why?
5. What information does the postal clerk fill in on a postal money order? What parts does the purchaser fill in?
6. In what ways is an express money order different from a bank money order and a postal money order?

7. What is the procedure for sending money by telegraphic money order?
8. Why are traveler's checks better for the traveler to carry than personal checks or cash?
9. What are the steps taken by the bank to certify a personal check?
10. What is the major difference between a bank draft and a cashier's check?
11. If you are not sure which type of special money payment to use in a certain situation, where can you find out?

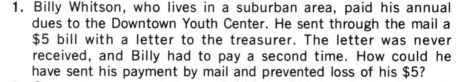

USING YOUR
BUSINESS
KNOWLEDGE

1. Billy Whitson, who lives in a suburban area, paid his annual dues to the Downtown Youth Center. He sent through the mail a $5 bill with a letter to the treasurer. The letter was never received, and Billy had to pay a second time. How could he have sent his payment by mail and prevented loss of his $5?
2. Suppose you want to send $18 to Old Car Parts, Inc., in another city for repair parts needed in fixing up an old car. You have no checking account. Would you make the payment with a certified check, a money order, or a bank draft? Explain.
3. Tell how you would buy and send a postal money order for $7.28 to Burlo Mills, Inc., for a knitted cap.
4. Billie Jo and Tom Reid are moving to a distant city where Billie Jo has been transferred by her employer. The moving company has instructed them to have a cashier's check ready to pay the driver when their furniture is delivered. What reasons can you give for the company wanting a cashier's check?
5. Listed below are some of the money payments that the Garcia family of Albuquerque made during a six-month period. In each case, tell what method of making payment you would recommend.
   (a) Mrs. Garcia paid the telephone bill at the local office.
   (b) Mr. Garcia made the monthly payment on their house at the local bank.
   (c) The Garcias paid their federal income tax.
   (d) Mr. Garcia bought his automobile license.
   (e) The Garcias paid $125 for goods they ordered from a Chicago mail-order house. They wanted the goods shipped at once, but they had never bought goods from that firm before.
   (f) Mr. Garcia had an automobile accident 300 miles from home. Mrs. Garcia sent him $250 by the fastest method.
   (g) Mr. Garcia paid $14.75 for repairs at a local garage.

SOLVING
PROBLEMS
IN BUSINESS

1. Wes Langhorne ordered a tape of the best of country-western music to add to his collection. The tape was advertised on TV as available only through the station address. Customers could send a check or money order for $7.95. Or, if they preferred, the order could be shipped C.O.D. (collect on delivery) at an additional charge for postage and handling. Since Wes did not have a checking account, he decided to send a postal money order for the tape. The cost of the money order was 50¢.
   (a) What was the total cost of the tape?
   (b) If postage and handling charges for delivery to Wes's home were $2.64, how much would the tape cost if it were shipped C.O.D.?
   (c) How much did Wes save by sending payment with his order?

2. Mrs. Kane bought traveler's checks from her bank for her family's vacation. She must pay a fee of 1 percent of the value of the checks. The denominations she chose were: $300 in $50 checks and $200 in $20 checks.
   (a) How many $50 checks did she receive? How many $20 checks?
   (b) How much was the bank's charge for the checks?
   (c) What was the total cost of Mrs. Kane's checks?

3. Andy Wexler's ability to repair bicycles has developed into an after-school business. He finds he can get parts cheaper by ordering them from wholesale houses in several cities. He pays by postal money order. During the last three months, he made the following payments:

   National Cycle Co. $7.42, $18.12, $31.04
   Wheels, Inc. $41.74, $3.19, $67.18, $10

   The post office fee schedule is as follows:

Amount of Money Order	Fee
$ 0.01 to $ 10.00	$ .55
$10.01 to $ 50.00	.80
$50.01 to $400.00	1.10

   (a) What was the cost of each postal money order? List the payments in a column and write the fee beside each.
   (b) What was the total cost of Andy's postal money orders for the three months?
   (c) What was the total cost of the bicycle parts Andy ordered, including the cost of the money orders?

4. On September 11 Allen Hutton of Oakland suddenly remembered that it was the sixteenth birthday of his favorite nephews, twins Ron and Ray, of Cheyenne. He had forgotten to send his usual gift of $1 per year of age to each boy. To get his gift to

them on time, he decided to send a telegraphic money order for the total amount, addressed to both boys, and have it delivered to their home. He included this message: "Happy Birthday, Ron and Ray. Our love and a dollar per year." The fee schedule was as follows:

Base fee for office delivery		Additional for	
Amount	Fee	home delivery	Message
.01–$ 50.00	$6.20	$3.50	18¢ per word
$50.01–$100.00	$7.15		

(a) How much money was sent by money order as a combined gift?

(b) What was the fee for the delivered money order, not including the message?

(c) What was the charge for the message?

(d) What was the total cost of Mr. Hutton's gift to Ron and Ray?

5.

© 1965 United Feature Syndicate, Inc.

Suppose Linus measured Miss Othmar's journey for the day and found that she walked 1.5 miles. He then recommended to the school board that she be paid by this method. "But we've changed to the metric system, Linus," the official told him. "Figure the walk in kilometers and then give us your request again." To help Linus with his new request, answer the following questions:

(a) How many kilometers did Miss Othmar walk?

(b) Suppose Linus suggested that Miss Othmar be paid $10 per kilometer. How much would her salary be for a day's work?

EXPANDING YOUR UNDERSTANDING OF BUSINESS

1. List the name of at least one place in your community where each type of money order can be bought. What is the cost of each kind of money order for $10? For $50?

2. Certified checks are often required in real estate closings. Why might a personal check not be acceptable? A real estate agent, lawyer, or banker might help you with your answer.

3. Some people who live in large cities buy traveler's checks to

use even when they are not traveling. Why would they prefer traveler's checks instead of cash or personal checks?

4. Some banks include in their certifying stamp on certified checks the words, "Do not destroy." To whom is this addressed? Why are the words included? If the words are not included, is it all right to destroy the check?

5. There are several types of traveler's checks. Illus. 24-5 shows the American Express traveler's checks. Find out what other types are sold in your community. Is there a difference in cost among the types?

6. Certified checks sometimes are imprinted with the words, "collectible at par." Find out what the phrase means and whether a bank in your community issues certified checks including it.

The banking industry offers a variety of career opportunities. More than a million people are employed in over 47,000 banks and other financial institutions. Most of these workers are employed in commercial banks. Others work in specialized financial firms, such as savings banks, trust banks, Federal Reserve banks, clearinghouses, and savings and loan associations.

More than two thirds of all bank employees are clerical workers. Bank officers and managers make up about 30 percent of the total. A small percentage are professional workers, such as economists, lawyers, and marketing specialists. The remaining employees include guards, elevator operators, and other service workers.

WORKERS IN THE BANKING INDUSTRY

When you open an account in a bank, you usually do so with the aid of a new accounts clerk. This worker meets new customers, helps them select the types of accounts which suit their needs, and handles the paperwork involved in getting the new accounts in the bank's records.

When you make deposits or withdrawals, you go to a teller's window. During banking hours, tellers spend most of their time working directly with customers, receiving and paying out money. At the end of the day, the tellers must count the money and balance their cash drawers. They may then help to sort and file checks, notes, and other papers. In a large bank, tellers' duties may be specialized. A loan teller, for example, receives only loan payments; a payroll teller handles payroll accounts for firms that are customers of the bank.

Most clerical workers perform their jobs behind the scenes, handling routine paperwork and record keeping. They may operate machines, write computer programs, record transactions in customers' accounts, sort and file checks and other papers, or perform a variety of clerical tasks. Some clerks perform specialized duties. An interest clerk, for example, is responsible for keeping the records of notes on which the bank must collect or pay interest. A transit clerk is responsible for sorting, listing, and preparing for collection the checks and drafts drawn on other banks.

The bank may have many officers and managers. A loan officer is responsible for making loans to businesses and individuals. A trust officer manages the investments and other assets which certain customers place in the bank's care. The operations officer is responsible for seeing that the daily operations of the bank flow smoothly and efficiently. This officer usually directs the work of the tellers, clerks, data processors, and word processing specialists. All officers have the assistance of secretaries, stenographers, and typists.

Bank workers who meet the public must be able to communicate well. They must be tactful and have a neat, clean appearance. Most bank workers must be able to handle details and to work well under stress. Tellers must be able to handle money so well that they can account for every penny which passes through their windows. For most except the few executives, bank workers must be able to work at routine tasks for long periods.

EDUCATION AND TRAINING FOR BANKING JOBS

Most beginning jobs in banking require at least a high school education. The tellers, clerks, stenographers, and data processors often come from a background of high school business courses.

Some have had additional business training in community or technical colleges, especially the computer programmers and word processing specialists. Officers, professional personnel, and executives usually have college degrees.

Most beginning workers receive on-the-job training. Officers usually enter as management trainees. Most banks sponsor banking courses and encourage all employees to take advantage of them. Clerks and tellers, therefore, also have an opportunity for promotion to management positions. Most banks look for people who are willing to continue their education after employment.

LOOKING AT THE FUTURE IN BANKING

The banking industry grew rapidly during the past decade. As banks expand their services, it is expected that job opportunities in banking will continue to increase for several years. One estimate places the number of new banking employees needed for each of the next several years at 85,000.

Jobs are changing as technology changes banking procedures. Most banks now use computers and word processors for much of the record keeping and communications. More computer operators, programmers, and word processing specialists will probably be needed; fewer check sorters and bookkeeping machine operators will be needed. A person with the right combination of interest and training will find good prospects for a career in banking.

UNIT 7
Making Wise Credit Decisions

UNIT OBJECTIVES

After studying the parts in this unit, you will be able to:

1. Tell why credit is important to both the consumer and the business community.

2. Explain when loan credit should be used.

3. Identify several kinds of sales credit.

4. Discuss the proper use of installment sales credit.

5. Explain how to establish and maintain a good credit record.

25 UNDERSTANDING CREDIT

PART OBJECTIVES

After studying this part and completing the end-of-part activities, you will be able to:

1. Give examples of how credit is used by consumers, businesses, and governments.
2. State why creditors need information about debtors.
3. Give examples of questions that creditors might ask persons who apply for credit.
4. Discuss the three C's of credit.
5. Explain four advantages of buying on credit.
6. Explain three problems that unwise use of credit can cause.

If you buy something today and agree to pay for it at another time, you are using **credit**. When you receive credit, it is because someone believes your promise that you will pay at a future date. The use of credit is common in the business world — consumers, businesses, and governments rely on credit as a way of doing business.

For many consumers, credit is a part of everyday life. Look at the following events which happened in one week in the life of the Kinney family and see how they used credit:

Monday: Carol wanted to buy a record that was on sale. She borrowed $2 from her friend, Dorothy, and agreed to pay her back on Thursday.

Tuesday: Harold needed gas for his car and used his credit card to pay for his $10 purchase.

Wednesday: Mr. and Mrs. Kinney went shopping for an electric organ. They made a $50 payment and agreed to pay the rest of the price in monthly payments.

Thursday: John called from college with good news. He had been able to get a student loan for his senior year.

Friday: The family celebrated Eleanor's birthday by eating at a restaurant. Mr. Kinney charged the bill with one of his credit cards.

Saturday: Mrs. Kinney read in the paper that the city government was going to pay for $350,000 worth of buses with a ten-year loan.

As you can see, credit is used for a variety of purposes.

TRUST: THE BASIS FOR CREDIT

Anyone who buys on credit or receives a loan is known as a **debtor**. The one who sells on credit or makes a loan is called the **creditor**.

A credit system depends on trust between the debtor and creditor. The creditor trusts that the debtor will honor the promise to pay later for the goods and services that have been received and used. That is what happened when Carol borrowed $2 from Dorothy. Dorothy believed Carol's promise to pay back the $2.

When you borrow a large amount of money or buy on credit from a business, you usually will be asked to sign a written agreement. The agreement states that you will pay a certain amount in a certain period of time. For example, when Mr. and Mrs. Kinney agreed to buy the electric organ, they signed a paper which said that they would make a payment on the first day of each of the next 24 months. John had to agree to pay back his tuition loan in full within two years of his graduation. When Harold used his credit card to buy gas and signed the receipt form, he agreed to pay for his purchase when the bill came at the end of the month. Whether or not a written agreement is signed, a credit agreement means that the debtor promises to pay and the creditor trusts that the debtor will pay the amount that is owed.

WHO USES CREDIT?

As a typical American consumer, you will use credit for many purposes. You will frequently use credit to buy fairly expensive products that will last for quite a while, such as a car, furniture, or major appliances. You will also use credit for convenience in making smaller purchases, such as clothing and gasoline. You might also use credit to pay for medical care, vacations, taxes, or even to pay off another debt.

Illus. 25-1

Many consumers find using credit more convenient than paying cash for some everyday purchases.

Businesses also rely on credit. Business firms may borrow over a number of years to buy land and equipment and to construct buildings. They also use short-term credit, usually from 30 to 90 days, to meet temporary needs for cash. For example, merchants buy goods on credit, and manufacturers buy raw materials and supplies on credit. Businesses are willing to borrow on a short-term basis to get cash while they wait for goods to be sold and for customers to pay.

Local, state, and federal government units use credit often in providing for the public welfare. Government units may buy on credit such items as cars, aircraft, and police uniforms. They may also borrow to build hospitals, highways, parks, and airports.

They also borrow cash from banks to pay current expenses, such as payrolls, while they wait to collect taxes.

Although credit is very important to business and to government, most of the discussion in this unit will focus on consumer credit.

INFORMATION NEEDED TO GRANT CREDIT

Most businesses let their customers buy on credit because people tend to buy more goods and services when credit is available. But, if the persons who are granted credit do not repay the amounts when they are due, it costs the business money. Businesses must be careful in giving credit because they cannot afford to have credit losses.

You should not be hesitant to ask for credit. Credit is a two-way street; it is good for you and it is good for the business. But when you do request credit, be prepared to answer a number of questions. There is some information that is needed to help a business decide whether or not to give credit. You may be asked questions such as these: How much do you earn? How long have you worked? What property do you own? Do you have any other debts? Recent laws, such as the Consumer Credit Protection Act, regulate the kinds of information that can be asked when credit is being applied for. The questions listed above are all questions that can be legally asked.

Illus. 25-2

The person from whom you seek credit will need certain information about you before deciding.

You should be willing to give the required information readily and honestly. You very likely will be asked for **credit references**. Credit references are firms or individuals from whom you have received credit in the past. Your credit references will be contacted to check on information you have given and to see if you generally pay your debts on time.

THE THREE C's OF CREDIT

In deciding whether or not to allow you credit, there are three C's to be considered: character, capacity, and capital.

Character has to do with your honesty and willingness to pay. If you have a good reputation for paying bills on time, the seller will be likely to grant credit. How you will pay your bills in the future usually can be judged by how you have paid them in the past.

Capacity means your ability to earn. The seller must consider whether your income is large enough to let you continue to pay your bills promptly. If your income is too small or unsteady, it may not be wise to give you additional credit even though you may have had a good credit record in the past. On the other hand, your income may be very high, but if you have many debts already you may not be able to handle another one.

Capital has to do with what you own. All the money and property you own are your capital. You may have nothing except your present income. Or you might have a car that is paid for and a large amount paid on a house. You might have a checking account and some savings. The value of your capital helps give the lender some assurance that you will continue to be able to pay your bills.

WHY USE CREDIT?

Most businesses today would find it difficult to compete if they did not extend credit to their customers. Sellers believe that they can increase their sales and profits by using credit to attract customers. But credit is of benefit to the consumer, too. Here are some personal benefits that credit can give to you:

1. **Convenience**. Credit can make it convenient for you to buy. You can make purchases without carrying much cash. There may be times when you do not have enough

cash and need something very much. If your car needs emergency repairs, you may have to wait until payday unless you can have the work done on credit.

2. **Credit rating.** If you buy on credit and pay your bills when they are due, you gain a reputation for being dependable. You thus establish a good **credit rating**. This credit rating is valuable when you must borrow money to meet emergencies or to make a major purchase. It is also valuable in obtaining credit if you move to another community.

3. **Savings.** Credit allows you to buy an item when it goes on sale at a large saving, even if you do not have the cash at the time. Some stores, especially department and furniture stores, send notices of special sales to their credit customers several days before sales are advertised to the public. Credit customers thus have first choice of the merchandise and may obtain good value.

4. **Immediate possession.** Credit allows you to have immediate possession of an item that you want. A family can buy a dishwasher on credit and begin using it instead of having to wait until they save enough money to pay cash.

IS CREDIT ALWAYS GOOD FOR YOU?

Buying on credit is convenient and usually is beneficial. But there are some disadvantages if you are not careful in your use of credit. Some problems that you can encounter with the unwise use of credit include the following:

1. **Overbuying.** This is one of the most common hazards in using credit. There are several ways in which you may overbuy. One way is to purchase something that is more expensive than you can afford. It is easy to say, "All right, charge it," for a stereo that costs $495 when you would purchase one for much less than that if you had to pay cash. You probably have had the experience of looking in store windows or reading advertisements and seeing many things you would like to have. As a credit customer, you may also be tempted to buy items that you don't really need.

2. **Untimely shopping**. You may become a lazy shopper. You may stop checking advertisements and making compari-

sons and buy at the wrong time or the wrong place. Smart shoppers·know that at certain times of the year, prices of some goods go down. There may be special sales, such as the January and July shoe sales or end-of-season sales. Items are often priced higher when they are first put on the market than they are later after they become more common. Credit can tempt you not to wait for a better price on an item you want.

3. **Higher prices.** Stores that sell only for cash can sometimes sell at lower prices than stores which offer credit. Granting credit is expensive. It requires .a lot of bookkeeping to keep a record of each charge sale and each payment on account. And if a customer does not pay promptly, there ·is the extra expense of collecting what is owed. These increased costs are passed on to the customers of the store in the form of higher prices.

INCREASING YOUR BUSINESS VOCABULARY

The following terms should become part of your business vocabulary. For each numbered statement, find the term that has the same meaning.

capacity   creditor
capital   credit rating
character   credit references
credit   debtor

1. The factor in credit that has to do with a customer's honesty and willingness to pay.
2. One who buys or borrows and promises to pay later.
3. The factor in credit that has to do with a customer's ability to earn.
4. A person's reputation for paying debts on time.
5. Buying something today and agreeing to pay for it at another time.
6. Firms or individuals who have given credit to someone in the past and can give information on an individual's credit record.
7. The factor in credit that has to do with the property and money that a customer owns.
8. One who sells or lends on another's promise to pay in the future.

UNDERSTANDING YOUR READING

1. We say that our credit system is based on trust. Who does the trusting, the debtor or the creditor? What does this person trust?
2. If you make a credit agreement, what are you promising to do?
3. What are some typical uses of credit by consumers?
4. What are some goods and services which a business might buy on credit?
5. Give examples of things which local, state, and federal governments might buy on credit.
6. Why do creditors need information about debtors?
7. What kinds of questions might you be asked if you apply for credit?
8. What are the three C's of credit? Why is each one important?
9. Why would a business want to offer credit rather than selling for cash only?
10. What are four advantages for the person who uses credit?
11. Name three problems that unwise use of credit can cause.

USING YOUR BUSINESS KNOWLEDGE

1. If credit is based on trust, why does the borrower usually have to sign a written agreement to pay?
2. Some people think it is a good idea to buy a few things on credit, even if you would be able to pay cash for them. Do you agree? Why or why not?
3. Karl Wolfe buys all he possibly can on credit. If he doesn't have enough money to cover his payments when they are due, he borrows money to make them. His sister, Debbie, likes to buy things only after she has saved enough money to pay cash for them.
   (a) Whose plan do you think is better? Why?
   (b) What suggestions about the use of credit might you make to Karl and Debbie?
4. Rosie Cooper owns and operates a record shop. She is considering expanding her shop and selling radios, tape recorders, and stereos. At the present, Ms. Cooper sells for cash only. How might granting credit help or hurt this business?
5. Here are some statements that people have made about credit. Read each statement and tell whether you agree or disagree and why.
   (a) "I should buy as many things as I can on credit because credit increases sales and helps business."
   (b) "If things were sold for cash only, in the long run prices would be lower and everyone would be better off."

(c) "Buy on credit at least occasionally, make your payments on time, and keep a good credit rating which you might need in an emergency."

(d) "Credit only causes problems. It should be used only in case of emergency."

(e) "Credit should be used only in making expensive purchases, such as houses and cars, and never for everyday purchases, such as food and clothing."

SOLVING
PROBLEMS
IN BUSINESS

1. Clair Shively operates a small vegetable farm after his daily shift in a factory. He ordered 400 kilograms of fertilizer at 42¢ per kilogram. Clair agreed to pay the dealer for the fertilizer in four equal monthly payments.
    (a) How much was Clair's bill?
    (b) What was the amount of each payment?

2. Last year, O'Leary's Cycle Shop sold 2,180 ten-speed bicycles. The average sale price was $106, including tax. Seven out of every ten customers bought their bikes using O'Leary's credit plan.
    (a) What was the amount of the total sales of ten-speed bicycles?
    (b) What was the amount of total credit sales of ten-speeds?

3. The Capitol Area Transit System needs six new buses to expand its service to the suburbs. Each new bus will cost $300,000, which the company will have to borrow. It is estimated that each bus will earn about $3,500 per month. It will cost approximately $1,000 per month for fuel and repairs on each bus. How many months will it take to pay for the six buses?

4. Bob Maguire has a small leather shop. He would like to improve its appearance and add some special features. After checking several catalogs, here is what he would like to buy and the price of each:

New counter and work bench	$1,950
New set of tools	875
Tool rack	45
New display case	750

    (a) What will it cost Bob if he buys all of these items?
    (b) Bob has only $620 to invest in these items. If he borrows to pay the balance and agrees to pay back $100 per month, how many months will it take him to repay the loan?

5. Amy Markson would like to be an airline pilot someday. Right now, she wants to learn to fly and get a private license. Her

parents said that they would pay half the cost of the lessons if she would pay the other half. Amy checked with the Superior Air Service and was told that the cost would include:

44 hours of ground instruction	$ 8 per hour
25 hours of in-flight instruction	29 per hour
15 hours of solo flight time	17 per hour
Flight manuals and third-class student's license	60

(a) How much will it cost Amy to learn to fly and to get her license?

(b) If Amy borrows her share of the cost, how much will she borrow?

(c) If Amy pays back her loan in 50 equal weekly payments, how much will each weekly payment be? If she repaid $58 each month, how many months would it take to pay back her loan?

EXPANDING YOUR UNDERSTANDING OF BUSINESS

1. Some people speak of the four C's of credit. They include the three mentioned in this part and a fourth, collateral. Find the meaning of collateral as it is used in connection with credit and explain how it is used.

2. A family with a relatively low income and little property might have a better credit rating than a family with a large income and considerable property. Likewise, a small business might have a better credit rating than a much larger business owning millions of dollars worth of property. Explain the circumstances under which each of these conditions might exist.

3. Suppose that you and your parents decide to open a snack shop near your school to sell light lunches and snacks. Most of the customers will be junior and senior high school students. Since many students will forget to bring money or will want to treat friends when they haven't enough money, they will sometimes ask you to charge their purchases. Make up a set of rules for extending credit to your teenage customers.

4. Suppose everybody decided to stop granting credit to customers. What do you think would be the effects on each of the following:

(a) A recently married couple who have to buy furniture for their apartment.

(b) A small retail store which is trying to build up its sales.

(c) A large business which wants to expand its line of machines.

(d) A local school district similar to the one your school is in.

BORROWING MONEY

PART OBJECTIVES

After studying this part and completing the end-of-part activities, you will be able to:
1. Describe situations in which consumers need to borrow money.
2. List four types of businesses which lend money to consumers.
3. Compute simple interest.
4. Find the maturity date of a loan.
5. Tell what kinds of information you need when trying to compare loans.

At times when you want to make a purchase, you will decide to borrow money rather than buy on credit. Here are some examples of when such a decision might be made:

Terri Barrick has looked at a used car which sells for $2,000, but the seller wants cash.

Maurice Eberling is pleased that his daughter is going to college, but tuition and dormitory charges will be $4,000 per year.

Mary Bartow has to furnish her apartment, and the furniture and carpeting she wants will cost $2,350.

If you were Terri, Maurice, or Mary, would you buy on credit or borrow money for your purchases? Several factors might affect your decision. Maybe the seller will accept only cash. Or, perhaps the seller will not grant you credit because he or she does not know you and is unsure of your ability to repay. It may also be true that the cost of borrowing will be less than the finance charge for credit.

WHERE TO GO
FOR A LOAN

There are a number of businesses you can go to for a loan. Banks, credit unions, savings and loan associations, and consumer finance companies are the primary businesses that make consumer loans. Organizations which lend money earn a profit by collecting interest and making other charges on loans they grant. Where you should go for a loan depends upon a number of factors. It helps to know something about each of these types of lenders.

Banks, as you have learned, offer a variety of services to their customers. One of the important services provided by banks is making consumer and business loans. In general, banks are a good source of loans for the purchase of cars or other long-lasting items. Banks have lending requirements that are usually quite strict. They lend money only to persons who have very good credit ratings. You should also remember that banks are one of the least expensive sources of loans.

Credit unions are organized by groups of people who have something in common, such as the employees of a firm or the members of a labor union. Credit unions serve their members by accepting savings deposits and making small loans. They are good sources of loans because they know their customers well, and they are organized for the purpose of helping members with financial needs. Interest and other loan charges by credit unions are normally the lowest of any of the businesses which make consumer loans.

Illus. 26-1

This bank officer is helping a customer with his application for a car loan.

The funds of a **savings and loan association** or **building and loan association** are loaned to those who want to buy or build houses, apartments, or business buildings. A savings and loan association accepts savings deposits from its customers. It uses this money to make investments such as the loans described above. Loans are usually made for long-term periods of five years or more. The interest rates charged by savings and loan associations are competitive with banks.

You may also borrow from **consumer finance companies**. These companies make a business of lending small amounts of money, usually not more than $5,000. Many lending agencies will not make loans to people with weak credit ratings, but consumer finance companies take the risk of making loans to such people. For taking this risk, though, they usually charge higher interest rates than do banks, credit unions, or savings and loan associations.

KINDS OF LOANS AVAILABLE

There are two basic kinds of loans that you can get. One type of loan is called an **installment loan**. With this kind of loan, you have to make monthly payments in specific amounts over a period of time. The payments are called installments. The total amount you repay includes the amount you borrowed, called the **principal**, plus the interest on your loan.

Another kind of loan you might get is a **single-payment loan**. In this case, you do not pay anything until the end of the loan period, possibly 60 or 90 days. At that time, you repay the full amount you borrowed plus the interest.

OFFERING SECURITY

A lender must have some assurance that each loan will be repaid. If you have an excellent credit rating, you may be asked to sign a **promissory note**. This is a written promise to repay the amount borrowed, usually with some interest, on a certain date. Special names are given to the different parts of a promissory note. Illus. 26-2 will help you learn what these parts are called and what each means.

When you receive a loan by simply signing a promissory note, this is called a **signature loan**. In other cases, you may be asked

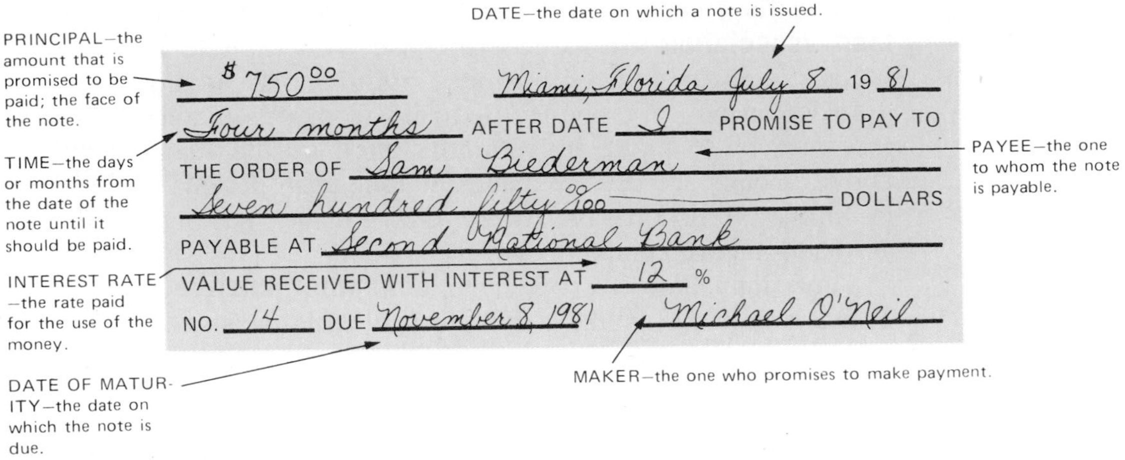

DATE—the date on which a note is issued.

PRINCIPAL—the amount that is promised to be paid; the face of the note.

TIME—the days or months from the date of the note until it should be paid.

INTEREST RATE—the rate paid for the use of the money.

DATE OF MATURITY—the date on which the note is due.

$750.00   Miami, Florida   July 8 19 81

Four months   AFTER DATE   I   PROMISE TO PAY TO

THE ORDER OF   Sam Biederman

Seven hundred fifty ⁰⁰/₁₀₀   DOLLARS

PAYABLE AT   Second National Bank

VALUE RECEIVED WITH INTEREST AT   12 %

NO. 14   DUE November 8, 1981   Michael O'Neil

PAYEE—the one to whom the note is payable.

MAKER—the one who promises to make payment.

Illus. 26-2

Study the parts of this promissory note.

to offer some kind of property, such as a car, a house, or jewelry, as **security**. This means that you give the lender the right to sell this property to get back the amount of the loan in case you do not repay it.

What if you do not have a credit rating established or any property to offer as security? In this case, you might get a relative or friend who has property or a good credit rating to cosign your note. The **cosigner** of a note is responsible for payment of the note if you do not pay as promised.

CALCULATING INTEREST

Interest, of course, is what you pay for the use of someone else's money. In calculating interest, there are three basic things to remember: (1) the rate of interest must be expressed in the form of a fraction; (2) interest is charged for each dollar, or part of a dollar, borrowed; and (3) the interest rate is based upon one year of time.

1. Interest is expressed as a part of a dollar. This part of a dollar, or percent, is called the rate of interest. For example, an interest rate of 6 percent means that 6 cents must be paid for every dollar borrowed. Before using a percent rate in a problem, you must change it to either a common or a decimal fraction. For example, a rate of

interest of 6 percent would be changed to a common fraction of 6/100 or a decimal of .06.

2. When a rate of interest is expressed as 6 percent per year, you must pay 6 cents for each dollar you borrow for a year. At this rate, if you borrow $1, you pay 6 cents. If you borrow $2, you pay 12 cents. If you borrow $10, you pay 60 cents, and so on. The amount of the interest charge is found by multiplying the principal by the rate of interest. Suppose that you borrow $100 for a year at 6 percent per year. The amount of interest is figured in this way:

$$\$100 \times 6/100 = \$6.00$$

3. If you borrow $100 at 6 percent for 1 year, you must pay back the $100 plus $6 interest, as you have just seen. If you borrow the same amount of money at the same rate of interest for 2 years, you pay twice as much interest, or $12. If the money is borrowed for 3 years, you pay $18, and so on. The amount of interest borrowed at 6 percent for 2 years would be figured in this way:

$$\$100 \times 6/100 \times 2 = \$12.00$$

How is interest found if you borrow money for less than 1 year? The amount of interest is calculated on the fractional part of the year. The fraction may be expressed either in months or in days. A month is considered to be one twelfth of a year, regardless of the number of days in the particular month. Suppose that you borrow $100 at 6 percent for 1 month. Here is how the interest is figured:

$$\$100 \times 6/100 \times 1/12 = \$.50$$

When a loan is made for a certain number of days, such as 30, 60, or 90 days, the interest is determined by days. To make the calculation easy, it is customary to use 360 days as being a year. Suppose that you borrow $100 at 6 percent for 60 days. Here is how the interest is figured:

$$\$100 \times 6/100 \times 60/360 = \$1.00$$

INTEREST CHARGED IN ADVANCE

Sometimes interest is subtracted from the amount borrowed at the time the loan is made. Interest paid in advance in this manner is called **discount**. When a note is discounted, you do not receive the full amount of your loan; you receive the amount less the interest that must be paid. The amount you actually receive is called the **proceeds**.

Suppose that on July 9 Ronald Stevens borrows $1,000 to be repaid in 60 days. Suppose also that the bank deducts interest at the rate of 6 percent. The discount will be $10 ($1,000 × 6/100 × 60/360 = $10). So the proceeds — the amount that Ronald will receive on July 9 — will be $990.

When interest is charged in advance, the agreement does not call for the payment of additional interest when the loan is due. But if you do not pay in full on the date of maturity, interest is charged from that date.

FINDING MATURITY DATES

How is the date of maturity found? When the time of the loan is stated in months, the date of maturity is the same day of the month as the date on which the loan was made. If a loan is made on January 15 and is to run 1 month, it will be due February 15. If it is to run 2 months, it will be due March 15, and so on.

When the time of the loan is given in days, the exact number of days must be counted to find the date of maturity. This can be done (1) by finding the number of days remaining in the month when the loan was made and then (2) by adding days in the following months until the total equals the required number of days. Suppose that you wanted to find the date of maturity of a 90-day loan made on March 3. Here is how it would be done:

> March 28 (31 − 3 = 28)
> April   30
> May   31
> June   1 (due date)
> _____
> 90 days

CALCULATING INSTALLMENT INTEREST

Simple interest, as you have just learned, is calculated on the basis of one year of time. Consumer lending agencies may charge a monthly interest rate on unpaid balances. You can see that interest of 1 percent a month is the same as 12 percent for a year. If you borrowed $100 at 2 percent for one year at simple interest, you would pay back $102 ($100 principal + $2 interest) at the end of one year. But if you borrowed $100 at a monthly rate of 2 percent, at the end of one month you would also pay back $102. Your interest charge, however, would be at the rate of 24 percent a year (2% × 12 months) since you had the use of the money for only one month.

On installment loans, interest may be charged only on the amount that is unpaid at the end of each month. Suppose that Armando Rivera borrowed $120 and agreed to repay the loan at $20 a month plus 1½ percent interest each month on the unpaid balance. Illus. 26-3 shows the schedule of payments that was set up. The interest rate on the loan was 18 percent a year (1½% per month × 12 months).

MONTH	UNPAID BALANCE	INTEREST PAID	LOAN REPAYMENT	TOTAL PAYMENT
1	$120	$1.80	$ 20	$ 21.80
2	100	1.50	20	21.50
3	80	1.20	20	21.20
4	60	.90	20	20.90
5	40	.60	20	20.60
6	20	.30	20	20.30
Totals	—	$6.30	$120	$126.30

Illus. 26-3

This schedule of payments was set up for Armando Rivera's loan.

When you borrow money from a bank, the amount of the interest is usually added to the amount you borrow, and you sign a note for the total amount. The note may then be repaid in equal monthly installments. Suppose that Sylvia Messinger borrowed $100, signed a note for $108, and agreed to repay the loan in 12 monthly installments of $9. What annual rate of interest did she pay for the use of the $100 that she actually received?

If Sylvia had borrowed $100 for one year and paid $8 interest, the interest rate would have been 8 percent ($8 ÷ $100 = .08, or 8%). But Sylvia repaid the loan in monthly installments, so she had the use of $100 for only one month and a smaller amount each succeeding month. For the entire year she had the use of only about half of the original amount. As a result, the actual interest rate was about twice the rate calculated on the full amount, or about 16 percent.

WHAT LOANS COST

Before you borrow money, you should know how much the loan is going to cost you. In addition to interest, there may be other loan charges. For example, it takes time and money to investigate your credit history, process your loan, and keep records of your payments. As a borrower, you are charged for these services. In addition, the lender may require that you pay for insurance that will repay the loan should you die or become disabled. The total cost of your loan, including interest and other charges, is called the **finance charge**.

By federal law, lenders are required to tell you in writing what the finance charges on your loan will be. To illustrate, if you wanted to borrow $4,000 for three years, you would be given the following information:

Annual Percentage Rate (*APR*)	Length of Loan	Monthly Payments	Total Finance Charge	Total Amount to be Repaid
11%	3 years	$131	$716	$4,716

When you know the total finance charge, you can better compare the costs of different loans.

MAKING THE FINAL DECISION

If you have to borrow money, you should shop for your loan just as carefully as you would for a new stereo, a car, or any major purchase. Borrowing money is expensive, so you want to make sure you get full value for your dollar.

Some of the things you should check when shopping for a loan are the annual percentage rate (APR), the length of the loan period, the amount of the monthly payments, and the total finance charges. As an example, suppose you want to borrow $4,000 to buy a car. After checking three lenders, you find the following information:

	APR	Loan Length	Monthly Payment	Total Finance Charge	Total Cost
Lender A	11%	3 yrs.	$131	$ 716	$4,716
Lender B	11%	4 yrs.	$103	$ 962	$4,962
Lender C	12%	4 yrs.	$105	$1,056	$5,056

Which of the loans would be best for you? The answer depends on whether you want the lowest monthly payments or the lowest total finance charges. Lender C would not be considered because it has the highest APR and the highest total finance charges. Lender B offers the lowest monthly payments, but Lender A has the lowest total finance charges. If you can afford the monthly payments, you will borrow from Lender A. If the monthly payments with Lender A are too high for your budget, you will borrow from Lender B.

INCREASING YOUR BUSINESS VOCABULARY

The following terms should become part of your business vocabulary. For each numbered statement, find the term that has the same meaning.

consumer finance company
cosigner
credit union
discount
finance charge
installment loan
principal

proceeds
promissory note
savings and loan association or
    building and loan association
security
signature loan
single-payment loan

1. A cooperative association which accepts savings deposits and makes small loans to its members.
2. The amount you borrow when getting a loan.
3. A written promise to repay borrowed money at a definite time.
4. A loan repaid with interest in a series of payments.
5. A loan repaid with interest by one payment at the end of a definite time.
6. A person who guarantees to pay a debt if the person who obtained the loan cannot do so.
7. The net amount of money a borrower receives after the discount is subtracted from the principal.
8. The total cost of a loan.
9. An organization that provides savings account services and makes loans to individuals, primarily for use in buying homes.
10. A company which specializes in making small loans to borrowers with weak credit ratings.
11. A small loan received by simply signing a promissory note.
12. Something of value pledged to insure payment of a loan.
13. Interest deducted in advance from the total amount borrowed.

UNDERSTANDING YOUR READING

1. Describe some purchases for which the buyer might borrow money rather than use a credit plan.
2. How does a business make a profit from lending money?
3. Name four types of businesses that make loans. How do these types of businesses differ?
4. Explain the difference between an installment loan and a single-payment loan.
5. What is the advantage to the lender if security is offered for a loan? What types of security are often used?
6. Why is knowing the total finance charge important to consumers?
7. What three basic things must you know in order to calculate interest?
8. How is the date of maturity found (a) when the time is stated in months, and (b) when time is stated in days?
9. What kinds of information do you need when deciding which loan is best?

USING YOUR BUSINESS KNOWLEDGE

1. The Flanigans are planning to buy a home freezer to help cut their costs on food. They can buy the size they need for $299.95. If they buy it on credit, the interest charge will be $24.00 for 12 months. They could wait for a year to buy and save money to pay cash, but it is likely that the price of the freezer will then be $319.00, due to inflation. What are the things they should consider before making a decision?
2. Find the date of maturity for each of the following notes:

Date of Note	Time to Run
March 15	4 months
May 26	3 months
July 31	5 months
April 30	30 days
October 5	45 days

3. What are some reasons why consumer finance companies charge higher interest rates than do banks or credit unions?
4. Jean Adams can borrow $100 at 12 percent for one year and repay the principal and the interest at the end of the year; or she can borrow $100 and repay it in 12 monthly payments of $9.50.
   (a) Under what circumstances might she prefer the first plan?
   (b) Under what circumstances might she prefer the second plan?

SOLVING PROBLEMS IN BUSINESS

1. Ted Jablonski makes $111.50 a week on his job. Some weeks he spends more than he makes and has to borrow a few dollars to get him through the week. Last week he needed $25. A friend offered to lend him $25 if Ted would pay him back $30 a week later.
   (a) How much interest would Ted pay in dollars?
   (b) If Ted had to borrow the same amount once a month for a year, how many dollars would he pay in interest?

2. Write three promissory notes, using the information given below. In each case, use the current year as part of the date.
   (a) Maker, Douglas Meyers, of Great River, Arkansas. Payee, Great River National Bank. Date, July 3. Time, 2 months. Principal, $275. Interest rate, 7%. Payable at the Great River National Bank. No. 5.
   (b) Clarence Petrey, of Hamilton, Rhode Island, borrowed $750 from Robert Posten. He gave Mr. Posten a 60-day note for this amount. The note (No. 13) was dated March 15, had an interest rate of 12%, and was payable at the New State Bank.
   (c) Maker, Anne McCarthy, of Seattle, Washington. Payee, Lawrence Brumfield and Associates. Date, October 3. Time, one year. Principal, $424.85. Interest rate, 8%. No. 8. Where the note was payable was not shown.

3. Calculate the interest charge on each of the following notes:

	Face of Note	Interest Rate	Time to Run
(a)	$225	8%	1 year
(b)	$650	6%	3 years
(c)	$240	8%	3 months
(d)	$520	7%	5 months
(e)	$460	9%	60 days
(f)	$720	6½%	90 days

4. Scott Ward owns a large ranch. He has a chance to buy a piece of land next to his property but some distance from his main ranch. Mr. Ward would need to put in a road so that he could move equipment onto the new property. The gravel road would be 3.3 kilometers long and would cost $800 per kilometer.
   (a) How much would the road cost?
   (b) If Mr. Ward had to pay 7 percent interest on a two-year loan to pay for the road, how much interest would he pay over that period?

5. Before borrowing $200, Laura Demetry visited a small loan company and the loan department of a bank. At the loan company, she found that she could borrow the $200 if she signed a note agreeing to pay back the balance in six equal

monthly installments of $36.25. At the bank, she could borrow the money by signing a note for $208 and repaying the balance in six equal monthly payments.

(a) What would be the cost of the loan at the small loan company?

(b) What annual rate of interest would Ms. Demetry be paying if she borrowed at the small loan company?

(c) What would be the cost of the loan at the bank?

(d) What annual rate of interest would she pay if she borrowed at the bank?

EXPANDING YOUR UNDERSTANDING OF BUSINESS

1. At some time or other, people will come to you and ask to borrow money. Perhaps they have already done so. These borrowers may be good friends.

   (a) How can you be reasonably sure that the money you lend to others will be paid back to you?

   (b) Would your attitude toward lending the money be any different if the borrower is a close friend or merely an acquaintance? Explain.

   (c) How would you feel about cosigning a note for a friend?

2. The federal government supports a plan by which college students can borrow money to finance their educations. Some state governments also have such a plan, and some banks offer educational loans. Write a report on sources of loans to finance education beyond high school. Give information about costs of such loans, repayment rules, and eligibility for the loans.

3. People borrow money for many different reasons. Some borrow money to consolidate their debts.

   (a) Find out what is meant by "consolidating debts."

   (b) Is there any advantage in consolidating debts and making a single monthly payment on a single loan?

   (c) How might consolidating debts reduce the amount of each payment? Does this mean that the borrower would be saving money?

4. Recent credit laws, designed to protect consumers, have imposed requirements on lenders to provide certain kinds of information. Find out from one of the businesses which lends money in your community if the business finds these laws to be a help to them in dealing with persons who want to borrow money from them. Ask for copies of forms that have been changed to comply with the new laws and note the changes that are on them. Find out what the APR and total finance charge would be for a loan of $1,000 for one year. Compare what you discover with information gathered by other students.

MAKING PURCHASES WITH CREDIT

"Will it be cash or credit?" Customers hear those words millions of times a year. Sellers offer credit so widely that you can buy and charge almost anything. For example, it is possible to buy food, stereo tapes, airline tickets, tennis balls, and ocean cruises on credit.

As a consumer, you are encouraged by business to use credit often. Here are some messages which lure you to buy on credit:

No payments due until February.
Travel to Bermuda now and pay later.
We accept all bank and major oil company cards.
We can arrange an easy-payment plan for you.
Use your credit to save on this sale.

To a newcomer on the credit scene, the variety of credit plans can be confusing. But learning about credit and how to use it is not difficult. There are really only a few basic types of consumer credit. Learn what they are and how they work, and you will be in a better position to choose the type of credit plan that is best for you.

TYPES OF CONSUMER CREDIT

There are two basic types of consumer credit: loan credit and sales credit. **Loan credit** is credit used to borrow money. For example, a father might borrow money from a bank to pay his daughter's tuition at college, or he might get a loan from a credit union to buy a motorcycle. Loan credit was discussed in Part 26. **Sales credit** is credit used to acquire goods and services and pay for them at a later time.

Credit can be obtained by either the installment plan or the noninstallment plan. **Installment credit** is a plan by which you can pay back a debt over a period of time in regular payments, such as monthly. For example, an automobile might be bought with monthly payments for 36 months. **Noninstallment credit** is a plan in which you agree to pay for a purchase with one payment.

Sales credit can be either installment or noninstallment. Perhaps the most familiar type of sales credit is that used to buy goods on a noninstallment basis. This usually takes the form of a charge account. With a charge account, you buy on credit during a month or other specified period of time and are expected to pay for your purchases in full at the end of the time period. If you do not pay in full, you may be assessed a finance charge. A finance charge covers the merchant's cost of handling a particular account.

There are many kinds of sales credit plans. Some of the most common plans are: (1) open charge accounts, (2) budget accounts, (3) revolving charge accounts, (4) bank credit card plans, (5) teenage accounts, and (6) travel and entertainment card plans.

OPEN CHARGE ACCOUNTS

With an **open charge account**, the seller agrees to let you purchase what you want during the "open" period and expects payment in full at the end of the period. The open period is usually a month. Sometimes the seller sets a limit on the total amount that may be charged during a given period. Open accounts are used mostly for everyday needs such as gasoline and clothing.

Merchants usually write out a sales ticket for each purchase and keep these sales tickets in the customer's file. Most merchants use **credit cards** to identify customers who have valid accounts. Credit cards are identification cards. They show that you are a person who pays on time and that you are entitled to charge your purchases. Sometimes the salesperson will call the credit office when you present a credit card. This call is to be sure that your account is in good standing and that you are not charging more than the credit limit set for your account.

Illus. 27-1

When you make a purchase with a credit card, you will sign the sales ticket.

BUDGET ACCOUNTS

Some merchants offer **budget accounts**. These are similar to open charge accounts but payments are made over several months. This arrangement helps consumers with their budgets. A common budget plan is the 90-day, 3-payment plan. Under this plan, you pay for your purchase in 90 days, usually in 3 equal monthly payments. There is generally no finance charge if payments are made on time. Advertising slogans for these plans might say, "90 days same as cash."

In another type of budget plan, an estimate is made of how much you will buy during a certain period of time, such as a year. You then agree to pay a certain amount each month to cover those purchases. For example, if you have a good credit rating, your public utility company might allow you to pay a certain amount of money each month to cover the cost of natural gas you use for heating and cooking. This plan avoids payments of large amounts during winter heating months, but you also pay the same amount during warm months when heating is not required. At the end of the year, if the total cost of the gas used is more than the total amount you have paid, you must pay the difference. If you have paid for more than you actually used, you will get a refund for your overpayment.

Many customers like budget plans because they spread the cost of large purchases over several months and also avoid finance charges. Such plans help customers average their monthly expenses. Many merchants like budget plans because they encourage large purchases which customers might postpone if they had to pay interest on an installment purchase or had to wait until they saved enough to pay in cash.

REVOLVING CHARGE ACCOUNTS

The **revolving charge account** is widely used. It is like an open account in some ways but also has some added features. You can charge any purchase, but there is usually a limit on the total amount that you can owe at one time. A payment is due once a month, but the entire amount owed need not be paid at one time. An interest charge is added to your bill if it is not paid in full when it is due. This charge is a percentage of the unpaid balance, which is the amount owed on the date you are billed. Interest charges are often as much as 1½ percent per month, or 18 percent per year.

Revolving accounts are convenient, but they can tempt you to overbuy. Since they are commonly used for low-priced, frequently purchased items, revolving accounts can be expensive unless you watch charges and payments carefully. Many customers do not pay the full amount when it is due and thus remain in debt for long periods of time.

BANK CREDIT CARD PLANS

Bank credit card plans have become very popular. It is estimated that over 70 million people have one or more bank credit cards. Most of the banks in the United States are part of a bank credit card plan.

A bank or group of banks sets up the plan and issues credit cards to people whose credit ratings meet the banks' standards. Such a credit card, in effect, guarantees that the credit rating of the cardholder is good. The banks make agreements with various merchants to accept the credit cards.

Here is how a bank card plan works when you make a purchase. The salesperson fills out a credit sales ticket. The merchant collects all credit sales tickets prepared during a day or other time period and sends them to the bank. At this point, two things happen.

First, the bank charges your account for your purchases and bills you once a month for all the purchases you made during the month. You usually do not pay a finance charge if you pay your bill in full. However, if you pay only part of your bill, you pay a finance charge on the unpaid balance. You are usually charged an annual fee for the privilege of using the card.

Second, the bank totals all the sales tickets from each merchant and pays the merchant the amount of the sales less the amount of a fee. This fee is usually about 4 percent. Thus, if a merchant turns in sales tickets totaling $1,000, that person gets back $1,000 less 4 percent ($40), or $960. This fee covers the bank's expenses of processing the sales tickets, billing and collecting from customers, and losing on the bills of customers

Illus. 27-2

With a bank credit card, customers can charge a variety of purchases. This couple is paying their restaurant bill with a bank credit card.

who do not pay. The bank is doing the work that the firm's own credit department would have to do otherwise.

Merchants like bank card plans for two main reasons. First, the bank decides if a customer is a good credit risk. Also, the bank takes over much of the trouble and expense of granting credit. Customers like bank cards because they are accepted by so many businesses throughout the United States and in many foreign countries. Bank credit card users also like the fact that they receive only one monthly bill rather than many.

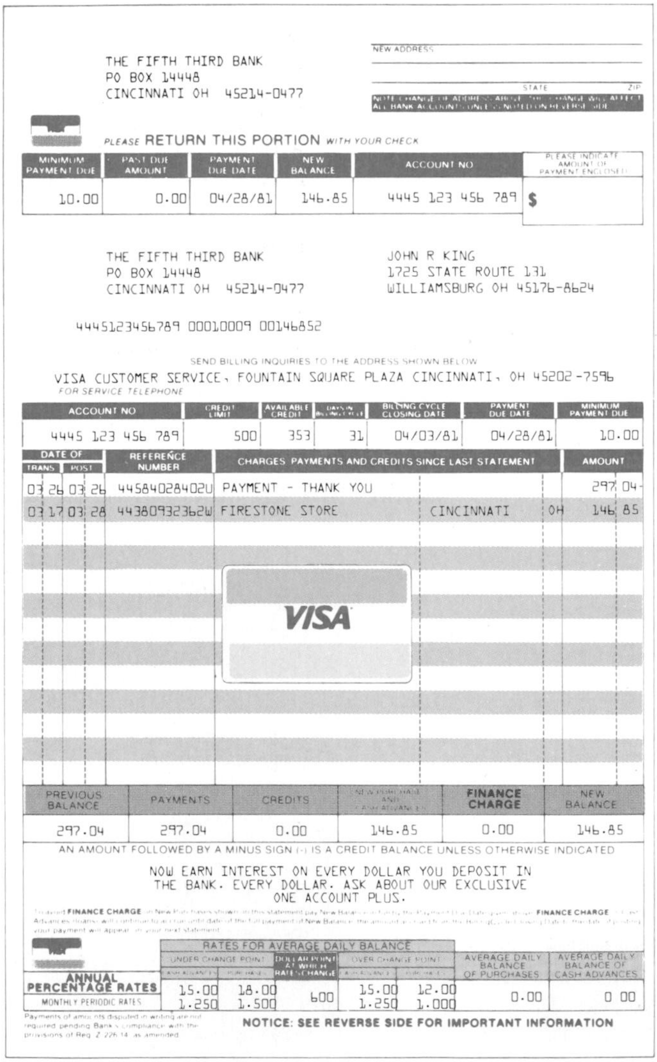

Illus. 27-3

This is the statement received monthly by people taking part in one bank card plan. Look at the kinds of information it contains. The two largest and best known bank card plans are MasterCard and VISA.

TEENAGE ACCOUNTS

As the teenage population has grown, teenagers have come to have more and more buying power. Some merchants today are granting credit to teenagers. Teenage accounts usually have a limit on the amount which can be charged during a given month. Generally a parent must agree to stand behind the debt, and sometimes the parent must also have an account with the firm granting the credit. But the teenager has a credit card and can buy an item without permission of the parents.

Teenage accounts give teenagers freedom in buying. But they need to learn to use this privilege wisely. This is especially true since it is often their first experience with credit.

TRAVEL AND ENTERTAINMENT CARD PLANS

Travel and entertainment (T&E) cards are something like bank cards. But in a T&E plan an independent firm performs the functions that a bank performs in a bank card plan. The T&E cards are used mainly to buy such services as lodging in hotels and motels, meals, and tickets for entertainment. Examples of nationally known T&E cards are Diners' Club, Carte Blanche, and American Express. A person who has a T&E card pays an annual fee for the privilege of having the card. Purchases are billed like those of the bank card plans.

Travelers especially like T&E cards because they do not have to carry much cash with them. The cards are good at many different businesses in all parts of the world. Firms who take part in T&E plans often find that their sales increase. They are able to attract more customers, and customers often buy more than they might buy if they had to pay cash.

INCREASING YOUR BUSINESS VOCABULARY

The following terms should become part of your business vocabulary. For each numbered statement, find the term that has the same meaning.

budget account   noninstallment credit
credit card   open charge account
installment credit   revolving charge account
loan credit   sales credit

1. Credit that is used to borrow money.
2. A type of credit in which a debt is repaid in one payment.

3. Credit that is used to acquire goods and services and pay for them at a later time.
4. A card which identifies a person and gives him or her the privilege of obtaining goods and services on credit.
5. A credit plan in which a customer may charge a purchase at any time but must pay the amount owed in full at the end of a specified period.
6. A credit plan in which purchases can be charged at any time and at least part of the debt must be paid each month.
7. A type of credit in which a debt is repaid in a series of payments.
8. A credit plan which is similar to an open charge account but spreads payment over a few months.

UNDERSTANDING YOUR READING

1. What are the two types of consumer credit?
2. What are the main differences between noninstallment credit and installment credit?
3. What are the six common types of sales credit plans?
4. In what ways does an open account plan differ from a budget plan?
5. Why do merchants and customers like budget plans?
6. What is the difference between an open account and a revolving account in terms of how much has to be paid each month?
7. What can be dangerous about using a revolving charge account?
8. Describe briefly how a bank credit card plan works.
9. What information is shown on a bank credit card statement?
10. If you have a teenage account and cannot pay your bill, what will the merchant normally do?
11. What are the advantages of having a travel and entertainment card?

USING YOUR BUSINESS KNOWLEDGE

1. Various attitudes toward the use of credit are found in the following statements. Tell whether you agree or disagree with each statement, and why.
   (a) "A bank card is nice to have. If I'm out of cash, I can still buy what I want."
   (b) "I don't believe in using credit for most purchases. I pay cash for everyday items and use credit only for big items like a new refrigerator, carpeting, or a new car."
   (c) "If I can't pay cash, I know that I can't afford it. I won't buy anything unless I can pay cash."

(d) "I often don't pay the full amount of my charge account when it is due; the interest charges are quite reasonable."
2. Many merchants would rather take credit cards than accept personal checks. Why do you think merchants feel this way?
3. Jerry Ripley owns a sporting goods store and is considering joining a bank credit card plan. He asks you to explain:
   (a) What advantages would there be for his business if he did join?
   (b) What will it cost him for the services the bank will provide?
   (c) In what ways are the services the bank provides important?
4. Some parents are opposed to the idea of their teenage children having charge accounts. Give reasons why:
   (a) a teenager might want such an account.
   (b) parents might favor their son or daughter having such an account.
   (c) parents might oppose such credit.

SOLVING
PROBLEMS
IN BUSINESS

1. Albert Belkus bought two gallons of paint on credit. The paint cost $8.40 a gallon. When he paid his account, a finance charge of $.25 was added to the purchase price of the paint. How much did his purchase cost him in total?
2. Charles Presley owns a pet store and hobby shop. He thinks he should join a bank credit card plan so that he can better compete with some large department stores. His credit sales each month on a bank card plan will be about $10,000.
   (a) If the bank plan he joins charges Mr. Presley 4 percent of his billings, how much would he pay for the bank's services in one month?
   (b) How much would the bank owe him for that month?
   (c) If his annual credit sales amount to $120,000, what would he pay for the bank's services for the year?
3. Sue Perkowski has a charge account with a department store. Her account is billed to her on the 20th of each month, and she is expected to pay in full by the last day of the month. If she does not, the store charges her 1½ percent on the balance of the account. This past month Sue made the following purchases: two skirts at $15.55 each; one pair of children's shoes at $16.95; costume jewelry at $11.15; and a lamp at $22.10.
   (a) What is the total amount for which Sue will be billed on the 20th of the month?
   (b) If she pays only $20 on her account this month, what will be the amount of the finance charge when her bill comes next month?

4. Norma Anderson charged the following items to her open account: 5 meters of wool plaid fabric at $5.90 per meter, and 2 meters of white lining fabric at $2.00 per meter. Sales tax on the purchase is 4 percent.

   (a) What was the total charge to Norma's account?

   (b) The pattern Norma was using showed the amount of material in yards. How many yards of the plaid and the lining did she buy?

5. Illus. 27-3 shows John R. King's VISA statement for April. It shows a balance of $146.85 and a minimum payment due of $10.00. As is shown at the bottom of the statement, the finance charge is figured at a monthly rate of 1.5 percent of the unpaid balance.

   (a) If Mr. King pays only the minimum payment, what will be the finance charge on his May statement?

   (b) If Mr. King charges no more purchases to his VISA before his May statement is prepared, what will be the balance on his May statement?

EXPANDING
YOUR
UNDERSTANDING
OF
BUSINESS

1. Businesses often give special names to their credit plans in order to attract customers. For example, a revolving charge account may be called a Basic Charge Account plan. Find two businesses in your community which offer at least two kinds of charge accounts. What names do these businesses give to their charge account plans? How do the plans differ?

2. Before revolving charge accounts became common, layaway plans were often used.

   (a) What is a layaway plan?

   (b) Is the layaway plan still used by businesses in your community?

3. Get an application form that is used by a bank when a person wants to apply for a bank credit card. Notice the information that is asked for and compare it with information that is requested when someone applies for a loan. Do you think that bank credit cards are easier to get than are loans? Why or why not?

4. In most states, the age of majority has been lowered from 21 to 18 or 19 years. This change means that those who reach age 18 or 19 have the legal rights and duties of adults. How does this change affect a 19-year-old's ability to get credit? Is a person of this age able to make wise credit decisions? Give reasons for your opinion from the point of view of both the seller and the 19-year-old.

28 USING INSTALLMENT SALES CREDIT

PART OBJECTIVES

After studying this part and completing the end-of-part activities, you will be able to:

1. Give an example of when installment sales credit would be better to use than an open charge account or a credit card.
2. Explain how installment sales credit differs from installment loan credit.
3. Identify the factors that contribute to the cost of installment sales credit.
4. State five questions you should answer before you sign an installment sales contract.

As you know, merchants offer many kinds of credit plans to make it easier for you to buy now and pay later. The kinds of sales credit plans you read about in Part 27 are what you use for purchasing things that you need daily. For example, credit cards and charge accounts are used to buy such items as clothes, gas, and birthday gifts. But when you want to buy something that is much more expensive and will usually last longer, a different kind of sales credit is needed. Suppose you want to buy an electric typewriter. You can wait until you save enough money and pay cash for it. You might be able to charge it to your regular account, but often such a large amount will be greater than your credit limit. In situations like this, you will probably use what is called installment buying or installment credit.

Illus. 28-1

When you want to buy something that is too expensive for you to pay all at once, you may be able to buy it on an installment plan.

Installment credit, as you learned in Part 27, is a plan by which a purchaser pays back a debt in a number of payments. Borrowing money and repaying the loan in monthly payments is one form of installment credit. When you borrow money in the manner explained in Part 26, you receive the cash from the lending agency. You take the cash to the seller to buy what you want or you use it to pay your bills.

INSTALLMENT SALES CREDIT

The kinds of sales credit you read about in Part 27 represent short-term credit. Installment sales credit is usually long-term, from 6 months to 5 years. An installment credit sale differs from a charge account or credit card sale in the following ways:

1. You sign a written agreement (a sales contract) which shows the terms of the purchase, such as payment periods and finance charges.
2. You receive and own the goods at the time of purchase. However, the seller has the right to **repossess** them (take them back) if payments are not made according to the agreement.
3. A **down payment** — a payment of part of the purchase price — is usually made at the time of the purchase.
4. A finance charge is made on the amount owed, because this amount is really a loan by the seller to you.
5. Regular payments must be made at stated times, usually weekly or monthly. For example, if a total of $120 is to be repaid in 12 monthly installments, $10 is paid in each

of the months. In some cases, a penalty is charged if a payment is received after the due date.

6. In some installment contracts, all remaining payments come due at once if only one payment is missed.

TYPES OF INSTALLMENT SALES CREDIT

Mark and Minnie Melton are furnishing their apartment. They went to a department store and bought a kitchen table with four chairs. They signed an installment contract to pay for the kitchen furniture and began making monthly payments. A few months later, Mark and Minnie returned to the same store and bought a stereo component system. They signed another sales contract. Not long after buying the stereo, the Meltons bought a microwave oven from the same store, and they then had three installment sales contracts. Each payment was due at a different time of the month, so the Meltons made three different payments to the department store each month. This type of installment sales credit plan is called the **one-time sale plan**.

Many stores offer a different plan called the **add-on plan**. With this plan, the Meltons would sign a sales contract for the kitchen set. Later, when they bought the stereo and microwave oven, these purchases would be added to their original contract. Each purchase amount would be added to the contract balance. The Meltons would have only one contract and one payment to make each month. Some stores call this plan the major purchase plan.

THE COST OF BUYING ON INSTALLMENTS

Installment purchases usually cost more than cash purchases because the seller is a lender that has money tied up for some time. As a lender, the firm will charge interest on the money that is loaned. Also, the firm has expenses in collecting money in small amounts and in recording payments. Sometimes businesses lose money because debts cannot be collected. All these costs must be shared by those who wish to make installment purchases.

Under the law, sellers must tell you the total finance charges in dollars and the annual percentage rate. This makes it easier for you to compare costs of installment loans and installment sales contracts. While it is no longer necessary for you to calculate the interest, you must still decide whether it would be better to pay cash. Here are some examples of typical purchasing situations. Consider whether you would have made the same purchasing decisions.

Stephanie Korick bought a color television set from a department store for $525.00 plus $19.80 tax, or a total of $544.80. She made a down payment of $30 and agreed to pay the balance of $514.80 in installments. The finance charge for the set on the installment plan was $100.31 with a period of 24 monthly installments. Her payments were $26.00 per month for 23 months with a final payment of $17.11. The annual interest rate in this situation was 18 percent. Her television set actually cost her $645.11.

Dick Swanson decided to buy a set of radial tires. The set cost $229.46, including tax. He decided to make a down payment of $29.46 and finance the remainder on an installment contract. The store gave him 24 months to pay. The finance charge was $40.00, so Dick owed a total of $240.00; his payments were $10.00 per month. He paid 20 percent annual interest for the privilege of buying on the installment plan. He actually paid $269.46 for the tires.

STUDY THE CONTRACT BEFORE SIGNING

Before signing a contract to buy on installments, there are certain questions you should answer listed on the next page:

Illus. 28-2

Before making an installment purchase, you must decide whether or not it would be better to pay cash.

1. Is this the best buy you can make or is someone else selling the same product, with better service, at the same price?

2. Can you make a bigger down payment? If you can, it will reduce the finance charges and thus the total cost of your purchase.

3. What part of your monthly income will the payments take? In the case of an emergency, will you still have enough money to make the monthly payments?

4. Does the contract include the cost of services you may need, such as repairs to a TV or a washing machine? If there is a separate repair contract, is its cost included in your sales contract or will you be billed separately?

5. Does the contract have the add-on advantage so that you can later buy other major items and have them added to the balance that you owe?

6. If you pay off the contract before its ending date, how much of the finance charge will you get back? (This is called a **rebate** — a refund of money you paid but did not really owe.)

7. If you pay off the contract within 90 days, will there be any finance charge or will it be as if you had paid cash?

8. Is the contract you are asked to sign completely filled in? (Do not sign if there are blanks.)

9. Under what conditions can the seller repossess the merchandise if you do not pay on time?

INCREASING YOUR BUSINESS VOCABULARY

The following terms should become part of your business vocabulary. For each numbered statement, find the term that has the same meaning.

add-on plan   *rebate*
down payment   *repossess*
one-time sale plan

1. An installment plan in which the cost of each item is paid for in separate monthly payments.

2. A refund of finance charges when an installment agreement is paid off early.

3. Part of the purchase price of an item that is paid at the time of buying.

4. An installment plan in which the costs of all time purchases are grouped together in one monthly payment.

5. To take back what was sold on the installment plan if payments are not made as agreed.

UNDERSTANDING YOUR READING

1. What kinds of items are most often bought on the installment credit plan?
2. What is the difference between an installment loan and an installment purchase?
3. What is a sales contract?
4. What is the difference between a one-time plan and an add-on plan?
5. Why are costs of buying on the installment plan more than those of paying cash?
6. Name several things you should ask yourself before signing an installment contract.
7. When would you expect to receive a rebate on an installment purchase?

USING YOUR BUSINESS KNOWLEDGE

1. Which of the following items might be wisely purchased on the installment credit plan? Which would you not advise buying on the installment plan? Give reasons for your answers.
   (a) vacation trip   (e) tropical fish aquarium
   (b) used car   (f) set of encyclopedias
   (c) suit of clothes   (g) refrigerator
   (d) TV set   (h) carpeting
2. How could buying on the installment plan improve a buyer's credit rating? How might it harm a credit rating?
3. Why would it not be wise to sign an installment sales contract that is not completely filled in?
4. If an item that was purchased on an installment contract has to be repossessed, what are the disadvantages to the purchaser? What are the disadvantages to the seller?
5. Explain why it is true that a retailer who sells on the installment plan is really lending you money.

SOLVING PROBLEMS IN BUSINESS

1. Sandy Wilson bought a rug for $350. She made a down payment of $50 and agreed to pay a total of $300 in 12 monthly payments of $25 each. The rug could have been purchased for cash for $330. How much did Miss Wilson pay for the privilege of buying on the installment plan?
2. Flora Ruiz can buy a TV set for $260 in cash. She has, however, only $60 to spend.
   (a) Flora could buy the TV on credit by paying $60 down and

then paying $225 over several months. How much would the TV cost her under this plan?

(b) Flora could also borrow the $200 that she needs in addition to her $60 to make the total cash payment. If she did this, she would have to repay a total of $244 on her loan. How much would she pay for the TV in this case?

3. A department store offers an easy-payment plan for installment purchases. Part of the payment schedule is shown below. Down payments are required for items costing more than $50.

Cash Price	Add for Easy Payments	Monthly Payments
No down payment required		
$ 30.01–$ 35.00	$ 3.50	
35.01– 40.00	4.00	
40.01– 45.00	4.50	$5.00
45.01– 50.00	5.00	
$5 down payment required		
$ 50.01–$ 55.00	$ 6.50	
55.01– 60.00	7.00	
60.01– 65.00	7.50	6.00
65.01– 70.00	8.00	
$10 down payment required		
$120.01–$130.00	$19.00	
130.01– 140.00	21.00	
140.01– 150.00	23.00	8.00
150.01– 160.00	26.00	

In one day, customers bought six articles on the installment plan. The cash price of each of the articles is shown below. In each case, the minimum down payment was made.

Article	Cash Price
Electric fan	$ 31.50
Metal kitchen cabinets	63.50
Bicycle	69.00
Record player	127.00
Bunk beds	133.00
Porch furniture	160.00

For each article find:

(a) The amount to be added for the privilege of buying on the installment plan.

(b) The total price to be paid on the installment plan.

(c) The amount of the down payment.

(d) The balance owed, to be paid in installments.

(e) The number of months over which installments will have to be paid.

4. William Schultz and his sister, Jean, were building a sailboat. To complete their project, they needed to buy some rope and some marine paint. After checking with several business places, they found the following prices: Rope at business A was 95¢ per foot, and at business B it was $3 per meter. At business C paint was $4.89 per liter, and at business D it was $5 per quart. They needed 80 feet, or 24½ meters, of rope, and 10 quarts, or 9½ liters, of paint.

(a) At which business place would the rope be cheaper? How much cheaper?

(b) At which business place would the paint be cheaper? How much cheaper?

EXPANDING YOUR UNDERSTANDING OF BUSINESS

1. It has been said that we are living in an "installment age." Almost everything we buy can be purchased on the installment plan: furniture, cars, houses, TV sets, vacation trips, insurance, education, and so on. If we go too deeply into debt, we can borrow money to pay the debts, and we can pay off the loan on the installment plan.

(a) Explain how this easy payment plan may be helpful to an individual. How may it be harmful?

(b) How may the easy payment plan be helpful to businesses? Under what circumstances may offering easy payment plans be harmful to business?

2. The Consumer Protection Act and Truth in Lending Law are important pieces of legislation. Many banks and other lending institutions have information about these laws. Your school library or business education department also might have folders which discuss and explain them. Find out what you can about each of these laws and make a list of the important provisions contained in each.

②⑨ KEEPING A GOOD CREDIT RECORD

PART OBJECTIVES

After studying this part and completing the end-of-part activities, you will be able to:
1. Tell why having a good credit record is important.
2. Explain how a credit record can be established.
3. Describe what a retail credit bureau does.
4. Identify the information shown on a statement of account.
5. Tell why receipts and credit memorandums are important.
6. Explain why it is important to keep accurate records.
7. Tell how credit laws have helped consumers.

American consumers use credit for millions of dollars worth of purchases every day. The use of credit is a privilege that you and others enjoy and can continue to enjoy as long as you maintain a good credit record. You see, when people grant you credit it means that they trust you and believe that you will pay your debts. Your personal history of paying or not paying on time is your credit record. Every person who has been granted credit has a credit record. Your credit record shows that you bought on credit, when and where you made each purchase, and how promptly you paid your bill. This record is very important because it follows you all of your life, no matter where you live.

Anytime you apply for credit, the seller will check your credit record. If you want to continue to obtain credit, you have to keep your record clean. To do this, you should know when to use credit and when not to use it.

BUILDING YOUR CREDIT RECORD

Starting to build your credit record can be a problem. You might apply for credit and find that you cannot get it because you have no credit record. Some businesses do not want to be the first to test your credit worthiness. However, there are several things you can do to begin building your credit record.

For one thing, it is good to have both a checking and a savings account. If you have a balance in each account and do not overdraw your checking account, that tells a lender that you can handle your money. Making regular deposits to your savings account also suggests that you will be a good credit risk.

Some persons establish credit records by making their first credit purchases small ones. For instance, if you buy a sweater on credit and make the payments according to the agreement, you have taken an important step toward proving you are a good credit risk. Or you may want to pay off your account within 30 days and avoid a charge for interest. Either way you will be building your credit record.

Having a good employment record also helps you to establish a good credit record. If you change jobs often, it does not look good to a creditor. Being on a job for two or more years is a positive part of a good credit record.

WHAT CREDITORS NEED TO KNOW

When you apply for credit, you will be asked to fill out a credit application form. The information on that form will be used to decide whether or not to grant you credit. Illus. 29-1 is an application for credit; look it over and notice the kinds of information requested.

Once you have completed the application form, the creditor may call those you list as references to see what kind of person you are. The creditor may also call your employer. This is done to be certain that you have a job and to see if your job is permanent or temporary.

Next, the creditor will probably check your record with a **retail credit bureau**. Retail credit bureaus are organizations that keep records on people in the area who have done business on credit. Each credit bureau is usually linked with similar organizations in other communities. If you are new to the area in which you are applying for credit, the local credit bureau can call

Bankard™ Application

THIS APPLICATION IS FOR VISA® AND MASTERCARD® (UNLESS OTHERWISE INDICATED) VISA ONLY □. MASTERCARD ONLY □.

IF YOU ALREADY HAVE A BANKARD ACCOUNT
PLEASE PROVIDE ACCOUNT NUMBER.

VISA: 4460-
M/C: 541169-

ABOUT YOU, THE APPLICANT
PLEASE PRINT YOUR NAME EXACTLY AS YOU WISH IT TO APPEAR ON YOUR CREDIT CARDS.

LAST NAME	FIRST NAME	INITIAL	DATE OF BIRTH	SOCIAL SECURITY NUMBER

STREET ADDRESS	CITY	STATE	ZIP CODE	NO. DEPENDENTS	AREA CODE/PHONE NO.

LENGTH AT PRESENT ADDRESS (YRS.) (MOS.)	PLEASE CHECK BUYING OR OWN □ LIVE WITH RENT □ RELATIVE □	MONTHLY PAYMENT	NAME AND ADDRESS OF LANDLORD OR MORTGAGE HOLDER

PREVIOUS ADDRESS	CITY/STATE	YEARS	MONTHS

PRESENTLY EMPLOYED BY	STREET ADDRESS	CITY/STATE	YEARS	MONTHS

POSITION/EMPLOYEE NO.	MONTHLY INCOME $	BUS. PHONE NO.	AMOUNT AND SOURCE OF OTHER MONTHLY INCOME Except Alimony, Child Support, or Maintenance (See ADDITIONAL INFORMATION Below) $

PREVIOUSLY EMPLOYED BY (OR UNIVERSITY IF RECENT GRADUATE)	CITY/STATE	POSITION (OR DEGREE)	HOW LONG (OR YR. GRAD.)

NAME AND STREET ADDRESS OF NEAREST RELATIVE NOT LIVING WITH YOU	CITY/STATE	RELATIONSHIP

NAME AND LOCATION OF YOUR BANK	SAVINGS ACCT. NO.	CHECKING ACCT. NO.

ABOUT JOINT APPLICANT (IF ANY)
RELATIONSHIP TO APPLICANT: _____

LAST NAME	FIRST NAME	INITIAL	DATE OF BIRTH	SOCIAL SECURITY NUMBER

STREET ADDRESS	CITY	STATE	ZIP CODE	AREA CODE/PHONE NO.

PRESENTLY EMPLOYED BY	STREET ADDRESS	CITY/STATE	YEARS	MONTHS

POSITION/EMPLOYEE NO.	MONTHLY INCOME $	BUS. PHONE NO.	AMOUNT AND SOURCE OF OTHER MONTHLY INCOME Except Alimony, Child Support, or Maintenance (See ADDITIONAL INFORMATION Below) $

NAME AND LOCATION OF YOUR BANK	SAVINGS ACCT. NO.	CHECKING ACCT. NO.

CREDIT REFERENCES (OPEN AND/OR CLOSED)

PLEASE LIST ALL DEBTS PRESENTLY OWING INCLUDING ALIMONY, CHILD SUPPORT OR MAINTENANCE PAYMENTS WHICH YOU ARE OBLIGATED TO MAKE. ATTACH ADDITIONAL SHEETS IF NECESSARY. AND INDICATE ANY OF YOUR ACCOUNTS LISTED UNDER ANOTHER NAME.

NAME OF CREDITOR OR INDIVIDUAL	CITY/STATE	ACCOUNT NO.	MO. PAYMENT	BALANCE
AUTO FINANCED BY				

ADDITIONAL INFORMATION

YOU ARE NOT REQUIRED TO DISCLOSE INCOME FROM ALIMONY, CHILD SUPPORT, OR MAINTENANCE PAYMENTS. HOWEVER, IF YOU ARE RELYING ON INCOME FROM ALIMONY, CHILD SUPPORT, OR MAINTENANCE PAYMENTS AS A BASIS FOR REPAYMENT OF THIS OBLIGATION, PLEASE COMPLETE BELOW

ALIMONY/MO. $ CHILD SUPPORT/MO. $ MAINTENANCE/MO. $

SIGNATURES
WHEN I RECEIVE MY CREDIT CARD(S), I AGREE AND UNDERSTAND THAT I AM CONTRACTUALLY LIABLE ACCORDING TO THE APPLICABLE BANKARD TERMS AND CONDITIONS. AND IF THIS IS A JOINT APPLICATION WE AGREE SUCH LIABILITY IS JOINT AND SEVERAL. YOU HAVE THE RIGHT TO TAKE ANY ACTION(S) YOU FEEL NECESSARY TO DETERMINE THE CREDIT WORTHINESS OF ANY PARTY SIGNING BELOW AND BY SIGNING BELOW I (WE) CONFIRM THAT THE INFORMATION GIVEN TO YOU ON THIS APPLICATION IS TRUE.

APPLICANT'S SIGNATURE X   DATE   DRIVERS LICENSE NO.

JOINT APPLICANT'S SIGNATURE X   DATE   DRIVERS LICENSE NO.

OTHER PERSONS PERMITTED TO USE ACCOUNT(S)
SIGNATURE(S)   RELATIONSHIP(S)

BANK USE ONLY

BANK NAME AND OR NUMBER

□ VISA
□ M/C
□ BOTH

TC	08	09	13	17	27	31	33
#							

APPROVED BY   DATE APPROVED

Illus. 29-1

An application for a
bank credit card.

the bureau in the community in which you formerly lived and check your record.

Your credit record with a bureau grades you as a credit risk. It describes what you owe now and how your payment record has been in the past. Your credit record is confidential. That is, it can be given out only to those who have a legitimate reason for seeing it.

There are times when your smallest actions can affect your credit rating. For example, you might be on vacation and fail to pay an auto insurance bill. Or, you might have delayed depositing money in your checking account so that your last check was returned for insufficient funds in your account. These actions on your part may become part of your credit record. One small blot on your record will not hurt you, but many will. You have a legal right to inquire about the contents of your credit record. If you find information which you feel is incorrect, you may write a statement that explains the situation from your point of view. Your statement becomes part of your credit report.

USING YOUR CREDIT STATEMENTS

You can help keep your credit record clean by keeping accurate records of your purchases and payments. When a merchant sells goods on credit, a record of the sale is made on a sales ticket. Usually two or more copies of the sales ticket are made. One copy is given to you, the customer, as a receipt. The other copy or copies are kept by the merchant for billing purposes.

At regular intervals, usually monthly, a business sends to each credit customer a record of the transactions that the customer has completed with the business during the billing period. This record is known as a **statement of account** or, more briefly, a **statement**. Your statement will show:

1. the balance that was due when the last statement was mailed.
2. the amounts charged during the month for merchandise or service you bought. Some sellers include copies of the sales tickets.
3. the amounts credited to your account during the month for payments or for merchandise returned.
4. the current balance, which is the balance from the last statement, plus interest charges and the amounts of any

new purchases, less the amounts credited to you (old balance + charges − payments = current balance).

Most statements are prepared by special accounting machines or by computers. Some statements list separately each item that was purchased. Some list only the totals purchased, paid, and owed. In any case, a statement serves two purposes: (1) it shows you how much you owe, and (2) it gives you a record of your transactions with the business.

You should prove the accuracy of the statement by comparing it with your copies of sales tickets and with your record of

Account number →

Purchase made during this billing period. →

The account balance last month. →

← The amount of purchase.

← The amount that must be paid.

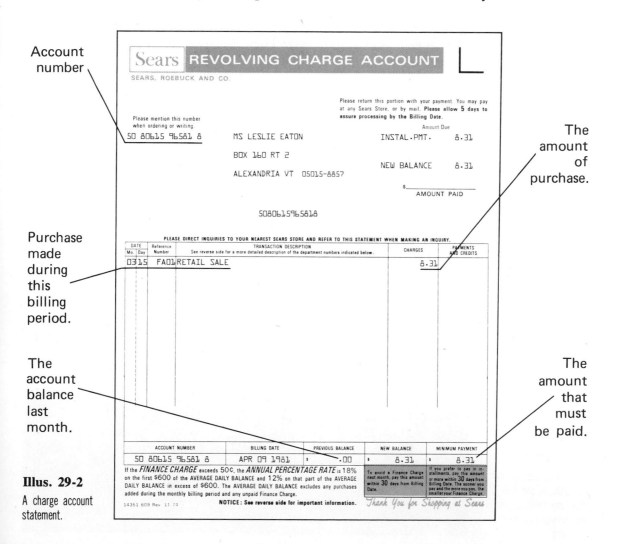

Illus. 29-2

A charge account statement.

payments and **credit memorandums** (written records the seller gives you when you return merchandise). If you discover an error on a statement, you should call it to the seller's attention at once.

KEEPING ACCURATE RECORDS

As soon as you receive a sales ticket or a monthly statement, you should examine it to make sure that it is correct. A business may mistakenly charge you for goods you did not actually buy. Or it may fail to give you credit for a payment or for goods that you returned. You should be sure to notice the date when each payment is due. When you are making a payment by check, write the date and the check number on the statement. Keep all such sales tickets and statements. They will be valuable in the future if any question arises as to whether or not they have been paid.

It is not enough for you to know that you have paid a bill. You should be able to prove that payment was made. Otherwise, you may be required to make payment a second time. In studying about checks, you learned that a canceled check is valuable as evidence that payment has been made because it has the endorsement of the payee on the back. When you do not pay by check, you need some other method of showing that you have made payment.

A written form that acknowledges that payment was made is called a **receipt**. Receipts are usually given to people who pay their bills by cash. Receipts are sometimes bound in books, along with stubs like check stubs. The receipt form provides spaces for entering the number of the receipt, the date, the name of the person making payment, the amount of the payment in words, the reason for the payment, the amount in figures, and the signature of the person receiving the payment. The stub is filled out to show the same information.

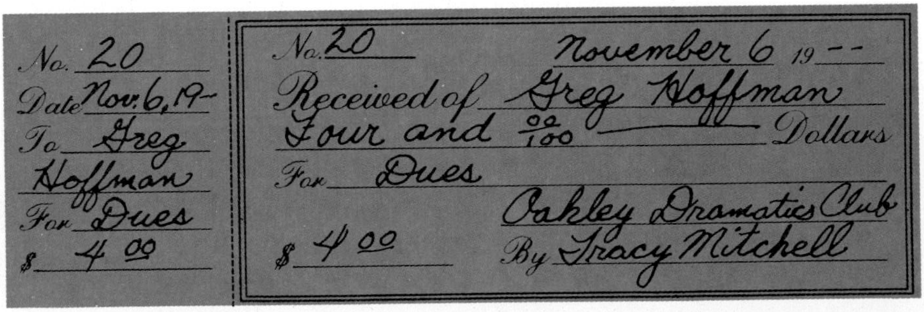
No. 20
Date Nov. 6, 19--
To Greg Hoffman
For Dues
$ 4 00

No. 20 November 6 19 --
Received of Greg Hoffman
Four and 00/100 Dollars
For Dues
$ 4 00
Oakley Dramatics Club
By Tracy Mitchell

Illus. 29-3

Study this receipt and its stub to see how they are filled out and the information each contains.

The information recorded on a receipt stub may later be needed by the one issuing the receipt to determine whether a customer paid and when. Each stub and receipt is numbered so that the customer's receipt can easily be compared with the stub if there is a dispute about the amount paid.

Sometimes a receipt is not given. Instead, acknowledgment of payment is written or stamped on the bill or statement. Usually, "Paid," along with the date and the initials or signature of the one who received your money, will be written on the statement. If you pay in cash, you should keep the cash register receipt or the sales ticket as evidence of payment. You will also need this if you have to return the goods.

CREDIT LAWS PROTECT YOU

In recent years a number of laws have been passed to protect you when you use credit. The Truth in Lending Act of 1968, for example, requires that you be told the cost of a credit purchase before you sign any agreement. You must be told the annual percentage rate, the amount of interest you will pay, and the total finance charges. The Equal Credit Opportunity Act prohibits sellers from denying credit because of age, race, sex, or marital status. And the Fair Credit Billing Act helps you if an error is made in your credit statement. When you bring an error to the attention of the creditor, you must receive an explanation for the error within 30 days.

GUIDELINES FOR USING CREDIT

You must personally decide whether you should use cash or credit for each purchase you make. No one can make these decisions for you, because no one else knows your personal financial situation. You know what your income is now and approximately what it will be in the coming months. You know how much you have saved or expect to save. Only you know what you feel you need now and what you believe you can get along without. All of these things will enter your purchasing decisions. They all affect the life-style you want to have.

In making your decisions about when to use credit, you may find the following guidelines useful.

1. Avoid using credit for small everyday items which you buy frequently. It is easy to use credit for small everyday

purchases and to spend your cash for luxuries, but it isn't practical. Use credit for those goods which have a much higher price than you can afford with one or two paychecks.

2. Use credit mainly for goods which have a useful life longer than the time you need to pay for them. It is discouraging to pay over many months for things which you use up quickly, such as a vacation.

3. Know what your income will be. If it varies from month to month, set a spending limit on yourself equal to the smallest paycheck you receive. Avoid buying on credit in the hope that you can make more money later in the year to pay for it.

4. Make as large a down payment as you can without robbing yourself of cash to buy necessities. Larger down payments can reduce the total amount of money you pay in interest for receiving credit.

5. Estimate your future income and expenses to be sure that you will have enough money in the future to pay a debt that you take on now. It is dangerous to use credit without knowing that you will have the money to pay debts when they are due.

Illus. 29-4

A shopping spree may be fun, but if you overuse credit, you may not be able to pay the bills when they are due.

6. Don't buy one item on credit just because you have finished paying for another one. For example, just because you have paid off your car is no reason to buy a new one. Instead, save the money you would have spent for payments so that you will have a fund with which to buy your next car, when it becomes necessary.

7. Avoid the temptation to use credit at times when you feel like splurging. For example, buying expensive Christmas presents on credit may be a real problem in January when the bills come due.

INCREASING YOUR BUSINESS VOCABULARY

The following terms should become part of your business vocabulary. For each numbered statement, find the term that has the same meaning.

credit memorandum   *retail credit bureau*
receipt   *statement of account or statement*

1. An organization that keeps records on people who have done business on credit.
2. A written acknowledgement that payment was made.
3. A record of the transactions that a customer has completed with a business during a billing period.
4. A written record the seller gives you when you return merchandise.

UNDERSTANDING YOUR READING

1. What is a credit record?
2. Why is having a good credit record important?
3. What are some of the things you can do to establish your credit record?
4. Where might a seller go to check up on your history of paying bills?
5. Why is more than one copy made of sales tickets? Of what value is a sales ticket to a customer and to a business?
6. What important information is usually shown on the statement of account?
7. What should you do with receipts and memorandums that you receive?
8. How can you prove the accuracy of statements you receive?
9. What evidence can a person give to prove that a bill has been paid if the payment was by check? by cash?

10. Name three credit laws that have been passed to protect you. What are the main features of each law?
11. Give seven guidelines for the proper use of credit.

USING YOUR BUSINESS KNOWLEDGE

1. Ms. Ballinger operates a retail grocery store. One day Mr. Stark, a total stranger, approaches her and asks if he may buy a week's supply of groceries on credit. Mr. Stark explains that he has just moved into town that day, that the moving expenses took all of his cash, but that he has a good job and will be able to pay Ms. Ballinger in a week or ten days. (a) What should Ms. Ballinger do? (b) If she decides to extend credit to Mr. Stark, what precautions do you think she should take?

2. Ms. Saxon wants to open an account in the Grandin Road Department Store. She objects, however, to giving the credit manager information about such things as where she has other charge accounts, whether she owns real estate, where she works, and in which bank she maintains an account. (a) Does the credit manager have a right to ask for this information? (b) Should Ms. Saxon object?

3. Donna Davis has been working on her first job for seven months. Her checking account has a balance of $159. She has put aside $50 in cash for a "rainy day." She wants to buy a clock radio which sells for $69.95 at a store that offers credit. Donna has never used credit and would like to establish a credit rating. What can she do to get a credit record started? What advice would you give her if she decided to buy this clock radio on credit?

4. Mrs. Leyman never saves the sales tickets listing merchandise that she buys for cash. Mrs. Dunbar saves her sales tickets for at least a month. Who is following the better business practice?

5. Below is a list of some everyday business transactions. Assuming that you are paying cash in each case, for which payments would you wish to have receipts and for which payments are receipts unimportant? Tell why in each case.
(a) Bought 10 gallons of gasoline.
(b) Bought a bus ticket.
(c) Bought a newspaper.
(d) Paid for shoe repairs.
(e) Paid to have the car repaired.
(f) Paid club dues.
(g) Bought a sandwich at a drive-in.
(h) Bought a ticket to a football game.
(i) Paid the telephone bill.

SOLVING
PROBLEMS
IN BUSINESS

1. The Polka Dot Market is a food store in a small town. It has been in the same location for many years and has been run by the same family. The owner gives credit to the people she knows who have been steady customers for years. Today she received checks in the mail from several customers. After applying the checks to the accounts as shown below, **(a)** what was the balance in each account and **(b)** how much in total was received from the charge customers?

Name	Amount Owed	Amount Paid
Jose Navarro	$ 44.22	$44.22
Lynne Goldberg	10.00	5.00
Eloise Little	102.67	50.00
Sam Nader	54.89	25.00
Ruth Smith	19.35	19.35

2. Joan Roman made the following credit purchases: gloves, $12; purse, $18; necklace, $25; shoes, $22. Later she returned the gloves and the purse and received a credit memorandum.
   (a) What was the total of Joan's purchases before she returned the gloves and the purse?
   (b) What was the amount of the credit memorandum?
   (c) What did she owe after she received the credit memorandum?

3. Wholesalers usually offer cash discounts to retailers to encourage them to pay their bills promptly. The following discount terms appeared on a bill received by Kane's Hardware: 5/10, 2/20, n/30. The term 5/10 means that a 5 percent discount will be allowed if the bill is paid within 10 days. The term 2/20 means that a 2 percent discount will be allowed if the bill is paid within 20 days. The term n/30 means that it is expected that the bill will be paid no later than 30 days after the date on the bill.
   (a) The amount of the bill was $526.70. If Kane's Hardware paid the bill within 5 days, what was the amount of the check written?
   (b) What was the amount of the check if the bill was paid on the 15th day? On the 25th day?

4. Po-ling Shen uses his bank credit card to charge merchandise he buys at several stores. During this past month, the following purchases were charged to his bank credit card account: Al's Clothing Store, 2 shirts, $18. Russ's Hardware Store, 2 gallons of paint, $21.50. Hislop's Family Restaurant, $24.75. A credit sales slip for $10.75 from Russ's Hardware Store was also received this month. Po-ling's statement shows a balance from

the previous month of $41.50, and a finance charge of $.42 was added by the bank this month.

(a) If Po-ling decides to pay his account in full, how much will he pay?

(b) If he decides to make a minimum payment of $10, how much will he still owe?

(c) If the finance charge is 1 percent per month, what will the next month's finance charge be if he pays only the $10 amount?

5. Billy Fitzgerald owns an apartment building consisting of six rental units. She lives in one unit and leases the other units to students at the local community college. She ordered new carpeting for the hallways. The cost was $9.20 per square meter installed. The amount of carpeting needed was 302 square meters.

(a) What was the total cost of the carpet?

(b) Billy signed a contract for the total cost and agreed to pay 8 percent interest for one year. How much interest will she pay?

EXPANDING YOUR UNDERSTANDING OF BUSINESS

1. When businesses have difficulty in collecting amounts that customers owe them, they sometimes hire collection agencies. Prepare a report on collection agencies. Tell what they do, how they collect, and what their services cost a business. You should be able to find most of the information you need in the library. However, you might call or visit a local collection agency to get additional information. Collection agencies are listed in the Yellow Pages of your telephone book.

2. *Usury* is lending money at a rate of interest that is greater than the limit established by law. Find out what the maximum allowable rate of interest is in your state. Are there any exceptions permitted to the maximum rate?

3. Find out what is meant by "attachment and garnishment of wages." What limits on garnished wages are established by the Truth in Lending Act?

4. The Equal Credit Opportunity Act permits lenders and creditors to use a credit scoring system. Such systems have been used by many businesses in the past. The credit scoring system assigns points to various factors which relate to whether or not a person is a good credit risk. The Equal Credit Opportunity Act, however, requires that the points that are used for each factor be assigned objectively and be based on the firm's actual experience in granting credit. Find out more about credit scoring systems by visiting your library and looking up articles

dealing with this system. Visit a retail store or a bank or some other lending institution and find out what you can about the experience that businesses have had with credit scoring. If you can, bring an example of a credit scoring system to class and discuss it with your class.

CAREER FOCUS

There are many career opportunities in the field of credit. Jobs in this career area fall under a broad heading of credit and collection. Jobs are available in manufacturing, wholesaling, and retailing as well as in banks, finance companies, credit unions, and savings and loan associations. Any organization that extends credit needs employees to handle various matters relating to granting credit and collecting the amount due.

Almost every business in the nation must have workers who can perform work required by credit transactions. All banks in our country must have employees to work in their loan and credit departments. Over 53,000 credit managers are needed to manage credit departments and supervise employees, and more than 64,000 workers are employed in jobs that deal with the collection of money that is owed on loans and credit accounts.

WORKERS IN THE CREDIT FIELD

Workers whose jobs are related to the use of credit do many different kinds of tasks. You have probably seen many of these people at work. Think about the people you could meet if you decided to apply for a charge account at a large department store.

Your first contact would more than likely be with a credit application clerk. This person would ask questions to help determine what kind of credit plan would best suit your needs. Your completed application form would probably be given to a credit investigator who would check to see if you should be given credit. The credit investigator would check the information on the application to see that it is accurate. The local credit bureau would be contacted to see if other businesses have had credit dealings with you.

The credit investigator would give the information to a credit analyst who would study your records and determine whether or not you are a good risk. If the credit analyst is satisfied, you would be extended credit and would receive your charge card.

When you go into a store and make a credit purchase, the salesclerk often will call the credit office to see that your record is okay. The salesclerk checks with a credit authorizer. If you fail to pay your account on time, a collection clerk will call or write to you to find out what the problem is.

All of these people are usually supervised by a credit manager who is responsible for all the credit activities of the business. In banks and some other financial institutions, this individual is called a loan officer.

Assisting the workers in the credit field are many clerical workers, secretaries, and data processing workers. As computers are used more and more to provide information upon which credit decisions are based, data processing workers are becoming increasingly important.

EDUCATION AND TRAINING
FOR CREDIT WORK

Workers in the credit field need at least a high school education for beginning jobs. Many of the jobs require education beyond high school. Practically all credit workers must know how to deal with people easily and tactfully. They also must be willing to take responsibility and make decisions. Naturally, they must be able to communicate well in both spoken and written form. Courses in English, mathematics, accounting, economics, insurance, and business law will help these workers develop the knowledge they need.

LOOKING AT THE FUTURE
IN THE FIELD OF CREDIT

It appears that job opportunities in the field of credit will grow rapidly in the next few years. As the use of credit continues to increase, more workers will be needed to handle the work that is involved. Expanded use of bank credit cards will create a need for more credit workers in banks but fewer in retail stores. The overall outlook for job openings in credit and collection is considered to be very good.

UNIT 8

Saving And Investing Money

UNIT OBJECTIVES

After studying the parts in this unit, you will be able to:

1. Give several reasons why planned savings are important to a consumer.

2. Describe several kinds of savings accounts to consider when investing money.

3. Explain how stocks and bonds fit into a savings and investment program.

4. State an advantage of real estate as a form of investment.

BUILDING YOUR SAVINGS

PART OBJECTIVES

After studying this part and completing the end-of-part activities, you will be able to:
1. Describe four different ways of saving money.
2. Explain how investments can increase your savings.
3. Tell how the safety of an investment affects the rate of return.
4. Describe a liquid investment.
5. Give an illustration of how investments serve our economy.

You have heard and read about many ways in which you can buy now and pay later. It is also important to know how to save money. As you know, saving means putting something aside for later use. Some people save things — like records, books, magazines, or stamps. These things often have special personal value. Occasionally saving things may be a hobby, such as saving postage stamps or rare coins.

A different kind of saving that is important for most people — whether they are rich or poor — is to save money. We save money now to buy things later that we cannot afford or do not need right away. We might save for a new car, a college education, or a vacation trip. We also save for a "rainy day," a time when some unexpected expense might occur. A savings plan is needed for us to buy many of the things we want and need and to prepare for emergencies.

Illus. 30-1

A trip to summer camp or buying your own car might be one of your reasons for saving money.

WAYS OF SAVING

People save money for different reasons and in different ways. Lettie Sherman's father believes in using his savings to buy land. In addition to making payments on the Shermans' home, he is making payments on an acre of land he bought in the mountains. Mr. and Mrs. Sherman also feel it is important to have some money in the bank. Every week, Lettie's mother takes a small part of the household money and puts it in a savings account. Lettie's older brother buys stocks and bonds. Lettie herself takes some of the money she earns babysitting and puts it in a piggy bank in her room. As soon as she saves enough, she wants to buy her own stereo set.

All of Lettie's family have one thing in common: savings. But each has a different savings plan. All except Lettie are investing their savings. Investing is doing something with your money that will provide an opportunity to make more money. Lettie is saving but not investing. A piggy bank is a good way to save but it offers no opportunity to earn money. In this unit you will learn how to save and invest your money.

INCREASING YOUR SAVINGS

Saving even a few dollars at a time is a good idea. Any amount of savings can be put to work to earn an income. Interest which is paid on your savings is one of the ways in which your money can earn more money. When savings are put to work to earn income, they are called investments.

When savings are invested and the income earned from them is in turn invested, the increase over a number of years is larger than many people might think. Suppose that David Skinner, a mechanic, can save $50 a month. In a year, his savings will amount to $600; in 10 years, $6,000. He finds that he can deposit his money in a savings account and receive interest of 6 percent. If he does this, he will have at the end of 10 years, not $6,000, but about $8,200. He will have increased his savings by over $2,200.

As an investor, David realizes the importance of this increase in his savings. He does some more figuring to see how much the increase will be if he saves for a longer period. He finds that by saving $50 a month his savings and interest will be over $14,500 in 15 years. If this amount continues to earn interest at 6 percent, the interest received by the 15th year will be more than $50 a month. This means that he could then start withdrawing $50 each month without decreasing his investment. He would have a permanent income of $50 a month. Often people do not think in terms of 15 years from now. But, as you can see, it does pay to think ahead. Illus. 30-2 shows how the amount of interest received on savings increases over a period of years.

In David's case, the interest he earns will be added to the amount saved. Then the next time interest is calculated, interest will be paid on the amount saved plus the interest earned. When

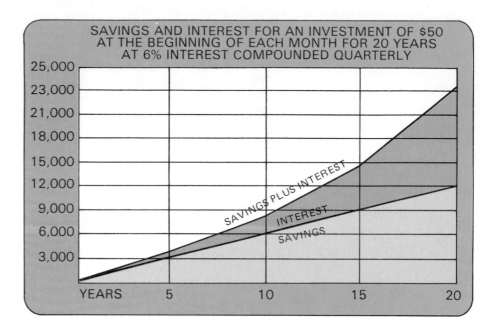

SAVINGS AND INTEREST FOR AN INVESTMENT OF $50 AT THE BEGINNING OF EACH MONTH FOR 20 YEARS AT 6% INTEREST COMPOUNDED QUARTERLY

Illus. 30-2

Money kept in a drawer or in a sugar bowl is not an investment, but it is when deposited in a savings account.

interest is added to the total invested before future interest is calculated, it is called **compound interest**. Interest may be compounded daily, monthly, quarterly, **semiannually** (twice a year), or yearly. Illus. 30-3 shows how rapidly monthly savings of different amounts increase when interest is compounded quarterly at 6 percent.

INVESTING SAVINGS PROMPTLY

You usually do not receive at one time a large amount of money to invest. In fact, you may build up your savings a dollar

Illus. 30-3

This table shows deposits made at the beginning of each month with interest at 6 percent compounded quarterly for a selected number of years.

MONTHLY SAVINGS	END OF FIRST YEAR	END OF SECOND YEAR	END OF THIRD YEAR	END OF FOURTH YEAR	END OF FIFTH YEAR	END OF TENTH YEAR
$ 5.00	$ 61.98	$ 127.76	$ 197.76	$ 271.68	$ 350.32	$ 822.16
10.00	123.95	255.52	395.15	543.35	700.47	1,644.32
25.00	309.89	638.79	987.87	1,358.38	1,751.62	4,110.79
30.00	371.86	766.55	1,185.45	1,630.05	2,101.94	4,932.95
35.00	433.84	894.30	1,383.02	1,901.73	2,452.26	5,755.11
50.00	619.77	1,277.58	1,975.74	2,716.75	3,503.24	8,221.59

or two at a time. You may wait until you have a large sum, perhaps $100, and then invest the whole amount at once. This plan is usually not the best because you earn no interest until the sum is actually invested.

Many financial institutions allow you to invest money in small amounts as you save it. Deposits are accepted whenever you want to make them, and interest is paid at regular periods. Banks, credit unions, and savings and loan associations welcome savings deposits of any size.

INVESTING SAVINGS CAREFULLY

Savings that you invest do increase in amount, but only if you invest them wisely. Suppose that you lend $40 to a friend with the understanding that you will be repaid with 6 percent interest at the end of a year. If the payment is made, you will receive $42.40 at the end of the year. But if the borrower has no money at the end of the year, you may get nothing. You may lose both the $40 loaned and the $2.40 interest. Investments are satisfactory only when the safety of the amount invested and the interest are sure.

Not all investors need the same degree of safety. Suppose that a person has enough money to make 100 different investments. If one of them is lost, the investor still has the other 99; and that one loss may not be very important. On the other hand, suppose that a person has only a small amount of money and is able to make only one investment. One loss would be very serious to that person. A person with limited funds should be very careful to make investments that will be as safe as possible.

THE RATE OF RETURN
MAKES A DIFFERENCE

A good investment should earn a reasonable income. That is, it should have a satisfactory rate of return. The **rate of return** is the percentage at which your savings earn money. The higher the rate of return, the more your savings will earn over a period of time. Illus. 30-4 shows the value of an original investment of $100 in 20 years at several different rates of return.

Usually the higher the rate of return offered by an investment, the greater the risk of loss. Loans to the federal government are safer than any others. If investors lend to individuals or businesses, regardless of the risk involved, they usually do so because they receive higher interest rates than those paid by the government. For example, when the government is paying 5 percent interest, one business may be paying 6 percent and another business may be paying 8 percent.

The offer of a low rate of interest does not guarantee safety, because investors are sometimes mistaken about the risk involved. Similarly, the offer of a high rate of interest does not mean that loss is bound to occur. The high rate does mean, though, that investors believe that the loan involves considerable risk. A borrower with a good credit record would not offer to pay a high rate of interest if a loan could be obtained for less interest.

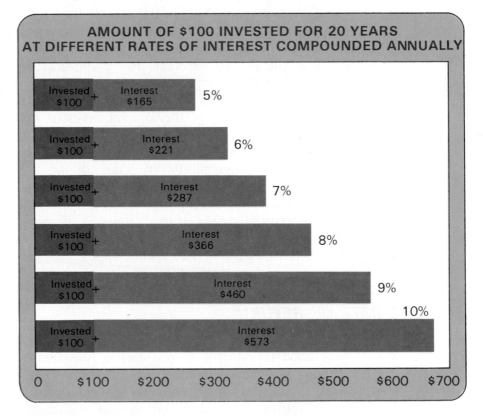

Illus. 30-4

The rate of return on an investment is important. Compound interest causes the amount invested to grow substantially over a period of years. Compound interest accelerates growth.

HAVING SOME LIQUID SAVINGS

When an investment can be turned into money quickly, it is said to be **liquid**. This feature of an investment is important if you may need money quickly to take care of emergencies. Suppose, for example, that you have $1,000 on deposit in a bank. If you need money right away, you can withdraw it from the bank. On the other hand, suppose that you own a piece of land which you bought for $1,000. The land may be a safe investment and may eventually return a satisfactory income; but if you need money at once, you may not be able to get it. You may have trouble selling the land, or you may be able to get only part of the price you paid for it, perhaps $700. In this case, you will lose $300, not because the investment was unsafe but because it could not be quickly turned into money.

A person making a number of investments need not have all the investments in a liquid form. All of the money invested is seldom needed at one time. There should be enough investments in liquid form, however, to get money at once if it is needed.

INVESTMENTS AND THE ECONOMY

No matter how you invest, remember that all such investments serve a very useful economic purpose. Invested money is used to operate businesses, governments, and other organizations. A business, for example, sells bonds or stocks to investors to raise money in order to grow. We as individuals borrow money from banks and other organizations to buy what businesses produce. Keep in mind that the money we borrow is usually someone's invested funds. Without sources for borrowing and investing, the economic system would be greatly hurt. Your investments, then, contribute much to keeping our economic system healthy.

INCREASING YOUR BUSINESS VOCABULARY

The following terms should become part of your business vocabulary. For each numbered statement, find the term that has the same meaning.

compound interest   rate of return
liquid investment   semiannually

1. Interest added to the total invested before the interest is calculated.
2. The percentage at which your savings earn money.
3. An investment which can be turned into money quickly.
4. Twice a year.

1. What are four different ways of saving?
2. When does money saved become an investment?
3. Why is interest that is compounded seminannually better than interest compounded annually?
4. What will be the total savings if $10 is deposited monthly at 6 percent interest compounded quarterly for a period of 10 years? (Use the table on page 374).
5. Suppose that you want to invest $3 a week. Should you wait until the end of a year and invest $156 at that time, or should you invest $3 each week?
6. Is an investment that pays a high rate of interest usually safer than an investment that pays a low rate of interest?
7. Cindy Redmond has $500 in a savings account that is paying her 6% interest. A friend, Rosalind Tate, knows of a project where the $500 could be invested at 8% interest. What might be the advantages and disadvantages for Cindy of taking her money out of savings and putting it in this other investment?
8. Does the offer of a low rate of interest guarantee safety?
9. Tell which of the following investments might be called liquid: (a) land, (b) a deposit in a bank, (c) a loan made to a friend in exchange for an oral promise to pay.
10. What are some advantages of savings and investments for you as an individual? For the economy?

USING YOUR BUSINESS KNOWLEDGE

1. Sandy Malone opened her own beauty shop near the local high school. She put the cash she made each day in a heavy fireproof safe in the back of the shop. Though there was more money in the vault than was needed to run the shop, she believed the money was safe and immediately available if she suddenly needed it. What advice can you give her?
2. Donna Gorski has been saving her money for the last two years since she started working part time in her father's grocery store. The money is kept in a metal candy box in her bedroom. Donna's mother has agreed to give her $10 more for every $100 saved in order to help Donna pay for a new car when she graduates from high school. Is Donna investing as well as saving? Explain.
3. Frank Brokaw, a man of considerable wealth, invests $5,000 in a newly organized manufacturing company. Ella Chapman owns her home and also has $5,000 in a savings account. She knows of Mr. Brokaw's investment. Because Mr. Brokaw has a reputation for being a good businessperson, Ms. Chapman decides to make a similar investment. Is the fact that the

investment may be a good one for Mr. Brokaw sufficient indication that it may be a good one for Ms. Chapman?

4. Jill Young worked hard all summer and earned $2,000. She wants to go to college in three years, so she decides to put $500 of her earnings in a savings account. With the balance, she is thinking of buying a piece of land outside of the city that her father mentioned the other day as being a pretty good investment. What advice would you give to Jill?

5. Freida Reibling wanted to borrow $1,000 from Cliff Mathis. Ms. Reibling offered to pay 10 percent interest although the usual bank rate at that time was 6 percent. Suggest why the higher rate was offered.

SOLVING PROBLEMS IN BUSINESS

1. People save in many different ways. No matter how you save, saving a certain amount — no matter how much — on a regular basis is an excellent practice. Even small amounts build up to large sums in a short time. How much would each person below have saved in just one year if he or she saved the following amounts without interest being added?
   (a) Charles Jasons — 10¢ a day
   (b) Carla Spivak — 75¢ a week
   (c) Alice Farney — $5 every two weeks
   (d) Nolan Robinson — $10 a month

2. Brenda Nolan has an account at a bank that is 5 kilometers from her apartment.
   (a) If it costs her 10¢ per mile to operate her car, how much would it cost her to drive to the bank?
   (b) If on her way home she drove an extra 6 kilometers, how much would her return trip cost?

3. Rhonda Fess lends $500 to Bill Hedges, who is to pay interest of 7 percent a year in return for the use of the money.
   (a) How much interest does Mr. Hedges have to pay Miss Fess each year?
   (b) If the interest is to be paid semiannually at the rate of 7 percent per year, how much would Mr. Hedges pay on each interest date?

4. Yoko Hori deposited in a bank $30 each month for 5 years.
   (a) What is the total amount that she has invested?
   (b) How much do the deposits amount to if they earn 6 percent compounded quarterly? (See the table on page 374.)
   (c) What is the total amount of interest earned?

5. Brian Jordan deposited in a bank $5 a month for 10 years; Karen Griffin, $10 a month for 5 years; and Joe Walters, $35 a month for 1 year. According to the table on page 374:

(a) Which of these three people earned the most interest?

(b) How much more interest did he or she earn than was earned by each of the others?

6. Barbara Maxwell finds that she can save $25 a month.

(a) If she receives no interest on her savings, how much will her savings amount to in 1 year? In 10 years?

(b) If she deposits her money in a savings account and receives an income of 6 percent compounded quarterly (the rate used in the table on page 374), how much will she have at the end of 1 year? At the end of 10 years?

(c) At the end of 10 years, how much of the value of the savings as found in (b) will be made up of interest?

EXPANDING YOUR UNDERSTANDING OF BUSINESS

1. If you deposit money in a savings account with a bank, the bank will protect it and will return it to you when you ask for it. In the meantime, the bank will pay you interest on the amount deposited. (a) Is it fair for you to receive this interest? (b) If so, what service are you providing for which you should be paid?

2. Susan Bella has decided to save $30 monthly from her job and to invest the money in a bank that pays 6 percent interest compounded quarterly. While she does not know how many years she will be saving and investing this money, she would like some idea as to the total amount she will have each year up to five years. Using the table in Illus. 30-3, prepare a rough chart for Ms. Bella much like that shown in Illus. 30-2.

3. Suppose that everyone only saves money and no one buys such things as cars, furniture, household equipment, and new houses. If no one is buying, merchants will not be making sales, factories will not need to produce goods, and many people will lose their jobs as a result. Under these circumstances, do you think that it is a good idea for a person to save part of what is earned, or would it be better if everyone spent it all?

4. Lending institutions now compute interest for many differing time periods. Visit some lending institutions in your area and find out how much interest you could receive if you were to deposit $500 for one year. Find out what rates of interest would be paid and on what time basis they would be compounded. Report back to your class; compare answers that various members of your class receive.

5. Find out from your local banks or savings and loan associations what kinds of investments they have made in your community with the money that has been placed in savings accounts in their institutions.

31 USING A SAVINGS ACCOUNT

PART OBJECTIVES

After studying this part and completing the end-of-part activities, you will be able to:
1. Explain how to open and use a savings account.
2. Describe a certificate of deposit and explain what advantages it has.
3. Name four things you should consider in choosing a place to invest.
4. State the advantages of investing in a savings account.

You can get much satisfaction from saving money. It gives you a feeling of pride knowing that you chose to set aside for future purchases or for other investments part of the money you earn.

Millions of people use savings accounts to help them save. One of the reasons for this is that even small amounts of money can be invested in savings accounts. And small amounts saved regularly grow into important sums.

USING A REGULAR SAVINGS ACCOUNT

A savings account may be opened in a commercial bank, a savings bank, a savings and loan association, or a credit union. The way in which you open a regular savings account is much the same in all of these institutions. You fill out a signature card, make a deposit to your account, and receive a savings account passbook or a savings account register. A passbook, as shown in Illus. 31-1, shows your deposits, withdrawals, interest earned, and the balance of your account. If a register is used, you must record each deposit or withdrawal when it is made. The bank then sends out a statement at the end of each month or quarter. This statement shows deposits and withdrawals, the addition of interest (if any), and the balance of the account.

When you make a deposit, you fill out a deposit slip much like the ones used in making a deposit in a checking account. You present this slip, your passbook, and the money or checks you are depositing to the bank clerk. The clerk then enters the deposit in your passbook. If your bank uses savings account registers or electronic funds transfers, you will be given a receipt for your deposit. You must then enter the deposit on your register.

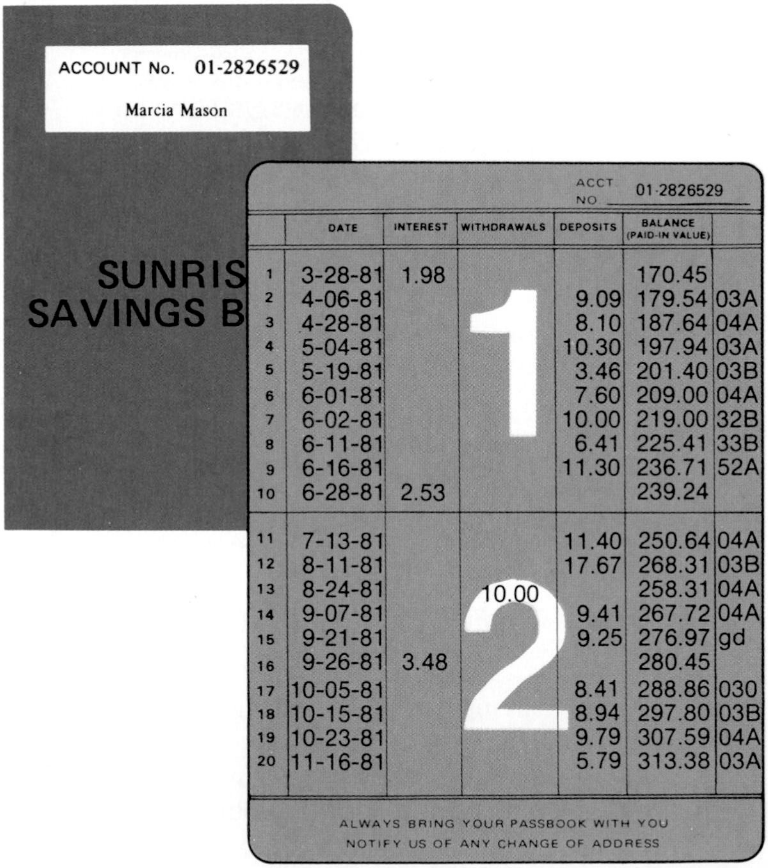

ACCOUNT No. 01-2826529

Marcia Mason

SUNRIS
SAVINGS B

ACCT NO. 01-2826529

	DATE	INTEREST	WITHDRAWALS	DEPOSITS	BALANCE (PAID-IN VALUE)	
1	3-28-81	1.98			170.45	
2	4-06-81			9.09	179.54	03A
3	4-28-81			8.10	187.64	04A
4	5-04-81			10.30	197.94	03A
5	5-19-81			3.46	201.40	03B
6	6-01-81			7.60	209.00	04A
7	6-02-81			10.00	219.00	32B
8	6-11-81			6.41	225.41	33B
9	6-16-81			11.30	236.71	52A
10	6-28-81	2.53			239.24	
11	7-13-81			11.40	250.64	04A
12	8-11-81			17.67	268.31	03B
13	8-24-81		10.00		258.31	04A
14	9-07-81			9.41	267.72	04A
15	9-21-81			9.25	276.97	gd
16	9-26-81	3.48			280.45	
17	10-05-81			8.41	288.86	030
18	10-15-81			8.94	297.80	03B
19	10-23-81			9.79	307.59	04A
20	11-16-81			5.79	313.38	03A

ALWAYS BRING YOUR PASSBOOK WITH YOU
NOTIFY US OF ANY CHANGE OF ADDRESS

Illus. 31-1

A savings account passbook.

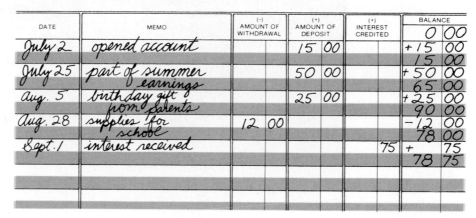

DATE	MEMO	(-) AMOUNT OF WITHDRAWAL	(+) AMOUNT OF DEPOSIT	(+) INTEREST CREDITED	BALANCE
					0 | 00
July 2	opened account		15 | 00		+ 15 | 00
					15 | 00
July 25	part of summer earnings		50 | 00		+ 50 | 00
					65 | 00
aug. 5	birthday gift from parents		25 | 00		+ 25 | 00
					90 | 00
aug. 28	supplies for school	12 | 00			- 12 | 00
					78 | 00
Sept. 1	interest received			75	+ | 75
					78 | 75

Illus. 31-2

A page from a savings account register.

Normally, checks cannot be written against a savings account. If you need money that is on deposit in your savings account, you must fill out a withdrawal slip. A **withdrawal slip** is a written request to take money out of your account. You give the withdrawal slip and your passbook to the bank clerk. Your withdrawal is then recorded in your passbook and your new balance is shown. Usually money cannot be withdrawn from a passbook savings account unless the passbook is presented.

If savings account registers are used, the clerk will check the bank's records to make sure your balance is large enough to cover the withdrawal. After the clerk records the withdrawal on the bank's records, you will be given your money and a duplicate copy of the withdrawal slip for your records. You should record the withdrawal on your register to make certain that your balance is current.

Banking by mail for savings accounts has become very popular over the past few years. Most financial institutions allow you to make deposits and withdrawals by mail as long as the necessary forms are completed. Special bank-by-mail envelopes are usually provided.

SPECIAL SAVINGS ACCOUNTS

Regular savings accounts allow you to deposit small amounts of money and to withdraw your savings whenever you want to. The savings institution pays interest on the invested money. Commercial banks, savings banks, and savings and loan associations usually offer special savings accounts in addition to regular accounts.

Illus. 31-3

At many banks, you can make deposits and withdrawals conveniently at a drive-in window.

Special savings accounts are given different names by different banks, but they all pay a higher rate of interest than do regular accounts. To earn this higher rate, you must accept certain rules. Three common rules are:

1. A fixed minimum, or any amount above that minimum, must be deposited. This amount may be $100, $250, $500, $1,000, or more.
2. The money must be left on deposit for a certain period of time. This period varies from three months to four years or more.
3. If the money is withdrawn before the stated time, much of the interest is lost.

The savings placed in these special accounts may be recorded on forms called **certificates of deposit**. Or they may be recorded in special passbooks that are similar to the passbooks provided for regular accounts.

SAVING IN COMMERCIAL BANKS

Commercial banks, as you read in Part 19, offer more services than other financial institutions. That is why they are sometimes called full-service banks. In addition to regular and special savings accounts, for example, commercial banks provide safe-deposit boxes; sell U.S. savings bonds, traveler's checks, and money orders; offer Christmas and vacation club accounts; and make loans.

One of the most popular services of commercial banks is the

checking account. Generally, checks may not be written on savings accounts. Some banks, however, have plans that allow you to write checks on savings accounts or will pay you interest on money in your checking account. Still other banks are allowing depositors to have funds automatically transferred from a checking account to a savings account or vice versa. As you know, this is true for banks using electronic funds transfer systems.

SAVING IN SAVINGS BANKS

You deal with savings banks in about the same way that you deal with commercial banks. Savings banks operate much like commercial banks in that they offer such services as savings accounts and real estate loans. Savings banks also perform other services such as check cashing, renting safe-deposit boxes, and selling savings-bank life insurance.

The maximum interest rate allowed by law for a savings bank to pay is usually slightly higher than for a commercial bank. Of course not all banks pay the maximum interest rate allowed.

SAVING IN SAVINGS AND LOAN ASSOCIATIONS

Savings and loan associations do not offer as many services as commercial banks. They are, nevertheless, important financial institutions.

As you read in Part 26, they lend money to people for use in building or buying homes. They also assist small investors by handling savings accounts in much the same way that banks do. Many savings and loan associations also offer check-cashing services, rent safe-deposit boxes, and sell traveler's checks and U.S. savings bonds. As with savings banks, the maximum interest rate that savings and loan associations can pay is slightly higher than at commercial banks.

SAVING THROUGH CREDIT UNIONS

A credit union is another kind of financial institution that offers special savings opportunities to its members. As you know, credit unions are organized by specific groups, such as labor unions or the employees of a company, to serve only those groups.

Investing and borrowing are the main services that credit unions offer their members. However, many credit unions are expanding their services so that they now provide members with checking accounts, traveler's checks, and consumer advice.

Credit unions obtain their funds through deposits made by their members. These deposits are often referred to as **ownership shares** because the depositors are actually co-owners of the credit union. Funds collected in this way are available for making loans to credit union members.

The maximum rate of interest that may be paid by credit unions is usually higher than that for regular savings accounts in banks and savings and loan associations. Because depositors are co-owners, the interest paid is properly called a dividend.

Illus. 31-4

Credit unions offer special savings services to their members.

DECIDING WHERE TO INVEST

In which institution should you open a savings account? The answer will depend on your personal needs. The amount of interest that you can earn will be very important. Just as important will be how often the interest is compounded. Other things must also be considered, such as other services you may want, convenient location for making deposits, and hours of operation. Like other investors, you will have to compare financial institutions on rates and services before deciding where to invest your savings.

ADVANTAGES OF INVESTING IN A SAVINGS ACCOUNT

Savings accounts have certain advantages. Here are some:

1. You can find a place to invest in nearly any community.
2. You can make deposits of almost any size, as small as $1.
3. You can withdraw money from a regular savings account easily at any time.
4. The interest or dividends paid are reasonable. You usually earn 6 percent or more on your savings. This is a fair return on an investment with such a high degree of safety.
5. Investments are quite safe since they are usually insured by agencies of the federal government. In banks, each account balance of $100,000 or less is insured through the Federal Deposit Insurance Corporation. The **Federal Savings and Loan Insurance Corporation** insures deposits in savings and loan association accounts up to $100,000. And amounts up to $100,000 are insured in most credit unions by an agency of either the federal or state government.

When you have built up your savings account, you may want to think about investments which offer better opportunities for even greater income. Some of these investments are discussed in Parts 32 and 33. However, even when large sums of money are available to invest, it is considered wise to keep part of your funds in a savings account.

INCREASING YOUR BUSINESS VOCABULARY

The following terms should become part of your business vocabulary. For each numbered statement, find the term that has the same meaning.

certificate of deposit   *ownership shares*
Federal Savings and Loan   *withdrawal slip*
Insurance Corporation

1. An organization that insures accounts in savings and loan associations up to $100,000.

2. A written request for a bank to take money out of a savings account.
3. Deposits made to credit union savings accounts.
4. A special form of savings which requires a large amount of money to be invested and requires that the deposit be left for a certain period of time.

UNDERSTANDING YOUR READING

1. What are the four kinds of financial institutions in which you may open a savings account?
2. What steps would you follow in opening a savings account?
3. How does a depositor withdraw money from a savings account?
4. What are three common rules that a depositor must accept in order to earn a higher rate of interest in a certificate of deposit?
5. How do commercial banks differ from other financial institutions?
6. What are the two main services of savings and loan associations?
7. Why are deposits in credit unions sometimes called ownership shares?
8. What are four things that you should consider in choosing a place to invest?
9. What are five advantages of savings accounts?
10. For how much are account balances insured in most banks and savings and loan associations?

USING YOUR BUSINESS KNOWLEDGE

1. What advantages of savings accounts make them especially good for students?
2. Financial institutions commonly pay a higher interest rate on special savings accounts than they do on regular accounts. Give reasons why they could afford to pay a higher interest rate on special accounts.
3. Give the name of a commercial bank and a savings and loan association in your community. What rate of interest does each pay on regular savings accounts?
4. What are some procedures that you should follow if you receive a savings account register rather than a passbook for your savings account? When should withdrawals and deposits be recorded in your register? How should the monthly or quarterly statements be used?
5. What is wrong with each of the following statements made by students who were discussing investing their savings:

(a) You can only invest in a savings and loan association if you plan to buy a house.

(b) Credit unions are run by labor unions.

(c) All financial institutions are required to pay the same rate of interest.

(d) Banks are the safest place for your money because their accounts are insured by the government.

6. Melody Krider has $6 to invest; her older brother, Harmon, has received a gift of $2,000 which he wants to invest. Why should Melody consider a regular savings account rather than a special account? Why should Harmon consider a special savings account rather than a regular one?

SOLVING PROBLEMS IN BUSINESS

1. Three people had the following amounts deposited in regular savings accounts at different places: Dawn Schweizer, $10,000 in a commercial bank; Margaret Zimmerman, $20,000 in a savings bank; and Steven Nudo, $45,000 in a savings and loan association. Each financial institution has insurance on account balances up to $100,000.

(a) What was the total amount of money invested by all three depositors?

(b) How much would be lost (if anything) by each depositor if all of these savings institutions went bankrupt?

2. Joanne Olson plans to deposit $6 a month in a savings account.

(a) How much will she deposit in the first 6 months?

(b) If she then increases her monthly deposit to $8, how much will she deposit in the next 6 months?

(c) How much will she have deposited in the first 12 months of her savings plan?

3. Maynard Monnat, a retired person, owns an old car that will only start if the outside temperature is 32° Fahrenheit or higher. Since he has to get to the bank to withdraw money from his savings account, he checked his thermometer. But his thermometer, a gift from his grandson, read 5° Celsius.

(a) What is the Fahrenheit temperature?

(b) Should Mr. Monnat try to start his car?

4. Curtis Okura is trying to decide in which of two branch offices of the same bank he should invest his savings. The branches are the same except the distance to each is different. He will deposit his money in the closest branch. Branch A is 3 miles away and Branch B is 4 kilometers away.

(a) How many miles is 4 kilometers?

(b) How many kilometers is 3 miles?

(c) Which branch is closer and by how many kilometers?

5. The table below shows the amount of money in savings deposits in four types of organizations for 1973 and 1978:

	Savings Deposits (in billions of dollars)	
	1973	1978
Commercial banks	$318.4	$505.0
Savings banks	96.3	111.5
Savings and loan associations	227.3	385.3
Credit unions	24.6	53.1

(a) What were the total deposits in all four types of organizations in 1973? in 1978?

(b) Which two organizations had the largest deposits in 1978?

(c) In which type of organization did deposits increase the most in dollars from 1973 to 1978?

(d) What was the percent of increase between 1973 and 1978 in credit unions?

EXPANDING YOUR UNDERSTANDING OF BUSINESS

1. Most savings institutions have a rule that permits them to delay the withdrawal of money from savings accounts if necessary. One bank has the following provision: "While it is extremely unlikely, the bank reserves the right to require depositors to give 30 days written notice of intent to withdraw funds." Why would they have such rules if they are seldom used?

2. The government does not provide insurance that all investments will be successful. For example, it does not provide insurance for investments in land, stocks and bonds, or a small business. Since it does not provide insurance against loss in other investments, why should it set up the Federal Deposit Insurance Corporation and the Federal Savings and Loan Insurance Corporation to insure deposits in banks and in savings and loan associations?

3. A savings bank advertises its services under these headings: Business Services, Special Services, Savings Plans, Checking Accounts, and Loan Services. Under savings plans, it lists: Golden Passbook, Certificates of Deposit, Regular Passbook, Individual Retirement Account, and Statement Savings Account. Each of these savings plans has special features and earns a different rate of interest. Visit one of your community's banks, or get some descriptive literature from them, and make a report to your class on the different kinds of savings plans which they offer. Find out what rules affect each of the plans and what the interest rates are for each plan.

32 INVESTING IN STOCKS AND BONDS

PART OBJECTIVES

After studying this part and completing the end-of-part activities, you will be able to:

1. Tell why organizations sell bonds.
2. Explain how investing in bonds is different from investing in stocks.
3. State what investment services are offered by brokers.
4. Explain how an investment club operates.
5. List the factors that should be considered when deciding whether to invest in stocks.

You learned in Part 31 that the savings account is a popular way to invest money. But there are other ways for you to invest, too, such as buying stocks and bonds. Some people do not consider investing in stocks and bonds because they do not know very much about them. Take Manuel Lopez for example.

Manuel earns $20,000 a year as a computer programmer for an insurance company. He and his wife have $5,000 in a savings account and, of course, plenty of insurance coverage. One of his friends suggested that Manuel put some of his savings in **securities** — another word for stocks and bonds. Manuel, however, is not sure about investing in securities. He has heard about people who have lost money by investing in stocks and bonds.

Manuel is right in being concerned about the safety of investments. If savings are small, they should be invested where they are very safe. They should also be very liquid. But Manuel could increase the earnings on his savings and still have safe investments. After he learns more about stocks and bonds, Manuel will be in a better position to decide whether to invest in securities.

INVESTING IN BONDS

Bonds are sold by the federal government, by local and state governments, and by many corporations. Because there are so many types of bonds, it is helpful to know the answers to two questions: What is a bond? Why are bonds sold?

A **bond** is a printed promise to pay a definite amount of money, with interest, at a specified time. Bonds are therefore similar to the promissory notes discussed in Part 26. Except for Series EE savings bonds, which you will soon learn about, interest is usually paid twice a year. Each bond has printed on its front the amount it promises to pay. This is called its **face value**. Bonds of corporations and local and state governments are normally sold in $1,000 amounts. Government bonds often pay a lower rate of interest than corporation bonds because government bonds are usually safer investments.

Organizations sell bonds when they need to raise large sums of money for some special reason. A corporation may want to build a new office building. A city may want to build a new park. When you buy a bond, you are really lending money to the organization selling the bond and become its creditor. Bonds issued by city and state governments are called **municipal bonds** and have an added advantage for the investor. The advantage is that income tax does not have to be paid on the interest earned. That encourages people to buy municipal bonds even though the interest rate is not as high as that offered on corporate bonds.

FEDERAL SAVINGS BONDS

One of the safest investments in securities, especially for small investors, is to buy savings bonds from the federal government. Series EE savings bonds are the most popular though there are other types of government bonds. Series EE bonds can be purchased for as little as $25 or as much as $5,000.

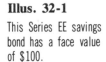

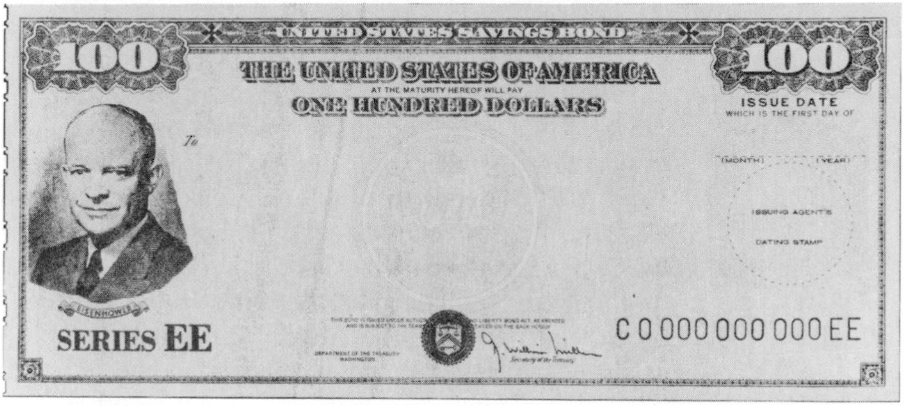

Illus. 32-1

This Series EE savings bond has a face value of $100.

Savings bonds are bought at a lower price than their face value. For example, Series EE bonds are bought at half their face value. A $50 Series EE bond costs $25. When the bond is cashed (redeemed) at the end of the stated period, the government will pay the face value. The difference between the cost ($25) and the face value ($50) is interest earned. A lower rate of interest is earned if these bonds are cashed in before the end of the stated time period. The stated time period for Series EE bonds is 9 years. A Series EE bond held beyond 9 years continues to accumulate interest.

Manuel can purchase Series EE bonds at his local bank. Or he may wish to have an amount deducted by his employer from his paychecks to go toward the purchase of savings bonds. For example, Manuel could have $5 deducted from each week's paycheck. At the end of 5 weeks his employer would use the $25 collected to buy him a $50 bond. This payroll savings plan is a convenient way to invest.

INVESTING IN STOCKS

Investing in stocks is quite different from investing in bonds. When you invest in bonds, you lend money. When you invest in stock, you become a part owner of a firm. As you learned in Part 6, you become a stockholder when you buy one or more shares in a corporation. Ownership is shown by a printed form known as a **stock certificate**. If a business is profitable, part of the profits may be paid to the stockholders in the form of dividends.

The chance to earn a high rate of return is what attracts many people to invest in stocks. But the risk is usually greater with stocks than with bonds. A company must pay bondholders the rate of interest promised before it can pay any dividends. However, it may not make enough money to pay dividends. Or it may make money but decide to keep the money for business expansion and not to offer the stockholders a dividend.

There is no guarantee that a stockholder will get back what was paid for the stock. On the other hand, the value of the stock might increase. The **market value** is the price at which a share of stock can be bought or sold. The market value of the stock of a business which is doing well usually goes up. Market value drops when the record of a business is not good. If a company goes out of business, a stockholder may get little or nothing back from the investment. Bondholders, on the other hand, are more certain of getting back the amount invested plus interest.

TWO MAIN CLASSES OF STOCK

There are two main classes of stock issued by corporations: preferred and common. **Preferred stock** has preference over common stock in the payment of dividends. A preferred stockholder, for example, is paid first if profits from which to pay dividends are available. The dividends paid to preferred stockholders are usually limited to a certain rate, such as 6 percent. Preferred stock may also have a preference on the return of the amount invested if the firm goes out of business.

Common stock has no stated dividend rate. Common stockholders receive dividends only after preferred stockholders are paid their share of any dividends. Yet, if the profits of a company are large, the common stockholders may receive more in dividends than preferred stockholders. For example, suppose there is a company that issues $100,000 worth of common stock and also $100,000 worth of preferred stock that pays a dividend of 6 percent. Also suppose that one year the company makes a profit of $20,000. The preferred stockholders will receive $6,000 ($100,000 × 6%) in dividends. The remainder, or $14,000 ($20,000 − $6,000), will be available for dividends to the common stockholders. If all of the profits are paid out in dividends, the common stockholders will receive a return of 14 percent.

BUYING STOCKS AND BONDS

If Manuel Lopez decides to buy some stocks or bonds, he will probably contact a broker. A **broker** is someone who helps investors buy and sell stocks and bonds. For their services, brokers charge a fee, called a **commission**. Brokers work through **exchanges**, which are places of business that specialize in the buying and selling of securities. While there are several exchanges in the U.S., the two best known are the New York Stock Exchange and the American Stock Exchange. Brokers throughout the nation deal directly with these exchanges by telephone and computer lines.

Illus. 32-2

These brokers are buying and selling stocks over the telephone for their investors.

The prices at which stocks and bonds are bought and sold are continually changing. Through their brokers, stockholders state prices at which they are willing to sell their shares. Interested buyers tell their brokers what they would be willing to pay for shares in the same company. The brokers then work out a price that is acceptable to both. The highest and lowest prices at which stocks sell are listed in the newspaper for every business day, as shown in Illus. 32-3.

Before selecting a stock to purchase, an investor should study the history of the firm. Has the company usually been profitable? Does its management seem to make good decisions? Is the company likely to grow in the coming years? Brokers spend much of their time studying stocks, so they are able to provide helpful information and recommend stocks to purchase.

The current dividend rate in dollars per year.

The hundreds of shares sold during the day.

The highest price in dollars at which a sale was made during the day.

The lowest price at which a sale was made during the day.

The last price at which a sale was made during the day.

The net change between the closing price and the closing price of the preceding day.

Div.	Sales in 100's	Hi	Lo	Clo.	Net Chg.	Div.	Sales in 100's	Hi	Lo	Clo.	Net Chg.
DaytPL 1.74	93	13¼	13	13	-⅛	Getty 1.50e	508	77	74½	74¾	-2¾
Deere 1.80	638	31½	d29⅞	30¾	-⅞	Getty pf1.20	8	13⅝	13¼	13⅝	+⅜
DelmP 1.48	141	11¼	10⅝	10⅝	-⅛	GiantPC	25	5¾	d5⅝	5⅝	-¼
DeltaA 1.20	268	35⅜	34¼	34¼	-1⅛	GibrFn .60	110	7¾	7½	7½	-¼
Deltec	1	7⅛	7⅛	7⅛	-⅛	GidLew 1	78	26⅜	24⅝	24¾	-1½
Deltona	87	10⅞	10	10	-1	GiffHill .92	41	13	12½	12½	-½
DenMfg 1.16	19	16⅛	16½	16⅛	+¼	Gillette 1.72	544	20⅛	d19⅜	19⅞	-⅛
Dennys .88	57	12¼	12	12¼	....	Ginosinc .44	27	9½	9¼	9¼	-⅛
Dentsply .88	75	15⅜	14¾	15	-⅝	GleasW .80	32	17¾	17½	17½	-¼
DeSoto 1	24	11⅝	11½	11½	-¼	GlobMar .20	236	45¼	43	43	-2⅝
DetEd 1.60	486	11½	11⅜	11¼	-⅛	GldWFn .54	119	13¼	12¾	12¾	-⅛
DetE pf9.32	z300	65½	64	64	-½	Gdrich 1.56	88	18⅛	17½	17¾	-⅛
DetE pf7.68	z10	51½	51½	51½	....	Goodyr 1.30	649	11⅜	11¼	11⅜	....
DE pfF 2.75	13	19¾	19⅜	19⅜	....	GordJw .72	69	21¼	20	20	-1½
DE pfB 2.75	3	19¼	19¼	19⅜	....	Gould 1.72	253	22¼	22	22⅛	....
DetE pr2.28	6	15⅜	15⅜	15⅜	-¼	Grace 2.05	1294	35	34¼	34¼	-1⅛
Dexter 1	126	23¼	22¾	22¾	-½	Graingr .92	77	30¼	30	30	....
DiGior .56	150	9⅛	8¼	8¼	-¾	Granitvl 1	10	10¾	10¼	10¾	-⅛
DiGior pf2.25	1	19½	19½	19½	-½	GrayDr .80	26	9½	9¼	9¼	-⅛
DialCp 1.20	36	14¾	14⅛	14⅜	....	GtAtPc	64	5⅞	5¾	5¾	-⅛

Illus. 32-3

Quotations for a few of the stocks listed on the New York Stock Exchange.

INVESTING IN STOCKS WITH A GROUP

Another way for Manuel Lopez to invest regularly would be to join others in forming an investment club. An **investment club** is a small group organized to invest money for its members. An agreement is usually prepared stating how often the club will meet and how much the members will put into the club each month to be invested. At the meetings, members report on stocks they have studied and make decisions on what stocks to buy. The club's earnings are shared in proportion to the members' investments. Most brokers will help groups form investment clubs.

One advantage of an investment club to Manuel is that it encourages regular savings. Another advantage is that he would learn a great deal about how to judge a stock. Manuel will also be spreading his risk because the combined funds of all members are used to buy stocks in a number of corporations. If the club lost money on one investment, the loss might be offset by other investments that do quite well.

Illus. 32-4

Members of investment clubs like this one meet to decide which stocks to buy with the club's funds.

INVESTING IN MUTUAL FUNDS

Manuel may not wish to select stocks on his own or to join an investment club. Often people do not have the time needed to study stock choices carefully. A good understanding about stocks is needed to purchase wisely. A mutual fund may be an excellent way to buy securities while taking some of the worry and problems out of investing.

A **mutual fund**, also known as an **investment company**, is a corporation that sells its own stock to the public and buys stocks and bonds of other corporations. It receives interest and dividends from its investments. From these amounts it first pays its operating expenses. The amount that is left is distributed as dividends to its stockholders.

An investor may choose a mutual fund because of the kinds of securities it buys. Some mutual fund companies invest in bonds, preferred stocks, and common stocks (balanced funds). Some buy only the common stock of young, fast-growing companies (growth funds). Some companies invest only in securities that pay good dividends and interest (income funds). A few investment companies invest in bonds only. There are hundreds of funds available. It should not be difficult for Manuel to find a fund that will meet his needs.

DECIDING WHETHER
TO BUY STOCKS

The decision to buy stocks should be made carefully. It would be possible for Manuel Lopez to increase his savings quite a bit if he made the right stock purchases. But Manuel could also lose all or most of what he invests in stocks. That is a risk he must be willing to take.

One important guide in the decision to buy stocks is whether you can afford to lose part or all of your investment. If you have to sell your stock quickly, it could sell for much less than what you paid for it. Before investing in stocks you should have adequate savings in a safe place, such as in a savings account or in bonds. You should have sufficient insurance coverage, too. You should not need the money invested in stocks to meet basic living expenses.

HELPING YOURSELF
THROUGH WISE INVESTING

Before investing, ask yourself which of these factors are most important to your personal investment plan: safety, liquidity, or rate of return? From your answer, an investment goal can be determined. As shown in Illus. 32-5, no one investment can give you the highest possible return and still be very liquid and safe.

If you have little savings, for example, you will want a very safe and liquid investment, such as a savings account. Most of your funds should be safe and liquid. Bonds could be part of your investment plan. If your savings are more than adequate for your basic needs, then investing in stocks where a higher rate of return is possible could be your investment goal.

Illus. 32-5

Five common investments can be compared roughly as to safety, liquidity, and rate of return. At any time, ratings might change slightly based on economic conditions.

WHICH INVESTMENT?	HOW SAFE?	HOW LIQUID?	HOW IS RATE OF RETURN?
Savings accounts	Excellent	Excellent	Fair
Savings bonds	Excellent	Very good	Fair
Other bonds	Very good	Good	Good
Preferred stocks	Fair to good	Good	Very good
Common stocks	Fair	Good	Poor to excellent

INCREASING YOUR BUSINESS VOCABULARY

The following terms should become part of your business vocabulary. For each numbered statement, find the term that has the same meaning.

bond
broker
commission
common stock
exchange
face value
investment club

market value
municipal bonds
mutual fund or *investment company*
preferred stock
securities
stock certificate

1. A printed form that shows ownership in a corporation.
2. A specialist in buying and selling securities.
3. Bonds issued by city and state governments.
4. Another name for stocks and bonds.
5. A printed promise to pay a definite amount of money, with interest, at a specified time.
6. Stock that has preference in payment of dividends and in return of the investment.
7. A fee paid to a broker for services in buying and selling securities.
8. A corporation that sells its own stock to the public and buys stocks and bonds of other corporations.
9. The price at which a share of stock can be bought and sold.
10. Stock that has no stated dividend rate but shares in the profits of a firm.
11. A small group organized to study stocks and invest members' money.
12. A special place of business where stocks and bonds are bought and sold.
13. The amount printed on the front of a bond.

UNDERSTANDING YOUR READING

1. Why do businesses and other organizations sell bonds?
2. How much does a $50 Series EE bond cost? What is the difference between the purchase price and the face value called?
3. What are two ways in which you might buy Series EE bonds?
4. In what ways is investing in bonds different from investing in stocks?
5. When might common stock pay more dividends than preferred stock?
6. What are some of the services that a broker offers persons who are interested in buying stocks?

7. Who selects the stocks that are purchased through an investment club?
8. What are the advantages of a mutual fund?
9. What are some important points to consider when deciding whether to purchase stocks?

USING YOUR BUSINESS KNOWLEDGE

1. Explain how bonds are similar to promissory notes.
2. Why does the government pay a higher rate of interest on Series EE bonds held for their full time than if cashed in earlier?
3. Why do municipal bonds usually pay a lower rate of interest than corporation bonds?
4. Company A wants to borrow $1,000. Company B wants to borrow $10,000. Company C wants to borrow $1,000,000. Which business is most likely to issue bonds? Why?
5. Why do people buy stocks even though they are not as safe as savings accounts or bonds?
6. Why might a broker be interested in helping a group of people form an investment club?
7. One mutual fund is advertised as a growth fund. Another is advertised as an income fund. What would you expect to be the difference in the investment practices of the two funds?
8. Sally Thompson put $75 in gold mining stock a few years ago. Last week she received a letter saying that the company went out of business. It could not find a gold mine. How much of her investment might Miss Thompson lose?
9. Kurt Iverson wants to invest in stocks that will be very safe, highly liquid, and earn an excellent income. What is wrong with his investment plans and goals?
10. On January 1, Tina Smith purchased one share of stock for $107 plus a broker's commission of $7. At the end of the year the stock's market value was $114. Has Tina earned an income on her investment, at least on paper?

SOLVING PROBLEMS IN BUSINESS

1. Mary Kozak bought the following Series EE bonds: two $50 bonds, and one $100 bond.
   (a) How much will the bonds be worth when the stated time period is reached?
   (b) How much did she pay for the three bonds?
   (c) How much interest will she have earned when the stated time period is reached?
2. Stanley Dickson owns five Morgan Enterprises bonds, each with

a face value of $1,000. Morgan Enterprises pays 8 percent interest on the bonds it has issued.

(a) How much interest does Stanley receive each year on each bond?

(b) What is the total amount of interest Stanley receives each year?

(c) If the interest payments are made semiannually to each bondholder, how much interest does Stanley receive every 6 months?

3. At the stock exchange, the Speedy Auto Corporation closed at 9½. The next day it opened at 10¼ and then closed at 11.

(a) How much was the "net change"?

(b) By what percent did the stock increase in value between the close of the first and the close of the second day?

4. You are trying to decide whether to invest in gold mining stock of a foreign company. The only information you have is the table below. The table shows the weight in kilograms of the gold mined during the last five months.

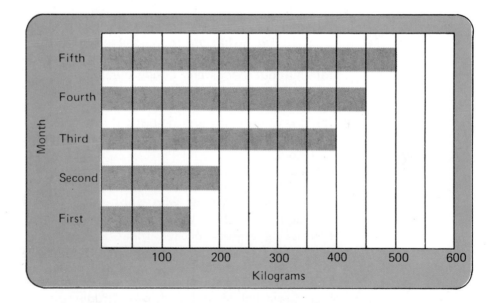

(a) How many kilograms of gold were mined each month?

(b) How many pounds of gold were mined in the first month? the third month?

(c) By about how many pounds did the amount of mined gold increase between the fourth and fifth months?

5. The table below shows the price paid and the annual dividend on six different stocks:

	Price Paid	Annual Dividend
Consolidated Engineering	$48	$2.40
Electro-Jet Company	50	3.00
Federated Industries	30	1.60
Instrumentation, Inc.	30	1.30
Magus Corporation	38	1.90
Seaboard Steel	65	2.60

What is the rate of return on each of these stocks?

EXPANDING YOUR UNDERSTANDING OF BUSINESS

1. Federal government savings bonds at one time paid interest of less than 3 percent a year on bonds held to maturity. Later the rate was increased several times. Why do you think the interest rate was increased?
2. Within a few weeks the market price of a stock dropped from $110 to $85. What are the possible causes for such a drop?
3. Check the library to find what each of the following pairs of terms about stocks and bonds means:
   (a) registered bond and coupon bond
   (b) callable bond and convertible bond
   (c) par value stock and no-par value stock
   (d) cumulative preferred stock and noncumulative preferred stock
   (e) load fund and no-load fund
4. The National Association of Investment Clubs can be of great assistance to persons who want to form an investment club. Through research in your library, by writing to the NAIC, or by contacting a stock broker, make a report on the specific aids available for persons interested in organizing an investment club.
5. The financial or business section of many daily newspapers includes a list of mutual funds. Study such a list; then answer these questions:
   (a) Which fund has the highest price per share? The lowest?
   (b) What is the difference in meanings between the headings "bid" and "asked"? (Check the library for your answer.)

33 INVESTING IN REAL ESTATE

PART OBJECTIVES

After studying this part and completing the end-of-part activities, you will be able to:
1. Tell why renting is sometimes better than buying a house.
2. Explain how owning a mobile home is similar to owning a house.
3. Describe at least three costs, other than the purchase price, of owning a house.
4. Give an example of how real estate is purchased as an investment by an individual or group.
5. Explain how real estate brokers, appraisers, and lawyers can be helpful when you are buying real estate.

Besides the many types of investments discussed earlier, there is another that concerns most people — real estate. **Real estate** is land and anything that is attached to it. To most people, real estate means a house, mobile home, apartment, or some other building. In one way or another, we are all users, buyers, or sellers of real estate. Real estate is usually the most expensive investment that people make.

Since nearly two out of three families own real estate, it is very likely that you, too, will someday own real estate. And, because real estate is so important, it will be helpful for you to understand as much about it as possible.

You can learn about real estate through the experiences of others. When Jim and Janet Brumfield were first married, one of their problems was meeting their housing needs. Buying a house was out of the question because of the cost. They decided to rent an apartment as their first real estate transaction.

RENTING A PLACE TO LIVE

There were several advantages that Jim and Janet considered when they decided to rent. One advantage that a family has when it rents is that they are free to move at almost any time. They may want to move because of a change in the family's size or because of a change in job location.

A family that rents is also freed of much of the work of keeping a house in good repair. In addition to the work involved, renters are not burdened with the costs of maintaining a house.

Renting also makes it easier to keep money available for immediate use. When a family puts all of its savings in a house, it may not have enough money to meet emergencies or to pay bills during times when family income is low. Those who buy a house need some savings in addition to the amount they pay for the house.

OWNING A MOBILE HOME

During the first few years of married life, Jim was getting valuable experience as a mechanic. Janet worked as a computer operator. They saved as much of their incomes as possible. Jim changed jobs several times to get experience, so renting was ideal. Then they both got good jobs working for a big corporation. They were ready to settle down but could still not afford a house. So they used part of their savings, borrowed some money, and bought a mobile home.

To the Brumfields, the biggest advantage of the mobile home was owning a place of their own. There were other advantages. The mobile home was less expensive than a house, so their monthly payments were smaller. They could still save much of their incomes. The Brumfields planned to use their savings, plus the money they would get from selling the mobile home, to buy a house someday. Mobile homes are also easier and less expensive to maintain than houses. Many Americans have bought mobile homes for the same reasons as the Brumfields.

OWNING A HOUSE

After saving their money for a number of years, the Brumfields believed they were ready to buy a house. They now had two children and needed more space.

The advantages of owning a house are similar to those of owning a mobile home. The owners have pride of ownership. Also, they can remodel or improve as they like. Owning a home gives people a feeling of security, too. When a family owns a house, it usually plans to stay there without moving frequently.

An important advantage of owning your own house is that you build up equity. **Equity** is the difference between what your house is worth and what you owe on your mortgage. For instance, after Jim and Janet lived in their house for five years, the balance of their mortgage was $27,500. By that time their house, which had cost them $45,000, was worth $50,000. Their equity, then, was the difference between $50,000 and $27,500, or $22,500. The amount of increase in value of property is known as **appreciation**. Appreciation and equity are important factors when considering the purchase of a house as an investment.

COSTS OF OWNING A HOUSE

The actual cost of buying and owning real estate includes more than just the purchase price. The most important yearly costs are taxes, insurance, upkeep, and interest. The Brumfields, like other homeowners, had to take care of the following costs while owning their house:

1. **Taxes.** Local property taxes are one of the certain costs of home ownership. Taxes are not the same in all

Illus. 33-1

Buying a house is the most important investment many families make. This couple is selecting the style of house they want to buy.

communities, and they tend to increase from year to year. On the average, they are about 2 percent of the value of the property.

The tax rate is not based on the actual value of the property, but rather on its **assessed value**. This is the amount which the property is determined to be worth for tax purposes. The assessed value is often quite a bit less than the actual market value of the property. For example, if a house can be sold for $60,000, its assessed value may be only $30,000.

The property tax rate is stated as so many dollars per $1,000 of assessed value. If the tax rate is $40 per $1,000 of assessed value, the annual taxes on property assessed at $30,000 would be $1,200. This is 4 percent of the assessed but only 2 percent of the $60,000 actual value of the property in the example.

Before you buy a house, you should find out from local government officials what is or will be the assessed value of the property. You should also learn about the tax rate and the amount of taxes actually paid in previous years. This will tell you about how much you must allow in your budget to cover the cost of taxes.

2. **Insurance.** The cost of insurance is usually much less than the cost of taxes, but it is still an important expense of home ownership. The cost of insurance is affected by the value of the house, the material from which it is made, how near it is to other buildings, and the availability of fire protection. The annual cost of insurance is about ½ of 1 percent of the value of the house, or $5 for each $1,000 of value.

3. **Upkeep.** Homeowners find that keeping their property in good condition brings frequent expenses. These annual **upkeep** costs average about 2 percent of the value of the house. The costs do not necessarily occur every year. Many repairs and replacements can be put off so that for a year or two it seems that the costs of upkeep are small. But if repairs are delayed too long, the house will fall into poor condition and the cost of bringing it into good repair will increase.

4. **Interest.** When a family buys a house, it usually borrows part of the money. The amount borrowed often is quite large, and the house is used as security for the loan. In

that case the lender receives a **mortgage**. A mortgage is a legal paper giving the lender a claim against the house in case the principal, the interest, or both are not paid as agreed. The borrower usually agrees to make a payment every month over the life of the mortgage. The amount of the monthly payment varies according to the amount of the mortgage and how quickly it is to be paid. The monthly payment includes repayment of part of the principal plus interest. Some mortgages also include payments to cover property taxes and insurance.

When the Brumfields bought their house at a cost of $45,000, they paid $15,000 down and borrowed $30,000 for 20 years at an interest rate of 12 percent. The monthly payment to the bank was $330.33, determined from the table shown in Illus. 33-2. A payment table of this kind is usually used by lenders to determine the monthly rate on mortgages.

Illus. 33-2

A partial schedule of monthly payments for various amounts borrowed at 12 percent interest. For example, if you borrowed $20,000 for 25 years, the monthly payments would be $210.65.

MONTHLY HOUSE PAYMENTS AT 12% INTEREST				
AMOUNT BORROWED	5 YEARS	10 YEARS	20 YEARS	25 YEARS
$ 5,000	$ 111.23	$ 71.74	$ 55.06	$ 52.57
10,000	222.45	143.48	110.11	105.33
20,000	444.90	286.95	220.22	210.65
30,000	667.34	443.42	330.33	315.97
40,000	889.78	573.89	440.44	421.29
50,000	1,112.23	717.36	550.55	526.62

CONDOMINIUM LIVING

After living in their home for nearly 30 years, Jim and Janet Brumfield found that their housing needs had changed again. Both children were married and had moved away. There was much more space than Jim and Janet needed. And caring for the house was not as easy as it was when they were younger. So they sold their house. They received much more than they had paid for it, so the Brumfields believed their investment had been a good one.

They considered renting an apartment again. But owning a place of their own was still important to them. They decided against another mobile home because they did not want the responsibility of caring for the yard. So they bought a condominium. A **condominium** is an individually owned unit of an apartment-like building or complex.

Condominiums give people the advantages of home ownership without some of the difficulties. Upkeep of the lawns and shrubbery is usually done by others in return for a service fee. And condominiums are sometimes less costly than houses.

OTHER REAL ESTATE INVESTMENTS

There are many types of real estate investments. Buying a home to live in is only one type. Some people buy two-family houses and live in one half while renting the other. The rented half helps to pay for the property. The homeowner, of course, then has additional duties in caring for the rented half. Real estate investors may also buy an apartment building and hire someone to run it. Still other investors buy land and then hope to sell it when the market value goes up.

Some people join with others to form a group to purchase real estate as an investment. They combine the money each member of the group has available for investing. Then they purchase apartment buildings or shopping centers or other buildings. The money they receive from rents and the increases in the value of the properties held make this kind of investment attractive to some investors.

GETTING HELP WITH REAL ESTATE TRANSACTIONS

Whatever type of real estate investment you make, buying and selling are complicated. Because most people buy only a few homes during their lives, they are not likely to be experts in such matters. As a result, it is a good idea to hire specialists to help you avoid problems.

Many real estate buyers work with realtors. A **realtor** is an expert in buying and selling real estate. Realtors receive special training and are licensed to do business. Land, houses, apartments, condominiums, and other properties are listed for sale with realtors. Realtors can help buyers compare the different real estate investment opportunities that are available. The realtor helps work out a purchase price that is acceptable to both the

Illus. 33-3

When buying a new home, many families use the services of a realtor.

buyer and the seller. The realtor may also help a buyer get a mortgage.

Before signing any papers and before deciding on how much to pay for a house, you should get an appraiser's report. An **appraiser** is an expert who estimates the value of property. The appraiser will also report on the quality of construction and identify repairs that may be needed. An appraiser who finds a major defect may prevent you from paying more than a house is worth. The lending company also has the property appraised. But this estimate is made after you agree to buy the property at a given price.

To prevent legal problems, hire a lawyer. One is needed during all the stages of buying. For instance, when you are buying real estate you should be certain that you are obtaining a good title to the property. In other words, get a lawyer's opinion that you are obtaining complete and clear ownership of the property. Even though the seller does own the property, there may be claims against it for which the new owner will be responsible. If there are unpaid taxes on the property, these taxes are a claim against the property itself. If they are not paid, the property may be taken and sold so that the government may collect the taxes. A lawyer can help you avoid these and other legal problems.

INCREASING YOUR BUSINESS VOCABULARY

The following terms should become part of your business vocabulary. For each numbered statement, find the term that has the same meaning.

appraiser	*mortgage*
appreciation	*real estate*
assessed value	*realtor*
condominium	*upkeep*
equity	

1. Land and anything attached to it.
2. An expert in buying and selling real estate.
3. An individually owned unit of an apartment-like building or complex.
4. The amount of increase in the value of property.
5. Keeping property in good condition.
6. An expert in estimating the value of property.
7. The difference between what your house is worth and what you owe on your mortgage.
8. The amount which property is determined to be worth for tax purposes.
9. A legal paper giving the lender a claim against property if the principal, interest, or both are not paid as agreed.

UNDERSTANDING YOUR READING

1. What are some advantages of owning a house and some advantages of renting an apartment?
2. What advantages are similar in owning a mobile home and owning a house?
3. What items, in addition to the original cost, are included in the cost of owning a house?
4. On the average, the annual cost of taxes is about what percent of the market value of the property?
5. What should you find out from local governments about taxes on property you are considering buying?
6. What factors help determine the amount charged for insurance on a house?
7. What percent of the market value of a house do the annual costs for upkeep average?
8. Will a monthly payment be larger or smaller if the house is paid off in five years rather than ten? Refer to Illus. 33-2 for your answer.
9. What are some ways of investing in real estate other than buying a house or condominium in which you will live?
10. In what ways are the services of a realtor, an appraiser, and a lawyer important in a real estate buying transaction?

USING YOUR BUSINESS KNOWLEDGE

1. Blair West owns a house which has a value of $40,000. For the past three years, the upkeep has averaged less than $200 a year. Can Mr. West assume that $200 is a fair estimate of the annual expense for upkeep?
2. Why is a condominium often desirable for retired people?
3. What can you do to help assure the increase in value of a home you purchase?

4. Robin Greer has decided to purchase a house. She also decided to take care of all the details herself and save some money by not having to pay a realtor, an appraiser, or a lawyer. Why might Robin find that her decision is not a good one?

SOLVING PROBLEMS IN BUSINESS

1. The Brocks own a house valued at $60,000 and they have a balance on their mortgage of $40,000. Last year they had the following expenses:

Interest on mortgage	$4,000
Upkeep	600
Insurance	300
Taxes	1,200

What was the total of their expenses for last year?

2. Don Smith invests $15,000 in a group that is buying some apartments as an investment. At the end of the first year, he receives earnings of 10 percent.
   (a) What is the amount that he receives the first year?
   (b) If he receives the same amount for the next 6 years, what is the total he will receive?

3. Jan Jaworski is about to paint the walls and ceiling of one of the rooms of her house. One gallon of paint is needed for every 500 square feet. Disregarding doors and windows, the room measures as follows:

   Each of two walls measures 2.4 meters high and 6 meters wide.
   Each of the two other walls measures 2.4 meters high and 4.8 meters wide.
   The ceiling measures 4.8 meters by 6 meters.

   (a) What are the dimensions of the room in feet? (Figure your answers to the nearest whole foot.)
   (b) How many gallons of paint are needed? (Figure your answer to the nearest gallon.)

4. Billie Fields has been renting an apartment for 3 years and pays $250 per month for rent. She has an opportunity to buy a house which will require her to pay $320 per month as a mortgage payment.
   (a) In one year, how much more will she have to pay for house payments compared to the rent she now pays?
   (b) During the first year, 90 percent of her payment will be for interest and 10 percent will be for principal repayment. What will be the amount she pays for interest for the year? For principal repayment for the year?

EXPANDING YOUR UNDERSTANDING OF BUSINESS

1. The Perez family is renting an apartment for $330 a month. Mr. Perez read in the newspaper that the tax rate on real estate for the coming year will be increased by 40¢ per $100. Since Mr. Perez is a renter and pays no real estate taxes, will this increase in the tax rate make any difference to him?

2. Cooperatives are places to live that are somewhat like condominiums. Through research in your library, find out what cooperatives are and how they are like and unlike condominiums. Make a report of your findings.

3. Visit a local realtor's office or invite a realtor to come to speak to your class. Find out what you can about the changing values of real estate in your community. Also find out about some of the problems that people are having today with the purchase of houses and condominiums.

4. Call or visit a bank or savings and loan association. Ask for information about getting a mortgage on a home costing $50,000. Get answers to these questions and make a report to your class:

    (a) What is the minimum down payment needed?

    (b) What is the average interest rate for a mortgage?

    (c) What is the monthly payment on a 25-year loan at the current interest rate if the minimum down payment is made?

    (d) If you decide to pay off the loan early, will there be a financial penalty?

5. Title insurance is recommended to most home buyers. Either from your library research or from a talk with a lawyer, find out what title insurance is and why a homeowner needs it. Also find out how much title insurance costs for an average home in your community.

CAREER FOCUS

You are already familiar with many of the career opportunities in saving and investing. These jobs exist in banks, credit unions, savings and loan associations, real estate firms, and securities brokerage houses. For those interested in helping others save and invest their money, there are thousands of jobs available. Some of the careers were mentioned in the Career Focus on banking on pages 310 to 312. Some other careers you might want to consider are presented here.

WORKERS IN SAVING
AND INVESTING

As you know, workers in the trust departments of banks manage the investments and other assets that customers have placed in the banks' care. But banks, credit unions, and savings and loan associations also invest their own funds. Investment experts are needed to make their investments. These experts study the investments available and choose the ones that will best accomplish the goals of the financial institution for which they work.

Over 90,000 people are involved in selling stocks and bonds. These securities salesworkers are employed by brokerage firms, mutual funds, and insurance companies. Some of these sellers work for the stock exchanges that are located in major cities, such as the New York Stock Exchange. It is their duty to aid buyers and sellers from all over the nation in completing stock purchases and sales. Of course, if you wanted to buy or sell stocks or bonds, you would not go to a stock exchange. Instead, you would go to a brokerage firm. There you would find many professional investors ready to serve you. You would probably talk with a stock broker. That person would want to know what your investment goals are. The broker might then suggest some possible investments for you.

More than 450,000 people are employed full-time as either real estate brokers or salesworkers. Many others work as part-time brokers and agents. Many of these experts specialize in commercial real estate. If you are interested in investing money in real estate, they can help you find the kind of property that will serve your needs. If you think you might like to own an apartment building, a retail store location, or even a warehouse, a real estate broker can help you.

Many large private businesses and government agencies also have investment specialists on their staffs. If a firm decides it wants to sell stock to raise some money, its investment experts will judge how much stock they can sell and how it can be sold. Often they will work with investment bankers who specialize in raising large sums of money for businesses by selling stocks and bonds. Even if a business is not planning to sell any more stocks or bonds, it will usually have investment specialists to see that dividends are paid to stockholders and that interest is paid to bondholders. These investment experts are also responsible for investing the funds of the business that will not be needed until sometime in the future. The investors may buy stocks or bonds of other businesses or they may buy government securities.

EDUCATION AND TRAINING FOR SAVING AND INVESTING

You can see that workers in saving and investing have great responsibilities. Employers need persons who are entirely honest because they deal with other people's money. They must have a natural liking for math. To be successful working in the investment field, you should have a pleasant personality, be neat in appearance, get along well with others, and have enthusiasm for your job.

Some beginning positions in saving and investing require only a high school education. But this must be only a starting point. For example, there are some selling positions where an individual with a high school education could start. However, to advance and to be truly successful, additional education and training are necessary. College training is preferred by many employers and will probably prepare you for jobs in this field in the fastest way. One way to get college training is to go to school part-time while working in the field and gaining valuable practical experience.

Courses that will be most helpful are accounting, finance, advanced mathematics, business law, investments, public speaking, and economics. You should also know that many positions in the investment field require that the specialists pass a formal examination in the field and be licensed by the state in which they work.

LOOKING AT THE FUTURE IN SAVING AND INVESTING

Future employment prospects look very bright for saving and investing workers. For example, in real estate, the need for brokers and salesworkers is expected to increase because of our growing population. In the securities investment field, more workers will be needed because people's incomes are rising and they have an increased amount of money to invest. If our population continues to increase and incomes rise, there will be many careers available for those who are interested in saving and investing.

UNIT 9

Protecting Yourself With Insurance

HOW INSURANCE WORKS

PART OBJECTIVES

After studying this part and completing the end-of-part activities, you will be able to:

1. Tell how insurance provides protection against economic loss.
2. Name at least four kinds of insurance that are important to most people.
3. Name two things which affect the cost of insurance.

When you get ready to buy your first car, it will probably take you a long time to save the money for the purchase price. In fact, it is quite likely that you will need to borrow part of the money. That means you will have to make monthly car payments. Think about how you would feel if on the day after you made your last payment you had an accident that totally destroyed your car. All the work you did to earn the money and all the sacrifices you made to save to buy the car would be wasted.

Or suppose some night while you are at a movie a thief breaks in, steals your possessions, and sets fire to your home. You could be left without food, clothes, or a place to live. Or consider what would happen if after getting your first full-time job you have an accident while skiing and break your leg so badly that you cannot work for three months. How would you support yourself?

Unfortunate events like these do happen to people all the time. Hopefully they won't happen to you, but you cannot be certain that you won't experience at least some of them. While you may not be able to avoid such tragedies, you can protect yourself against the economic losses that they may cause.

SHARING ECONOMIC LOSSES

All these risks of loss of property or earning power are called **economic risks**. That is, when any one of them happens, it will cost someone money to repair the damage or solve the problem.

Illus. 34-1

The damage caused by a flood is one type of economic risk. This homeowner is reporting the damage done to her property during a recent flood.

No matter how careful you are, you cannot completely remove the risks that may cause financial loss. You can, however, avoid a large financial loss all at once by sharing the loss with other people. Suppose you and 49 other people form an organization called the Broken Arm Insurance Club. The purpose of the club is not to protect its members against broken arms but to protect them against the large economic loss of paying the medical bills resulting from broken arms. In order to provide that protection, each member agrees to share the medical cost of a broken arm for any of its members. So, if you break your arm and the total of the medical bills is $500, each member, including you, will chip in $10 to pay the bill.

Illus. 34-2

This is how an advertisement for the Broken Arm Insurance Club might appear.

You can easily see that if you are not a club member you will have to pay the whole $500 medical bill. But if you are a member, your broken arm will cost you only $10. Under the Broken Arm Insurance Club plan whenever a member breaks an arm, each member suffers only a small economic loss. In that way the members help one another by sharing the risk of economic loss.

USING INSURANCE TO SHARE LOSSES

It would not be practical to handle all loss sharing as the Broken Arm Insurance Club did. There are too many kinds of risks and too many people to be protected. Loss protection must be carefully planned. **Insurance** is the name for planned protection provided by sharing economic losses. The companies that provide this protection service are called **insurance companies**.

An insurance company, like the Broken Arm Insurance Club, agrees to take on a certain economic risk for you and to pay you if and when a loss occurs. The person for whom the risk is assumed is known as the **insured** or the **policyholder**. To show that risk has been assumed, the company gives the insured a policy. A **policy** is a contract stating the conditions that the insurance company and the policyholder have agreed to. For example, the policyholder may agree not to keep gasoline in the house, not to allow an unlicensed person to drive the insured car, or not to go skydiving.

In return for taking on a risk, the insurance company requires that the policyholder pay a certain amount of money. The insured may make payments once a month, once every six months, once every year, or sometimes even less often. The amount that the policyholder must pay is called a **premium**. The premiums from all the policyholders make up the funds from which the company pays for losses.

KINDS OF INSURANCE

You can buy insurance against almost every economic risk if you are willing to pay the premiums for it. Organizers of a county fair, for example, can buy insurance against rain. Singers can insure their voices, and professional baseball players can insure themselves against injuries on the diamond. The kinds of insurance that will be important to most people, however, are insurance for automobiles and homes, life insurance, health insurance, and insurance for income security.

Policyholders should know exactly what protection is provided by the kinds of insurance they have. Some people have failed to tell their insurance companies about losses for which they should have been paid just because they did not know their policies covered those losses. Other people have assumed that losses they suffered were covered by their insurance, only to find out by reading their policies that the losses were not covered.

DETERMINING INSURANCE COSTS

Claims are the requests of policyholders for payment for losses. An insurance company must collect enough money in

Illus. 34-3

Business owners as well as individuals need the protection of insurance against loss.

premiums to pay its claims, to pay its operating expenses, and to make a profit. The premium for each policy is determined partly by the experience of insurance companies in paying for losses of the kind covered in that policy. For example, it is more likely that a 20-year-old driver will have an auto accident than it is for a 40-year-old driver. Therefore, the car insurance premiums for 20-year-old drivers are higher than they are for older drivers. In general, the greater the risk insured and the more claims the company has to pay, the higher will be the premiums.

The money that an insurance company keeps to pay for losses that may occur in the future is invested. The earnings from these investments make it possible to provide insurance at lower cost. Premium rates charged by insurance companies are reviewed by a state **insurance commission**. This is a state agency which acts to assure that insurance premium rates and practices are fair.

Insured people also play an important part in determining how much insurance will cost. They can reduce property losses by being careful in everything they do. Locking doors and driving defensively, for example, will help to reduce losses associated with thefts and accidents. Practicing good health habits will reduce life and health insurance claims. On the other hand, if losses paid by insurance companies increase because of policyholders' carelessness or poor health habits, premiums will usually increase.

Everyone benefits if the losses covered by insurance are decreased. Assume that fewer losses are caused by fire and that fire insurance premiums are reduced. If your family owns a house and has fire insurance on it, you gain directly because you pay lower premiums. If a business owner pays lower premiums, expenses will be less and prices on goods may be less. Anything that you can do to reduce losses covered by insurance helps you and the entire community.

BUYING INSURANCE

Individuals can buy some kinds of insurance through their employers, but most people buy insurance through an **insurance agent**. The insurance agent works for an insurance company or for an independent agency which sells many kinds of policies from a number of different companies. You can learn a lot about insurance by reading about it, but it is hard for anyone to know about all the types that are available. The best thing to do is to choose an agent who can explain the various policies to you.

INSURANCE FOR EVERYONE

Insurance is important to everyone because it provides economic security. If you had no insurance, you could probably take care of small losses such as those resulting from minor accidents. However, a large loss from a fire or serious illness could be a real financial hardship. Protection against major hazards gives everyone a feeling of security.

Insurance is also important because it helps our economy. Insurance makes it possible for many people and businesses to do things they otherwise could not consider. Suppose that someday you want to buy an $80,000 home but can make only a $10,000 down payment. You will need to borrow $70,000. It is very doubtful that anyone will lend you this amount at a reasonable rate unless the house is insured. Money to buy a new car can't be borrowed at a reasonable rate unless the car is insured against such risks as theft and collisions.

You have learned that part of the money collected in premiums is invested. Many insurance companies, mainly life insurance companies, use premiums to make loans. The loans are used to build government and private business projects which help our economy grow.

Insurance companies also perform educational services by conducting campaigns on safety, health, and accident prevention. They conduct these activities to help reduce losses and premiums.

INCREASING YOUR BUSINESS VOCABULARY

The following terms should become part of your business vocabulary. For each numbered statement, find the term that has the same meaning.

claim
economic risk
insurance
insurance agent
insurance commission
insurance companies
insured or policyholder
policy
premium

1. A person who sells insurance.
2. The amount that a policyholder must pay.
3. A request for payment due to loss.
4. The planned protection provided by sharing economic losses.
5. A contract between one who buys insurance and the company which provides it.
6. Businesses that make insurance available to others.
7. The person for whom risk is assumed by an insurance company.
8. A state agency which acts to assure that insurance premium rates and practices are fair.
9. The chance of losing the financial value of something.

UNDERSTANDING YOUR READING

1. What are some types of economic risks that people face each day?
2. How does insurance provide protection against financial losses?
3. What are some unusual kinds of economic loss against which people may be insured?
4. Name at least four kinds of insurance that are important to most people.
5. What uses does an insurance company make of the premiums it collects?
6. What is the purpose of the state insurance commission?
7. Give some examples of how people benefit from fewer insurance claims.
8. How can insured people play a part in determining how much insurance will cost?
9. How does insurance provide economic security?

USING YOUR
BUSINESS
KNOWLEDGE

1. Willie Jones and Dorothy Sanchez are discussing insurance. Willie feels that one should have insurance to cover small as well as large financial losses. Dorothy feels that most people can handle small losses. She favors insuring against the risk of large losses. Whose opinion do you agree with? Give your reasons.

2. The residents of a subdivision of 100 homes decide that they can save money by providing their own fire insurance. Since the houses in the area are of about the same value, each owner agrees to contribute $500. The money is to be placed in a savings account in a bank. When a homeowner suffers a fire loss, the loss would be paid out of this account. Do you think this is a wise plan? Why or why not?

3. Why do you think an insurance company would be willing to spend large amounts of money on health and safety education?

SOLVING
PROBLEMS
IN BUSINESS

1. May Barclay's auto insurance company believes it can reduce its premiums by an average of 10 percent. This reduction is possible because of lowered speed limits with fewer and less costly accident settlements. Miss Barclay's last annual premium was $300.
   (a) How much will she save if the proposed premium reduction is put into effect?
   (b) What will be the amount of her new premium payment?

2. The Franklin family pays the following insurance premiums every year: first life insurance policy, $200; second life insurance policy, $230; insurance on house and household goods, $120; automobile insurance, $225.
   (a) What is the total cost of the insurance premiums?
   (b) If the Franklin family keeps a monthly budget, how much should the monthly allowance for insurance be?

3. In a recent year the residents of a small town held the following numbers of insurance policies:

Life insurance	1,240
Health insurance	1,280
Automobile insurance	1,434
Property insurance	1,358
Other	188

   (a) What was the total number of policies in effect?
   (b) What percent of the total number of policies were automobile policies?

4. Charley Wendel's home is 2 kilometers from a fire station. Maria Corey's is 8 kilometers from the station. If fire trucks average 40 kilometers per hour, including starting time, how long would it take a fire truck to reach each of the two homes in case of a fire? How much longer would it take to reach Maria's home than Charley's?

5. In a recent year, one city had 950 fires. The number of fires for which the causes were known is shown below:

Cause	Number
Electrical	220
Heating and cooking equipment	188
Smoking and matches	176
Deliberate	156
Children and matches	180

(a) For how many of the fires were the causes known?
(b) For what percent of all fires were the causes known?
(c) What percent of the known-cause fires was accounted for by each cause?

EXPANDING
YOUR
UNDERSTANDING
OF
BUSINESS

1. It has been said that some people are "insurance poor." That means that they are insured against so many possible economic losses that paying all of the premiums is a financial hardship for them. How do you think the condition of being "insurance poor" might develop?

2. Some states carry no insurance on state-owned buildings. Why do you think they do this? What would they do in the case of a loss?

3. In a recent year, 32 percent of all drivers were under 30 years of age. However, police reports showed that 50 percent of all accidents involved drivers in this age group. What effect might these facts have on insurance rates for people under 30?

4. Examine two or three issues of your local newspaper. Look for news items reporting injury to people or damage to property. Think about the types of mishaps reported and the cost of injury or damage. Which of the situations may have been covered by insurance? Prepare a short report on your findings.

5. Contact a representative of the insurance commission of your state. Report on its purpose and the types of activities in which it is involved. Find out whether it investigates complaints from policyholders.

35 INSURING VEHICLES

PART OBJECTIVES

After studying this part and completing the end-of-part activities, you will be able to:
1. Identify the two types of financial losses for which vehicle insurance provides protection.
2. List the six basic coverages provided by auto insurance.
3. List the factors which determine the cost of vehicle insurance.
4. Explain what no-fault insurance is.

Driving and owning a car or other vehicle is usually a pleasure, but it is also a risky activity. Each year there are more than 25 million auto accidents in the United States. Close to 50,000 people die and 5 million are injured in these accidents. Of special interest to you is the fact that more than 35 percent of the drivers involved in accidents are under age 25.

Financial losses resulting from traffic accidents have risen steadily and now amount to more than $50 billion annually. The costs of treating injured people and repairing damaged property can easily bring financial ruin to the people who must pay. Court action is costly, and awards to injured people and to owners of damaged property have increased tremendously. The purpose of vehicle insurance is to provide protection from the financial risks involved in owning and driving a car or other vehicle.

FINANCIAL RESPONSIBILITY LAWS

All states have **financial responsibility laws**. These laws provide that if you cause an accident and cannot pay for the damages either through insurance or through your savings or by selling property you own, your driver's license will be suspended or taken away. These laws do not state that you must have insurance, but they do make you legally liable (responsible) for any damage you do to people or their property.

COMPULSORY INSURANCE LAWS

Several states have gone one step further than passage of financial responsibility laws and have adopted laws requiring you to carry certain types of automobile insurance before your car can be licensed. In those states that have a **compulsory insurance regulation**, you may not register a car or obtain a license to drive without presenting proof of having the minimum amounts of insurance coverage required.

PROTECTION PROVIDED BY AUTOMOBILE INSURANCE

Insurance protection for both you and your car is available through an automobile insurance policy. You can buy insurance to protect your car from almost everything that could happen to it except wearing out. More important, however, you can buy insurance to protect yourself against financial loss if you injure someone else or damage someone else's property in an automobile accident. This protection is referred to as **liability insurance**.

Sometimes an accident is unavoidable; that is, no one can be directly blamed for it. In most cases, however, someone is at fault. The person who is found to be at fault is responsible for damages which result from the accident. Although you may think you are completely innocent, you can be sued. If you are insured, your insurance company will provide legal defense for the suit. If the court decides that you are legally liable for injuries and damage to property, your insurance company will pay the costs up to the limits stated in your insurance policy.

The kinds of protection that are available through automobile insurance are explained in the following paragraphs. These coverages are available in different combinations and for different

Illus. 35-1

Unless you are protected by auto insurance, injuries and damages from an accident can result in serious financial loss.

amounts. Although some of the coverages can be bought separately, many car owners prefer a package policy which includes most or all of the coverages.

TYPES OF AUTOMOBILE INSURANCE

There are six basic automobile insurance coverages to protect you against risk. Three are classified as bodily injury insurance: (1) bodily injury liability, (2) medical payments, and (3) protection against uninsured motorists. The other three are called property damage insurance: (1) property damage liability, (2) collision, and (3) comprehensive physical damage. The protection available with each type of coverage is explained in the following paragraphs.

BODILY INJURY LIABILITY INSURANCE

Bodily injury liability insurance protects you from claims resulting from injuries or deaths for which you are found to be at fault. This kind of insurance covers people in other cars, guests riding with you, and pedestrians. It does not cover you or, in most cases, your immediate family.

Dollar amounts of bodily injury coverage are generally expressed as 10/20, 25/50, 100/300, and so on. The first number refers to the limit, in thousands of dollars, that the insurance company will pay for injuries to any one person in an accident. The second number is the maximum, in thousands of dollars, that will be paid for all the injuries resulting from any one accident.

For example, if you had bodily injury coverage of 10/20 and had an accident for which you were found at fault, the insurance company would pay a maximum of $10,000 if just one person were injured. If more than one person were injured in the accident, the insurance company would pay a maximum of $20,000 no matter how many persons were injured.

Although the minimum liability coverage that state financial responsibility laws require is usually 10/20, car owners should consider carrying much larger amounts. It is not unusual for juries to award an injured person $50,000 or more. If this happened to you and you only had 10/20 coverage, your insurance company would pay the $10,000 limit and you would have to pay the rest.

MEDICAL PAYMENTS INSURANCE

Most car owners who have bodily injury liability insurance also purchase medical expense protection for themselves and their families by buying **medical payments insurance**. This coverage applies to the policyholder and family members if they are injured when riding in the car or in someone else's car, or if they are walking and are hit by a car. Guests riding in the insured car are also protected.

With medical payments insurance, the insurance company agrees to pay the costs of medical, dental, ambulance, hospital, nursing, and funeral services. Payment, up to the limit stated in the policy, is made regardless of who is at fault in the accident. Medical payments coverage is available in the minimum amount of $500 for each person. For rather small additional costs, the coverage may be increased.

UNINSURED MOTORISTS PROTECTION

Sometimes injuries are caused by hit-and-run drivers or by drivers who have no insurance and no money to pay claims. Therefore, insurance companies make available a coverage called **uninsured motorists protection**. This coverage is available only to those people who carry bodily injury liability insurance. In addition to covering the policyholder and family members, it also covers guests riding in the policyholder's car.

The dollar amount of coverage provided by uninsured motorists protection is limited to the liability that state financial responsibility laws require — usually 10/20. Unlike medical payments coverage, which pays regardless of who is at fault in the accident, uninsured motorists protection covers the insured person only if the uninsured motorist is at fault.

PROPERTY DAMAGE LIABILITY INSURANCE

Property damage liability insurance protects you if your car damages someone else's property and you are at fault. The damaged property is usually another car, but it may also be such property as telephone poles, fire hydrants, and buildings. Property damage liability insurance does not cover damage to the insured person's car.

Car owners often buy property damage insurance to provide at least $5,000 worth of protection in any one accident. Additional coverage may be bought for little extra cost.

COLLISION INSURANCE

Collision insurance pays for damages to your car caused by a collision with an object or by turning over. It does not cover injuries to people or damage to the property of others. Most collision coverage is written with a $100 or $200 **deductible clause**. This means that the car owner agrees to pay the first $100 or $200 of damage to his or her car in any one collision, and the insurance company agrees to pay the rest. Larger deductible amounts are available at a substantial saving to the policyholder.

Collision coverage does not provide for payment of damages greater than the car's value. Suppose your car receives $1,000 in

Illus. 35-2

If your car is damaged in a collision, an insurance claims representative may examine it to determine the extent of damage.

damages in a collision with another vehicle. If your car has a value of only $500, the collision coverage would pay $500, not $1,000. Collision coverage should not be carried on cars that are of little value.

COMPREHENSIVE PHYSICAL DAMAGE INSURANCE

Even if you do not have an accident with another vehicle, your car can still be damaged or destroyed. The car could be stolen or damaged by fire, tornado, windstorm, vandalism, or falling objects. **Comprehensive physical damage insurance** protects you against all losses except those caused by a collision or turning over.

If your car is totally destroyed or stolen, the amount paid to you is not necessarily equal to the cost of the car. Rather, it is equal to the car's estimated value at the time of the loss. Suppose your car costing $5,000 is stolen soon after you buy it. The insurance company will probably pay you almost as much as the car cost, perhaps $4,700. However, if the car is stolen two years after you buy it, the insurance company may pay you only $3,000. The car has grown older, and its value has decreased.

A SUMMARY CHART OF AUTOMOBILE INSURANCE COVERAGES

TYPES OF COVERAGE	COVERAGE ON	
Bodily Injury Coverages	Policyholder	Others
Bodily Injury Liability......................................	NO	YES
Medical Payments	YES	YES
Protection Against Uninsured Motorists	YES	YES
Property Damage Coverages	Policyholder's Automobile	Property of Others
Property Damage Liability	NO	YES
Comprehensive Physical Damage.....................	YES	NO
Collision..	YES	NO
Source: Insurance Information Institute		

Illus. 35-3

A summary of automobile insurance coverages.

COST OF AUTO INSURANCE

The cost of automobile insurance is not the same for everyone. Some of the factors that an insurance company considers in determining the cost of your coverage are:

1. Your age and other characteristics.
2. The purpose for which your car is used.
3. The value and type of car.
4. The community in which you live.
5. Types of coverage and deductibles.

Since some drivers are more likely to have accidents than others, they must pay higher rates. To determine the rates, drivers are classified according to age, sex, marital status, driving record, and scholastic achievement. The lowest rates are reserved for the best risks. The cost of insurance is usually higher when one of the drivers in the insured's family is under 30 than it is if all family drivers are over 30. The extra amount charged for young drivers may be decreased if they have completed approved driver education courses. Also, in most states companies offer young people who have good scholastic records a good student discount. The discount may amount to as much as 25 percent of the premium. When you buy insurance, you should check several companies to see what discounts they give.

The purpose for which a car is driven and the miles it is driven in a year are also important in determining insurance rates. Cars used for business purposes are generally driven more miles in a year than are cars driven for pleasure and so are more likely to be involved in an accident. Insurance companies often give you a reduced rate if you drive your car fewer than 20 miles a day to work or use it only for short pleasure trips.

The value of your car naturally has an important effect on the cost of insurance. Premiums for collision coverage and comprehensive physical damage coverage must be higher for a car worth $3,500 than for a car worth only $1,000. The insurance company runs the risk of paying out much more to the insured if the $3,500 car is destroyed or stolen. The type of car also affects the rate. If you have a high-performance car or an expensive sports car, you may have to pay higher rates.

Basic rates for automobile insurance are not the same throughout the country. The rates vary from state to state and from city to city within a state. Auto insurance rates are affected by the population in a particular area, the number of cars, whether it is a rural or urban area, and the number of accidents that occur over a certain period of time in the area. Insurance companies gather statistics on the dollar amount of claims paid for an area and base their insurance rates on this information.

The cost of your auto insurance will also vary according to the types of coverages you have and the amounts of the deductibles you choose. Naturally, the more coverages you carry the higher will be the cost. And, as you will recall, the larger the deductibles you have the more you will save on your premiums.

SUGGESTIONS FOR BUYING AUTOMOBILE INSURANCE

1. Decide on the types and amounts of coverage you need.
2. Check with several reputable insurers, keeping in mind that the least expensive coverage is not necessarily the best for you. Consider also such things as the company's reliability and its reputation for service including claims handling. If you're in doubt about a company, check with your state insurance department.
3. Consider the savings in premiums available through the purchase of a higher deductible — you may find it pays in the long run to take care of small losses yourself.
4. Check with your agent regarding your eligibility for premium discounts for:
   - safe driving.
   - graduates of recognized driver education courses.
   - good students.
   - students attending school over 100 miles from where the family car is garaged.
   - drivers over 65.
   - low annual mileage.
   - farmers.
   - multi-car families with all cars insured on the same policy.
   - car pools.
5. Consider special coverages or higher policy limits if you frequently drive other commuters to work or groups of children to school or special events.
6. Consider dropping collision coverage as cars get older.

Source: Insurance Information Institute

Illus. 35-4

Suggestions for buying automobile insurance.

INSURANCE FOR MOTORCYCLES AND OTHER VEHICLES

Insurance on motorcycles, motorbikes, and snowmobiles is similar in some respects to automobile insurance. For example, bodily injury liability, property damage, collision, and comprehensive physical damage insurance are the most important coverages on these vehicles. The engine size in cubic centimeters and value of the vehicle are the important factors in determining the cost of insurance. Generally, the larger the vehicle, the higher the insurance cost.

Insurance can also be obtained on other types of recreational vehicles. These include dune buggies, campers, antique cars, and modified cars. Special insurance can be obtained, at extra cost, on racing vehicles such as stock cars.

NO-FAULT INSURANCE

A major reason for the long and costly accident court cases is proving who is at fault, that is, who is legally to blame for the accident. The average settlement time in a serious injury case is about 16 months. Some cases, however, take as long as 5 years. Meanwhile, injured persons or their families may have very heavy medical expenses and loss of pay because of time off the job.

In an attempt to speed up the payment of claims and reduce the hardship of long delays, **no-fault insurance** is being adopted by a growing number of states. Under this plan, people injured in auto accidents can collect for their financial losses — such as their medical bills, loss of wages, and other related expenses — from their own insurance companies no matter who is at fault.

Let's look at an example. Bob Watson, who is insured with Autosurance Company, and Phil Spagnola, who is insured with All-Nation Company, are injured in a serious two-car accident. Watson would collect from Autosurance, and Spagnola's claims would be paid by All-Nation. It would not be necessary to decide whether Watson or Spagnola caused the accident.

No-fault laws vary in some ways from state to state. Ordinarily the right to sue is kept for the more serious injury cases and for death.

INCREASING YOUR BUSINESS VOCABULARY

The following terms should become part of your business vocabulary. For each numbered statement, find the term that has the same meaning.

bodily injury liability insurance
collision insurance
comprehensive physical damage
  insurance
compulsory insurance regulations
deductible clause
financial responsibility laws

liability insurance
medical payments insurance
no-fault insurance
property damage liability
  insurance
uninsured motorists protection

1. Insurance coverage which pays for damages to the insured's car caused by collision or by turning over.
2. Insurance coverage which provides medical expense protection for the policyholder, immediate family members, and guests while in the insured person's car.
3. A plan in which people injured in auto accidents can collect for their financial losses from their own insurance companies no matter who is at fault.
4. A clause in an insurance contract that says the car owner agrees to pay the first $100 or $200 of damage to his or her car and the insurance company will pay the rest.
5. Laws providing that if you cause an accident and cannot pay for the damages through insurance or through your savings or property, your driver's license will be suspended or taken away.
6. Laws that say you may not register a car or obtain a license to drive without presenting proof of having the minimum amounts of insurance coverage.
7. Insurance coverage which protects the policyholder against losses resulting from injuries caused by a hit-and-run driver or by a driver who has no insurance or no money to pay claims.
8. Insurance coverage which provides protection against claims if your car damages someone else's property and you are at fault.
9. The general term used to describe insurance you buy to protect yourself against financial loss if you injure someone else or damage someone else's property in an automobile accident.
10. Insurance that protects you from claims resulting from injuries or deaths for which you are found to be at fault.
11. Insurance coverage which pays for damages to your car caused by events other than a collision or by turning over.

UNDERSTANDING YOUR READING

1. Do financial responsibility laws make automobile insurance compulsory? What can happen to an uninsured motorist who is found to be at fault in an accident and does not have enough money to pay for the damages?
2. What are the two types of financial losses for which vehicle insurance provides protection?
3. What are the six basic coverages provided by auto insurance?
4. Who is covered by bodily injury liability insurance?
5. What does 100/300 mean in terms of bodily injury liability coverage?
6. If a driver carries medical payments coverage, in which of the following situations will benefits be paid?
   (a) A passenger in the driver's car is injured.

    (b) The driver is injured in an accident.

    (c) The insured person is crossing the street and is injured by a passing car.

7. Under what circumstances does uninsured motorists protection pay losses?

8. What type of property is covered by property damage liability coverage?

9. What kind of protection is provided by collision insurance?

10. What factors determine the cost of insurance coverage?

11. Some automobile insurance companies give premium discounts to certain drivers. List two types of such discounts.

12. What is no-fault insurance?

USING YOUR BUSINESS KNOWLEDGE

1. Which type of automobile insurance coverage would Tom Hood need in order to be covered in the following situations?

    (a) Tom, in an attempt to avoid hitting a dog in the street, ran into a parked car.

    (b) Tom's daughter, who was riding in the back seat, was injured when he ran into the parked car.

    (c) During a storm, a heavy tree branch damaged Tom's car, breaking the windshield and denting the hood.

    (d) Tom was found to be at fault in an accident in which a pedestrian was injured.

2. Carey Lindquist was the driver at fault in an accident in which her three passengers were badly hurt. The court awarded two of the injured people $15,000 and it awarded the third person $20,000. Carey had bodily injury liability coverage in the amount of 20/40. Was this enough insurance to protect her from financial loss? Why or why not?

3. John Bronsky is a traveling salesperson and usually drives his $7,000 car over 500 kilometers per week. His twin sister, Eve, drives a $3,500 economy car and seldom goes farther than the local shopping center. Who probably pays higher insurance rates? Why?

4. Jerry Johnson ran through a stop sign and hit another car, injuring both the other driver and himself. Both cars were badly damaged. Jerry had no car insurance and no money to pay for the damages and medical expenses. What types of insurance would have paid the other driver's expenses of the accident?

5. Kay Silverstein purchased a new car five years ago. She has always carried collision insurance. Now the car's value has decreased to the point where it is worth very little. Kay feels

that it would be wise to drop the collision insurance. Do you agree that she should? Why or why not?

6. Phil Sanborn is involved in a three-car accident which injures many people. How would claims be settled in a state with no-fault insurance? What would happen in a state without no-fault?

1. Paul Antonio purchased his car new six years ago for $3,500. The present value of the car is $800. This is the figure Paul uses in deciding on insurance coverage.
   (a) By how much did Paul's car decrease in value over the six-year period?
   (b) On the average, how much did the car's value decrease each year?

2. When Nancy Thompson drove 60 kilometers round-trip to work each day, her auto insurance premium was $200 a year. Nancy changed jobs and now drives 28 kilometers round-trip. Her insurance company gives a 10 percent premium discount to policyholders who drive less than 32 kilometers round-trip to work each day.
   (a) How much will she save per year?
   (b) How much is Nancy's present premium?

3. In a recent month, an insurance company reported receiving the following numbers of claims for losses:

       65 bodily injury liability
       40 medical payments
       10 uninsured motorists protection
       80 property damage liability
      120 collision
       85 comprehensive physical damage

   (a) What was the total number of claims made to this company?
   (b) If the total amount the company paid out to satisfy the claims was $160,000, what was the average settlement per claim?

4. Audrey Hadley is a college student. She took driver training in high school. She also earned an overall scholastic average of A in her college work. These things qualify her for a driver-training discount of 20 percent of the premium and a good-student discount of 15 percent of the premium for her auto insurance. If the standard premium for her policy is $240 per year, how much will Audrey pay for her auto insurance this year? How much will she save?

5. Peter Borsch lost control of the car he was driving and ran into a small dairy and ice cream bar. In addition to $1,000 damage to the building itself, the owner presented a claim for the following losses:

> display window glass, 3 meters by 4 meters
> 150 liters of milk
> 200 liters of ice cream
> 100 kilograms of butter

The cost of the materials included in the claim were:

> window glass, $5.20 per square meter
> milk, 35¢ per liter
> ice cream, 70¢ per liter
> butter, $1.45 per kilogram

(a) What was the total amount of the dairy owner's claim?
(b) What type of insurance coverage would Peter need to pay for this claim?

EXPANDING YOUR UNDERSTANDING OF BUSINESS

1. Does your state have a no-fault insurance law? If so, what are its provisions? If your state does not have such a law but is considering it, report on the plan being considered.
2. Summarize the provisions of the financial responsibility law in your state. Does your state have a compulsory insurance regulation?
3. Choose an insurance agent to find out what should be done about insurance coverage if:
   (a) You sell your car and buy a new one.
   (b) You sell your car four months before your policy expires and you do not plan on getting another car.
   (c) Conditions of driving change, such as use of the car, number of drivers of the car, or a move to another location.
4. Ricardo and Norman had an accident in which one person was slightly injured. Although there appeared to be great damage to the two cars, Ricardo suggested that they give each other their license numbers and driver's license information, and then leave. Norman felt that they should call the police and wait for an officer to come. Whose position do you agree with? Check with your local police and report to the class on what to do at the scene of the accident. Check with an insurance agent to find out what the procedure is in reporting the accident to your insurance company.

LIFE INSURANCE

PART OBJECTIVES

After studying this part and completing the end-of-part activities, you will be able to:
1. Explain the main reason why people buy life insurance.
2. Describe how you obtain life insurance.
3. Identify the three major types of life insurance.

Maria and Roberto Garcia are the parents of a young family. They have insurance on their car in case of an accident. Also, their home is insured should it catch on fire. However, the Garcias do not have protection against a risk of financial loss even greater than their car and home. They have no insurance on the two wage earners.

Maria earns $1,000 a month while Roberto earns $1,100. If either of them were to die, how could the family keep up the payments on their home, pay fuel bills, buy food and clothing, and meet other expenses? The loss of either salary would cause the family great financial hardship. The Garcias want to protect their family from such a loss through life insurance. Life insurance would provide the money needed to meet the family's living expenses.

In planning their life insurance program, Maria and Roberto need to answer many questions, such as the following: How can they get life insurance? What type of life insurance should they buy to best meet their financial responsibilities?

OBTAINING AN INSURANCE POLICY

To obtain life insurance, you usually apply for a policy through an insurance agent. Normally you will be required to take a physical examination so that your state of health can be determined. Assuming that you have no serious health problems, you then pay a premium to get your life insurance policy. If you are in poor health or work in a dangerous occupation, you may be considered a poor risk. For example, if you drive racing cars to earn a living, you are in a dangerous occupation. Even if you are in poor health or work in a dangerous job, you may be able to obtain insurance, but you will have to pay higher premiums than other people who are in good health and in ordinary kinds of work.

RECEIVING INSURANCE BENEFITS

When you buy life insurance, you will be asked to name a beneficiary. A **beneficiary** is the person named in the policy to receive the insurance benefits.

You may insure not only your own life but also the life of any other person in whom you have an **insurable interest**. To have an insurable interest in the life of another person, you must receive some kind of financial benefit from that person's continued life. You have, for example, an insurable interest in the lives of your parents. You do not have an insurable interest in a stranger's life. A partner in a business has an insurable interest in the life of his or her partner. The insurable interest must exist at the time the policy is started, but generally it need not exist at the time of loss.

DIFFERENT POLICIES
FOR DIFFERENT NEEDS

People have many different life insurance needs. A recent high school graduate would not have the same life insurance needs as someone who is getting ready to retire. A young single person has insurance needs that are different from those of a married person with small children. To provide for the different types of protection that are needed, insurance companies offer a variety of policies. But the three basic types of life insurance are term insurance, whole life insurance, and endowment life insurance.

Illus. 36-1

With the help of an insurance agent, customers can choose a policy that best meets their needs.

TERM LIFE INSURANCE

Term insurance provides protection against loss of life for a definite period, or term, of time. It is the least expensive form of life insurance. Policies may run for a period of one year, five years, ten years, twenty years, or more. If the insured dies during the period for which the insurance was taken, the amount of the policy is paid to the beneficiary. If the insured does not die during the period for which the policy was taken, the insurance company is not required to pay anything. Protection ends when the term of years expires.

By paying a slightly higher premium, a person can buy term insurance that is renewable or convertible or both. If the policy is **renewable**, the policyholder can continue it for one or more terms without taking a physical examination to determine whether she or he is still a good risk physically. If the policy is **convertible**, the insured can have it changed into some kind of permanent insurance without taking a physical examination.

Term insurance policies may be level term, increasing term, or decreasing term. With **level term insurance**, the amount of protection remains the same during the time the insurance is in effect. With **increasing term insurance**, the premiums remain the same but the amount of insurance gets larger each year. With

decreasing term insurance, premiums remain the same during the term but the amount of protection gradually becomes smaller.

An example of decreasing term insurance is **mortgage insurance**. It protects homeowners from losing their homes in case the insured person dies before the mortgage is paid off. Suppose the Campbell family bought a $40,000 house on which they paid down $10,000 and took a 30-year mortgage for the remaining $30,000. The Campbells want to be sure that the mortgage will be paid off if one of them should die, so they buy a $30,000 mortgage insurance policy. The amount of coverage decreases as the Campbells repay what they have borrowed, so the coverage corresponds to the balance of the debt.

WHOLE LIFE INSURANCE

Whole life insurance is permanent insurance that extends over the lifetime of the insured. One type of whole life insurance is called **straight life insurance**. Premiums for straight life insurance remain the same as long as the policyholder lives. Some whole life insurance policies are intended to be paid up in a certain number of years and are called **limited-payment policies**. They may also be designated by the number of years the insured agrees to pay on them, such as 20-payment life policies. They are like straight life policies except that premiums are paid for a limited number of years — 20 or 30, for example — or until a person reaches a certain age — say, 60 or 65. Limited-payment policies free the insured from paying premiums during retirement when his or her income may be small.

ENDOWMENT LIFE INSURANCE

Endowment life insurance is really a savings plan which also gives insurance protection. An endowment policy may provide a fund of money for the insured at the end of a certain period, such as 10 or 20 years, or at a certain age, such as 60 or 65. If the insured dies before the end of the endowment period, the face value of the policy is paid to the beneficiary.

Assume that Jan Tefler wants to make sure that money will be available to send each of her children to college. When each child is born, she takes out a $10,000 endowment policy on her own life. Each policy is to mature in 17 years and will be payable to Jan if she is living at the end of the 17-year period. If she dies before that time, it will become an educational fund for the child. In either case, the face value of the policy — $10,000 — will be available for the child's education.

CASH VALUES

As long as they are kept in force, whole life policies and endowment policies accumulate a cash surrender or loan value or, simply, **cash value**. The longer you keep your policy, the higher its cash value will be. If you give up or surrender your policy, you are paid the amount of the cash value. If you need money but do not wish to cancel your policy, you can borrow from the insurance company an amount up to the cash value. If you should die before the loan can be repaid, the amount yet unpaid will be deducted from the face value of the policy.

COMBINING POLICIES TO MEET SPECIAL NEEDS

The basic life insurance policies you have just learned about can be combined or modified to meet special needs. A combination plan that is popular with many couples with young children is the **family income policy**. This plan combines straight life insurance with decreasing term insurance. The family income plan pays a monthly income to the policyholder's family if he or she dies within a period of time specified in the policy. The monthly income payments are provided through the decreasing term insurance part of the policy. In addition, the family receives the full amount of the straight life part of the policy.

Fred and Marie Lynch have two small children. The Lynches buy a family income policy with a face amount of $20,000. The policy also provides that in the event of death the beneficiaries will receive a monthly income of $150 for 15 years from the date of the policy. If Mr. Lynch were to die five years after buying the policy, Mrs. Lynch and the children would receive $150 a month for the next ten years. They would also receive $20,000 from the straight life part of the policy.

GROUP LIFE INSURANCE

Group life insurance gives protection to each individual in a certain group, with the group acting as a single unit in buying the insurance. Most group life insurance contracts are issued through employers. Some policies, though, are available through unions, professional associations, and other similar organizations.

Group life insurance is almost always issued on a term basis, but whole life policies may be offered. When employees leave the group in which they are insured, they usually do not have to drop their insurance. They can convert the group insurance to some kind of individual policy if they do so within a given period of time, such as 30 days. No physical examination is required; the premium will be based on the age of the person when the conversion takes place.

The cost of group life insurance is less than the cost of a similar amount of protection bought individually. This lower cost is possible because insurance for many people can be handled economically in one policy. The employer and the employee usually share the cost under some plans. The amount of protection available to an individual under a group insurance plan is generally limited. Many people, therefore, supplement their group insurance with policies of their own.

LIFE INSURANCE COSTS

In general, the cost of a life insurance policy depends on the type of life insurance and the age of the person being insured.

Premiums for straight life insurance are higher than those for term insurance, but the annual premium stays the same throughout the insured's life. The premiums on limited-payment life insurance are higher than those for straight life insurance, but they are payable for only a limited number of years. Although the premiums on a 20-payment life policy are payable for only 20 years, the policy remains in force for the lifetime of the insured.

The premiums on endowment policies are higher than the premiums for limited-payment life, straight life, or term insurance policies. Endowment policies are payable on the death of the insured and are also payable to the insured at the end of the policy period. Thus, the insurance company must collect enough in premiums to: (1) give the insured protection in case he or she dies before the end of the policy period, and (2) pay to the insured the amount of the policy if she or he is living at the end of the period.

INCREASING YOUR BUSINESS VOCABULARY

The following terms should become part of your business vocabulary. For each numbered statement, find the term that has the same meaning.

beneficiary   insurable interest
cash value   level term insurance
convertible policy   limited-payment policies
decreasing term insurance   mortgage insurance
endowment life insurance   renewable policy
family income policy   straight life insurance
group life insurance   term insurance
increasing term insurance   whole life insurance

1. Term life insurance on which the premiums remain the same during the term but the amount of protection gradually decreases.
2. Permanent life insurance on which premiums are paid only for a stated number of years.
3. Life insurance issued to members of a group as a unit.
4. Permanent insurance that extends over the lifetime of the insured.
5. The person named in an insurance policy to receive the insurance benefits.
6. Term life insurance on which the amount of protection remains the same during the term.
7. A policy that combines a standard whole life insurance policy with decreasing term insurance.
8. Having some kind of financial benefit in the continued life of someone.
9. A life insurance policy that assures the payment of debts on real property if the insured dies.
10. A term life insurance policy that the policyholder can continue for more than one term without taking a physical exam.
11. The amount that an insurance company will pay to the insured if a policy is given up.
12. A life insurance policy that protects against risk only for a specified period of time.
13. Permanent life insurance on which the insured pays unchanged premiums throughout his or her life.
14. A term life insurance policy that may be changed into another type of insurance.
15. A life insurance policy payable to the beneficiary if the insured should die, or payable to the insured if he or she lives beyond the number of years in which premiums are paid.

16. Term life insurance on which the premiums remain the same during the life of the policy but the amount of coverage increases.

UNDERSTANDING YOUR READING

1. What is the main reason why people buy life insurance?
2. What must you do to obtain life insurance?
3. What determines whether you have an insurable interest in someone else's life?
4. What are the three basic types of life insurance?
5. How do term insurance and whole life insurance differ?
6. What does it mean if a term life insurance policy is convertible and renewable?
7. What is mortgage insurance?
8. In what way is a limited-payment policy different from a straight life policy?
9. Explain why a family income policy is referred to as a combination plan.
10. Why is the cost of group life insurance less than the cost of insurance that is bought privately?
11. What two factors determine the cost of life insurance?

USING YOUR BUSINESS KNOWLEDGE

1. Why does an insurance company ordinarily require that a person who wants to buy life insurance have a physical examination?
2. Does Christine Abbott have an insurable interest in the life of:
   (a) her mother, who is the financial support of the family?
   (b) her uncle, who is going to pay Christine's college expenses?
   (c) her best friend at school?
3. Why is loss of income usually more serious to a family than loss of property?
4. What happens to the insurance protection of a whole-life policy if the insured borrows the cash value of the policy?
5. Fred and Mary Alonzo have two young children. For an annual premium of $150 they can obtain a five-year, $15,000 term life insurance policy. For the same premium, they can obtain an $8,000 whole life policy. What factors would you take into account in advising the Alonzos which policy to buy?
6. Why should a term policy that is renewable or convertible cost more than one which is not?
7. What kind of life insurance policy would you recommend for each of these people?

(a) Dan Phelps, age 26, wants to buy a policy on which the premiums will be as low as possible for the next ten years.

(b) Donald Watkins, who works as a mechanic, wishes to have maximum protection for his invalid and widowed mother in case anything should happen to him.

(c) Barbara Jensen, age 35, wants to buy a policy that will not require payment of any premiums after she retires.

8. Endowment insurance is sometimes called an insured savings plan. Can you explain why it is given this title?

9. When a person buys life insurance as a member of a large group, no physical examination is ordinarily required. Why do you think this is so?

SOLVING PROBLEMS IN BUSINESS

1. Bill Mason has a $10,000 life insurance policy which has built up a cash value of $4,000. He recently borrowed $2,000 on this policy.

   (a) If Bill should die before the loan is repaid, how much would his beneficiary receive?

   (b) If Bill repays the loan in one year at 10 percent annual interest, what is the total amount he will pay back?

2. When Vicki Fennell took out a life insurance policy, she was told that she could pay the premiums quarterly, semiannually, or annually. Quarterly premiums were $53; semiannual premiums were $105; and annual premiums were $205.

   (a) How much would Vicki save by paying the premiums annually instead of semiannually?

   (b) How much would she save by paying the premiums annually instead of quarterly?

3. Aaron Snyder is having the physical examination required for his life insurance policy. His height is 185 centimeters, and his weight is 115 kilograms. The doctor's chart shows that the best weight for someone of Aaron's height is 92 kilograms. The insurance company charges 10 percent more than standard rates for overweight people.

   (a) If the standard annual premium for the insurance that Aaron wants is $365, what will his annual premium be?

   (b) Approximately how many pounds must he lose to qualify for the standard premium?

4. Robin Reed borrowed $2,000 to finish her college education. She agreed to pay $500 on the principal each year, plus interest of 10 percent a year on the unpaid balance. To be sure that her debt would be paid if she should die, she took out a $2,000, four-year decreasing term insurance policy with an annual premium of $15.

(a) How much did Robin pay in premiums and interest each year?

(b) What was the total cost of premiums and interest for the four years?

5. The average amount of life insurance in force per family in three states for the years indicated were as follows:

	1976	1978
Alabama	$29,100	$34,100
New Hampshire	28,300	34,700
Washington	26,700	30,900

(a) In which state was there the greatest dollar increase in coverage over the period?

(b) In which state was there the greatest percentage increase? (Round your answer to the nearest whole percent.)

(c) If the people of the state of Washington increase their coverage by the same percentage over the next two-year period as they did for the 1976–1978 period, what will be the average amount of the insurance per family in 1980?

EXPANDING YOUR UNDERSTANDING OF BUSINESS

1. How did the life insurance business begin? Prepare a report for the class on the early history of life insurance.

2. A traveler can purchase life insurance for the length of a trip. Such policies are often sold in vending machines or booths at airports and terminals. Why would someone be interested in travel insurance? How would such insurance differ from whole life insurance? If possible, obtain a travel insurance policy to show the class.

3. Life insurance premiums are sometimes higher for people who work at hazardous jobs. Consult an insurance agent to find the answers to these questions:

(a) What jobs are considered hazardous?

(b) How much more will the premium be on a policy for a person working in such an occupation than for the same person working in a standard occupation?

4. Kevin and Mary Tyson were recently married. They are discussing the type of insurance they need. The couple is trying to decide between having separate whole life policies on each of them or putting all their insurance payments into policies on Kevin's life, since he will be the principal wage earner. What do you feel would be best? Can you think of a better alternative?

37 HEALTH INSURANCE

PART OBJECTIVES

After studying this part and completing the end-of-part activities, you will be able to:

1. Identify the two types of losses for which health insurance provides protection.
2. Discuss the six basic coverages available in health insurance policies.
3. Describe two methods of obtaining health insurance.
4. Explain the kinds of protection workers' compensation insurance provides.

One day while trying to install a television antenna on his roof, Larry Cornell fell and was seriously injured. An ambulance was called and Larry was taken to the hospital. He was admitted, examined, X-rayed, and taken to his room. The examination revealed that he had internal injuries, a broken leg, and two broken ribs. Larry spent three weeks in the hospital and was not able to return to his job for three months. Total expenses and lost income from this accident amounted to nearly $10,000. If you had an accident like Larry's, how would you pay the costs?

You have many health care needs. Sometimes you need regular physical and dental checkups. At other times you are sick or injured and need medicine and perhaps even hospital care and surgery. In the future if you become sick or disabled for a long period of time, you may lose a great deal of income. Health insurance provides protection against the cost of medical care and the loss of income when you cannot work because of injury or illness.

Health insurance policies can provide six basic coverages: (1) hospital expense, (2) surgical expense, (3) regular medical expense, (4) major medical expense, (5) dental expense, and (6) loss of income. These coverages may be bought separately or in a combination policy.

HOSPITAL EXPENSE INSURANCE

Hospital expense insurance pays part or all of the charges for room, food, and certain other hospital expenses. Payments are also made for such items as use of an operating room, anesthesia, X rays, laboratory tests, and drugs. More people carry hospital expense insurance than any other kind of health insurance.

Hospital expense insurance can be purchased from insurance companies or from nonprofit corporations. The best known nonprofit organization that offers hospital insurance is Blue Cross. Blue Cross plans usually pay hospitals directly for care provided to their policyholders. If expenses go beyond what is covered by the Blue Cross contract, the patient must pay the hospital directly for the extra charges.

SURGICAL EXPENSE INSURANCE

Surgical expense insurance is frequently bought in combination with hospital expense insurance. Surgical expense insurance pays part or all of a surgeon's fee for an operation. The typical surgical policy gives a list of the types of operations that it covers and states the amount allowed for each. Some policies allow larger amounts for operations than others do. This, of course, requires that a higher premium be paid.

Surgical expense insurance can be purchased from insurance companies or from nonprofit organizations such as Blue Shield. Unlike Blue Cross, Blue Shield plans cover mainly medical and surgical treatment rather than hospital care. Most Blue Shield plans list the maximum amounts that will be paid for different types of surgery. They also cover the doctor's charges for care in the hospital and some pay doctor's charges for office or home care.

REGULAR MEDICAL EXPENSE INSURANCE

Regular medical expense insurance pays part or all of a doctor's fees for nonsurgical care given in the doctor's office, the patient's home, or a hospital. The policy states the amount payable for each call and the maximum number of calls covered. Some plans also provide payments for X ray and laboratory expenses. This type of insurance is often bought along with hospital and surgical insurance. The protection provided by these three coverages is referred to as **basic health coverage**.

MAJOR MEDICAL EXPENSE INSURANCE

Major medical expense insurance provides protection against the very large costs of serious or long illness or injury. In a sense, it takes over where other medical insurance leaves off. It helps pay for most kinds of health care prescribed by a doctor. It covers the cost of treatment in and out of the hospital, special nursing care, X rays, psychiatric care, medicine, and many other health care needs. Maximum benefits range from $10,000 to $250,000 and higher, amounts that most people could not afford to pay out of their earnings and savings.

All major medical policies have a deductible clause similar to the deductible clause in automobile collision insurance. In this clause, the insured agrees to pay the first part — perhaps $100 or $500 — of the expense resulting from sickness or injury. Major medical policies also usually contain a **coinsurance clause**. This means that the insured person will be expected to pay a certain percentage — generally 20 or 25 percent — of the costs over and above the deductible amount.

The deductible clause helps discourage the filing of minor claims. The coinsurance clause encourages the insured to keep his or her medical expenses as reasonable as possible. Thus, both clauses help to make lower premiums possible because they help to keep down insurance payments.

DENTAL CARE INSURANCE

Dental expense insurance helps pay for normal dental care, including examinations, X rays, cleaning, fillings, and more

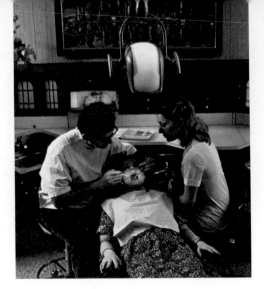

Illus. 37-1

Expenses for routine dental care are covered by dental expense insurance.

complicated types of dental work. It also covers dental injuries sustained through accidents. Some dental plans contain deductible and coinsurance provisions, and others pay for all claims.

DISABILITY INCOME INSURANCE

Disability income insurance provides the insured with weekly or monthly payments when she or he is unable to work as a result of an illness or injury covered by the policy. Disability income policies frequently include a waiting period provision which requires that the insured wait a specified length of time after the disability occurs before payment begins. The purpose of the waiting period is to keep people from making frequent claims for small losses, thus reducing premium costs.

OBTAINING HEALTH COVERAGE

You can buy health insurance as an individual or as a member of a group. Applicants for individual policies may have to take a physical examination and to give their medical history. In some cases, people with a long history of illnesses or injuries may be insured only at higher premium cost.

Most Americans are protected under **group health insurance**. Like group life insurance, such policies are made available by employers to their employees, by unions to their members, and by other organizations to their members. The company, union, or other organization receives a master policy or contract. Those insured under the plan get certificates to indicate their participation in the plan. Companies that sponsor group policies often pay part or all of the premium costs for their employees.

The cost of group health insurance is lower than the cost of a comparable individual policy. This is possible because insurance companies can administer group plans more economically, thus lowering costs for each person in the group.

HEALTH MAINTENANCE ORGANIZATIONS

There has been much concern with finding new ways of dealing with rising medical costs. One way is through **health maintenance organizations**. A health maintenance organization provides complete health care to its members for a fixed regular payment. A wide range of medical and hospital services are available to members. Health maintenance organizations emphasize preventive care and early detection and treatment of illnesses.

HELP FROM STATE GOVERNMENTS

Our local, state, and federal governments are involved in activities that improve the health of the entire nation. An especially important health insurance program provided by our state governments is **workers' compensation**. Accidents may occur on almost any job, but some jobs are more hazardous than others. Employees may suffer injuries or may get some illness as a result of their working conditions. Thus, all states have passed legislation known as workers' compensation laws. These laws provide medical benefits to employees who are injured on the job or become ill as a direct result of their working conditions. Under these laws, most employers are required to provide and pay for insurance for their employees.

The benefits provided through workers' compensation vary from state to state. In some states, all necessary expenses for medical treatment are paid. In others, there is a stated limit of payment. Usually there is a waiting period of a few days before a worker is eligible for loss-of-income benefits. If the worker is unable to return to the job after this waiting period, he or she is paid a certain proportion of wages as benefits. This proportion often amounts to about two thirds of the worker's normal wages. Payments are also made to dependents if the worker is killed in an accident while on the job. Benefits for injury to or death of a worker are usually paid without regard to whether the employee or the employer was at fault.

State governments also provide a form of medical aid to low-income families known as **Medicaid**. The federal government shares with the state the cost of providing health benefits to medically needy families. A medically needy family has been defined as one whose income provides for basic necessities but who could not afford adequate medical care or pay large medical bills.

The services covered by Medicaid include hospital care, doctors' services, X rays and lab tests, nursing home care, diagnosis and treatment of children, home health care services, and family planning. States may provide additional services if they wish.

Illus. 37-2

Workers' compensation insurance will pay loss-of-income benefits to an employee who is injured on the job.

HELP FROM THE FEDERAL GOVERNMENT

The nation's social security laws provide a national program of health insurance known as **Medicare**. It is designed to help people age 65 and over and some disabled people to pay the high cost of health care. Medicare has two basic parts: hospital insurance and medical insurance.

The hospital insurance plan includes coverage for hospital care, care in an approved nursing home, and home health care up to a certain number of visits. The medical insurance portion of Medicare is often called supplementary or voluntary insurance. The services covered under this plan include doctors' services, visits by nurses and other health workers to the patient's home, and certain other services.

For the hospital insurance, no premium payments are required, and almost everyone 65 and over may qualify. The medical insurance requires a small monthly premium. The federal government pays an equal amount to help cover the cost of the medical insurance. Some features of the Medicare plan are similar to the deductible and coinsurance provisions in other health policies.

INCREASING YOUR BUSINESS VOCABULARY

The following terms should become part of your business vocabulary. For each numbered statement, find the term that has the same meaning.

basic health coverage
coinsurance clause
dental expense insurance
disability income insurance
group health insurance
health maintenance organization
hospital expense insurance

major medical expense insurance
Medicaid
Medicare
regular medical expense insurance
surgical expense insurance
workers' compensation

1. A provision in which the insured agrees with the insurance company to pay a certain percentage of his or her medical expenses.
2. Health insurance provided by the federal government for aged and disabled people.
3. Insurance that provides protection against the very large costs of serious or long illness or injury.
4. Insurance that pays part or all of the charges for room, food, and other hospital expenses that the insured person incurs.
5. Medical expense assistance provided by state governments to medically needy families.
6. Health insurance available to members of a group.
7. Insurance that provides benefits to cover part or all of a surgeon's fee for an operation.
8. State government insurance that provides payments to employees for injuries or loss of income caused by accidents on the job.
9. Insurance that pays for normal care of and accidental damage to teeth.

10. A combination of hospital, surgical, and regular medical expense insurance.
11. An organization which provides complete health care to its members for a fixed regular payment.
12. Insurance that pays part or all of a doctor's fees for nonsurgical care given in the doctor's office, the patient's home, or a hospital.
13. Insurance that provides a worker with weekly or monthly payments when he or she is unable to work as a result of an illness or injury covered by the policy.

UNDERSTANDING YOUR READING

1. What are the two types of losses for which health insurance provides protection?
2. What are the six basic types of coverage provided by health insurance? Explain what kinds of expenses each covers.
3. What is the purpose of a deductible clause in a health insurance policy?
4. Why is a health insurance policy with a coinsurance clause less expensive than one without a coinsurance clause?
5. What types of dental care are covered by a dental expense policy?
6. Why is being insured under an individual health insurance policy more expensive than under a group policy?
7. What three health insurance programs are operated by government agencies?
8. What is the purpose of workers' compensation insurance? Is this a state or federal program?
9. Explain what Medicaid is.
10. What are the two basic parts of the Medicare plan?

USING YOUR BUSINESS KNOWLEDGE

1. Patty Kelly is studying to be an electrical engineer and has a part-time job to help pay her college expenses. She does not have health insurance because she feels she cannot afford it. She also feels that she does not really need health insurance. (a) Do you think Patty should protect herself with some type of health insurance? (b) Where might she find a policy at a reasonable premium?
2. Kevin Strand found that he could buy major medical expense insurance with a maximum coverage of $10,000 for about the same cost as regular medical expense insurance with a maximum coverage of about $2,000. Why is the cost of the two types of insurance about the same when the maximum coverage is so different?

3. The O'Haras are trying to determine which kinds of health insurance coverage would best fit their family's needs. On one hand, they feel that a Blue Cross hospital expense plan and a Blue Shield surgical expense plan would be sufficient insurance for a family. On the other hand, a major medical plan might better serve their needs. What advice would you offer this couple relative to their health insurance needs?

4. Dental insurance is a form of insurance that is gaining in popularity. Why do you suppose that this form of insurance is being so widely accepted?

SOLVING PROBLEMS IN BUSINESS

1. Julie Kemper wants to buy hospital expense insurance. From the Mid-American Insurance Company, she can purchase this coverage for monthly premiums of $45. The Drake Insurance Agency offers the same coverage for premiums of $125 paid quarterly (every 3 months). From which company should Julie buy her insurance?

2. The following shows the health insurance carried by Maria Flores and the monthly cost for each kind of coverage:

Blue Cross	$25.00
Blue Shield	$ 5.50
Major Medical	$ 5.75

(a) What is the total cost of her health care coverage each month?

(b) How much does each of the coverages cost her annually?

(c) What is the total cost annually?

3. Wayne Polus was hospitalized as a result of a skiing accident. His medical expenses were:

10 days in hospital	$100 per day
Lab tests and X rays	$185
Surgeon's fees	$975

Wayne was covered by hospital expense insurance which pays the cost of his hospital room for up to 120 days for any one illness. Coverage for lab tests, X rays, and other hospital extras is limited to $300. His surgical expense insurance plan limits benefits to $600 for the type of surgery involved.

(a) What was the cost of all Wayne's medical services?

(b) How much of this total cost was paid for by insurance?

(c) How much of the medical cost did Wayne have to pay?

4. Many companies which have group health insurance also have blood bank plans for their employees. One of these blood banks had a drive for blood donations and the following numbers of

employees gave blood:

First day	26 donors
Second day	19 donors
Third day	33 donors

(a) Each donor gave 1 pint of blood. What was the total amount of blood contributed to the blood bank?

(b) What is this amount of blood in milliliters?

5. In a community with a population of 5,000, the following numbers of people are covered by the types of health insurance indicated:

Hospital expense	4,600
Surgical expense	3,200
Regular medical expense	3,000
Major medical expense	3,900
Dental expense	2,000
Disability income	3,000

(a) What percent of the people in the community are covered by each type of insurance?

(b) In one year, 235 people covered by surgical expense insurance presented claims totaling $176,250. What was the amount of the average claim?

EXPANDING YOUR UNDERSTANDING OF BUSINESS

1. Dental insurance is a relatively new type of insurance which is being rapidly accepted. Other forms of protection that are beginning to receive attention are eye care insurance, home care services insurance, and prescription drug insurance. What kinds of expenses would likely be covered under such policies? Do you think there is a need for these types of protection?

2. Mail-order sales of health and accident insurance plans are growing. Find two or three mail-order health insurance ads in your newspaper or magazines. Examine and compare the ads. What coverages do the policies offer?

3. Health maintenance organizations are trying to help people meet the costs of health care. Are there any health maintenance organizations in your community? If there are, find out what services are provided by one of them.

4. Schools often arrange with an insurance company to provide students with coverage that protects the students in case of accidents on the way to and from school and on school grounds. They also provide coverage for members of school athletic teams. Does your school provide such coverage? If so, how much does it cost? What coverage is provided?

38 HOME AND PROPERTY INSURANCE

PART OBJECTIVES

After studying this part and completing the end-of-part activities, you will be able to:
1. Identify three kinds of economic losses property insurance protects against.
2. Explain the difference between real property and personal property.
3. Explain how the three types of homeowners policies are different.
4. Give five factors that affect the cost of property insurance.
5. Tell why a homeowner should keep an inventory of insured personal property.

Anyone who owns anything is in danger of losing it. Consider these situations:

Vandals broke into the Milligans' apartment, slashed furniture and draperies, and stole jewelry.

The Alonzos returned from a two-week vacation trip to find that their house was flooded because a frozen water pipe burst.

Erin drove a golf ball through a neighbor's picture window, injuring a child.

A fire started by a careless camper destroyed the Stevensons' summer cottage in the mountains.

Bill returned to his college dorm and found that his stereo was missing.

In each of these situations, the owners of the property involved would suffer considerable financial loss without the protection of insurance. Fire, theft, vandalism, floods, windstorms, and other hazards cause a lot of personal and financial hardship. On the average, a residential fire breaks out every 35 to 40 seconds somewhere in the United States. The resulting property damage totals close to $4 billion each year. More than $3 billion a year is stolen by thieves. Property owners also run the risk of being sued by people who are injured on their property. Because the risks of loss in such situations are high, property owners should — and most do — carry property insurance.

LOSSES COVERED BY HOME AND PROPERTY INSURANCE

Home and property insurance provides protection against three kinds of economic losses: (1) damage to your home or property, (2) the additional living expenses involved when you must live someplace else because your home was badly damaged, and (3) liability losses.

If your home and its contents are damaged by fire, lightning, vandalism, earthquake, or some other disaster, home and property insurance will pay for the repairs or replacement. When you suffer a loss to your property, there may be additional expenses because you can no longer use that property. These losses are also covered by home and property insurance. For example, if your home were badly damaged by fire, your insurance would pay for the higher than normal living expenses you would have from living in a hotel and eating in restaurants.

The third kind of losses, liability losses, are protected by personal liability coverage. **Personal liability coverage** protects you from claims arising from injuries to other people or damage to other people's property which are caused by you, your family, or your pets. If your dog bites the letter carrier, for example, personal liability coverage will pay for any medical and legal costs involved. Or if you should hit a baseball through a neighbor's window, claims will be paid through the provision in your policy that covers the liability for physical damage to the property of others.

Illus. 38-1

If your home were destroyed by fire, home and property insurance would pay for the repairs and for temporary living expenses.

KINDS OF PROPERTY INSURANCE POLICIES

When you are considering the purchase of property insurance, you must first decide what should be insured and what perils it should be insured against. Property attached to land, such as a house or a garage, is known as **real property**. Property not attached to the land, such as furniture or clothing, is known as **personal property**. Real and personal property may be protected by separate policies or by a combination policy.

A property owner can buy separate policies which insure against certain perils. For example, a **standard fire policy** insures against losses caused by fire or lightning. **Extended coverage** can be included in a standard fire policy. This expands the coverage to include such risks as damage caused by wind, hail, smoke, and falling aircraft, among other things. Also, insurance companies may offer separate policies for protection in areas with frequent flooding or a high crime rate.

Today, however, most people buy a package policy that is known as a **homeowners policy**. The number of perils covered by a homeowners policy depends on whether the insured chooses the basic form, the broad form, or the comprehensive form.

FORMS OF HOMEOWNERS POLICIES

The basic form of homeowners policy insures property against the first 11 perils listed in Illus. 38-2. The broad form, which is very widely purchased, covers 18 different risks. The comprehensive form covers all perils shown in the illustration and many more. It is sometimes referred to as an all-risk policy. Actually, such a policy insures against all perils except those named in the policy. Personal liability coverage is included with all forms of the homeowners policy.

PERILS AGAINST WHICH PROPERTIES ARE INSURED
HOMEOWNERS POLICY

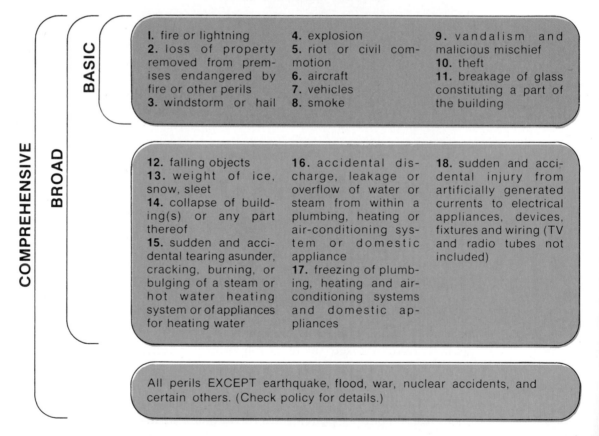

BASIC

1. fire or lightning
2. loss of property removed from premises endangered by fire or other perils
3. windstorm or hail
4. explosion
5. riot or civil commotion
6. aircraft
7. vehicles
8. smoke
9. vandalism and malicious mischief
10. theft
11. breakage of glass constituting a part of the building

BROAD

12. falling objects
13. weight of ice, snow, sleet
14. collapse of building(s) or any part thereof
15. sudden and accidental tearing asunder, cracking, burning, or bulging of a steam or hot water heating system or of appliances for heating water
16. accidental discharge, leakage or overflow of water or steam from within a plumbing, heating or air-conditioning system or domestic appliance
17. freezing of plumbing, heating and air-conditioning systems and domestic appliances
18. sudden and accidental injury from artificially generated currents to electrical appliances, devices, fixtures and wiring (TV and radio tubes not included)

COMPREHENSIVE

All perils EXCEPT earthquake, flood, war, nuclear accidents, and certain others. (Check policy for details.)

Source: Insurance Information Institute

Illus. 38-2

Perils against which property is insured by a homeowners policy.

With a homeowners policy, you are protected as you would be if you bought several different policies. Yet the cost of a homeowners policy is usually 20 to 30 percent less than if the same amount of coverage were obtained by buying separate policies. Also, there is the convenience of having only one policy and one premium to be concerned about. If you live in a rented home or apartment, you can get a similar package policy. This is called a **tenants policy** and covers household goods and personal belongings.

INSURABLE INTEREST

If you will lose money because a certain piece of property is damaged or destroyed, you are said to have an insurable interest in that property. If you have no insurable interest in a property, you are not paid for any damage to that property, even though you may have paid for an insurance policy on it. It is not enough that an insurable interest existed when the policy was bought. The insurable interest must exist at the time of the loss.

Suppose you own a house which you have insured for $55,000 under a policy that expires on September 30. If you sell this house on June 1, your insurable interest ends at that time. If the house is destroyed by fire on July 15, you cannot collect any insurance, even though the policy is still in effect, because you no longer have an insurable interest in the house. If the insurable interest expires before the policy does or if the policy is canceled, you may be able to obtain a partial refund of the premium you paid.

An insurance company agrees to pay you for any losses covered by your policy. However, the company does not agree to pay you more than the amount of your loss, no matter what the amount of your insurance. Suppose you own a house that is valued at $55,000 but is insured for $70,000. If your house burns to the ground, you will receive not more than $55,000.

GETTING THE RIGHT PROTECTION

If homeowners want adequate protection, the amount of insurance on their property should be based on the property's current value. Suppose that Mary Wong built her house in 1980 for $60,000 and that she has it insured for that amount. It might cost $75,000 to build a similar house today, so the house has a current replacement value of $75,000. Yet if Ms. Wong's house is completely destroyed by fire, the insurance company will pay her only $60,000.

Building costs and property values have increased greatly in recent years. Property owners should review the value of their property and insurance coverage every few years. They should determine the cost of replacing their property and make sure that their insurance policies give enough protection. Some insurance companies provide for automatic increases in property coverage as the price level increases.

Special care should be taken to accurately estimate the value of personal property. Since personal property includes many different items, some may be overlooked if a careless estimate of value is made. Most homeowners policies provide personal property coverage at 50 percent of policy value. For example, if your home is insured for $50,000, your personal property is insured for 50 percent of $50,000 or $25,000. The value of personal property that you collect bit by bit over the years is often surprisingly high. In many cases a homeowner's personal property is worth considerably more than 50 percent of the coverage on the home. Additional coverage is available for a small increase in premium.

FACTORS AFFECTING PROPERTY INSURANCE COSTS

The price that homeowners pay for insurance on homes and furnishings is based on a number of factors. One of the most important is the estimated danger of loss based on the insurance company's past experiences. In addition to the loss experiences, an insurance company considers the following factors in determining homeowner insurance premiums:

1. The type of policy (basic, broad, or comprehensive).
2. The amount of coverage.
3. The amount of deductibles (the higher the deductibles, the lower the premium).
4. The construction of the building, that is, whether it is made of brick, wood, or concrete, and what the roof is made of.
5. The distance to the nearest fire department and water supply.

PROVIDING PROOF OF LOSS

As soon as possible after you discover a loss, you should file a claim with your insurance company. However, before the company will pay, you must provide proof of your loss. This is not a problem with real property. With real property a representative of the insurance company can look at the damaged property, determine the extent of loss, and pay you according to the terms of the policy. The destroyed contents of a house, however, would pose a problem. In order to prove the amount of personal property loss, you must know the value of each article damaged or destroyed.

In order to show proof of loss, you should keep a list of personal property that is insured. The list, called an **inventory**, should include: (1) the original cost of each article, (2) when the article was purchased, and (3) how long the article is expected to last. The age of an insured article of personal property is quite important. As most property becomes older, it gradually wears out and decreases in value. This decrease in value, called **depreciation**, affects the amount the insurance company will pay if the property is destroyed.

Illus. 38-3

Keeping an up-to-date inventory of your personal property makes it easier to provide proof of loss in case of theft or damage.

Let's take an example. Bill and Wanda Duvall buy a sofa for $600. The sofa is expected to last ten years. The average yearly depreciation, then, would be $60 ($600 ÷ 10). After four years, the sofa is destroyed by fire. The amount of the Duvalls' claim will be about $360 ($600 less the four years of depreciation).

In addition to maintaining an up-to-date personal property inventory, some insurance companies suggest taking photographs of furniture and other property. These photos can be used to support claims. Insurance companies can provide you with inventory forms and information about how to make claims for losses.

INCREASING YOUR BUSINESS VOCABULARY

The following terms should become part of your business vocabulary. For each numbered statement, find the term that has the same meaning.

depreciation   personal property
extended coverage   real property
homeowners policy   standard fire policy
inventory   tenants policy
personal liability coverage

1. Property not attached to land.
2. A decrease in the value of property as it becomes older and wears out.
3. A package policy covering a wide range of risks for the owners of homes.
4. Property attached to the land.
5. A basic type of property insurance that protects against loss resulting from fire or lightning damage to a home.
6. Insurance on household goods and personal belongings for those who rent.
7. Insurance to protect against claims arising from injuries to other people or damage to other people's property which are caused by you, your family, or your pets.
8. A list of goods showing the cost of each item, when it was purchased, and how long it is expected to last.
9. Additional protection of property against losses from such causes as windstorms, hail, and smoke.

UNDERSTANDING YOUR READING

1. What are the three types of economic losses for which home and property insurance provides protection?
2. What kind of protection is provided by personal liability coverage?
3. What is the difference between real property and personal property?
4. Give five examples of perils against which property owners can purchase insurance protection.
5. How does extended coverage affect the standard fire policy?
6. Why do most people buy a homeowners policy to cover the perils for which they want to be insured rather than buy a separate policy to cover each peril?
7. How does the broad form of the homeowners policy differ from the basic form? From the comprehensive form?
8. What kind of policy would renters buy to protect their household contents and personal belongings?
9. What is an insurable interest? In order to make a property insurance claim, when must you have an insurable interest?
10. What factors affect the cost of property insurance?
11. Why should the owner of a homeowners policy keep an inventory and photographs of the property that is insured?

USING YOUR BUSINESS KNOWLEDGE

1. Jill Fritsch's dog attacked a neighbor who entered Jill's yard while Jill was at work. The neighbor was seriously injured and is suing Jill for payment of damages. Will Jill's homeowners insurance policy cover these damages?
2. Ronald Winfield insured his house under a broad form homeowners insurance policy. He sold the house three months before his insurance policy expired. Following the sale, a hailstorm seriously damaged the house. Mr. Winfield attempted to claim benefits for the damages because his policy was paid for. Will the insurance company pay? Why or why not?
3. Joseph Stein's property is covered by the basic form of homeowners insurance. Which of the following losses is he insured against? Which would be covered if he had the broad form?
   (a) A smouldering fire breaks out in a bedroom closet and his clothing is damaged by smoke.
   (b) His home is broken into and vandalized, but nothing is stolen.
   (c) A storm knocks out the electricity for two days in midwinter and the water pipes burst, causing flooding.

(d) A heavy windstorm tears some shingles from the roof of the house.

(e) A heavy buildup of wet snow causes his porch roof to collapse.

(f) An unusually heavy rain causes a nearby creek to overflow and flood his basement.

(g) Several windowpanes are broken by children throwing rocks.

4. Frank Polewski recently bought a house and lot for $70,000. Before moving into his new home, he wants to take out an insurance policy covering both the house and his personal property. In order to determine the amount of coverage needed, Frank needs to make an estimate of the value of his real and personal property. How should he proceed in estimating the value of his house? In estimating the value of his personal property?

5. Helen Fossi and Maria Fernandez were playing golf together. Helen hit a ball which accidentally struck and injured Maria. On the way to the hospital, Helen told Maria that she would pay Maria's medical expenses. Maria answered that she would pay her own expenses since Helen had hit her accidentally. Then Helen remembered that she was covered by personal liability insurance. Will this insurance cover Maria's medical expenses?

SOLVING PROBLEMS IN BUSINESS

1. When Michael Logan was having an additional room built onto his house, one of the carpenters dropped a board which hit and injured a neighbor girl. The girl's medical expenses amounted to $975. However, Mr. Logan's personal liability coverage in his homeowners policy stated that the amount of protection provided was limited to $500 per person.

(a) How much would the insurance company have to pay?

(b) How much would Mr. Logan have to pay?

2. Kathy Hampton owns a home that is valued at $50,000. It is 80 percent destroyed by fire. What will be the amount of the claim against the insurance company?

3. Someone broke into the garage of Paul Wilcox and stole the following items:

15 liters of oak stain, valued at $3.25 a liter
6 liters of motor oil, valued at $1.25 a liter
3 kilograms of 2.5 cm finishing nails, valued at 75¢ a kilogram
68 meters of 2.5 cm × 30.5 cm pine shelving, valued at $3.50 a meter

Since Mr. Wilcox had recently bought these items and had not yet used any of the material, for what amount should he make his claim under his homeowners policy?

4. Sylvia Long lives in an apartment. Her furniture and other personal property are covered under a tenants policy. Miss Long's apartment was broken into and the following things were stolen:

> A stereo, bought 3 years ago for $250 and estimated to last 5 years.
> A camera, bought 4 years ago for $160 and estimated to last 10 years.
> A suede jacket, bought 2 years ago for $80 and estimated to last 5 years.

If the insurance company pays Miss Long the estimated present worth of the lost articles, what amount will she receive?

EXPANDING YOUR UNDERSTANDING OF BUSINESS

1. Some insurance companies offer lower rates on fire insurance policies if the members of the insured family do not smoke. What do you think that the personal habit of smoking would have to do with insurance rates? Find out whether any companies in your area offer this discount.

2. Draw an inventory form that you can use to keep a record of your personal property. You may find samples of inventory forms in accounting or record keeping books. Fill in the form with a few of the items that you own.

3. Because certain areas of the U.S. are subject to flooding, the federal government has begun to sponsor government-backed flood insurance. Before flood insurance can be offered, however, the area must be approved by a government agency.
   (a) What is meant by government-backed insurance?
   (b) What types of losses are covered under flood insurance?
   (c) Is your area approved for flood insurance?
   (d) Is flood insurance available there?

4. Property insurance policies usually set certain limits on the amount of protection allowed for such personal property as stamp and coin collections, jewelry, furs, and rare paintings. Why are such limitations established? If a person wants to be covered for the full value of such property, what can he or she do?

39 INSURING YOUR FUTURE INCOME

PART OBJECTIVES

After studying this part and completing the end-of-part activities, you will be able to:
1. List five ways to insure future income.
2. Identify the purpose of state unemployment insurance.
3. Explain what pensions are.
4. Tell how an annuity differs from an insurance policy.
5. Discuss how social security provides protection for future income.

At all stages of your life, you are directly concerned with whether there will be enough money to live on. As a youth, you are affected if your parents lose the ability to earn an income. As a young adult, you will be concerned about how you will get along if you lose your income because of an injury or sickness. If you have a family, you will want to feel that your children will be supported and educated if you or your spouse dies or becomes disabled. And when you grow older, you might worry about whether your retirement income will be enough to meet living expenses. Everyone should be aware of the source of his or her financial support and of ways of assuring a continuing income. In this part, you will study ways by which income security is provided.

INSURING AGAINST LOSS OF INCOME

One way to insure against loss of income is by having disability income insurance. As you learned when you studied health insurance in Part 37, disability income insurance helps replace income that stops when you cannot work because of illness or injury. There are many different individual and group disability income policies available. The provisions for the amount of each payment, the length of the waiting period before benefits are paid, and the length of time that payments are desired should be chosen on the basis of the needs of each family. The more benefits provided for, the higher premiums will be.

STATE UNEMPLOYMENT INSURANCE

When you lose your job, your income may be cut off entirely. You may be out of work at different times due to such causes as business failures, strikes, changes in methods and in equipment, and the temporary or seasonal nature of certain jobs.

To cut down the risk of financial loss because of unemployment, every state has an **unemployment insurance** program which it operates in cooperation with the federal government. Through this plan, if you are unemployed you will be helped to find a new job. But if no suitable job is found, you may receive payments to replace part of your lost wages. The duration of this payment varies, but most states will pay for as long as 26 weeks of unemployment after a one-week waiting period. Ordinarily, the amount you will receive when you are unemployed is based on your previous earnings.

PENSION PLANS

Other organized programs also contribute to your income security. Most employers offer plans that provide monthly payments, or **pensions**, to retired workers. Similar plans are often established by professional and trade associations or unions.

To qualify for a pension under most private plans, you must work for the same company or belong to the same organization for a minimum number of years. Pensions are commonly paid not only to retired workers of industries but also to retired workers of institutions such as schools, hospitals, and government units. It is possible for some workers to retire on pensions which together with their social security benefits give them an income of up to half or more of their earnings during employment.

The Employee Retirement Income Security Act of 1974 lays down rules for company pension plans. The act assures that people under pension plans will receive their pensions even if the companies they work for go bankrupt. Also, most workers who change jobs will keep some of their pension rights instead of losing them as many workers have in the past. This law also makes it possible for self-employed business and professional people and for employees not covered by a pension plan to set aside some tax-free income to provide for their retirement.

ASSURING FUTURE INCOME WITH ANNUITIES

You can enter into a contract with an insurance company to provide you with a regular future income. You pay the insurance company a certain amount of money either in a lump sum or in a series of payments. In return, the company agrees to pay you a regular income beginning at a certain age and continuing for life or for a specified number of years. The amount of money that the insurance company will pay at definite intervals to a person who has previously deposited money with the company is called an **annuity**.

Annuity contracts are sold by life insurance companies and are often thought to be a form of life insurance. However, they are really quite different. You buy life insurance mainly to protect your dependents; you buy an annuity to protect yourself against not having an adequate income in retirement years. It has been said that life insurance insures against dying too soon and an annuity insures against living too long.

PROTECTION THROUGH SOCIAL SECURITY

Important protection for income security is provided through the federal social security system. More than 110 million American workers are covered by social security. And in one recent year, nearly 35 million people received almost $120 million in benefits.

The Medicare program which you learned about in Part 37 is one part of the social security system. The other important part is **retirement, survivors, and disability insurance**. This insurance provides pensions to retired workers and their families, death benefits to dependents of workers who die, and benefits to disabled workers and their families.

Illus. 39-1

Many Americans receive retirement benefits in the form of monthly social security checks.

The basic idea of social security is not difficult. During working years, employed people pay social security taxes. The taxes are deducted from the employees' paychecks. Employers match the amounts paid by their employees. Self-employed people, such as farmers, retail merchants, and professional people, pay the entire tax themselves. But the amount they pay is less than the total amount paid by both the employer and the employee on the same income. Self-employed people pay their tax when they file their income tax returns.

The taxes collected are put into a special trust fund. When a worker retires, becomes disabled, or dies, monthly payments are made to replace part of the income the family has lost.

APPLYING FOR SOCIAL SECURITY BENEFITS

Social security benefits are not automatically paid when you are entitled to them. To receive any benefits, you must apply at a social security office. The amount of the benefits you receive depends to a great extent on the amount of wages you earned during your working years. Social security monthly benefits increase automatically as the cost of living rises.

Those who are covered by social security can receive the full amount of the monthly payments to which they are entitled when they reach age 65. But if they choose, they can retire as early as age 62 by accepting lower payments. Workers may be entitled to full benefits if they become disabled at any age before 65. If an insured worker dies, a lump-sum payment is made to help take care of burial expenses, even though monthly benefits are also payable.

GETTING A SOCIAL SECURITY NUMBER

If you work in a job covered by social security, you must have a **social security number**. This number is used to identify your record of earnings. The social security benefits that you and your dependents may someday receive will be determined by this record of earnings.

A social security number is also needed by anyone who fills out a federal income tax return. The Internal Revenue Service uses this number as a taxpayer identification number for processing tax returns. People who receive interest or dividends also need social security numbers.

To get a social security number, you must fill out an application form. You may get a form from your employer, from a social security office, or from a post office. The federal government then issues a **social security card** which shows your number. You use the same social security number during your entire life. If you lose your card, you can get a duplicate from a social security office. When a woman marries, she can obtain a new card showing her married name with her account number.

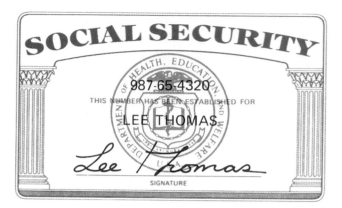

Illus. 39-2

A social security card.

INCREASING YOUR BUSINESS VOCABULARY

The following terms should become part of your business vocabulary. For each numbered statement, find the term that has the same meaning.

annuity
pension
retirement, survivors, and disability insurance

social security card
social security number
unemployment insurance

1. Payment made to a retired worker under a privately organized plan.
2. The number used to identify one's record of earnings under social security laws.
3. An amount of money that an insurance company will pay at definite intervals to a person who has previously deposited money with the company.
4. The document showing one's social security number.
5. Government insurance that provides, among other things, for benefits to be paid to retired workers and their families.
6. Insurance that provides cash payments for a limited time to people who are out of a job.

UNDERSTANDING YOUR READING

1. What are five ways by which you can insure or protect your future income?
2. What is the purpose of state unemployment insurance?
3. What is a pension?
4. What are some of the ways the Employee Retirement Income Security Act of 1974 helps workers?
5. What is the difference between an annuity and an insurance policy?
6. Explain how the social security system works.
7. What three groups of people receive monthly incomes from social security?
8. What does the federal government do with social security taxes after it collects them?
9. Even if you do not have a job, what is one reason why you might need a social security number?
10. How can you get a social security card?

USING YOUR BUSINESS KNOWLEDGE

1. What type of insurance for future income would each of the following people be likely to benefit from?
   (a) Rick Timmons loses his job when the department store he works for goes out of business.
   (b) Nancy Elton, who has worked for 40 years in a city hospital, retires.
   (c) Hazel Collins retires and receives monthly checks from an insurance company under a plan bought with a lump-sum payment.
2. Sarah Martin has a small flower shop. She pays her social security taxes but is concerned that social security will not be enough to support her when she is too old to run her business any more. What alternatives does she have for providing for income security in her old age?
3. A requirement for drawing state unemployment insurance usually is that the applicant must be available for work and must be making reasonable efforts to find work. Why would states have this requirement?
4. Most states have a one-week waiting period before a person can collect unemployment payments. What purpose do you think this waiting period serves?
5. With unemployment insurance available in every state, why would anyone want to buy loss of income insurance from a private insurance company? Does loss of income insurance provide any benefits that unemployment insurance does not?

SOLVING
PROBLEMS
IN BUSINESS

1. Frank Williams works in the accounting department of a business firm. Both he and his employer are taxed for social security benefits. Each month, $75.50 is taken out of Mr. Williams' paycheck as his share of the social security tax. How much does his employer pay each year to match Mr. Williams' tax?

2. As the cost of living increases, Congress increases the social security benefits for retired and disabled workers. In one year, Congress approved an 8 percent increase in March. Darlene Meyer, a widow, received a monthly check for $225 before the increase went into effect. What was the amount of Darlene's monthly check after the March increase?

3. Suzanne Louis is planning to buy disability insurance with a 15-day waiting period. To get monthly benefits of $300, her semiannual premium will be $30.60. To receive $400 per month, the premiums are $40.80; and to receive $500 per month, $51.00.

   (a) By how much do the premiums increase for every $100 the benefits increase?

   (b) Ms. Louis could instead buy a plan with a 45-day waiting period and benefits of $300 per month for a semiannual premium of $23.10. How much would she save as compared with the 15-day waiting period?

4. James Parrish is about to retire. He will collect social security and a pension from the gas and electric company where he has been employed in a town in New York. Mr. and Mrs. Parrish have always planned to retire to Florida, but they are worried about missing their children and grandchildren they will leave behind in New York. They plan to return to New York twice a year by car for a visit. If the distance from the New York town they live in now to their new home in Florida is 2050 kilometers, how many kilometers will they travel the first year, counting the first trip to Florida? How many miles is this?

5. Walter Barrow, who has worked for 24 years in occupations covered under social security, became disabled as a result of an accident. His average monthly earnings covered by social security amount to $650. The social security office used the following percentages to decide the amount of the monthly check to which Mr. Barrow is entitled:

   114% of the first $110 of average monthly wage
   42% of the next $290
   38% of the next $150
   25% of the next $100

   For how much will Mr. Barrow's monthly disability check be?

EXPANDING YOUR UNDERSTANDING OF BUSINESS

1. Since most workers are protected by workers' compensation, isn't unemployment insurance for these same workers an unnecessary type of coverage? Explain your answer.
2. Although many people retire and begin collecting social security at age 65, one may retire at age 62 and receive smaller benefit checks. Explain why a person retiring at age 62 would receive less per month than a person retiring at age 65.
3. Some insurance companies offer variable annuities as a protection against inflation. What is a variable annuity? Which do you think is better, fixed or variable annuities?
4. There are some types of workers who are not covered under social security. Find out from your local social security office who these workers are. What types of protection for income security are available to them?
5. Savings, insurance, and investments in a home and other property contribute to economic security as well as to a better life-style. All of us can count on a happier and more successful life if we start planning now for our economic well-being. This might be called estate planning. How can you start estate planning while you are still in high school? How can you continue this estate planning early in your working career?

CAREER FOCUS

The insurance industry employs many clerical, secretarial, accounting, data processing, and distributive workers. There are approximately 5,000 insurance companies in the United States, and these companies provide jobs for one and one-half million people. Most of the people in insurance are employed in clerical or sales jobs. Almost one third of all insurance workers are sales agents.

WORKERS IN THE INSURANCE BUSINESS

Workers are needed by insurance companies to perform a variety of tasks. Some must keep records of insurance sold and of payments made by those who own the insurance policies. Good records help an insurance company provide services when needed and make payments for claims as promptly and accurately as possible. Each of the offices must be operated efficiently, and that requires good workers in all jobs.

Many positions in insurance involve frequent contact with the public, either policy owners or potential customers. Claims adjusters and claims examiners, for instance, must meet policy owners when they investigate a claim and decide how much, if anything, should be paid. They must treat the policy owners fairly and courteously. Sales agents, those workers who find customers and sell them the kinds of insurance needed, also may deliver claim checks to those who have had a loss. Sales agents must be very good in getting along with people. All workers who have contacts with the public should have pleasant manners and should be the kind of people who can talk in a polite and friendly way with a great variety of people. An honest desire to help people is also important for workers in this category.

Some specially trained workers must be very good in math and statistics. These workers are called actuaries. They are responsible for determining the risks taken on by the insurance companies when they sell policies. Actuaries do complicated work involving mathematical formulas and computations. Accountants and data processing managers also are important in seeing to it that appropriate records are maintained and analyzed. Actuaries, accountants, and data processing managers work together as an important management team.

EDUCATION AND TRAINING
FOR INSURANCE WORK

Insurance offers job opportunities for people having a variety of educational backgrounds and talents. Graduation from high school is adequate for many beginning office positions. Courses in typewriting, bookkeeping, general business, and office machines are valuable to beginning workers. Some clerical positions in insurance are very responsible jobs and must be filled by people who know a good deal about insurance and the company for which they work. Some jobs are specialized and require college degrees as well as special training for office employees and for sales agents. The insurance industry itself has several courses of study for office employees as well as for sales agents.

LOOKING AT THE FUTURE
IN INSURANCE

The employment outlook in the insurance industry is very good. An expected increase in the need for additional workers results in part from a rapidly growing volume of business. Our growing population, as well as new services offered by insurance companies, make the future for workers look good. Insurance workers also have a generally good prospect for regular employment without layoffs. Even during bad economic periods, people must keep their property, liability, and other kinds of insurance policies in force. There are good employment prospects for those who prepare themselves for insurance careers.

UNIT 10

Moving People, Ideas, And Goods

UNIT OBJECTIVES

After studying the parts in this unit, you will be able to:

1. Tell the advantages of each of the four principal means of travel in the United States.

2. Explain what telephone services are available and how each is used.

3. Describe the characteristics of a good business letter.

4. List the advantages of shipping by mail, truck, bus, plane, ship, and pipeline.

40 HOW AMERICANS TRAVEL

PART OBJECTIVES

After studying this part and completing the end-of-part activities, you will be able to:
1. List the four principal means of travel in the United States.
2. Tell why many people prefer to travel by automobile rather than any other means.
3. Explain what the main advantage of plane service is.
4. Describe the four kinds of information needed to properly plan a trip.
5. Tell what sources of information are available about means of transportation and travel services.

When the American people were moving West, during the winters many suffered from what was called "cabin fever." This meant they became very irritable and were easily provoked into fighting because they spent so much time living alone in cabins in remote areas. Often there were no other people nearby to break the monotony or boredom. They had no telephones with which to call family or friends and no roads or modern vehicles to use for visiting or shopping. Fortunately, our economy has overcome most of the obstacles that caused cabin fever. Now if you are lonely or bored, you can pick up the telephone and talk with someone. Or you can turn on the radio or television to be entertained or informed. In addition, it is probably not unusual for you and your family to receive several letters each week from relatives and friends. And few people live where there are no roads for cars, buses, or other means of transportation.

Much of the strength of the American economic system is based on good transportation and communication services. Through these services we can quickly and easily move people, ideas, and goods from one place to another. To give you some idea of how much we use these services, consider that every day there are over 575 million telephone calls made and close to 165 thousand letters sent. In addition, Americans travel over 1.5 trillion miles a year, and most of that is in private automobiles. This is, indeed, a nation of continual movement — of people, thoughts, and things.

As you read about moving people, ideas, and goods, there are three basic terms you need to keep in mind. The first is **communication**, which is simply the exchanging of information. The other two terms, travel and transportation, are sometimes considered to be the same thing. In this discussion, however, think of **travel** as the movement of people and **transportation** as the movement of goods. In this part you will take a look at how you and other Americans travel. Communication and transportation will be discussed in later parts.

MODERN MEANS OF TRAVEL

People used to do most of their traveling on foot, horseback, stagecoaches, or ships. None of these means offered much comfort or speed, but travelers had little choice if they needed to get from one place to another. Now you can choose to travel by the means that suits you best: automobiles, planes, buses, or trains.

1. Americans rely more on the automobile for travel than on any other means. There are about 120 million automobiles registered in this country, which is about one for every two people. When someone travels between cities, almost nine times out of ten it will be in a passenger car. Many families prefer to drive their cars on vacations because cars are convenient and generally less expensive than other means of travel. Business and professional workers may prefer to use cars because this frees them from having to depend on plane, bus, and train schedules.

People traveling on business often fly to a city and then rent a car to use while they are there. Vacationers may also rent cars, perhaps for as long as several weeks. Rental costs are based on the kind of car desired, the length of time the car is kept, and usually on the number of miles driven.

The driving habits of Americans have changed significantly in the last several years. Because of the shortages of oil and gasoline, people have tended to drive fewer miles and have been inclined to buy smaller cars than when gasoline was plentiful. Also, the increased cost and sometimes limited availability of gasoline have caused many families to take fewer long vacations by car. Nevertheless, the automobile remains the most important method of travel for the majority of people.

2. Flying is the second most popular means of travel, especially for executives and others who have limited time to get to distant places. The main advantage of air travel is its speed. If you are going on a vacation, air travel can enable you to spend extra time at your vacation spot. For business executives, air travel can mean spending less time away from their firms.

Illus. 40-1

Airline terminals like this one serve many people who prefer flying as a means of travel.

3. Buses are most popular as a means of traveling to smaller towns and cities. Bus transportation is usually less costly than the fares for train or air travel.

4. Over the past few decades, railroads have declined in importance as a means of travel. There was a time when you had the choice of several trains a day when you wanted to travel from one city to another. For the most part, this is no longer true. Because of this decline in service by railroads, passengers have been switching to airplanes, buses, and their own cars. Passenger trains now account for less than 1 percent of all travel between cities.

PLANNING A TRIP

Planning a trip is as important as planning any other activity. The better your planning is, the better your chances of having a successful trip will be. While there are many ways to plan a trip, in general you should carefully consider each of the following:

Where do you want to go? Will you be going to a place where no additional transportation will be needed once you reach your destination? For example, if you plan to spend a spring vacation in Florida, once you get to the beach you may not want to go any place else that will require transportation. In that case, your only problem is how to get to the Florida beaches.

On the other hand, perhaps you plan to visit several different cities and towns on your trip. Or maybe you will be going to only one city, but the people and things you want to see are widely scattered. In either of these situations, you would need to think not only about how to get to your initial destination but also how to get to the other places you want to visit.

How much time do you have available? If you have a limited amount of time and your destination is some distance away, you will probably have to fly in order to avoid spending all or most of your time traveling. Again considering the example of going to Florida for your week-long spring vacation, if you live in Minnesota, driving will take you at least four days (two days each way). That will leave you only three days to lie in the sun. If you go by plane, it will take only a few hours to go each way.

How much can you afford to spend? If the cost is of no importance to you and you want both speed and convenience, for a long trip you might fly to your destination and then rent a car.

If you want the least expensive means of travel and have plenty of time available, you may take a bus.

In considering the costs of travel, however, transportation costs are not the only factor to be figured. You need also to plan carefully how much you will need for lodging, food, admissions, and the many incidental costs you have when traveling. By planning you can avoid ending up 1,000 miles from home with no money.

Where will you stay when you get to your destination? Perhaps you will be able to stay with relatives or friends. Or you may stay in a motel or hotel. If you are planning to stay in a motel or hotel, you may need to make advanced reservations. Going to Florida without reservations during the time when universities and other schools take their spring vacations may cause you to arrive and have no place to stay.

Illus. 40-2

Traveling by bus can save you money.

SOURCES OF INFORMATION FOR THE TRAVELER

There is no shortage of information about travel. If you are planning a trip, begin your planning early so that you will have adequate time to search for the information you need.

Many magazines and books are devoted completely to travel and vacation topics. Before planning trips, it would be a good idea to check bookstores and libraries for such publications. Directories of information about motels, hotels, trailer courts, and campsites are also available. Some directories have complete information about the accommodations provided and the prices charged. These directories may be obtained from several different sources: city chambers of commerce, automobile clubs, travelers' information booths, and service stations, among others.

Also, don't forget to talk with relatives and friends who have taken the same or similar trips. They may be able to give you some very valuable advice.

USING THE SERVICES OF TRAVEL BUREAUS

If you need help in planning a trip, you can contact a travel bureau. Travel bureaus offer vacation ideas, trip suggestions, and information on costs of transportation and lodging. Travel bureaus will also make reservations, obtain tickets, and provide other services. Some vacationers like group tours where a guide takes care of tickets, baggage, hotel accommodations, and many other matters. Of course, many people prefer to travel independently. Travel bureaus will make trip arrangements to suit your special needs. The services of a travel bureau can help make a trip more enjoyable and perhaps less expensive than if you were to work out all the details yourself.

Travel bureaus receive their incomes mainly from airlines, car rental companies, hotels, and other such organizations. This income comes in the form of commissions on the tickets and services sold. Because they receive their incomes from other sources, travel bureaus usually do not charge travelers for their services.

TRAVELING IN OTHER COUNTRIES

Millions of Americans travel overseas every year. To travel in most countries, you need a **passport**. This is an official government document that identifies you (by photo and a brief description) as a citizen of the United States and permits you to leave the country and to return to it at a later date. Passports are good for five years. Applications for passports may be obtained from the federal building in most major cities and from main post offices. A **visa** is a permission granted by a government to enter a country and is required by most foreign nations. This is usually stamped on the passport by a consular representative of the country to be visited. When applying for a passport, you can find out about the inoculations (shots) that will be needed before traveling in certain foreign countries.

When you are planning a trip to a foreign country you can obtain information about the country from transportation companies, travel bureaus, and often from banks and other financial institutions. These firms are glad to help you since they may sell tickets, traveler's checks, and other services as a result. Large cities may also have offices of consular officials and other foreign government representatives who can give information about travel in their countries.

When traveling in a foreign country, you must have your American money changed into the currency of that country. You can make the exchange at banks, American Express offices, and many hotels and business firms.

INCREASING YOUR BUSINESS VOCABULARY

The following terms should become part of your business vocabulary. For each numbered statement, find the term that has the same meaning.

communication   travel
passport   visa
transportation

1. The movement of goods from one place to another.
2. The exchanging of information.
3. An official government document identifying a traveler and giving that traveler permission to leave and return to a country.
4. Permission granted by a government to enter its country.
5. The movement of people from one place to another.

UNDERSTANDING YOUR READING

1. What are the four principal means of travel in the United States?
2. Why do many people prefer travel by car rather than by other means of transportation?
3. How has the shortage of gasoline changed the driving habits of Americans?
4. What is the main advantage of air travel?
5. For what types of travel are buses most popular?
6. What kinds of information do you need in order to plan a trip?
7. If you want the least expensive means and have plenty of time, how should you travel?
8. Where can you get information about means of transportation and travel services?
9. Describe some of the services of travel bureaus.
10. What is the purpose of a passport?
11. What sources of information are available if you are planning a trip to a foreign country?

USING YOUR BUSINESS KNOWLEDGE

1. Airlines give fare discounts to certain travelers, such as children and military personnel. Why do you think this is done?
2. Mr. and Mrs. Reddington are planning to drive from Laredo, Texas to Caribou, Maine. Make a list of the expenses they should consider in preparing their vacation budget.
3. Harriet Engel, a cattle buyer for a supermarket chain, rents a car in Tulsa and at the end of three weeks returns the car in Denver. It would have been less expensive for Harriet to fly to Denver instead of driving. What reasons might Harriet have had for driving a rented car this distance and length of time?
4. Donald Brunsman is planning to go to a summer resort in Vermont for his vacation. He would like to know what services are offered by the different hotels at this resort before making reservations. From what sources can Donald obtain this information?
5. Suppose that you want to take a trip and are not sure whether you ought to go by plane, train, or bus. Make a list of the information you ought to have about each method of transportation before you make a decision.

SOLVING PROBLEMS IN BUSINESS

1. A car rental agency rents compact cars for $140 a week. If the car is kept longer than 7 days, an additional charge of $35 a day is made. If you want to rent a car for 10 days, how much will it cost you?

2. Maxine Hightower wants to take pictures with her camera while she is on vacation. The film for her camera costs $3.00 a roll. To have the roll of film developed costs $4.40.
   (a) What is the total cost for the film and developing of each roll of film?
   (b) If a roll of film has 20 pictures on it, what is the cost of each picture?

3. Henry and Wilma Ritchie are planning a 7-day driving vacation. They have budgeted the following amounts for each day of the trip:

Hotels and motels	$30.00
Gasoline and oil	15.00
Meals	25.00
Admissions and entertainment	20.00
Incidentals	10.00

   (a) How much will it cost the Ritchies for each day of the trip?
   (b) How much do the Ritchies expect to spend during the entire trip?
   (c) If they stay for 10 days rather than 7, how much will they spend?

4. The Varela family is planning a two-week vacation trip by car. They plan to travel 2400 kilometers. The Varelas' car averages 6 kilometers per liter of gasoline, and the average cost of gasoline is 40¢ per liter. How much will the Varelas spend for gasoline on their vacation?

5. When you apply for a passport, you are asked the reason for your trip out of the country. In a recent year, approximately 3,200,000 Americans applied for passports. They stated their reasons as shown below:

Government	590,000
Personal reasons	1,570,000
Pleasure	820,000
Business	165,000
Education	75,000

   To the nearest whole percent, figure the percent of people who traveled for each reason. Present your results in a table. Be sure that your figures add up to 100 percent.

EXPANDING YOUR UNDERSTANDING OF BUSINESS

1. Camping has become a very popular vacation activity for many families. Make a list of resources available to campers that would provide information on public and private campsites, the facilities that are available, and the costs.

2. Select a place in a nearby state that you would like to visit for one week. Report to the class on the following:
   (a) What types of transportation to this place are available?
   (b) What are the comparisons in cost and travel time among the possible methods of transportation?
   (c) Which method of transportation would you choose? Why?
   (d) Make an estimate of what a one-week trip would cost you. Include your transportation, food, lodging, entertainment, and any other expenses you might have.

3. Obtain an up-to-date map of your state. Pick a city and then plan a route for an automobile trip to that city. You might also plan alternate routes, for example, the quickest route and the most scenic route.

4. Most hotels in this country are operated on the European plan. However, hotels in resort areas are often operated on the American plan. Find out what these two plans mean. Why do you think resort hotels favor the American plan?

5. At one time, railroads were the most important means of long-distance travel in this country. Through research in the library, find out what caused the decline of passenger rail service. Present to your class a report on your findings.

41 USING TELEPHONE SERVICES

PART OBJECTIVES

After studying this part and completing the end-of-part activities, you will be able to:

1. Tell what kinds of information are found in telephone directories.
2. Explain the difference between a person-to-person and a station-to-station telephone call.
3. Give the four factors that determine the cost of a long distance call.
4. Tell why a business would use a Data-Phone.
5. List three reasons why you might want to send a telegram.
6. Explain how mailgram service works.

Suppose you have a summer job working at a resort on an island off the Georgia coast. In late August a hurricane hits the area and does a tremendous amount of damage. When your parents in Mississippi see the report of the storm on television, they become very anxious to know if you have been injured. What is the fastest means you can use to let them know that you are all right? The telephone, of course, is the answer.

No doubt you have used the telephone many hundreds of times. As you know, the telephone makes it possible for you to have pleasurable conversations with your friends and relatives. And, as in the example of the hurricane, it can also be an important lifeline in times of emergency. In addition, it is an essential tool in conducting business. It is no wonder that almost every home in the nation has at least one telephone.

As you can see, the telephone is very important to your way of living. Since it is so important to you, you should make sure you know how to use it so that it can serve you best.

THE TELEPHONE BOOK

You might not have looked at it this way before, but did you know that your telephone book is the set of instructions for your telephone? If you want to know how to use your telephone or what services are available, look in the front of your telephone book.

The telephone directory usually has two parts: an alphabetical directory and a classified directory. These may be separate books if you live in a large city. The **alphabetical directory**, or the "white pages," lists all the people in your area who have telephones. The names are listed alphabetically, along with the addresses and telephone numbers. It is possible to have a telephone and not be listed in the alphabetical directory, but it costs extra to have an unlisted number.

The other part of the telephone book is the **classified directory** or "Yellow Pages." In this directory you will find a listing of businesses organized according to the goods or services they offer. For example, if you are looking for a baby-sitter for your dog, you would look in the Yellow Pages. By the way, if that is the case, you'd better look under "Dog Kennels" rather than "Babysitters." The fastest way to find information in the classified directory is to go to the index in front. The index will quickly tell you what goods and services are listed in the Yellow Pages.

KINDS OF TELEPHONE SERVICE

Telephone calls may be either local or long distance. Long distance calls are those made outside the area served by your telephone exchange. Your telephone book tells you which calls will be local and which will be long distance. Over 90 percent of all calls made are local calls. Most subscribers pay a fixed monthly rate for their telephone service and can make as many local calls as they want. In some cities, though, a subscriber may pay a lower monthly rate and then pay an extra amount for each local call over a certain number. In either case, a separate charge is made for each long distance call.

There are two kinds of long distance service. When you call **person-to-person**, the one you call must speak with you in order to complete the call. Charges begin when you start talking with that person. If that person cannot be located, there is no charge for the call. When you call **station-to-station**, you call a certain telephone number, and it is assumed that you are willing to talk with anyone at that telephone. Charges start from the moment the connection is made. Station-to-station calls are more easily and quickly completed than are person-to-person calls. For this reason, station-to-station calls are less expensive.

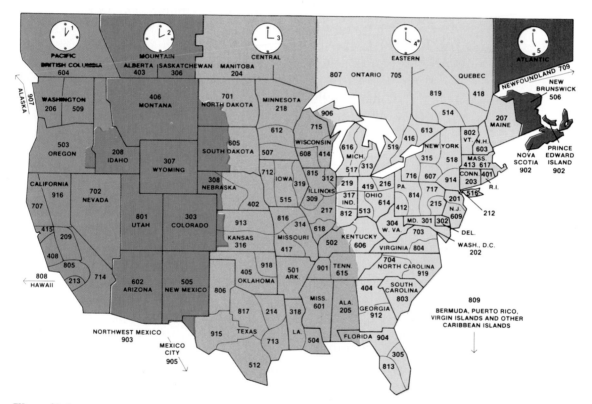

Illus. 41-1

Knowing the time and the area code of the place you want to call is important in calling long distance. This information is also available in your telephone book.

In many communities, a person-to-person call must be placed by an operator. In larger cities, however, person-to-person calls may be dialed directly by dialing the number and giving the operator the name of the person you are calling. Most station-to-station calls can be dialed directly by the caller rather than being placed by the operator. This is referred to as **direct distance dialing**.

The charges for long distance calls differ according to whether the call is made person-to-person or station-to-station, the distance of the call, the time of day the call is made, and how long the call lasts. The minimum charge is for a definite period of time, usually one or three minutes, depending on the type of call. An overtime charge is made for each extra minute used. Charges for long distance calls are usually less in the evening, on weekends, and on certain holidays.

Both person-to-person and station-to-station calls may be made as **collect calls**. This means that charges are billed to the telephone number being called rather than to the number from which the call is made. If you want to call your parents long distance from a friend's house, you can tell the operator you want to call collect. The long distance operator will ask your parents whether they will accept the charges. The charges will then be placed on your parents' telephone bill.

TELEPHONE SERVICES FOR BUSINESS

Since you know how important the telephone is in your life, you can easily imagine how essential it is to business. Business transactions are constantly being discussed and completed by telephone. Telephone companies offer special kinds of telephone equipment and services to all customers, but particularly to businesses.

You probably have seen some of the switchboards used in business. These help direct incoming and outgoing calls to the correct people. There are also telephones that dial certain frequently called numbers automatically. To make a call on such a phone, you simply insert a card and push one button.

As you can probably guess, businesses usually pay more for their telephone services than do individuals. This is so because businesses use more equipment, use different kinds of equipment, and use it more often.

Ilus. 41-2
Telephone services are important to businesses of all kinds. Both this office supervisor and this doctor rely on the telphone in the work that they do.

SPECIAL COMMUNICATION SERVICES

There are times when businesses need to send written information very rapidly from one place to another. Perhaps they cannot wait for the mail. Two services that will fill this need are the Data-Phone and the telegraph system.

A **Data-Phone** enables computers to "talk" with each other over telephone lines. The computer machine language is changed into electrical tones that are sent over telephone lines, then changed again into machine language at the receiving end. The receiving computer can then print out the information. The charge for this service is about the same as it would be for a long distance call.

Messages, money orders, and many other kinds of information can be sent by telegraph service. On special occasions you may want to use a telegraph service. For example, you may want to send a special birthday greeting to someone, or maybe even flowers or candy.

Of course, the best known telegraph service is the telegram. If you or a business want to send a telegraph message, you can choose to send it as a full-rate telegram or as a night letter. A **full-rate telegram** is sent and delivered as quickly as possible. The cost is determined by the length of the message and whether it is being sent to another location within the state or out of state. Messages sent within the state are less expensive. Since the telegraph company is not as busy during the night as it is during the day, it offers a lower rate for relatively long messages sent at night. Messages sent during the night are called **night letters**.

At their destinations, telegrams are usually delivered by telephone. However, the telegraph company will provide a written

Illus. 41-3

A telegram is one of the fastest ways to send a message.

copy of the message if you ask them to do so. There is an extra charge for this service.

A rapidly growing service which combines the efforts of Western Union and the U.S. Postal Service is the mailgram. The **mailgram** is a message service that is designed to provide next-business-day delivery to any location within the continental U.S. Mailgram messages may be called in or delivered in person

```
MGMNWKB NWK
2-205617E158 06/07/81                 ши ши Mailgram
ICS IPMMTZZ CSP                       western union
2018251100 MGM TDMT UPPER SADDLE RIVER NJ 100 06-07 0929A EST
ZIP 60622-2596




     MARGARET R. BURMAN
     6492 EASTERN AVENUE
     CHICAGO, IL 60622-2596



     DEAR MS. BURMAN:

     YOUR ORDER FOR TWENTY DOZEN CARBON RIBBONS WAS SHIPPED TO YOU VIA
     APEX FREIGHT LINES TODAY. WE APPRECIATE THE OPPORTUNITY TO WELCOME
     YOU AS A NEW CUSTOMER.

     PLEASE GIVE US THE PLEASURE OF SERVING YOU WHENEVER YOU NEED OFFICE
     SUPPLIES.

     BENJAMIN HINTON
     ORDER DEPARTMENT
     MARTCO, INC.
     165 CRESCENT STREET
     UPPER SADDLE RIVER, NJ 07458-6284

     0932 EST

     MGMNWKB NWK
```

Illus. 41-4

A mailgram.

to a Western Union office, which then transmits the message to a post office near the destination address. At this receiving post office, the message is printed and placed in a special blue and white mailing envelope for delivery by a regular letter carrier.

Illus. 41-5

Some businesses have a mailgram terminal in their office. This enables a business to send a mailgram directly to another city.

INCREASING YOUR BUSINESS VOCABULARY

The following terms should become part of your business vocabulary. For each numbered statement, find the term that has the same meaning.

alphabetical directory	*full-rate telegram*
classified directory	*mailgram*
collect call	*night letter*
Data-Phone	*person-to-person call*
direct distance dialing	*station-to-station call*

1. A message service provided by Western Union and the U.S. Postal Service which gives next-business-day delivery to any location within the continental United States.
2. A long distance call which is made to a particular person.
3. A telephone that enables computers to send information over telephone lines.
4. A book listing all the people in an area who have telephones, arranged alphabetically.

5. A method of making a long distance call in which the caller dials the number and does not require help from the operator.
6. A telegram which is sent and delivered as quickly as possible.
7. A book listing all businesses which have telephones, arranged according to the goods or services they offer.
8. A long distance call which is billed to the number that is called.
9. A telegram sent overnight for a relatively low rate.
10. A long distance call in which the caller will speak with anyone at the number called.

1. Where can you find instructions on how to use the telephone?
2. How are names and telephone numbers arranged in the white pages? In the Yellow Pages?
3. How can you find out if a phone call you want to make is a local or long distance call?
4. What is the difference between a person-to-person and a station-to-station call?
5. What determines the charge for a long distance call?
6. What is the area code for Phoenix, Arizona?
7. Why might a business use Data-Phone service?
8. What are three reasons why you might want to send a telegram?
9. Why is the rate for a night letter less than the rate for a full-rate telegram?
10. How does mailgram service work?

1. You want to do something special to remember your grandmother's birthday, so you decide to send her a telegram. If your grandmother's birthday is the day after tomorrow, what kind of telegram would you send, and when would you send it?
2. You are in Logan, Utah, and you want to make a long distance call to Raleigh, North Carolina, about a job opening. You want your call to reach Raleigh by 3:00 p.m. in order to make sure the office will be open and the personnel director will be there. Using the time zone information in Illus. 41-1, what is the latest time you can place the call in Logan to reach Raleigh by 3:00 p.m.?
3. Paul Romito is a salesperson for the Bennington Paper Company. He travels a lot and makes many long distance calls. What kind of long distance service do you think Mr. Romito should use in placing the following calls?

(a) Mr. Romito will be unable to keep a promise to ship an order to one of his most frequent customers in a city 200 miles away. He wants to talk with the Purchasing Manager personally to explain why the order will be delayed.

(b) Mr. Romito is looking for new customers in a certain city. He wants to place long distance calls to these companies and speak with the person in charge of buying paper supplies, but he doesn't know who this person would be in each company.

(c) Away from home on a business trip, Mr. Romito wants to call home one evening because it is his son's birthday. He knows that the Bennington Company does not pay for personal calls while he is traveling.

4. Carolyn Arnold is the manager of an electronics repair shop. She ordered some special parts from a supply company in another city yesterday. Suddenly this morning, she realized that she ordered the wrong thing and she wants to correct the order before it is shipped today or tomorrow. The supply company will not accept telephone orders. What should Ms. Arnold do?

5. Rita Lofton placed a long distance call to her brother in Cedar Falls, Iowa. When she received her bill, she saw that she was not billed for a call to Cedar Falls, but she was billed for a call to Cedar Rapids, Iowa. She is not sure that she was billed for the call that she placed. What should Rita do?

SOLVING PROBLEMS IN BUSINESS

1. A telephone line used by only one subscriber is a private line. A party line serves two or more subscribers. In Bismarck, the monthly charge for a private line is $10.60. The charge for a party line is $8.50.
   (a) How much more per month does a private line cost in Bismarck?
   (b) How much more is that per year?

2. At the Commerce City Bank, each executive has a telephone on his or her desk. In addition, there is one telephone for every two clerical workers. If there are 15 executives and 20 clerical workers employed at the bank, how many telephones are there at the Commerce City Bank?

3. Patricia Graff is a telephone installer. She does a lot of driving on the job. In fact, last month, Patricia drove her installer's truck 2600 kilometers.
   (a) How many miles is that?

(b) The company performs maintenance service on its trucks every 3,000 miles. If Patricia's truck was serviced at the beginning of last month, about when will it need service again?

4. Dorothy Weaver, who lives in Owensville, Ohio, wants to call her cousin who lives in Parkersburg, West Virginia. A station-to-station call costs $1.85 for the first 3 minutes and $.30 for each additional minute. A person-to-person call costs $2.85 for the first 3 minutes and $.30 for each additional minute.

(a) What would be the cost of a 10 minute station-to-station call?

(b) What would be the cost of a 10 minute person-to-person call?

(c) What percent greater is the cost of a person-to-person call over a station-to-station call? (Round your answer to the nearest whole percent.)

5. Floyd Westfield works in Cincinnati, but often makes business trips to Houston. He sometimes needs to send telegrams to his office in Cincinnati. The telegram rates between these two cities are shown below:

> Full-rate telegram: $4.95 for the first 15 words, and $.18 for each additional word.
> Night letter: $4.45 for the first 50 words, and $.10 for each additional word.
> Mailgram: $2.80 for the first 50 words, and $.75 for each group of 50 words thereafter.

How much would each of the following telegrams cost Mr. Westfield?

(a) A full-rate telegram of 14 words

(b) A night letter of 14 words

(c) A mailgram of 14 words

(d) A full-rate telegram of 115 words

(e) A night letter of 115 words

(f) A mailgram of 115 words

EXPANDING YOUR UNDERSTANDING OF BUSINESS

1. Examine the white pages of your telephone directory to answer the following questions:

(a) How would you find out the telephone number of a friend living in another city?

(b) In your location, can you dial person-to-person and collect calls, or must an operator place these calls for you?

(c) What numbers would you call to report a police or fire emergency?

(d) At what time do evening, night, and weekend rates for long distance calls go into effect? Why do you think it costs less to make long distance calls during the evening, night, and weekends?

2. Using the index in the front of the Yellow Pages, tell what heading you would look under in the following situations. Give the name and phone number of one business in each category.
   (a) You want to call a movie theater to find out what time tonight's show starts.
   (b) You want to find out how much judo lessons cost.
   (c) Your grandfather will be coming home from the hospital after an operation, and you want to arrange to rent a wheelchair for him.
   (d) Your parents are planning a vacation trip and want to make plane reservations.
   (e) You need someone to repair your portable typewriter.

3. The rates charged by telephone companies are carefully regulated by the government. Why should the government be concerned with regulating the charges for telephone service when it does not regulate the prices of such things as food and clothing?

4. The needs of businesses for telephone equipment and services are different from those of most individuals. Listed below are several kinds of telephone equipment and services used by businesses. Explain what each kind of equipment is. The telephone company should be able to provide you with information about each.
   (a) Touch-Tone service
   (b) Call Director
   (c) conference call
   (d) mobile telephone service
   (e) WATS (Wide Area Telecommunications Service)

5. Several terms related to telegraph service are listed below. Define each of them. You will find some of the terms through library research, and the nearest Western Union office can help you define others.
   (a) radiogram
   (b) cablegram
   (c) telegraph tie line

42 COMMUNICATING BY LETTER

PART OBJECTIVES

After studying this part and completing the end-of-part activities, you will be able to:
1. List three purposes for which business letters are written.
2. Give the six characteristics of a good letter.
3. Explain how your letters help the readers form an impression of you.
4. List the six major parts of a business letter.
5. Tell what kinds of material should be sent by first-class mail.

Last Christmas Ron Lowrey, who lives in Silverton, Colorado, received a knitted ski hat from his grandmother who lives in Stowe, Vermont. Ron was very grateful for the gift and immediately began wearing the hat. He was also very prompt in thanking his grandmother for her thoughtfulness. He sent his thanks in a letter.

No doubt you have had many experiences just like Ron's, and you, too, have probably written letters of thanks. You have probably written other kinds of letters as well. Americans generally write many letters each year. In fact, the U.S. Postal Service delivers over 450 pieces of mail every year for each person in the United States. Mail is a very important way for us to communicate with others who are in different places from where we are. While it is slower than either the telephone or telegraph, the mail is also much less expensive.

In the years ahead, you are going to be writing letters

505

regularly. You will write thank-you letters, just as Ron Lowrey did, and also letters requesting information, letters applying for jobs, and letters to others with whom you want to share the experiences of your life. And if you enter the world of business, it is quite likely you will write numerous formal business letters.

Whether you are writing a letter for business or personal reasons, you should remember that your letters represent you. When others do not know you or cannot see and talk with you, they form an impression of you from your letters. Therefore, you want your letters to make a good impression. If your letters are neat in appearance and clearly written, they will usually make a favorable impression for you.

USING LETTERS IN BUSINESS

Much of the world's business is carried on through letters. Every day millions of letters flow through the business and government offices of our country. A large number of these letters are written to tell others about the products and services businesses are selling. Business letters are also written to answer customers' questions and complaints, to acknowledge orders, and to request information from suppliers of products.

Good letter communication is basic to the operation of almost any type of business. In fact, a letter may even mean the difference between success and failure in some business dealings. A well-written letter answering a customer's complaint, for example, can keep the customer's goodwill. A poorly written letter can mean that the customer will never come back to that business again.

WRITING A BUSINESS LETTER

To write an acceptable business letter takes skill and thought. A good letter needs to be: (1) carefully planned, (2) brief and to the point, (3) accurate, (4) complete, (5) courteous, and (6) attractive in appearance. Let's look at each of these six points.

     1. **Carefully planned.** Plan what you want to say before writing the letter. A good way to do this is to jot down on a piece of scrap paper the main points you want the reader to understand. If you start writing before you have in mind what you want to say, your letter may not be clear and you may leave out some important facts.

2. **Brief and to the point.** When you write a business letter, you will find that if you can write the way you talk, you will have a letter that expresses you. Watch carefully, though, that "write as you talk" doesn't make your letter something to be laughed at. Write in complete sentences and avoid slang. Your letters should say in simple and easily understood language what you have to say, and then close.

3. **Accurate.** Accuracy of facts, figures, directions, and descriptions is very important. An incorrect statement might require much additional correspondence to clear up misunderstandings. Check also to see that there are no errors in grammar or spelling. After you have written a letter, read it over carefully to be sure that what you have said makes sense.

4. **Complete.** A letter may be accurate in terms of what is included and still leave out essential information. Suppose you write to the manufacturer of your clock radio with a question. If you forget to mention the model of clock radio that you own, additional letters will probably be needed to get the information you want.

5. **Courteous.** Courtesy and tact in a letter show your consideration for the person to whom you are writing. Remember, the reader of your letter can't see you. Your letter has to be the reader's picture of you. The tone of your letter is just as important as the tone of your voice over the telephone.

6. **Attractive in appearance.** When you meet someone for the first time, you form impressions from the way that person speaks and looks. A business letter, too, creates a first impression. If the letter is attractive, the first impression is good. If the letter is unattractive, the first impression is bad. Before sending out your letter, check the following: Is the letter placed neatly on the page? Is it free from messy erasures? What about smudges, fingerprints, or pencil marks?

HOW THE LETTER LOOKS

Though there are many styles of business letters, most firms choose one style for their correspondence. Two styles, one for handwritten letters and one for typewritten letters, are shown in Illus. 42-1 and 42-2.

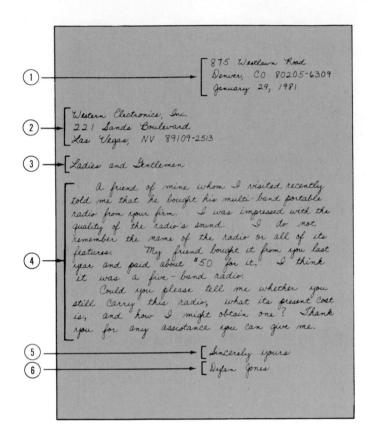

875 Westlawn Road
Denver, CO 80205-6309
January 29, 1981

Western Electronics, Inc.
221 Sands Boulevard
Las Vegas, NV 89109-2513

Ladies and Gentlemen

A friend of mine whom I visited recently told me that he bought his multi-band portable radio from your firm. I was impressed with the quality of the radio's sound. I do not remember the name of the radio or all of its features. My friend bought it from you last year and paid about $50 for it. I think it was a five-band radio.

Could you please tell me whether you still carry this radio, what its present cost is, and how I might obtain one? Thank you for any assistance you can give me.

Sincerely yours

Dylan Jones

① The *heading* contains the writer's address and the date. Place the ZIP code after the state abbreviation.

② Write the *address* to which you are sending the letter a little below the heading at the left side of the page.

③ Begin the *salutation* at the left margin. No punctuation is required after the salutation, but a colon is often used. When a letter is addressed to an individual, the salutation usually includes "Dear" and the name of the person addressed. The words "Ladies and Gentlemen" are ordinarily used as the salutation when the letter is addressed to a business.

④ Indent the first line of each paragraph in the *body* of the letter about one-half inch. Follow the rules of English writing in paragraphing and punctuating the body of the letter.

⑤ Begin the *complimentary close* at about the middle of the line of writing. If a colon is used after the salutation, use a comma after the complimentary close.

⑥ The *signature* is the handwritten name of the writer.

Illus. 42-1

An acceptable form for
a handwritten business
letter.

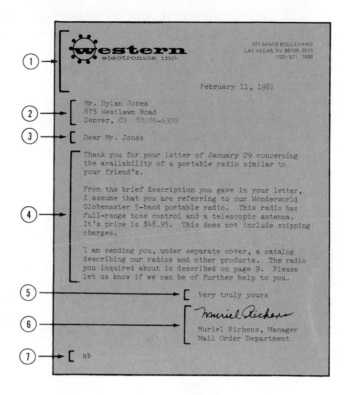

① The name and address of the business are printed on a **letterhead.** Notice the placement of the date.

② The address is typed on the fourth line below the date. Each line of the address begins at the left margin. No period follows the **two-letter state abbreviation,** which is in capital letters. (The state abbreviations were specially designed for use with an optical character reader, a machine that helps post offices speed up the handling of mail.)

③ The salutation begins at the left margin and is separated by a blank line from the address and the body of the letter. It may be followed by a colon, although no punctuation is required.

④ The body of the letter is typed with single spacing, and a blank space is left between paragraphs. The first line of each paragraph may start at the left margin or may be indented.

⑤ The complimentary close starts at the center of the page, one double space below the last line of the body. If a colon is used after the salutation, a comma follows the complimentary close.

⑥ The name and title of the writer are usually typed below the handwritten signature.

⑦ When a letter is typed by someone other than the writer, the typist's initials, called **reference initials,** are placed in the lower left corner.

Illus. 42-2

An acceptable form for a typewritten business letter.

An extra copy (a carbon copy or photocopy) of each business letter should be made and filed. This copy serves as a record of what has been said and done. Having an extra copy is especially important for letters referring to times and dates for appointments, payment of bills, travel reservations, orders for products and services, and job applications. Having the extra copy will often save time, expense, and further letter writing.

The address on an envelope should be the same as the address in the letter. The writer's address should also be on the envelope, usually in the upper left-hand corner.

Illus. 42-3

A letter that is carefully written makes a good impression for you.

POSTAL CARDS

Postal cards are sometimes used to send brief messages. They are typed in a style similar to the form of a business letter. Usually the address of the person to whom the card is being written is placed only on the front of the card. No extra space is left between paragraphs. Stamped government postal cards may be purchased from post offices for less than the postage cost of a letter.

MAILING LETTERS PROPERLY

It takes time and effort to write a good letter. If you go to that much trouble, you should then make sure that you use the correct postal service to deliver your letter. Using the correct postal service will get your letter where you want it, when you want it there, and at the lowest possible cost.

Ordinary letters and postal cards are sent by **first-class mail**. First-class mail includes typewritten and handwritten material that is sealed against postal inspection. In addition to letters and postal cards, you would use first-class mail to send a savings book to a bank, football or theater tickets to a friend, or a check to a firm to which you owe money.

First-class mail may be sent anywhere in the United States and its possessions for a small charge for each ounce or fraction of an ounce. The rate for first-class mail sent to Canada and Mexico is the same as that for similar mail sent within the United States. Letters to all other countries require a higher amount of postage. Unless you are certain about rates and other regulations for foreign mail, you should check at the post office for correct information.

It is very important that correct postage be placed on each envelope. If no postage is used, the envelope is returned to the sender. Mail without enough postage is delivered to the person addressed upon payment of "postage due." Needless to say, annoyance and loss of time occur in both cases.

INCREASING YOUR BUSINESS VOCABULARY

The following terms should become part of your business vocabulary. For each numbered statement, find the term that has the same meaning.

first-class mail
letterhead
reference initials

1. The initials of the person who types a letter, placed in the lower left corner of the letter.
2. Mail that includes handwritten or typewritten material that is sealed against postal inspection.
3. A sheet of paper with the name and address of a business printed on it.

UNDERSTANDING YOUR READING

1. List three of the purposes for which business letters are written.
2. List and explain briefly six characteristics of a good letter.
3. In what ways does a business letter create a first impression of the writer?
4. What are the six major parts of a business letter?
5. What information is commonly printed on a letterhead?
6. What salutation would you use in a letter to the Humber Investment Company? In a letter to Mr. Arthur Humber?
7. Why should an extra copy of each business letter be kept?
8. In what ways may the form of a message written on a postal card be different from that of a message written on business stationery?
9. What kinds of material should you send by first-class mail?
10. What happens if you mail a letter, but forget to put a stamp on the envelope? If you put only half of the required amount of postage on the envelope?

USING YOUR BUSINESS KNOWLEDGE

1. Bring the class two letters that you or someone you know has received recently from business firms. Examine them, using as a basis the six characteristics of a good letter presented in this part. How would you classify these letters according to their purposes?
2. Florence Grant is preparing to write a letter requesting a reservation at Rainbow Lodge for a weekend holiday. What facts should Florence include in her letter?
3. Bring to class a few letterheads from local businesses. Point out what information the letterheads contain, the size and style of type used, and the arrangement of the information on the page. Can you offer any suggestions for improving the letterheads?
4. What advantages and disadvantages do postal cards have for communicating business messages?
5. Millions of letters are typed every day. Typing a salutation and a complimentary close on all these letters costs a lot in time and money. Some people feel that these two parts of the letter are unnecessary and costly, and therefore they should be omitted. Do you agree? Why or why not?

1. In one recent year, it was calculated that the average business letter cost about $6.10 to produce. This figure included the cost of the executive's and secretary's time, the cost of supplies, and several other costs. One business writes an average of 120 letters each five-day week.
   (a) What does it cost this business each week to write letters?
   (b) What does it cost this business each day to write letters?

2. One typist at the Hanna Manufacturing Company earns $4.50 an hour. The typist works 8 hours a day and 5½ days a week.
   (a) How much does the typist earn in one week?
   (b) How much would the typist earn in four weeks?

3. Write or type the following letter properly on a sheet of paper 8½ by 11 inches. Use today's date and your address. Sign your name. The New World Foundation, 709 Franklin Boulevard, Wilmington, Delaware 19808-6359. Ladies and Gentlemen: Thank you for sending me a copy of "The Air Around Us." Before I read this leaflet, I had never fully realized the great need for us to solve the problems of air and water pollution in our country today. (New paragraph) This leaflet will help me to prepare my term paper on "Conserving Our Natural Resources." I appreciate your answering my request so quickly. Sincerely yours.

4. You are the president of your high school business club. The club has decided to ask Dr. Emily Quinn, a professor of business communication at a university in a nearby city, to give a short talk at the regular monthly meeting of the club. The meeting is to be held on Wednesday afternoon of next week. Dr. Quinn is to be in your city that day to address a meeting of the American Business Writing Society. Write a letter to Dr. Quinn asking her to speak to your club. Use paper measuring 8½ by 11 inches. Use your school address and sign your name. For Dr. Quinn's address, use a real or imaginary name of a university and the name of a nearby city. Tell Dr. Quinn that the meeting will be held in the school auditorium at 3:00 and that at least 100 people will be there.

5. In the United States, the most commonly used size of stationery is 8½ by 11 inches. In countries using the metric system, the size of stationery in common use measures 210 by 297 millimeters.
   (a) Which sheet is wider, the metric sheet or the U.S. standard sheet?
   (b) Which sheet is longer?

EXPANDING YOUR UNDERSTANDING OF BUSINESS

1. Even though your letters are well written and neatly typed, they may still make a poor impression if they are not folded and placed properly in their envelopes. Demonstrate to the class the proper method of folding a standard letter (8½ by 11 inches) for a large envelope and for a small envelope. Also, show how a small or half sheet should be folded for a small envelope. A typewriting or business communication textbook will help you.

2. By visiting an office using mail-handling equipment or by obtaining advertising literature on the equipment, prepare a brief report on one or both of the following topics:

   (a) How a folding machine operates.

   (b) Sealing and stamping envelopes by machine.

3. Interoffice correspondence is an important part of written communication in businesses. Obtain samples of their interoffice communication forms from at least two businesses and at least two government offices. Report on the similarities and differences of the forms.

4. Prepare a short oral report for the class on one of the following questions. For information or examples, refer to postal service publications or talk with local post office officials.

   (a) Under what conditions may a sealed letter be opened by postal authorities?

   (b) What is the difference between registered mail and certified mail? What is the advantage of paying an additional fee for a return receipt on registered or certified mail?

   (c) When and why would you use special delivery service?

   (d) If you were planning to drive across the United States this coming summer, how could you plan to have mail forwarded to you?

   (e) What does the term "franked mail" mean? Who uses it?

SHIPPING GOODS

The last time you were on an interstate highway, did you happen to notice how many trucks were also on the road? It may have seemed as if there were more trucks than passenger cars. However, think for a minute about why those trucks were there and what they were doing. They were transporting goods to all parts of the nation so that you and others can conveniently get the things you need to live. They may have been transporting food, clothing, washing machines, cattle, or mobile homes. In fact, you probably saw trucks carrying all of those goods and more.

Trucks are just one method of transporting goods. In this country there is a need for many different means of transportation. In addition to trucks, there are trains, planes, ships, and pipelines. These different shipping services are available to you and to business to move goods from one place to another. While you may never ship anything by train or pipeline, you should have some idea of what services are available and what the special features of each are.

CHOOSING A MEANS OF TRANSPORTATION

Choosing a way to transport goods is not always easy, especially since there are thousands of companies that provide transportation services. Goods that are transported are called **freight** or **shipments**. The person or company sending the shipment is known as the **shipper**. An individual or company that transports goods or people is called a **carrier**.

There are two main types of carriers: private and public. **Private carriers** are used by their owners to move their own products. The truck a farmer uses for hauling supplies or products is a private carrier. So is the truck that a retailer uses to deliver customers' orders. **Public carriers** are used by their owners to move goods for others.

Before choosing a means of transportation, the following factors should be considered:

1. **Nature of the goods.** Do the goods have certain features that limit how the shipment might be made? For example, what are the size, shape, and weight? Are the goods in solid or liquid form? Are they fragile?

2. **Distance.** How far must the goods be sent? Sending something across town means something quite different from sending it across the country.

3. **Speed.** How fast should the goods be delivered? Deliveries are made quickly by air and slowly by ship. Speed is of little importance for an order of snow shovels placed in the summer. But a special medicine that is needed to save a life must be sent quickly.

4. **Service.** What types of service do you need? Will the goods be picked up at your home, or must you take them to the carrier? Is insurance on the shipment provided?

5. **Cost.** What is a fair and reasonable price to pay for shipping the goods? Of course, the kind of item you are shipping, the distance you are sending it, and the services provided will help determine the cost.

SHIPPING BY MAIL

Suppose you wanted to send a friend in another city a box of candy as a birthday present. The best method would probably be to send it by mail. The particular service you would use to send the candy would be **fourth-class mail** or **parcel post**. This class includes all packages that weigh one pound or more and that may be opened for postal inspection. Parcel-post rates change according to the distance the package is to be sent, as well as according to its weight. There are limits to the size and weight of packages that can be sent by parcel post. Ask someone at your post office if you are not sure about whether a package will be accepted.

USING PRIVATE PARCEL DELIVERY COMPANIES

If you were away from home on a long visit and decided you wanted your parents to send your guitar to you, they couldn't send it through the mail because it would be too big. In that case, they might send it by one of the private parcel delivery companies, such as United Parcel Service. There are several private parcel delivery companies that provide this service to both individuals and businesses. These companies operate their trucks and planes mainly between and around large cities. Parcel delivery services are often used by retail firms that send small packages to customers. Private parcel delivery companies have quick and convenient service that usually includes pickup and delivery.

SHIPPING BY BUS

Did you know that you can send small packages by bus? Many bus lines carry shipments on their regular passenger schedules. Shipping this way will give you very fast service. Of course, the town to which you want to send the package must be on the bus route. Packages shipped by bus must be taken to and picked up from the bus station.

SHIPPING BY TRUCK

Sometimes you will have a very large box or other item to ship. In those instances you might consider calling a trucking company. Many trucking companies will pick up packages at your home. Some companies offer special express service between major cities, often overnight.

SHIPPING NEEDS OF BUSINESSES

As you can probably guess, the transportation needs of businesses are different from those of individuals. Businesses must usually ship more items over greater distances than do individuals. Many times, however, business firms will use the same methods of shipping as individuals. For example, most firms make great use of parcel post, private delivery services, bus express, and trucking companies. Many organizations have their own trucks.

But some kinds of businesses have need for methods of transporting items that are very large or in great quantity. This is especially true for manufacturing and processing companies.

SHIPPING BY TRAIN

A great network of railroad lines extends throughout our country. Rail transportation is best suited to handling bulky, heavy goods in large quantities at reasonable speed. It often has cost advantages for such items, especially over long-distance routes.

Railroads also offer the shipper many special facilities. For example, a railroad can build track right up to a new factory. The railroad can then give door-to-door pickup and delivery service to shippers. Railroads also build cars especially for certain goods with special requirements, such as refrigerator cars for fresh foods.

Illus. 43-1

Trains are the most efficient means of shipping heavy freight such as coal over long distances.

Most railroads have adopted a policy of not accepting shipments of less than a full carload. Shippers sending smaller items may turn them over to firms known as **freight forwarders**. These firms group many small shipments into a full carload.

USING TRUCKS IN BUSINESS

There are over 30 million trucks on our streets and highways. Trucks have increased their share of cargo hauling in recent years because of a number of advantages. First, they can go almost anywhere to almost any town, right to the doors of the shipper and the receiver. Second, their time schedules are very flexible. A truck can begin its run as soon as a load is picked up; a railroad or an airline operates on a fixed schedule. Trucks also accept small shipments and consolidate a number of them to make a truckload. For fragile cargo, trucks offer the advantage of less handling of the shipment and thus lessen the chance of breakage.

Illus. 43-2

Trucks carry the second largest quantity of goods in the U.S.

CARRYING GOODS BY SHIP

Cargo being shipped by water often goes by barge or small ship on inland waterways and by larger ships in ocean trade. Ships travel our major rivers and the Great Lakes. Ships also carry goods from one coastal city to another and handle most of the freight across oceans. Oil from the Middle East, for example, comes to us by ship.

The greatest advantage of shipping by water is that its cost is relatively low. Water is ideal for shipping bulky cargo, such as coal, lumber, and grains, to cities that can be reached by water. The disadvantage is that water traffic is slow and waterways do not go everywhere.

COMBINING METHODS OF TRANSPORTATION

A service offered by trucks and railroads together is called **piggyback service**. Goods are loaded into a trailer at the factory or some other point. The trailer is hauled by truck to a railroad siding and is lifted onto a flatcar. When the shipment reaches its destination, the trailer is lifted off the flatcar and moved by truck to the receiver. A similar service, called **fishyback**, is available for water shipments. An adaptation of piggyback and fishyback is called **containerization**. With this service, goods are packed by the shipper in large containers which can be carried on railroad cars, trucks, or ships. These containers are not as heavy or bulky as the trailers used with piggyback and fishyback.

SHIPPING BY PLANE

Even though air shipments account for less than 1 percent of the nation's total transportation, this service is very important.

Illus. 43-3

In this shipyard, large containers of cargo are stored until they are ready to be shipped.

Special planes can carry shipments of more than 100 tons. Smaller shipments often go aboard regular passenger planes. A shipment between any two cities in the continental United States usually takes no more than two days.

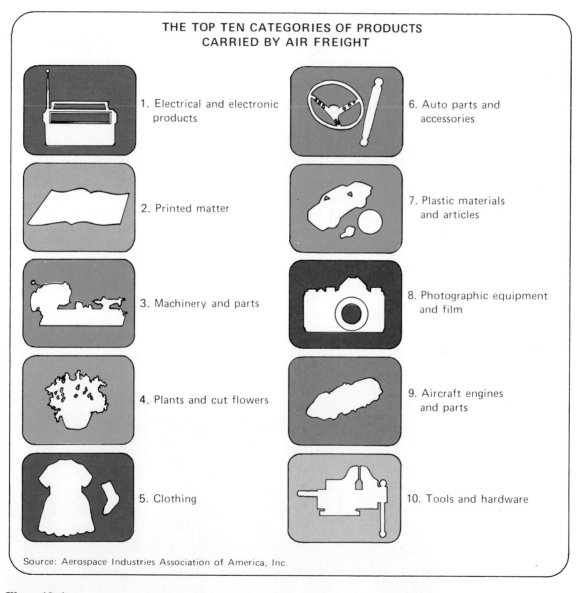

THE TOP TEN CATEGORIES OF PRODUCTS CARRIED BY AIR FREIGHT

1. Electrical and electronic products
2. Printed matter
3. Machinery and parts
4. Plants and cut flowers
5. Clothing
6. Auto parts and accessories
7. Plastic materials and articles
8. Photographic equipment and film
9. Aircraft engines and parts
10. Tools and hardware

Source: Aerospace Industries Association of America, Inc.

Illus. 43-4

This illustration shows the products most commonly shipped by plane.

Air freight is more expensive than other means of transportation, but things other than rates alone need to be considered. Air freight may actually be less expensive than other forms of transportation when the time factor is important. For example, it may be the best method of shipping perishable merchandise.

Most airline companies offer air freight service. In addition, many private parcel delivery companies handle air freight shipments. Pickup and delivery are usually part of their service.

SENDING GOODS THROUGH PIPELINES

Pipelines are used to transport the third largest quantity of goods in the U.S. Only trains and trucks carry a greater volume of freight than do pipelines. Pipelines are mostly used to ship liquid products, especially oil. On a small scale, solid goods such as coal, wheat, and wood chips can be sent by pipeline.

An advantage of a pipeline is that, once it is built, operating costs are low. The cost of moving petroleum products by pipeline is much less than by rail. The chief drawback, however, is that pipelines are still mostly restricted to sending products that are in liquid form.

Illus. 43-5

We rely on pipelines as a means of shipping liquid goods inexpensively.

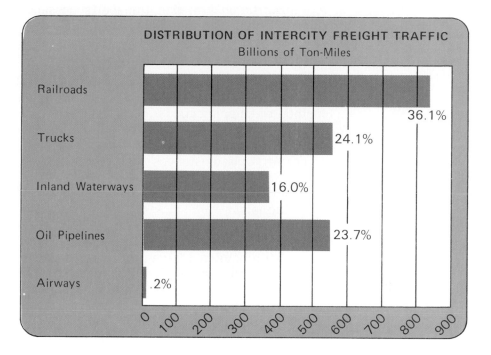

DISTRIBUTION OF INTERCITY FREIGHT TRAFFIC
Billions of Ton-Miles

Railroads 36.1%
Trucks 24.1%
Inland Waterways 16.0%
Oil Pipelines 23.7%
Airways .2%

Illus. 43-6
This bar graph shows how much cargo is moved by the various types of carriers. A ton-mile represents one ton of freight carried one mile.

INCREASING YOUR BUSINESS VOCABULARY

The following terms should become part of your business vocabulary. For each numbered statement, find the term that has the same meaning.

carrier
containerization
fishyback
fourth-class mail or parcel post
freight or shipments

freight forwarder
piggyback
private carrier
public carrier
shipper

1. A shipping service in which loaded trailers are carried on ships.
2. A transportation unit used by its owner to move his or her own products.
3. A firm which groups small shipments to make a full railroad car-load.
4. A shipping service in which specially designed containers can be carried on railroad flatcars, trucks, or ships.
5. Goods that are transported.
6. Mail that includes all packages weighing one pound or more that may be opened for postal inspection.
7. An individual or company that transports goods or people.
8. A shipping service in which loaded trailers are carried on railroad flatcars.

9. A transportation firm that transports passengers and goods for others.
10. The person or firm who ships something.

1. What five factors should a shipper consider in choosing a method of shipping goods?
2. What two factors determine the charge for mailing a parcel post package?
3. Under what circumstances might you use the services of United Parcel Service?
4. How are the shipping needs of businesses different from those of individuals?
5. Name three advantages that railroad shipping offers.
6. What advantages of truck transportation will likely cause trucks to continue hauling a large proportion of all freight?
7. What is the chief advantage of shipping by water?
8. What is the most expensive method of transporting goods?
9. What is the biggest disadvantage of transportation by pipeline?
10. Which means of transportation carries the greatest volume of intercity shipments?

1. If you lived in Medford, Oregon, and wanted to send a box containing a dozen apples to a relative in Spokane, Washington, which method of shipping would you use? Which method would you use if the relative lived in Honolulu, Hawaii?
2. Prepare a list of 10 companies that carry shipments from your city to other cities. Include in the list as many different kinds of companies as possible. If you live in a community which has fewer than 10 transportation companies, list all that are available.
3. A manufacturer wants to ship three refrigerators weighing about 200 pounds each to a retail appliance store in a small town about 100 miles away. (a) How should the manufacturer decide which transportation means offers the kind of service needed for this shipment? (b) What kind of shipping service do you think the manufacturer should use?
4. Ben Kunkel has an antique table weighing 150 pounds that he wants to ship to his brother who lives in a city 200 miles away. Which method of shipping would you recommend that he use?
5. Dolly Schilling owns a concrete mixing company. In order to deliver concrete to her customers, Dolly owns 25 trucks. Are the trucks that Dolly owns public or private carriers?

SOLVING PROBLEMS IN BUSINESS

1. The Lancaster Department Store operates four delivery trucks. Each truck uses an average of 20 gallons of gasoline a day.
   (a) How many gallons of gasoline must the department store purchase each day?
   (b) If the department store delivers on days Monday through Saturday, how many gallons of gas will the trucks use in one week?

2. The rates for shipping 30,000 pounds of books 800 miles by 2 different carriers are:

Truck	$3.90 for each 100 pounds
Rail	5.65 for each 100 pounds

   For each carrier, figure the total freight charge.

3. The table below shows the amount of cargo carried on inland waterways in the United States. Draw a pie chart showing the percent of cargo carried by each waterway.

Atlantic coast	8%
Gulf coast	10%
Pacific coast	4%
Mississippi River	53%
Great Lakes	25%

4. A carrier received some live plants for shipment. The shipping instructions said that to avoid damage the plants should be kept at temperatures between 20°C and 30°C. What are the temperatures expressed in degrees Fahrenheit?

5. Cheryl Thomas is shipping a valuable bracelet to a friend in a distant city. Cheryl is using a private parcel delivery service which automatically insures all packages for $100. Additional insurance can be purchased for 50¢ for each $100 of insurance desired. The bracelet is valued at $800. How much will it cost Cheryl to insure the bracelet for $800?

EXPANDING YOUR UNDERSTANDING OF BUSINESS

1. When goods are shipped by freight, several different forms must pass between the shipper and the receiver. Find out what the following forms are and be prepared to describe them to the class:
   (a) bill of lading
   (b) freight bill
   (c) waybill
   (d) notice of arrival

2. In this part, you learned that a public carrier moves goods for others. Public carriers are divided into common carriers and

contract carriers. Find out what these terms mean, and give some examples of each.

3. Assume that you are sending three packages to the same destination, a place of your choice within 400 miles of your home. Compare the charges of three or four transportation services available in your area for the shipment of these packages:
   (a) a two-pound box of candy
   (b) books weighing 8½ pounds
   (c) a box containing clothing and personal items, weighing 18 pounds

4. If United Parcel Service is available in your community, find out the following information about it:
   (a) Does it pick up and deliver shipments?
   (b) When delivery service is offered, what are the limitations on distance?
   (c) For what amount does United Parcel Service insure shipments without making an extra charge?
   (d) What limitations are placed on the amount for which a United Parcel Service shipment can be insured?

5. Some carriers, including the U.S. Postal Service, allow packages to be shipped COD. Find out what these letters stand for and why a package would be sent COD. Is there any additional charge to the shipper when a package is mailed COD?

CAREER FOCUS

As with all other industries, very large numbers of clerical, secretarial, accounting, data processing, and distributive workers are needed in the travel, communications, and transportation industries. However, each of these industries has some careers that are different because of the special services performed by the industry.

CAREERS IN TRAVEL

The traveling American creates thousands of jobs. You have probably seen some of the many attendants ready to serve you in service stations, restaurants, hotels, and motels. It takes a lot of people with many different skills to help you travel with comfort and pleasure.

The management of hotels, motels, and restaurants is very complex. It requires advanced training and usually years of experience in the business. But a person with little or no training beyond high school can also find a rewarding career in the travel industry. Reservations clerks at travel agencies, airlines, railroads, and bus companies help you plan your trip. Room clerks help you check in at hotels and motels. And cashiers collect your money as you leave. When you visit amusement centers such as Disneyland, Six Flags, or Kings Island, you will not even see the computer operators, secretaries, and accounting workers who help you enjoy yourself. But all these people have business skills that allow them to serve you.

Business education subjects like typing, business arithmetic, business English, and office procedures can help you prepare for many of the occupations in the travel industry. No matter how much education you have before seeking employment, you will surely receive some training as you begin your job. You will need to learn the particular procedures of the business you choose.

If you want a career in the travel industry, you must have skill at detail work and must make few mistakes. What would you think of a reservations clerk who made arrangements for you to go to Rome, New York, when you wanted to go to Rome, Georgia? Travel businesses build their reputations on providing quick, accurate service.

CAREERS IN COMMUNICATION

Communication is important to every business. Also, communication with the public is the main function of many businesses. Newspapers, magazines, and radio and television stations and networks are such businesses. In addition, advertising and public relations agencies specialize in helping many other businesses communicate with the public.

There are many careers for those who are effective in both spoken and written communications. Newspapers and magazines need reporters to go out and gather information, copy editors to prepare the information for the public, and artists to present the information in an attractive form. The broadcast industries need these people plus news broadcasters and disc jockeys to carry their messages to the public. A great number of typists, file clerks, secretaries, and various clerical workers are needed to help these specialists perform their jobs.

Some of the careers in communications require only a high school education followed by some special training on the job.

Many communications workers are needed to operate a television broadcast studio.

Careers in publishing and broadcasting often require some college training with special emphasis on journalism and language arts. The artists who work in communications have usually attended art schools or academies after high school. Anyone interested in a career in communications needs to be good in English and like people.

CAREERS IN TRANSPORTATION

The transportation industry offers careers with trucking companies, airlines, railroads, bus companies, and shipping lines. When you think of careers in these industries, you probably think first of pilots, engineers, and drivers. These people are highly skilled. Behind these people are thousands of other individuals in business-related careers who help to make things go correctly.

If you enjoy working with schedules, are able to plan thoroughly, and can handle emergencies calmly, you might consider a position as a dispatcher, scheduler, or traffic agent. People in these jobs must plan for the most profitable way to use the vehicles available to move goods where and when they are supposed to move.

If you would prefer a career with less pressure, you might be more satisfied working as a stock clerk, shipping clerk, or receiving clerk. Stock clerks prepare goods for use by making certain that the goods are in the proper department when needed. Shipping clerks must see that the correct goods are packed and shipped to the ordering customer. Receiving clerks check goods in as they arrive and sometimes prepare them for sale or use.

A high school education is needed for most careers in transportation. The ability to follow instructions carefully is important, as is good handwriting. There are many positions in supervision and management in the transportation field. Although many people work their ways up to these positions, college training would be of great value in reaching such positions.

UNIT 11

Government And Labor In Your Economy

UNIT OBJECTIVES

After studying the parts in this unit, you will be able to:

1. Explain how government serves business and the individual in our free enterprise system.

2. Tell how the cost of government is met.

3. Describe the role of labor and its contribution to the economy.

44 HOW GOVERNMENT SERVES YOU

Many people enjoy attending auction sales. Not only do these sales often make bargain purchases available, but the competitiveness of auction bidding provides a source of entertainment. Usually before the sale starts, the auctioneer will announce the terms of sale and the rules under which the auction will be conducted. These rules are not intended to interfere with anyone's freedom, but rather to make sure that all people involved are treated fairly. In business as well as in other activities, the government often needs to serve as a kind of referee.

Business activities need to be conducted according to rules of fair play. No one person or group should be allowed to have an unfair advantage over others. For this reason, government regulates and works with business in many ways. In the example that follows, you can see the interest that government has in the operation of a small business.

Charles and Peggy Enders decide to start a health food store in a new shopping center. They are free to start a business of their own, but government requires that they follow certain rules so that the well-being of others will not be harmed. For example, Charles and Peggy's business must meet certain standards set up by the local department of health. Their building must have the approval of the fire department. Working conditions and wages of their employees must comply with state labor laws. These and other requirements will also be of benefit to Charles and Peggy as owners of a business. Because of government regulations, other similar stores will have to compete fairly and honestly with them.

GOVERNMENT SERVING THE PEOPLE

The American people vote "yes" or "no" on questions that are placed on ballots. Voters elect men and women to speak and act for them in running the government. Locally they elect mayors, sheriffs, supervisors, and school board members. Elected state officials include governors, legislators, and other leaders. And in national elections the president, vice-president, representatives, and senators are chosen.

Government officials serve you; you do not serve them. They are responsible to you and to all citizens for passing and enforcing laws needed for the good of all. What are some of the services they provide? They operate public schools, hospitals, and libraries. They build and maintain streets, highways, and water supply systems. They provide parks and other facilities for recreation. They maintain police and fire departments and the

Illus. 44-1

Sponsoring sports events is just one of the many services government provides for you.

armed forces. They collect and deliver mail, print and coin money, and develop programs to conserve natural resources.

Such services are necessary for your welfare, and government can perform them better than any individuals. The government assumes many other responsibilities for you. Business, too, must depend on these services of government in order to succeed.

PREVENTING UNFAIR COMPETITION

Most business people operate fairly and honestly, but a few may try to take unfair advantage of their customers or competitors. Government seeks to prevent this. For example, many businesses ship goods by truck. If a trucking company gives one shipper a lower rate, that shipper has an unfair advantage over other shippers. Government regulations prevent this inequality. They require that a trucking company charge all customers the same rate for the same kind of shipment over the same route.

Many laws have been passed to prevent unfair business practices. Some cities and states regulate the purity and quality of certain food products, such as milk and meat, that are sold by local businesses. Most local and state governments also provide for regular inspection of food products and of scales, gas pumps, and other devices used to weigh and measure products.

LIMITING COMPETITION AMONG PUBLIC UTILITIES

A **public utility** regularly supplies a service or a product that is vital to the public welfare. Examples are telephone companies, railroads, and companies that provide water and electricity. Government limits competition among public utilities. This is done so that the citizens may be better served. One electric company can give a city better service than could several companies. If your city had six different electric companies instead of one, each with its own utility poles, lines, and expensive equipment, the service you would get would probably be more expensive and less efficient. And think of how unsightly your environment would be with all the extra poles and wires.

Governments give special privileges to public utilities. For example, cities give permission for their streets to be used by electric, telephone, and telegraph companies for their wires; by natural gas and water companies for their mains; and by bus companies for their buses. The right of privately owned public utilities to use the streets is usually limited so that no more than one company of each kind will serve a certain city. The city gives the utility the right to supply certain services and keeps out all competing companies.

LIMITING MONOPOLIES

You will recall that when a business has control of the market for a product or service, a monopoly exists. Some monopolies are needed; others are not. Although one electric company can give you better service than six could, the same is not true for most other businesses. For example, it would not be good for one firm to be the only seller of groceries in a city. That firm might have stores in all parts of the city so that each family would be near a store. But because of lack of competition, customers might receive poor quality merchandise, prices might be too high, and service might be poor.

When there are many similar businesses competing for the customer's dollar, each business will do all it can to attract customers and give them quality merchandise and good service. For this reason, government forbids monopolies in most lines of business. When government does permit a business, such as an electric company, to operate as a monopoly, it has the right to regulate the monopoly and its prices so that public interests are served.

ENFORCING CONTRACTS

An agreement to exchange goods and services for something of value is called a **contract**. The enforcement of contracts is a vital function of government. If you promise to pay $25 to have work done on your car, when the work is completed you know you must pay for it. Similarly, the auto mechanic must do the promised work for the $25 payment. If you do not pay when the work is completed, you can be taken to court and forced to pay. Businesses could not operate successfully if government did not use its authority to enforce contracts in the courts.

Illus. 44-2

Government helps to maintain order by providing a police force.

PROTECTING PROPERTY RIGHTS

You learned in Part 2 that anything that you lawfully acquire and that you may freely use or sell is known as private property. **Public property** is made up of those things owned in common by the people of a city, state, or nation. Post offices, public schools, public playgrounds and parks, and streets are some examples of public property.

Government protects your right to private property. The city, state, or nation can take private property for public use only when it is necessary to do so for the public good. The owner is paid a fair price for the property taken. The power to purchase private property at a fair price for necessary public use is known as the right of **eminent domain**.

GIVING SPECIAL PROPERTY RIGHTS

Patent and copyright laws were passed to encourage and reward people who create useful things. A **patent** gives an inventor the exclusive right to make, use, or sell an invention for a period of 17 years. A **copyright** gives an author, composer, or artist the exclusive right to use what he or she has produced. This right exists for the life of the person and for 50 years after that person's death. Inspect the front pages of your textbooks, and you will see examples of copyright statements.

Businesses may also be given the sole use of **trademarks** in marketing their products. Trademarks are words, letters, or symbols used in connection with products and which indicate the origin or ownership of the products. Many automobile manufacturers, insurance companies, and food processing companies have trademarks which you recognize. Trademarks are registered with the government, and no business may use the registered trademark of another business.

PROTECTING HUMAN RIGHTS

Government is concerned not only with the protection of property rights; it is also greatly concerned with the protection of human rights. For example, government does not permit businesses to pay employees wages that are below an established minimum. You have also learned that through unemployment compensation laws government provides unemployed people with money to assist them in supporting themselves and their families until they can find jobs. In some cases government will provide them with the training needed to get new jobs. Also, it will help them locate jobs.

Government forbids certain other business practices that would harm human rights. The federal government, states, and cities have passed laws forbidding discrimination against people because of their race, religion, sex, or age.

HELPING PRIVATE BUSINESS

Local, state, and national governments aid private business in many ways. One important service is the collection and reporting of information that business people can use in planning for the future. The Bureau of Labor Statistics, the Small Business Administration, the Department of Agriculture, and many other federal agencies collect information on a nationwide scale. They make available information on how people earn, save, and spend their incomes; on employment and unemployment; on business failures; on the cost of living; and on many other phases of economic life.

Direct aid is also given to business. Through agencies of the federal government, loans may be granted to small business firms and to farmers. Homebuilders, veterans, and others may also borrow needed funds from federal agencies and some state government agencies.

THE NEED FOR GOVERNMENT

You can rightfully boast that you live in a free country. You really have the freedom to do almost anything you wish except for things that might harm others or deny freedom to others. But in order to be sure that you enjoy and keep your freedom, rules are needed for fair play. Government helps enforce these rules. Without government, the economic activities of your country could not be carried out in an orderly way. Without government, it is doubtful that an economic system could even exist.

INCREASING YOUR BUSINESS VOCABULARY

The following terms should become part of your business vocabulary. For each numbered statement, find the term that has the same meaning.

contract   public property
copyright   public utility
eminent domain   trademark
patent

1. The exclusive right given to an inventor to make, use, or sell an invention for a period of 17 years.
2. A word, letter, or symbol used in connection with a product and which indicates the origin or ownership of the product.
3. The right of the government to purchase private property at a fair price for necessary public use.
4. An agreement to exchange goods and services for something of value.
5. A business that supplies a service or product at prices usually determined by government regulation rather than by competition.
6. The exclusive right of an author, composer, or artist to use what he or she has produced for life and for 50 years after death.
7. Things owned in common by the people of a city, state, or nation.

UNDERSTANDING YOUR READING

1. Name some ways in which government affects small business owners.
2. List six services provided by government.
3. How does government act to prevent unfair competition in the shipping business?
4. Why can one public utility serve a city better than several similar public utilities?
5. When is a monopoly considered to be not in the best public interest?
6. How does the enforcement of contracts aid business?
7. What is the difference between private property and public property? Give two specific examples of each.
8. Why does the government give special copyright and patent rights?
9. What are three things government will do to help people who are unemployed?
10. What are some aids government gives to private business?

USING YOUR BUSINESS KNOWLEDGE

1. In this part you learned about many of the services that are provided by government. Make a list of at least five government services that you or a member of your family received during the past week. Tell whether each service came from your local, state, or federal government.
2. Make a list of the public utilities that serve your community.
   (a) What services do they provide?
   (b) Do you think it would be better for these services to be offered by several competing businesses? Explain your answer.
3. Under the right of eminent domain, the government buys private property to be converted into public property. Of course, sometimes people have to sell their property when they would rather not. What are some reasons that you think would justify a government's exercising its right to eminent domain?
4. Two students are discussing the fact that "government is our biggest business." Cindy feels that some government activities are in direct competition with private business and that this is unfair. She feels that government should limit its activities to only those that private business cannot or will not undertake. Chuck thinks that government should undertake any business activities that it can perform better or less expensively than private business. What do you think? Give some examples of business activities undertaken both by private business and by government.

5. In protecting human rights, the government places certain restrictions, such as minimum wages, on private businesses. Do you think that in protecting human rights the government is unfairly restricting the rights of business? Explain your answer.

SOLVING PROBLEMS IN BUSINESS

1. The first census of the United States was taken in 1790. Based on that census, the membership of the United States House of Representatives from each state was as follows:

Connecticut	7	New York	10
Delaware	1	North Carolina	10
Georgia	2	Pennsylvania	13
Kentucky	2	Rhode Island	2
Maryland	8	South Carolina	6
Massachusetts	14	Tennessee	1
New Hampshire	4	Vermont	2
New Jersey	5	Virginia	19

(a) How many members were there in the House of Representatives in 1790?

(b) By 1980 the membership of the House of Representatives had grown to 435. How many more members were there in 1980 than there were in 1790?

2. In a recent year, the U.S. Patent Office issued patents for almost 70,000 items. Of those patents, 45 percent were issued to corporations and the rest to individuals.

(a) How many patents were issued to corporations in that year?

(b) How many patents were issued to individuals?

3. So that an interstate highway can be completed, 12 families in the town of Clarksville will have to move from their homes and sell their property to the government. The lots involved are each 150 feet wide. If the highway goes straight across the property, how many meters of highway will replace the 12 homes?

4. In a city in which there are 90,000 employed workers, 18,000 are public employees. Of this number, 6,000 are employed by the federal government, 8,000 by the state government, and 4,000 by the city.

(a) What percent of all workers are public employees?

(b) What percent of the public employees are employed by the federal government?

(c) What percent of all employees are employees of the federal government?

5. Listed on the next page are the cash income and expenditures for one year for the Public Library of Randolph:

Income

Cash on hand, beginning of year	$ 1,250
Town and state appropriations	52,000
Income from investments	1,795
Gifts	1,645
Fines on overdue books	550
Miscellaneous income	325

Expenditures

Salaries	$23,500
Books and periodicals	6,775
Utilities	1,525
Insurance	780
Equipment and supplies	1,455
Cleaning and repairs	420
Community service programs	1,800
Library binding	675
General administrative expenses	715

(a) What was the total amount of cash on hand and received during the year?

(b) How much was paid out during the year?

(c) What percent of the total cash received was accounted for by town and state appropriations? (Round your answer to the nearest percent.)

(d) What percent of total expenditures was accounted for by salaries? (Round your answer to the nearest percent.)

EXPANDING YOUR UNDERSTANDING OF BUSINESS

1. In this part you learned the importance of carefully selecting elected officials. Elected officials have specified terms of office. Find out the terms of office for:
   (a) A United States Senator
   (b) A state legislator
   (c) The governor of your state
   (d) The mayor of your city or town, if there is one

2. You have seen many trademarks on products themselves as well as in advertisements on television, on billboards, and in newspapers and magazines. Make a display of about 10 trademarks you recognize to show to the class. See if your classmates can tell the name of the company represented by each trademark. You can then see why trademarks are so valuable to businesses.

3. What is the difference between interstate and intrastate commerce? Which one is regulated by the federal government? Why is this so?

4. The salaries paid to government employees are matters of public record; that is, the public can know what these people are paid. Do you think it is fair to these employees for you to know how much money they make? Why or why not?

5. Government control of monopolies in the U.S. has an interesting history. Around the beginning of this century, many important laws were passed relating to monopoly control. Through library research, find out what were the major provisions and some of the results of these laws:

   (a) Sherman Antitrust Act

   (b) Clayton Act

   (c) Federal Trade Commission Act

45 MEETING THE COST OF GOVERNMENT

PART OBJECTIVES

After studying this part and completing the end-of-part activities, you will be able to:

1. Give at least five examples of services that citizens believe can be better provided by government than by citizens as individuals.
2. List six kinds of taxes levied by government.
3. Tell which government unit collects most property taxes.
4. Explain how government can meet its expenses if taxes do not provide enough revenue.
5. Tell in what ways government income depends on business conditions.

Many ways have been used to pay for the costs of government. In early times, taxes were paid not in money but in goods by peasants who farmed the land for their rulers. A farmer, for example, might have paid taxes by delivering six pigs and a fourth of the grain and fruit crop. Rulers sometimes taxed displays of wealth such as fancy doorways, beautiful robes, and fireplaces. At one time in Holland a tax was levied according to the number and size of windows in an owner's house. In order to avoid paying this tax, people were soon building houses that were short on windows, light, and air.

SHARING THE COST OF GOVERNMENT SERVICES

If you want telephone service, electricity in your home, or milk delivered to your door, you pay the bill. But suppose you want to protect your home against fire. Should you buy your own fire-fighting gear? Should everyone in a neighborhood join together and buy a fire engine? Or should everyone in the community buy protection by helping to pay for a well-equipped, well-staffed fire department?

The most practical way to get protection, of course, is for everyone in the community to share the cost of maintaining the fire department. The same idea applies to sharing the cost of protection provided by the police and the armed forces. Everyone also agrees to pay a part of the costs of paving roads, operating schools, and supporting other government services.

More than 15 million Americans — about 1 out of every 6 workers — are employees of the government. These include office workers, engineers, teachers, judges, members of the armed services, senators, truck drivers, tax collectors, and many other kinds of workers employed by the federal, state, and local governments. All these employees must be paid from government funds. Firms that are hired by the government to build freeways, dams, airports, and school buildings must be paid for their services. And the government must buy paper, office machines, bricks and cement, trucks, and airplanes.

HOW GOVERNMENT GETS ITS MONEY

To pay for public expenses, the various levels of government must have income. Government income is often referred to as **revenue**. Much of the government's revenue comes from taxes. Taxes are the payments that you and everyone else are required by law to make to help cover the costs of government services. Taxes of various kinds are also paid by businesses. In a recent year nearly $420 billion was collected in taxes by federal and state governments and by local government units such as counties, cities, and school districts. If these taxes had been divided equally among all the people in the United States, your share would have been about $1,900. An average family of four would have paid about $7,600 in taxes for just one year. The federal government is the biggest collector of taxes, as is shown in Illus. 45-1.

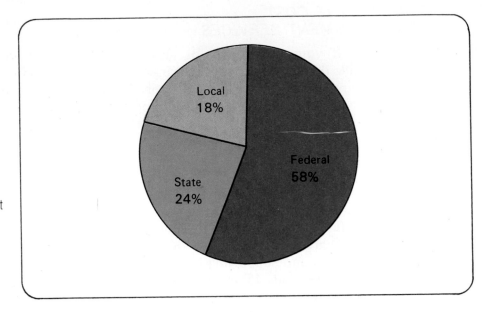

Illus. 45-1

The federal government collects almost 60 percent of all taxes. The remainder is divided between state and local levels of government.

To pay for most of the services it provides, government places taxes on: (1) income, (2) payroll for social security purposes, (3) property, (4) goods and services, (5) imports, and (6) estates, inheritances, and gifts.

TAXES ON INCOME

Taxes on the earnings of individuals and corporations are known as **income taxes**. Income taxes produce the largest part of the federal government's total income. Most states also impose income taxes. In addition, some cities levy taxes on the earnings of workers.

Under the present tax law, employed people pay all or a large part of their federal income tax during the year in which they receive their income. Employers are required by law to withhold the tax from employees' earnings and forward the tax to the government. People who receive much income from sources other than wages and salaries estimate the amount of their income for the year. They pay the tax on their estimated income directly to the government, either in one amount or in quarterly installments. Every taxpayer must file an income tax return each year. At that time an adjustment is made for any overpayment or underpayment of the total tax due.

Illus. 45-2

Many taxpayers use the services of agencies such as this one for help in preparing their income tax returns.

The corporation income tax applies to a corporation's yearly profits and is paid directly to the federal government. This results in a kind of double taxation. The corporation must pay taxes on its profits, and the stockholders must pay taxes on the share of the profits they receive as dividends. Partnerships and sole proprietorships do not pay a federal income tax in the same manner. Instead, each partner and each proprietor pays an individual income tax only on his or her share of profits from the business.

SOCIAL SECURITY TAXES

As you learned in Part 39, social security taxes are levied on both employers and employees. These payroll taxes provide funds for unemployment compensation and for retirement benefits for workers. Employers deduct the social security taxes from their employees' wages and forward the taxes, along with their share, to the government.

TAXES ON PROPERTY

Taxes on property are of two types: (1) taxes on real estate, which includes land and anything permanently attached to the land, such as homes, factories, and stores; and (2) taxes on personal property, such as farm machinery, automobiles, furniture, merchandise, and livestock.

Property taxes are collected by several different types of taxing units, mainly county and city governments and school districts. Most property taxes are collected and used by local governments.

TAXES ON GOODS AND SERVICES

In most states and in some cities you pay a **sales tax** on many of the things you buy. This is a tax that is added to the purchase price of many goods and services. Consumer goods in general are taxed, but in some places foods and medicines are not included. Sales taxes range from 2 percent to 8 percent of the amount of each purchase. If you buy a can of paint for $5.00 and the state sales tax is 6 percent, the merchant collects $5.30 from you. The merchant then will pay 30¢ to the state, but you were the one who provided the money for the tax.

Another type of tax that consumers pay on the purchase of certain goods and services is known as an **excise tax**. This tax is imposed only on certain goods and services such as gasoline, cigarettes, and air travel.

Excise taxes are generally included in the price of the item being purchased, while the amount of the sales tax is added to the price of the purchase. Excise taxes are federal taxes; sales taxes are city and state taxes. You might pay both an excise tax and a sales tax on some things.

TAXES ON IMPORTS

The right to collect taxes on imports is reserved for the federal government. States cannot impose taxes on goods that are imported from foreign countries or shipped in from other states.

As you learned in Part 8, taxes on imports are called tariffs. At one time, these made up a large share of the federal government's income. About a hundred years ago tariffs provided more than 90 percent of the federal government's total income. Today the amount collected from tariffs is little more than 1 percent of the federal government's total income.

Illus. 45-3

This customs officer examines goods that are imported into the U.S.

TAXES ON ESTATES, INHERITANCES, AND GIFTS

Taxes on estates and inheritances are levied by both the federal government and state governments. They are payable at the time of a property holder's death. The **estate tax** is based on the total amount of property left by the owner when she or he dies. The **inheritance tax** is based on the amount left to a particular person by someone who dies.

To avoid estate and inheritance taxes, some people used to give their property to whomever they wanted to have it before they died. To prevent this practice, the government passed the **gift tax**. Now whenever a large amount of property changes hands, before or after the death of the owner, it is subject to a tax.

WHAT IF TAXES AREN'T ENOUGH?

In some years the money government receives from taxes may not be enough to pay all its expenses. In fact, in just one recent year the federal budget deficit (the difference between proposed spending and expected revenue) was over $65 billion. When its expenses are more than its income, government may borrow from individuals, banks, insurance companies, and other organizations. It borrows by issuing short-term notes or long-term bonds. When government borrows money on such notes or bonds, it is not receiving income. The money it receives is strictly a loan. The money must be paid back to the lenders with interest. Part of your taxes must be used to pay this interest. Tax money must also be used to pay off the government's debts.

Government income depends to a considerable extent on business conditions. When there are thousands of prosperous businesses employing millions of workers, government collects great sums in taxes. For example, when large amounts of goods are made and sold, government income from sales taxes increases. When business is good and corporation profits and personal incomes are large, the receipts from income taxes are large. But if many businesses fail and many workers lose their jobs, the amount of taxes that can be collected decreases.

GETTING AND SPENDING THE FEDERAL BUDGET DOLLAR
FISCAL YEAR 1981

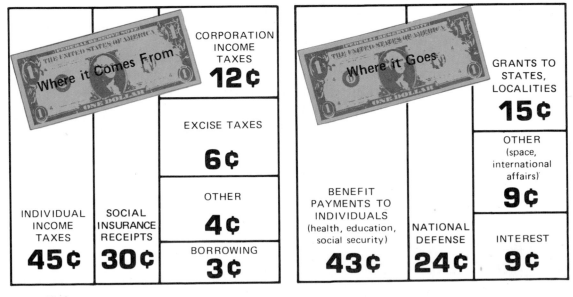

Illus. 45-4

This chart shows where the federal government gets its revenue and how that revenue is spent.

DECIDING HOW TO USE TAXES

As a taxpayer, you should insist that good business management be followed in the conduct of government. Those we elect to run the government should:

1. Decide the purposes for which government money is to be used.
2. Decide how much money will be needed for these purposes.
3. Decide how to raise the money needed.
4. Make sure that money set aside for a particular purpose is used for that purpose and no other.
5. Prepare careful budgets and operate within these budgets.

You can help see that these things are done by:

1. Being interested in government affairs.
2. Electing capable, honest people to government positions.
3. Studying and then voting intelligently on the issues presented.
4. Expressing your views to elected officials.

Long ago, taxes were forced on the people by their rulers. The people themselves had little or no voice in deciding what would be taxed and how much. Today, though some people may object to being taxed, all citizens decide by their votes what to tax and how to tax. If you demand more in services from the government, you must be willing to pay for these services through higher taxes.

INCREASING
YOUR
BUSINESS
VOCABULARY

The following terms should become part of your business vocabulary. For each numbered statement, find the term that has the same meaning.

estate tax	*inheritance tax*
excise tax	*revenue*
gift tax	*sales tax*
income taxes	

1. A tax on consumer purchases in general, added separately to the cost of the items taxed.
2. Taxes on the earnings of individuals and corporations.
3. A tax on the total amount of property left by a person who dies.

4. A federal tax on certain goods and services, generally included in the prices quoted to purchasers.
5. A tax imposed on large amounts of property given away.
6. Income that the government receives from taxes and other sources.
7. A tax on the amount inherited by an individual.

1. Give five examples of services that many citizens believe can be better provided by government than by citizens as individuals.
2. List six kinds of taxes levied and collected by government.
3. How is a corporation income tax a form of double taxation?
4. How are social security taxes paid?
5. Which government units collect most property taxes?
6. What is the difference between a sales tax and an excise tax?
7. Who may impose tariffs?
8. Why was the gift tax passed?
9. How can government meet its expenses if taxes do not provide enough revenue?
10. In what ways does government income depend on business conditions?
11. How can you help make sure that good business management is practiced in government?

1. In this part, you learned that only the federal government can impose import taxes. What do you think would happen if states were permitted to place import taxes on goods brought in for sale from other states? What kind of situation would result?
2. How is money received by government through the sale of bonds different from money received through taxes?
3. Below is a list of some of the public services provided by government. For each service, tell whether federal, state, or local governments (or more than one of these) would most likely have the major responsibility for financing the service.

(a) fire protection	(h) sewage and trash disposal
(b) education	(i) public buses
(c) parks and recreation	(j) police protection
(d) water supply	(k) public libraries
(e) highways between cities	(l) urban renewal
(f) airports	(m) city streets
(g) aid to low income groups	(n) national defense

4. Income taxes are withheld from your wages throughout the year. Why do you think the government collects the taxes in this way rather than just once a year, such as when you file your tax return?

5. People with expensive jewelry are usually well able to pay taxes. If the government needs additional revenue, would you recommend a large annual tax on jewelry?

SOLVING
PROBLEMS
IN BUSINESS

1. When Amelia Delgado received her first paycheck, she was quite upset. She had been hired at a rate of $150 a week. However, her check was for an amount much less than that. The stub of the check showed that the following deductions were made from her pay:

Federal income tax	$18.60
Social security tax	9.20
State income tax	1.00
City income tax	3.00

   (a) What was the total amount of deductions from Amelia's check?
   (b) What was the amount of her paycheck?

2. Larry Reed wants to buy a camera that costs $90, plus 6 percent sales tax. Larry has saved $100 with which to make the purchase.
   (a) What will be the amount of the sales tax?
   (b) What will be the total cost of the camera?
   (c) How much money will Larry have after buying the camera?

3. James Harrell has an annual income of $12,600. Of this amount, he spends $5,000 for items subject to sales tax. Michelle Landon has an annual income of $19,600. Of this amount, she spends $6,200 for items subject to sales tax. In each case, the sales tax is 4 percent.
   (a) Which person used the greater percent of income for sales taxes?
   (b) How much is the difference between the percents required for sales taxes? Round your answer to the nearest tenth of a percent.

4. The Mt. Sherman School District is located in a city of 20,000 people. The student enrollment is 4,000. The property tax rate is $42.00 per $1,000 of assessed valuation. Of this tax rate, $20.16 is for educational needs. The assessed valuation of all property in the city is $126 million.

(a) How much revenue should the city receive this year from the property tax?

(b) What percent of the property tax is budgeted for education?

(c) How much of the total annual revenue is budgeted for educational needs?

(d) What is the average amount of revenue received by the school district per student enrolled?

5. The state in which Thomas Sheehan lives has a 4 percent sales tax on all consumer purchases except food. At the supermarket one day, Mr. Sheehan bought the items shown below.

> 2 kilograms of peaches, 75¢ per kilogram
> 1 box of sandwich bags, 72¢
> 2 liters of milk, 60¢ per liter
> 1 can tomato juice, 76¢
> 2 rolls of paper towels, 65¢ per roll
> 1 box of detergent, $2.43
> 1 package frozen fish, $1.78

What was the total of Mr. Sheehan's bill, including sales tax?

EXPANDING YOUR UNDERSTANDING OF BUSINESS

1. Taxes are sometimes classified as "proportional," "progressive," or "regressive" taxes. From a dictionary or a textbook on economics, find the meanings of these terms. In which category does the federal income tax belong? State sales taxes? Property taxes?

2. Tom Lee earns a salary of $11,000 a year and rents an apartment.

   (a) Which of the kinds of taxes discussed in this part does Tom probably pay?

   (b) Which of these kinds of taxes are paid by others but are passed on to him as part of the cost of goods he buys?

3. Through library research, prepare a report on *social goods*. Find out what they are, who they benefit, and who pays for them.

4. The federal income tax is levied against taxable income. When you file an income tax return, taxable income is determined by subtracting certain deductions and exemptions from your total income. Through library research, find out what some allowable exemptions and deductions are. Why do you think the government allows these exemptions and deductions?

5. Besides using them as a source of revenue, government can use taxes as a means of control. If a product is scarce and the government wants to discourage consumers from buying that product, the government can place an additional tax on that product. Is this a good means of controlling shortages?

46 LABOR AND BUSINESS

PART OBJECTIVES

After studying this part and completing the end-of-part activities, you will be able to:
1. Tell why labor is such an important economic resource.
2. Explain who is included in the U.S. work force.
3. List at least five groups of organized workers.
4. Tell what conditions contributed to the rise and growth of unions.
5. Explain the difference between closed shop and union shop agreements.
6. Tell why collective bargaining is more effective than individual bargaining.

In this country there are literally thousands of jobs you could have to earn a living. In fact, one book, *The Dictionary of Occupational Titles*, lists 20,000 different jobs that people do. These jobs range from circus ringmaster to gold miner. But also included are workers in jobs that you see every day, such as secretaries, teachers, police officers, retail store clerks, truck drivers, and factory workers. All of these people are producing goods and services for you and everybody else. Each person's job is important in helping to keep our economy healthy and growing.

LABOR: A KEY ECONOMIC RESOURCE

In Part 1, you learned that three kinds of economic resources are needed to produce the things that we need and want. These are natural resources, capital resources, and human resources or labor. Natural and capital resources would be of little value without labor to make use of them. Without labor, our tools, machinery, and buildings would not be built. And without labor, this equipment could not be put to good use in producing goods and services.

The term **labor** includes all human effort, both mental and physical, exerted to produce goods and services. It includes all men and women who grow or take products from nature, convert raw materials into useful products, and sell these products.

It includes people who provide services to others, services ranging from baby-sitting to brain surgery. Labor also includes those who supervise others and who manage business operations.

MEMBERS OF THE WORK FORCE

The total work force is made up of all people 16 years of age or older who are working or looking for work. In the United States there are over 100 million people in this large group. You are likely to spend many years of your life as part of the work force.

Most workers are employed either part-time or full-time in business, industry, or government. But the work force also includes professional people, such as doctors and lawyers, and other self-employed people, such as farmers. In the ranks of the work force are machinists, janitors, clothing workers, teachers, accountants, company executives, government officials, artists, and fashion designers.

Another way to describe the work force is to look at those who are not included in it. Such people as students, homemakers, retired people, those under 16, and those unable or unwilling to work are not considered part of the work force. Students are included in the work force if they are over 16 and if they work part-time or look for work while going to school.

WORKERS UNITING TO ADVANCE
THEIR INTERESTS

At some time as a member of a team or perhaps just for fun with some friends, you may have been involved in a tug of war. Usually there are several members on each team at opposite ends of a rope. The object, of course, is for one team to pull the other team across a certain point on the ground. It can be a very strenuous activity. However, if all team members do not pull at the same time and in the same direction, it is almost impossible to win. Team members must join together in a united effort if they want to win.

As workers, many people unite for causes that are important to them. Almost every worker belongs to some special organization that is concerned with the welfare of its members. Doctors belong to the American Medical Association. Lawyers join the American Bar Association. Millions of farmers are members of the American Farm Bureau or the National Farmers Organization. Employers are active in local employers' councils and merchants' associations. Many business people belong to the Chamber of Commerce and the National Association of Manufacturers. There are also special societies for sales managers, actors, secretaries, and countless other groups.

Having a strong group speak for its members is a common means of expression in a democracy. Many people in the work force — over 21 million of them — express themselves through labor unions. Almost 17 million of these workers belong to unions that are affiliated with one very large labor organization. This is the American Federation of Labor — Congress of Industrial Organizations, or the AFL-CIO. There are also strong independent unions. The International Brotherhood of Teamsters, the United Mine Workers, and the United Auto Workers are some of them.

THE START AND GROWTH
OF LABOR UNIONS

Before the 1800's, we had largely an agricultural economy. Most businesses were small. Each business owner hired only a few workers, and the owner knew them all personally. Problems of salary and working conditions were usually settled between the owner and each worker individually. In the 1800's, the widespread use of machinery and mass production enabled businesses to grow larger and larger. Small shops grew into large factories. When hundreds or perhaps thousands of workers were on the payroll, it was impossible for owners and managers to know each one personally.

In those times, many factory workers labored under conditions that today we would consider unbearable. Work days of 12 or 14 hours were common. Working conditions were very often unsanitary and sometimes unsafe. Pay was frequently so low that workers could buy only the bare necessities. Workers who complained about such conditions were often fired. They were also usually "blacklisted"; that is, their names were circulated among other businesses as being troublemakers. If employees banded together to express their discontent, they were sometimes prosecuted in court. Some of the early conflicts between employers and employees were violent.

Despite opposition, groups of employees kept trying to organize unions in order to improve their working conditions. They gained strength when the AFL was established in 1886. In 1935 a group broke away from the AFL and formed the CIO, but the two were reunited in 1955. In 1935 the legal status of unions in the United States was firmly established. In that year the National Labor Relations Act, sometimes called the Wagner Act, was passed. This act assures the right of employees to join unions. It says that employees have the right to hold fair elections to decide which union they want. It also states that employees have the right to choose representatives from their unions to make agreements with employers about working conditions.

THE INFLUENCE OF LABOR UNIONS

After the passage of the National Labor Relations Act, unions grew tremendously in power and influence. For a time, unions seemed to be so strong that laws were passed to regulate their power. For example, one provision of the Taft-Hartley Act of 1947 forbids a **closed shop agreement**. This means that it forbids a business in which only members of a union may be hired by the employer. The law does permit a **union shop agreement**. This means that an employer may hire employees who are not union members, but the employees must join the union within a specified time.

The Taft-Hartley Act also permits states to pass **right-to-work laws**. These laws forbid making union membership a requirement for employment. Unions oppose these laws because in unionized firms, nonunion members get the same benefits as members even though they pay no union dues. Approximately 20 states have passed right-to-work laws.

In 1959 the Landrum-Griffin Act was passed to regulate the administration of unions. The purpose of this and several other laws was to protect workers' rights while preventing unfair practices by unions.

Even though unions are not always popular with employers, more than 20 percent of the work force are union members. For many years, union members were mostly from the blue-collar occupations. In recent years, however, unions have attracted some workers who used to show little interest in unions. For example, it is estimated that more than two million government employees belong to unions. Fifteen years ago only about one million government workers were union members. Workers holding white-collar jobs are joining unions in greater numbers than in years past. Also, the number of women belonging to unions continues to increase.

HOW UNIONS HELP
THEIR MEMBERS

The main goals of labor unions have been to get for their members higher wages, fewer hours in the standard workweek, and safer and more pleasant working conditions. Job security for members is another major concern of unions. Much unemployment is due to changes in business conditions. When business is good, many people are employed to produce the goods and services the public demands. But when business is poor, there is less need for so many workers, and some are laid off. Also, some employment is seasonal. In some fields, there is more demand for workers during one time of year than another. For example, more construction workers are needed in the summer than in the winter. Some unemployment is caused by changes in technology. For example, a new machine may be invented which will do the work of several employees.

Unions try to get job security for their members in several ways. They try to persuade employers not to discharge large numbers of employees suddenly. Unions may try to get employers to agree to retrain workers and place them in other jobs. Unions may ask employers to guarantee their workers enough employment to earn a minimum annual income. Unions also try to get employers to recognize **seniority rights**, that is, to consider the length of time a worker has been with the company.

In recent years, unions have given more attention to gaining for their members compensation other than salary or wages. The employee benefits they bargain for include sick leave with pay, paid vacations, life and health insurance, pensions, profit-sharing plans in which the employees share in the company's earnings, paid holidays, and free health services on the job. Unions have also worked for the passage of laws which provide other benefits for workers. By lobbying and by supporting candidates for political office, unions have prompted the passage of laws providing for workers' compensation, job safety, social security, and unemployment insurance.

HOW UNIONS GET RESULTS

Suppose that an employee in a large company is not satisfied with wages or working conditions. If the worker complains in person to the employer, he or she may not get much consideration. If the individual threatens to quit, the employer may not care. The employer can usually hire someone who will be satisfied with the present arrangements. A worker usually cannot get very far with individual bargaining.

On the other hand, if many workers present a united front, employers will generally hear their complaints. Negotiations between an organized body of workers and an employer, dealing with wages and working conditions, are called **collective bargaining**. If differences cannot be resolved through collective bargaining, the employees may threaten to **strike** and refuse to return to work until their demands are met. The strike is a powerful weapon of organized labor because it brings production to a halt. In many industries, most or all of the factory employees are members of unions. Work stoppage by a strike seriously affects both the business and the employee. It also affects the consumer because goods and services are not being produced during the work stoppage.

Illus. 46-1

During a recent mass transit strike, many people had to find alternate ways of getting to their jobs.

During a strike, employees may apply further pressure through **picketing**. Union members carry signs telling the public their complaints against the company. Many union members and others who sympathize with the union refuse to deal with the business that is being picketed. Sometimes union members refuse to transport and handle or buy the products of a business involved in a labor dispute with another union. This action is a **boycott**.

Because strikes are so costly to both workers and employers, both groups prefer to settle their differences through compromise. They often have long periods of bargaining in an attempt to establish a union contract between the two groups.

Illus. 46-2

Striking union members sometimes use picketing to tell the public their complaints.

WORKERS AND BUSINESS FIRMS AS PARTNERS IN PRODUCTION

When representatives of labor unions and of business firms sit around a conference table to bargain, they usually agree on certain basic points. Both sides want the firm to be successful. If it is not, it will not be able to pay dividends to owners, pay good wages to employees, or expand and create new jobs. With few exceptions, both sides want to safeguard the freedoms of our economic system.

INCREASING YOUR BUSINESS VOCABULARY

The following terms should become part of your business vocabulary. For each numbered statement, find the term that has the same meaning.

boycott   *right-to-work laws*
closed shop agreement   *seniority rights*
collective bargaining   *strike*
labor   *union shop agreement*
picketing

1. When employees refuse to work until their demands are met.
2. Laws which forbid making union membership a requirement for employment.
3. When union members refuse to transport and handle or buy the products of a business involved in a labor dispute.
4. An agreement requiring workers to join a union within a specified time after employment.
5. When union members walk in front of a place of business carrying signs telling of their complaints against the firm.
6. An agreement to employ only people who are already members of a union.
7. Negotiations between an organized body of workers and an employer dealing with wages and working conditions.
8. Recognition by an employer of the length of time a worker has been with the company.
9. All mental and physical effort directed toward the production of goods and services.

UNDERSTANDING YOUR READING

1. Why is labor such an important economic resource?
2. Who is included in the U.S. work force? Who is not included?
3. Name five or more groups, other than workers in labor unions, that have formed associations. Which of these organizations are likely to have members in your community?
4. What is the name of the largest labor organization?
5. What conditions in the past contributed to the rise and growth of unions?
6. Why is the Wagner Act of special importance to workers?
7. What is the main difference between a closed shop agreement and a union shop agreement?
8. What are right-to-work laws?
9. What methods do unions try to persuade businesses to adopt to provide job security for the workers?
10. Make a list of benefits that unions have helped to obtain for workers.
11. Why is collective bargaining more effective than individual bargaining?
12. Why do both workers and employers generally prefer to settle disputes by collective bargaining rather than by strikes or other tactics?

USING YOUR BUSINESS KNOWLEDGE

1. Some people are considered part of our total work force and others are not. Tell whether each person described below is or is not part of the work force.
   (a) an airline flight attendant
   (b) a bank president
   (c) a homemaker
   (d) a writer of mystery stories
   (e) an 18-year-old high school graduate interviewing for a job
   (f) a retired accountant
   (g) a dentist
   (h) your teacher
   (i) a disc jockey
   (j) a farmer
2. The workers at the Castleberry Sausage Company are on strike. What groups, other than the workers and the owners of the company, are affected by the strike? In what ways?
3. Many people feel that government workers who perform vital services, such as police officers and fire fighters, should not be allowed to strike. What do you think?

4. Certain products, such as clothing, have a "union label" on them which indicates the manufacturer is a unionized company. Members of unions are encouraged not to buy products that do not have union labels on them. Do you think this is fair?
5. "Workers and employers should solve their own problems without any interference from government." Do you agree with this statement? Explain.

SOLVING PROBLEMS IN BUSINESS

1. Recently, there were 100,000,000 people in the work force. Of those, 21 percent were members of labor unions.
   (a) How many people in the work force were members of labor unions?
   (b) How many people in the work force were not members of labor unions?
2. To join one union you must pay an initiation fee of $75 and monthly dues of $25.
   (a) How much will it cost to be a union member in the first year?
   (b) How much will it cost the second year?
3. The average hourly wages in 1970 and 1979 for several industries are shown below:

Industry	1970	1979
Manufacturing	$3.35	$6.54
Mining	3.85	8.32
Contract construction	5.24	9.02
Transportation, public utilities	3.85	7.90
Wholesale trade	3.44	6.25
Retail trade	2.44	4.47
Finance, insurance, real estate	3.07	5.19
Services	2.81	5.27

   (a) What was the amount of wage increase for each industry?
   (b) Which industry received the largest amount of increase?
   (c) Which industry received the smallest amount of increase?
   (d) What was the difference between the highest and lowest wages in 1979?
4. Members of the work force are not always paid by the hour. Sometimes they are paid by the amount of work they do. Consider the following two choices that were offered to a truck driver going from Washington, D.C. to Buffalo, New York, a distance of about 560 kilometers: (1) receive 16¢ per kilometer

for the entire trip; or (2) receive $14 per hour for the trip, driving at an average speed of 80 kilometers per hour.

(a) How much would the truck driver earn working by the kilometer?

(b) How much would the truck driver earn working by the hour?

5. Listed below are the hourly wages for printers in ten cities in a recent year. These were the union wage rates agreed upon through collective bargaining.

New York	$8.65
Chicago	8.27
Los Angeles	7.43
Philadelphia	6.72
Detroit	7.61
Houston	6.52
Atlanta	6.51
Denver	7.24
Washington, D.C.	8.51
Cleveland	6.96

(a) What is the average hourly rate for printers in these ten cities?

(b) In terms of percent, how much greater is the highest wage than the lowest wage?

(c) If a printer in Chicago works 40 hours a week for one year, what will be that person's yearly earnings?

EXPANDING YOUR UNDERSTANDING OF BUSINESS

1. American unions are organized basically as craft (or trade) unions or as industrial unions. Check your school or public library for references describing these two kinds of unions. Explain the differences between each and give examples of each type of union.

2. Discuss the questions below with acquaintances who are members of labor unions. Summarize in writing the information you receive from your discussions and be prepared to give an oral report to the class.

(a) What social and welfare advantages does the union provide for its members?

(b) What does it cost to maintain membership in the union?

(c) What voice does the membership have in the operation of the local union? In the national union?

3. The following are some terms that are frequently used in conversations and news stories about the activities of American

workers. Find out what you can about these terms and be prepared to explain their use to the class.

(a) arbitrator (e) mediation
(b) injunction (f) secondary boycott
(c) layoff (g) steward
(d) lobbying (h) wildcat strike

4. Make an appointment to talk with a union representative about that union's contract with a particular employer. Find out: (a) the length of time the contract is to run; (b) whether a grievance procedure is stated; and (c) what new provisions appear in the contract that were not included in the last one the union had with that company.
5. Unions have helped their members obtain important benefits. Have workers who are not members of unions shared in such benefits? Explain.

CAREER FOCUS

As you know, there are many career opportunities open to you. By exploring the career information that is available to you, you should be able to find the career that will satisfy the needs of your life-style. No area has more career possibilities than government service.

Over 18 percent of our nonagricultural work force is employed by government. More than 15 million workers are employed at the federal, state, county, and local levels. The federal government is the largest employer in the nation, with over 2.7 million workers.

Governments at the federal, state, and local levels employ just about every kind of worker you can think of. The illustration on page 565 shows the major categories of government workers in a recent year. Looking at the illustration will give you some idea of the kinds of career opportunities available to you. As you can see, governments hire over 6.5 million workers just for education. This is the greatest number of workers in any one area.

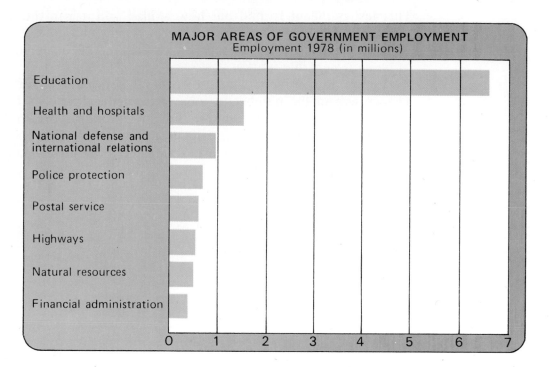

MAJOR AREAS OF GOVERNMENT EMPLOYMENT
Employment 1978 (in millions)

Education

Health and hospitals

National defense and
international relations

Police protection

Postal service

Highways

Natural resources

Financial administration

0   1   2   3   4   5   6   7

This chart of government workers includes federal, state, and local government employees.

A good way to get a quick idea of the kinds of workers needed by government is to look at the kinds of services government provides. You can do this by simply looking in the white pages of the telephone book. Look first under "United States Government," then under the name of your state, county, and city. If your telephone book does not list many departments, check at the post office, the state employment service office, the county courthouse, and city hall. Just by walking through these buildings you will get some idea of the many career opportunities available in government. You might also look at their bulletin boards for notices of job openings.

There are many beginning jobs for high school graduates in clerical and secretarial positions. For higher level jobs and for promotions, usually advanced education is expected. To get almost any government job you must first take a civil service test.

This test is meant to find out how skilled you are in the area for which you are applying. Once on a government job, the chances of promotions and increases in wages are very good if you prove to be an acceptable worker.

Future job prospects in government service are very good. The growth in the number of jobs at the federal level is expected to grow slowly because more and more federal programs are being taken over by state and local governments. This means, of course, that there will be more state and local government jobs available.

UNIT 12
Starting
Your
Career

UNIT OBJECTIVES

After studying the parts in this unit, you will be able to:

1. Discuss the personal qualities and characteristics you need to consider as you investigate careers.

2. Explain the steps to follow in locating and applying for a job.

PART 47   Beginning Your Role as a
           Worker
PART 48   Entering the World of Work

47 BEGINNING YOUR ROLE AS A WORKER

PART OBJECTIVES

After studying this part and completing the end-of-part activities, you will be able to:
1. Discuss nine areas that you should consider in looking at yourself as you investigate careers.
2. Explain how your experiences in school help you in making a career choice.
3. List five questions you should ask yourself when making a career choice.

You have now had an opportunity to look at your economic world and the many things in it. You know what business is and how it operates. You also know many ways in which you can fit into this world of business and economics. You should now begin to give more serious thought to what your future will be. Start to plan what you will do to attain the life-style you want.

In this book you studied information that may help you as you plan for your future. Unit 3, Finding Your Career, talked about the world of work and how you start preparing for it. At the end of each unit there was a Career Focus section that gave you specific information on career opportunities in various fields. It is time for you to get a better idea of the things you should do to get ready to take your place in the economic world.

PLANNING CAREFULLY

It has been mentioned many times that you must make careful plans if you are to find the career that is right for you. You know that it takes a great deal of thought and planning to do anything. For example, just think about how much planning is involved in having a surprise party for a friend. You have to decide whom to invite, what refreshments to serve, and what you will do at the party. And what may take the greatest amount of planning will be how to keep the party a secret and yet get the guest of honor there.

Determining the career you want to follow requires a great amount of careful planning. You need to learn what different careers have to offer you. You have to learn what special skills and abilities you have that might lead you to one career rather than another. You must find out what education and training you need for various careers. You should know what the future prospects are for the different careers you are considering. But one of your most important steps is to take a good look at yourself and see what you have to offer a potential employer.

LOOKING AT YOURSELF

Your work will make up a large part of your lifetime from about age 20 to age 65 or 70. Your enjoyment of life will depend in part on how successful you are in your work. People generally do best those things that they enjoy doing and for which they have the proper talent and training. To find the job that is best for you, you must understand yourself. As you look at yourself, consider the following:

1. Your likes and dislikes. Which do you like better — working alone or as part of a team? Does working with your hands satisfy your desire to create? Are you willing to move away from your home and family to find a certain job? Does work requiring attention to detail and accuracy appeal to you? Is it important to you to work outdoors? Do you prefer working with ideas rather than with tools and machinery?

2. Your abilities and special talents. Do you speak with ease before groups? Do you like arithmetic? Are you a good writer? Are you good at persuading people? Are you a

fast reader who knows what you have read? Do you have a good memory? Do you have special physical strength so that you can work long hours and still have energy?

3. **Your school record.** Do you do equally well in all subjects? What are your most difficult subjects? What are your easiest subjects? What subjects do you want to continue studying in school? Where do you want to continue your education after high school?

4. **Your physical qualities.** Some jobs require much more physical energy than others. For example, construction workers, mechanics, and factory workers often must have more than average physical strength. Other jobs require mental concentration for long periods of time or the physical endurance to travel and meet new people all the time.

5. **Your hobbies.** Hobbies can reveal special interests and abilities, and many hobbies can lead to careers later. Among such hobbies are music, writing, painting, and working with tools.

6. **Your dependability.** Can you get a job completed? Do you follow through on assignments? Is it necessary to remind you to do something after you have been told what has to be done? Will you be there when you are needed? What is your attendance record in school?

Illus. 47-1

A hobby that you enjoy now can lead to a fulfilling career later.

7. Your punctuality. Do you get to work on time? Do you do things when they are supposed to be done? Do you often have to give an excuse for why you are late? What is your school record for tardiness?

8. Your pride in your work. Are you satisfied with just getting by or do you always try to do your best? Do you feel a sense of accomplishment when you and others you work with do something well?

9. Your ability to get along with others. Can you work well with others? Are you willing to listen to others and learn from them? Can you take orders and be supervised without feeling annoyed? Are you willing to help others when they need help?

MAKING A CAREER CHOICE

Choosing your career is one of the most important decisions you will ever make. The world of work provides many opportunities for you if you take time to learn about careers and gain the necessary skills. Remember, your first choice may not be your last, but it is important to get started by choosing a field of interest. The following guidelines may help you do this.

Are you enthusiastic about this occupation? Is this what you really want to do? Will you enjoy doing this kind of work more than any other that you know about? Are you willing to learn as much as you can about this occupation?

What are the requirements of this occupation? What skills and abilities are needed? How much education is necessary?

Are you suited for this occupation? Do you have the physical, mental, and social qualities necessary for success in this occupation? If you do not have them, are you willing to develop them? Are you willing to spend the time, energy, and money needed to prepare yourself for this occupation?

Will you be able to advance yourself in this occupation? Does it lead to higher-level jobs with greater responsibility and higher pay?

What benefits are there in this occupation? Is it one that provides training even though the beginning salary is relatively low, or is it one with a high beginning wage but a dead-end job future? Are the skills of this occupation useful in others in case you want to change, or is the job one in which you will have to stay even though you may want a change?

Illus. 47-2

Some occupations require specialized training. These students are learning how to become chefs.

PUTTING YOUR PLAN INTO ACTION

Your investigation of careers should be interesting. Keep looking until you find a field that you really believe will fit the needs of your life-style. As you begin to narrow your choices, you will want to get some practical experience in one or several jobs. This will help you make your decisions. Part 48 will give you some ideas of how you can get work experience in order to make better career choices.

UNDERSTANDING YOUR READING

1. In looking at yourself as you plan your future career, what are nine areas you should consider?
2. How can your school record help you investigate careers?
3. What are some kinds of workers who need greater than average physical strength?
4. Why should you think about your hobbies as you think about careers?
5. What are five points you should consider in making a career choice?

USING YOUR BUSINESS KNOWLEDGE

1. Make a list of four jobs: one in an office, one in a retail store, one in a factory or on a farm, and one in a profession such as law, medicine, or teaching.
   (a) For each job, describe some ways in which you might get satisfaction from that job.
   (b) List the dissatisfactions that might come with each job.
2. Brenda Griffin is a freshman at McArthur High School. Brenda says that she doesn't want to be concerned about her career until after she completes high school. She thinks that she will have a better idea of what she wants to do then. Do you agree or disagree with Brenda? Why?
3. It has been said that you are known by the work you do. What does this statement mean to you? How will your occupation affect your home life, your community life, your health, and your recreation and hobbies?
4. Select a career in which you are interested. This career may or may not be one which you now think is the one for you.
   (a) Describe the duties of a worker in this career.
   (b) What special qualities must a person have or be willing to develop?
   (c) What training and education are needed?
   (d) Where may this training or education be obtained?

SOLVING PROBLEMS IN BUSINESS

1. Jack Shea likes to work with wood and wants a job in retailing as a career. He took a summer job working at a local lumber company. To prepare an order for a customer, Jack cut a piece of lumber that was 12 feet long into four equal sections.
   (a) How long was each section?
   (b) If the piece of lumber cost $6 before it was cut, how much did each of the four pieces cost?
2. In studying the work done in the stenographic department of the Hardin Company, it was found that the five secretaries could produce 1,000 lines of typed material per hour.
   (a) How many lines did each person produce?
   (b) How many lines could the department produce in 8 hours?
   (c) If production increased by 10 percent, how much would each person produce in an hour?
3. Word processing equipment was installed in a business office. The equipment consisted of two machines which cost $12,500 each. After the word processing equipment was installed, the business was able to sell four typewriters for $425 each.
   (a) After the sale price of the four typewriters was subtracted from the cost of the word processing equipment, what was the net cost of the installation?

(b) What was the net cost of each word processing machine?

4. Harry and Raymond are applying for summer jobs. In completing the information for which the employer asks, Harry writes that he weighs 150 pounds and is 68 inches tall. Raymond notes that he weighs 70 kilograms and is 175 centimeters tall.

   (a) Which of the two weighs more?

   (b) Which applicant is taller?

5. Teenagers were asked in a survey what factors they considered important for happiness in their future careers. In all, 860 teenagers were contacted. Of this number, 490 responded. The table below gives the facts about their responses.

Work Factor	Number Mentioning This Factor
Future salary	302
Good fellow workers	250
Good fringe benefits	191
Good supervisors	238
Good working conditions	297
Importance of the job	200
Job security	315
Personal interest in work	396
Opportunity for promotion	297
Serving others	300
Starting salary	199

   (a) What percent of the teenagers contacted responded to the survey? (Round your answer to the nearest whole percent.)

   (b) What four work factors appear to be most important to the teenagers surveyed?

   (c) For the four factors you indentified in (b), indicate the percent of respondents citing each factor.

EXPANDING YOUR UNDERSTANDING OF BUSINESS

1. To find out more about educational opportunities available to you, make a list of the types of educational institutions in your town or city or within easy driving distance. For each type of educational institution, state briefly the courses of study offered.

2. Locate a copy of the *Dictionary of Occupational Titles* in your school or community library. Look up the job titles and descriptions for five or more different occupations found in

business. Write down some of the interesting facts about each one. Be prepared to present this information to your class.

3. Studies made of why people fail in jobs show that many employees do not succeed because they lack certain personal traits. Some of the most important traits required for successful employment are described below. Make an analysis of your own employment traits by rating yourself on each one. Write the letters *a, b, c, d, e, f, g,* and *h* in a column. Then after each letter write the word *Excellent, Good, Fair,* or *Poor* to indicate your rating of yourself.

(a) *Attitude.* You make an effort to work as well as you can. You do not try to avoid work. You seldom complain about having to work.

(b) *Thoroughness.* You finish what you start out to do. You make an effort to be accurate. No one has to remind you that your work is incomplete.

(c) *Mental alertness.* It is easy for you to learn new things. You do not need to have instructions for work repeated frequently. It is easy for you to understand something that has been thoroughly explained.

(d) *Cooperation.* You work well with other people. You enjoy working with others on group projects. You do not criticize how other people do their work.

(e) *Promptness.* Work assignments are completed on schedule. You seldom ask for more time to complete your assignments. You never fail to be on time.

(f) *Initiative.* You can make your own decisions about what to do. You seldom need to be shown what to do. You do not wait for someone to tell you to do something that you know must be done.

(g) *Health.* You are not absent from school frequently because of minor illnesses. You have good health habits so that illness does not interfere with your activities. You seldom have long periods of illness.

(h) *Personal appearance.* You never wear messy clothing to school. You always make an effort to keep yourself and your clothing neat and clean.

48 ENTERING THE WORLD OF WORK

PART OBJECTIVES

After studying this part and completing the end-of-part activities, you will be able to:

1. State three ways in which work experience can help you prepare for a career.
2. Name five sources of help in finding jobs.
3. Write a letter of application for a job.
4. Develop a personal data sheet.
5. Explain why job applications are important.
6. Give at least four points to keep in mind during a job interview.

There are many ways in which you can learn about the world of work. Reading career materials and talking with workers are good ways to do that. Some career exploration activities help you to learn about yourself; others give you information about work opportunities and requirements. Each of these will be of value to you as you look ahead to your future career. Another important way for you to learn about the world of work is to get a part-time or full-time job. That could be a big step toward a career that is right for you.

A job will give you an opportunity to try out some of your skills and abilities. As you work you will discover what you like and dislike about certain kinds of work. You may learn, for instance, whether or not you really like to work with people. You can also determine if you are happy working with information or machines. Work experience can become an important part of your exploration of business careers.

LEARNING FROM WORK EXPERIENCE

As a student there are many ways in which you can get work experience. It may not be possible to get exactly the same kind of work you think you want to follow as a career, but there are many things you can learn from any job.

Right now you should be thinking in terms of part-time work experience. You could work after school and on weekends. In the summer you may be able to find a full-time job. Many schools have cooperative work experience programs for students. In these programs the students spend part of their time in school and part on the job. If none of these opportunities are available to you, consider getting work experience through volunteer service to a civic or religious organization.

Through work experience you will learn what employers expect of their employees. You will learn how to take directions and follow through on tasks assigned to you. You will learn more about the business world and how it operates. But most important of all, you may learn what career is the right one for you.

GETTING HELP IN FINDING A JOB

At this point in your life, you probably do not have a lot of experience in job hunting, and you may not know where to look.

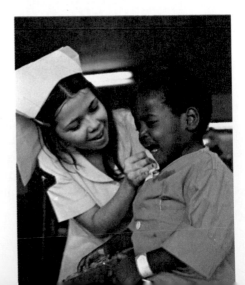

Illus. 48-1

Working as a volunteer is a good way to explore possible careers.

If that is the case, get help from those who have experience. Ask members of your family and friends how they found their jobs. Talk with your teachers and guidance counselors about possible job leads. Your business teachers often know many members of the business community and may know of businesses that have job openings. Watch the bulletin boards in your school for notices of jobs in which you might be interested. You should also register with the job placement service in your school, if there is one.

A very valuable source of job leads is the classified advertisements which are found in every newspaper. Read through these "help wanted" ads carefully at least once a week to see if there is a job for you. The Sunday paper usually has more ads than do the weekday editions.

You might also check with the local office of your state employment service. This is a state agency that aids people in finding work. Their services are available to you free of charge. The cost of maintaining these agencies is paid with taxes.

Another possible source of part-time employment if you have some special skill to offer is a private employment agency that specializes in temporary help. Kelly Services and Manpower are two examples of these organizations. If you do get a job through one of these agencies, it receives a fee for helping you.

As you can see, there are many sources of job information for you. If you really want work experience, you probably can find it. Remember that until you get some work experience in a particular area you may have to take a job that isn't too exciting and may have nothing to do with your future career goals. But any job you take will give you valuable work experience.

USING A LETTER OF APPLICATION

If you are answering a job advertisement or are following up a friend's lead, writing a **letter of application** may be your first step. The purpose of a letter of application is to get you a personal interview. The letter of application should be written so that it makes the employer interested in seeing you. It should be a simple, frank, and courteous sales letter.

Like any good sales letter, your letter of application should gain the employer's attention and interest. It should create a desire to see you. And it should urge the employer to take the desired action — inviting you to come for an interview. Examine

David M. Riggs' letter in Illus. 48-2 to see how the writer followed the basics of preparing a good letter of application. The letter is carefully and neatly prepared, courteous, and brief and to the point. A carelessly written letter may cause the employer to judge you as a careless worker. Remember, too, that your letter must compete with other letters for attention.

```
                                        501 Meadowlark Drive
                                        Iron Mountain, MI 49801-6295
                                        March 20, 1981


Ms. Elizabeth W. Chaffin
Personnel Manager
Tons O' Fun Amusement Park
Iron Mountain, MI 49801-5286

Dear Ms. Chaffin

In yesterday's Enterprise Journal I read your advertisement
for summer workers at Tons O' Fun Amusement Park.  I wish to apply
for one of the positions.

In your advertisement you mentioned that you are looking for
individuals who can act as cashiers at the ticket and refreshment
booths.  I believe I could serve you well in that position.  In
addition to studying subjects like English and mathematics, I
have taken typing and general business.  Therefore, I am
familiar with businesses and how they operate.  Also, I have
sold refreshments at my school's football games and served as
the treasurer of the youth group at my church.

Enclosed is a personal data sheet giving my qualifications in
more detail.  May I have an interview with you at your convenience?
I may be reached by telephone at 875-2129 after 4 p.m. on any
weekday.  Thank you for your consideration.

                                Sincerely yours

                                David M. Riggs

                                David M. Riggs


Enclosure
```

Illus. 48-2

A letter of application for a summer job.

PREPARING YOUR DATA SHEET

A **personal data sheet** is a summary of important information about you. It tells who you are, what education you have had, what work experience you have, and the names of people who know the kind of person you are. Anytime you apply for a job by mail, you should include a copy of your data sheet. If you apply in person you should have a copy of your data sheet with you. Data sheets should be short and should outline the information in brief, readable form. David Riggs' data sheet is shown in Illus. 48-3.

COMPLETING AN APPLICATION FORM

Most companies will ask you to fill out an **application form** if they are at all interested in you. The purpose of the application form is to get additional information about you. Most application forms ask for your name, address, educational background, work experience, the job for which you are applying, references, and other qualifications you may have.

The information on your data sheet will help you in completing the application form. Be careful to complete the application form neatly. A poorly prepared application form may give the wrong impression about you. The application form prepared by David Riggs is shown in Illus. 48-4.

PREPARING FOR
THE JOB INTERVIEW

If the company to which you apply believes you may be able to do the job, it will probably ask you to come for a personal interview. This gives you a chance to learn more about the job and the company. It gives the company interviewer a chance to make judgments about your dress, manners, use of English, and general suitability for the job. Plan your interview as carefully as you would plan a letter of application or a personal data sheet. Keep the following points in mind:

1. Be on time for the appointment.
2. Go alone to the interview. Do not ask friends or relatives to go with you.
3. Try to be calm during the interview. Do not talk too much. Answer questions completely. Ask questions intelligently. Let the interviewer guide the discussion.

4. Leave when the interviewer indicates that the interview is over. Thank the interviewer for the chance to present your qualifications.
5. After the interview, send a thank-you letter to the person who interviewed you.

```
                    PERSONAL DATA SHEET


NAME:        David M. Riggs              HEIGHT:   5'10"

ADDRESS:     501 Meadowlark Drive        WEIGHT:   150 pounds
             Iron Mountain, MI  49801-6295
                                         HEALTH:   Excellent
TELEPHONE:   875-2129

AGE:         16 years

EDUCATION:   1979 to present.  West High School.  I am presently
                               completing my sophomore year.  My
                               major is business.

                               Business Subjects Studied:
                                 General Business
                                 Typewriting

                               Activities:
                                 Member of the Pep Club.  Work
                                 at the refreshment stand for
                                 football games.

OTHER ACTIVITIES:

        Treasurer of the youth group at the First Methodist Church
        Member of the softball team in the Pike County League

REFERENCES:

        Miss Marilyn Skozak, Teacher
        West High School
        310 Seventh Street
        Iron Mountain, MI  49801-7322

        Dr. William L. Cryderman
        1287 Elder Boulevard
        Iron Mountain, MI  49801-5487

        Rev. David R. Crane
        First Methodist Church
        973 Culpepper Court
        Iron Mountain, MI  49801-8164
```

Illus. 48-3

A personal data sheet for a high school student.

Date *March 28, 1981*

Tons O' Fun
AMUSEMENT PARK

An Equal Opportunity Employer

Please Print All Information

Application For Seasonal Employment

For Office Use Only

Tel. _____ ☐ ☐ ☐ ☐
Due _____ Div. _____
Sec. _____ Area _____
Rate _____ Pl. _____

General
Use Full Name — No Nicknames Please

Last	First	Middle	Social Security Number
Riggs	David	Martin	301-44-0262

Number	Street	City	State	Zip Code	Home telephone number
501	Meadowlark Drive	Iron Mountain	MI	49801-6295	875-2129

Are you less than 18 years of age? Yes ☑ No ☐

If you are less than 18, what is your date of birth? *March 16 1965* Mo. Day Yr.

U.S. Citizen? ☑ Yes ☐ No If No, have you the legal right to remain permanently in the U.S.? ☐ Yes ☐ No

Have you ever been convicted of any crime(s) other than minor traffic violations? Yes ☐ No ☑

If yes, please explain when, where and disposition of the case(s) on reverse side of this form.

Have you been employed previously by Tons O' Fun? Yes ☐ No ☑

If yes, when and in what division?

The position(s) for which you are applying may require special physical abilities to safely and effectively perform the assigned duties and responsibilities of the position(s). Where there are questions in this regard, the interviewer will explain requisite abilities for specific positions. Please explain the nature of any illness, injury or disability which may restrict your ability to safely and effectively perform the duties of the position(s) for which you are applying:
If none, please check here ☑

Education

High School *West High School*   Present Grade Level (Circle) 9 ⑩ 11 12

College, Business, Tech or Trade School   1 2 3 4

List your special abilities, hobbies, awards, and honors received. *Treasurer of youth group; softball, swimming, skiing*

Availability

Will you be able to work weekends in: April & May? Yes ☑ No ☐ Sept. & Oct.? Yes ☑ No ☐

Date your school is out for summer *June 5*

Date your school begins in fall *Sept. 8*

Date you will be available to work daily *June 8*

Are you applying for weekend work only? Yes ☐ No ☑

Can you work an evening shift? Yes ☑ No ☐

Employment History

DATES	EMPLOYED BY	POSITION HELD	Last Rate Of Pay	Supervisor's Name	REASON FOR LEAVING
From	Employer		$		
To	Address of Employer		Per		
From	Employer		$		
To	Address of Employer		Per		

IN WHAT POSITION(S) AT TONS O' FUN WOULD YOU PREFER TO WORK

1. *Cashier*   2. *Ride Attendant*   3. _____   4. _____

Personal References
(Do not refer to relatives or former employers)

Name	Address

Miss Marilyn Skozak, Teacher, West High School, 310 Seventh St., Iron Mountain, MI

Dr. William L. Cryderman, 1287 Elder Boulevard, Iron Mountain, MI

Rev. David R. Crane, First Methodist Church, 973 Culpepper Court, Iron Mountain, MI

Illus. 48-4
A completed application form.

Illus. 48-5

In order to get the job you want, you will need to make a good impression in the interview.

YOUR FUTURE

In your lifetime you will probably hold many different jobs. You should learn something from each and you should get some satisfaction from each. After you have been in the world of work for some time, take a long look at yourself and where you are in terms of your career goals. Have you reached the goals you set for yourself? Have your goals changed? Are you still working to improve yourself? Are you still learning? The answers to these and similar questions will tell you of any changes you may need to make.

INCREASING YOUR BUSINESS VOCABULARY

The following terms should become part of your business vocabulary. For each numbered statement, find the term that has the same meaning.

application form   personal data sheet
letter of application

1. A written summary of a person's education, experience, and other information used in seeking employment.
2. A form filled out by each job applicant showing information the employer wants to know.
3. A letter expressing interest in a job and selling the prospective employer on the qualifications of a job applicant.

UNDERSTANDING YOUR READING

1. Name several ways that you can get some work experience while you are still a student.
2. In what three ways can work experience help you in your career planning?
3. Name seven sources you might go to for leads on possible jobs.
4. In what ways is a letter of application a kind of sales letter?
5. What kinds of information should you include on a personal data sheet?
6. Why should you be especially careful in filling out an application form?
7. What can a company learn about you during an interview?
8. What can you learn about a company during an interview?
9. What are five important points to keep in mind when going to an interview?
10. What are some questions you should ask yourself about your career goals after you have been on a job for several years?

USING YOUR BUSINESS KNOWLEDGE

1. Select an occupation in which you would be interested as a career. List as many part-time or summer jobs as you can think of that would give you skills and experience that would be helpful in this career.
2. If you were in charge of hiring people for jobs in your company, what information would you like to have about applicants? How would you get this information?
3. Your personal data sheet should list a few references. Many application forms also ask for references. These references may be teachers or former teachers, people you have worked for in the past, religious leaders who know you, or perhaps adult friends of your family. All of these people would know things about you which an employer would like to know. Make a list of three or more references for yourself. What type of information does each of your references know about you?

SOLVING PROBLEMS IN BUSINESS

1. Jackie Lippert worked 25 hours one week and 30 hours during each of the next two weeks.
   (a) What was the total number of hours she worked?
   (b) If she is required to work at least 100 hours during a four-week period, how many hours will Jackie have to work in the fourth week?
2. Gregory Ellison earns $3 an hour on his part-time job. During one week, he worked the following number of hours:

Monday	4 hours
Tuesday	3 hours
Wednesday	4 hours
Thursday	4 hours
Friday	5 hours
Saturday	8 hours

   (a) How many hours did Gregory work during that week?
   (b) What was the total amount that he earned?
3. Bill Bonkowski works as a volunteer helper at a children's summer camp near his home. This afternoon he set up some team races for the young children. He put four runners on a team and each runner was to run 50 meters.
   (a) How many meters did the winning team run?
   (b) How many feet did the winning team run?
4. You have received information about three jobs:
   (a) An office job, assembling and stapling papers, folding leaflets, and sealing and stamping envelopes.
   (b) A job in a refreshment stand at a movie theater.
   (c) A part-time job in a gift shop, stocking shelves, checking shipments, and preparing packages for mailing.
   Write a letter applying for one of these jobs. Supply the name and address of the employer. Refer to Illus. 48-2 as a guide for the necessary information to include in your letter.
5. Prepare your own personal data sheet that you might use to accompany a letter of application for a job. Use the personal data sheet in Illus. 48-3 as a guide.
6. Draw up an application form similar to the one in Illus. 48-4 (or use the form in your *Activities and Projects*) and supply whatever information you think necessary to apply for one of the jobs mentioned in Problem 4.

EXPANDING YOUR UNDERSTANDING OF BUSINESS

1. Find a copy of the classified advertising section of a Sunday newspaper from a medium- to large-size city. Examine the "help wanted" columns, particularly the advertisements of private employment agencies.
   (a) In the listing of the private agencies, what do the terms, "no fee" and "fee paid" mean?
   (b) Salaries for some jobs are listed as "open," "to $1,000," or "$550+." What do these terms mean?
2. Check the "help wanted" advertisements from your local newspaper over a period of one week. Make a list of the ten jobs for which you find the most ads. This list will tell you

something about the kinds of work which are most readily available in your community. Make another list of those jobs for which you think you could qualify. Do any of these jobs interest you?

3. Your text told you that volunteer work is a good way to get experience. Volunteer experience can also help you obtain a regular job at a later time. What are some agencies in your community that need volunteer workers? What kind of work do the volunteers do? How do these volunteer workers help themselves as well as the community?

CAREER FOCUS

In other sections of this book, you have read of career opportunities in various areas, such as credit, banking, insurance, government, and travel. Each of the Career Focus sections told you about jobs in those areas, ranging from the entry-level jobs to those in supervision and management. But there is another career opportunity you might consider — being in business for yourself. This is called being an entrepreneur, and it means that you own your own business. As you learned in Part 6, the business is then called a sole proprietorship.

There are over 11.4 million sole proprietorships in this country. They make up about 78 percent of all businesses. Most proprietorships are small businesses. You can find them in agriculture, construction, wholesaling, retailing, insurance, real estate, and in many of the personal service areas. Many barbers, doctors, beauticians, public accountants, and service station operators are proprietors.

When you decide to own your own business, you are saying that you want to be responsible for everything that happens in the business. You make all of the decisions and do most of the work. You are the one who buys and sells the products or services, orders items that are needed, takes care of the financial records, and perhaps even sweeps the floor. If the business succeeds, you get all of the profits; but if it fails, you must take the losses.

There are no educational requirements for those who want to go into business for themselves. When you have the money and an idea you think will work, you can start your own business.

However, many small businesses fail each year. To get off to a good start, you may want to do what many entrepreneurs have done: spend a few years working in another similar business. Working for someone else gives you many of the experiences you need to succeed when you start on your own.

Of course, there are many educational courses that will help you prepare yourself to be an entrepreneur. You should have some knowledge of accounting, economics, business law, and human relations. Also, you should have a great deal of preparation in the field in which you want to work. For example, if you want to open a tax consulting business, you will need to take tax courses.

If you want to start your own business but can't think of some new product or service to offer the public, you could buy a franchise from someone else. As you know, having a franchise means buying the right to provide a certain product or service within a specified area. Some examples of franchises are McDonald's, Baskin-Robbins 31 Ice Cream Stores, Bonanza Sirloin Pits, Holiday Inns, and Avis Rent A Car.

To become a franchise dealer you must pay for the right to be the exclusive agent in the area. Normally the franchise holder will then train you in handling the business. This has become a very popular way of going into business for yourself.

Another way to become the owner of a business is to buy an existing business from its owner. You might do this by finding a business owner who wants to retire. It is also possible that you might go to work for a small business and later be given the opportunity to buy part of the business.

USING INFORMATION SOURCES

Success in school, in your personal life, and at work often depends on how well you can locate and use information. It has been said, for example, that a good lawyer is not one who knows facts, but one who knows where to find the facts. In this appendix, a number of sources of information are described. By knowing what type of information is available in each source, you will be able to locate facts and figures quickly when you need them.

PUBLIC AND SCHOOL LIBRARIES

The services of public and school libraries are available to you. You are free to visit public libraries to read newspapers and magazines. Some libraries keep files of clippings on important topics. In some of the larger libraries, films and recordings of fine music can be borrowed. Public, school, and college libraries contain those reference books most likely to help you when you need to find specific information on almost any subject. Trained librarians will assist you.

In some parts of the country, traveling libraries called bookmobiles circulate through rural and suburban areas. Special libraries are maintained by many of the larger business firms, trade associations, and clubs. Microfilms of documents or technical and scientific reports may sometimes be obtained from government and university libraries. Also, many libraries now have back issues of major newspapers on microfilm.

GENERAL REFERENCE SOURCES

Many books are designed as sources of information. When you want information of any kind, consider first the possibility of finding it in a general reference book. If one of the popular reference sources does not contain the information needed, consult a librarian or the card index in the library.

Dictionaries. The dictionary is probably the most useful reference book. Its chief purpose is to give the spelling, pronunciation, and meaning of words; but most dictionaries provide other useful information. Some of the more commonly used types of dictionaries are listed below.

1. *Unabridged dictionary.* This is a complete dictionary giving more information about words and their meanings than smaller editions do. Unabridged dictionaries, often containing more than 2,800 pages, provide us with additional information such as the following:

   Guide to pronunciation | Forms of address
   Abbreviations | Drawings and illustrations
   Punctuation and grammar | Tables of measures and weights,
   Rules for spelling, forming plurals, and capitalizing | kinds of money used throughout the world, and common foreign language phrases

2. *Abridged dictionary.* This is a condensed or shorter version of a larger dictionary. It is usually the size of an average book and is handy for quick reference on the spellings and meanings of words. An abridged dictionary may contain some of the special features of the unabridged dictionary.
3. *Thesaurus.* This is a book of synonyms (words similar in meaning) and antonyms (words opposite in meaning).
4. *Special dictionaries.* Special kinds of dictionaries are published for use in such fields as medicine, law, and business. There are even dictionaries showing correct shorthand forms. Dictionaries of French, Spanish, Italian, and other languages are also available. Dictionaries of special interest to business people and students would include the *University Dictionary of Business and Finance* by Clark and Gottfried and the *Dictionary of Economics* by Sloan and Zurcher.

Encyclopedias. The most complete single source of general information is the encyclopedia, which contains information taken from all fields of knowledge. It is usually published in several volumes because it gives information on so many different subjects.

Encyclopedias, like dictionaries, are published in brief as well as in comprehensive editions. Both one-volume editions and complete sets are available. There are also junior editions published for the use of school-age children.

Encyclopedias are also published for special fields of interest such as business, education, engineering, sports, and religion. Munn's *Encyclopedia of Banking and Finance* is an example of one in the business area.

Almanacs. An almanac is a publication with facts and figures about government, population, industries, religions, museums, education, cost of living, national defense, trade, transportation, and many other subjects. The *World Almanac* and the *Information Please Almanac* are two books of facts that are published annually. They are among our most popular up-to-date references. Paperbound editions of these almanacs can be purchased at many bookstores.

Atlases. An atlas is a book containing maps of regions and countries of the world. It includes information on population, products, climate, history, and commerce. An atlas is very helpful in learning the location or the size of a city or a country, the pronunciation of a geographical name, or the agricultural and commercial products of an area.

Directories. A directory is a book listing names of people living in a certain place or engaged in a particular business, trade, or profession.

1. *Telephone*. The telephone directory gives the names, addresses, and telephone numbers of people and businesses who have telephones. Some telephone directories contain a civic section that provides a highway map of the city, information about the industry and commerce of the city, a list of parks and playgrounds, and a summary of traffic rules. Many telephone directories have a classified section — the Yellow Pages. This is a listing of the names, addresses, and telephone numbers of suppliers of goods and services. The names are arranged in alphabetical order under headings that describe the types of businesses and services.

2. *City*. A city directory lists the names, occupations, and addresses of persons 18 years old or older who reside in the city for which the directory is compiled. Other information usually given includes the names of business firms, streets, clubs, churches, museums, and other institutions in the city.

3. *Government*. The *Congressional Directory* contains information about the federal government and gives the names of members of Congress. The *Book of the States* and the *Municipal Yearbook* provide similar information about state and local governments. Another important source, published annually by the federal government, is the *United States Government Manual*. This is a valuable reference book for students, teachers, business people, lawyers, and others who need information about the functions, publications, and services of U.S. government agencies.

4. *Special types*. Special types of directories include those of national businesses, public schools, school teachers and administrators, clubs, associations, and newspapers and periodicals.

Books of Statistical Information. Statistics are facts that can be stated in the form of numbers. There are several excellent sources of statistical information. In addition to the almanacs previously mentioned, there are the *Statistical Abstract of the United States*, the *Statesman's Yearbook*, the *Census Reports*, and many others.

Guides to Reading. Magazines or periodicals contain many articles on various subjects not to be found in books. Because there are so many magazines, it is impossible for anyone to find all the desired information without some aid. This aid is supplied by guides — sometimes referred to as indexes. Perhaps the most commonly used guide is the *Readers' Guide to Periodical Literature*. This guide provides an index to articles appearing in almost 200 current magazines. It is published twice a month, except for one issue in February, July, and August. Once a year, one large volume is published that combines all the listings from the indexes issued during the preceding 12 months.

Another guide, the *Education Index*, cites articles that appear in journals of particular interest to educators. The *Public Affairs Information Service Bulletin* and the *Business Periodicals Index* will also assist you in locating articles and other literature on public affairs and business topics.

Some of the larger newspapers publish their own guides that assist readers to locate articles of interest in their newspapers. Examples of these are the *New York Times Index* and the *Wall Street Journal Index*. The *Newspaper Index* indexes news items and other articles in the *Chicago Tribune*, the *Washington Post*, the *New Orleans Times Picayune*, and the *Los Angeles Times*.

Newspapers. Almost everyone refers to daily newspapers for information on radio and television programs and for announcements of movies showing at the theaters. If you are planning a trip, you may check on weather forecasts and road condition reports. Newspapers also inform us of scheduled lectures, exhibits, concerts, school affairs, sports events, and other activities. Major newspapers print information about economic conditions, prices of commodities, cost of living, prices of stocks and bonds, and other information of interest to business people and consumers.

SPECIALIZED REFERENCE SOURCES

There is a wealth of information in almost any special field. You may be familiar with such special references as the *Official Baseball Guide* for baseball fans and the *Radio Amateur's Handbook* for ham radio operators. Directories, yearbooks, handbooks, and other references are available to hobbyists, artists, musicians, entertainers, workers in technical professions, ethnic groups, and many others. A few of the more widely used special reference sources are described in the following paragraphs.

Information for Travelers. Two commonly used sources of information for travelers are:

1. *Road maps.* In addition to highway routes, many road maps show places of interest, camping sites, parks, lakes, street layouts of larger cities, and other details.

2. *Guides and directories.* The *Hotel and Motel Red Book* gives information about the location and size of hotels and motels, room rates, and hotel services for more than 8,000 hotels and motels in the U.S. and in many foreign countries.

The *Official Airline Guide* contains airline schedules, fares, and information such as airmail rates, car rental services, and conversion of dollars to foreign currencies. The *Rand McNally Campground and Trailer Park Guide*, revised annually, contains a list of thousands of campgrounds and trailer parks in the U.S. and Canada.

Information for Consumers.

Two popular monthly magazines, *Consumer Reports* and *Consumers' Research Magazine*, contain facts and advice about products and services used most by consumers. Organized consumer groups and the federal government publish newsletters and other literature of particular interest to consumers.

Many useful government bulletins, some free and others available at little cost, can be ordered from the Superintendent of Documents, U.S. Government Printing Office, Washington, DC 20402. Many libraries have the *Monthly Catalog of U.S. Government Publications*, which lists by subject all federal government publications issued during the preceding month. Bulletins of value to consumers are often available from Better Business Bureaus, labor unions, colleges, government agencies, and other public and private organizations.

Information for Business.

The U.S. Department of Commerce issues many reports and studies of value to large and small business firms. It publishes *Survey of Current Business*, a monthly periodical with articles and statistics on business activity and economic conditions. The U.S. Department of Labor issues the *Monthly Labor Review* which gives information on prices, wages, and employment. National, state, and local chambers of commerce also provide many kinds of useful reports.

The *Economic Almanac* is prepared by the Conference Board. It is a standard source of facts on current business and economic developments.

Much information about business affairs can be found in the financial pages of daily newspapers. Other publications such as *Fortune* and *Business Week* are devoted primarily to business and its problems. A business can subscribe to special newsletter services, such as *The Kiplinger Washington Letter*, for information not usually published in newspapers and magazines.

Many handbooks describing principles, practices, and methods for certain specialized fields of business are available. Among the handbooks of special interest to business people are:

1. *Accountants' Handbook* — a general reference book in accounting, containing answers to accounting problems and presenting the principles of accounting.

2. *Financial Handbook* — a guide to solving financial problems such as financing the growth and operation of the business and raising new capital for expansion.
3. *Office Administration Handbook* — a comprehensive volume focusing attention on the human relationships involved in the management of offices. It includes chapters on testing, hiring, supervising, training, and promoting office workers; and on office systems, policies, work procedures, correspondence, layouts, equipment, and data processing developments.
4. *Marketing Handbook* — a reference book that discusses all phases of the marketing process such as advertising, sales promotion, and research.

Almost every field of business has its special trade directory. For example, special directories are published for people in such businesses as advertising, retailing, insurance, real estate, banking, plastics manufacturing, air transportation, and frozen food processing.

Information about People. Encyclopedias tell about great men and women of history. Other reference books give information about men and women now living. The best-known books of this type are *Who's Who* and *Who's Who in America*. *Who's Who* gives a summary of the lives and the achievements of outstanding people living throughout the world. *Who's Who in America* lists mainly those leaders living in the United States. Books similar to these are also published for special groups, such as *Who's Who in Finance and Industry*, *Who's Who of American Women*, and *American Men and Women of Science*. Another popular reference about people is *Current Biography*, which includes sketches about individuals, many of various nationalities, who have become prominent because of their recent accomplishments.

Information about Occupations. Two important government publications giving information on occupations are the *Dictionary of Occupational Titles* and the *Occupational Outlook Handbook* (see pages 118 and 125). Another very worthwhile reference for junior and senior high school students is the *Encyclopedia of Careers and Vocational Guidance*. This extensive compilation is published in two volumes. Volume I contains practical guidance material and broad articles on opportunities in some 70 major industries or areas of work. Volume II contains more than 200 articles on specific occupations, such as bank teller, stenographer, travel agent, hotel manager, buyer, economist, accountant, automobile mechanic, glazier, and watch repairer. These articles give detailed information about the nature of the work, requirements, methods of entry, earnings, and sources of additional information.

Because of the recent emphasis on career education, school libraries in particular have acquired more information on different occupations. This information is presented not only in book form, but also through films, microfilm, and games.

REVIEWING ARITHMETIC

This arithmetic review will be especially helpful to you in solving many of the end-of-part problems in this textbook and the common arithmetic problems you will encounter in your personal business. These suggestions deal with a few of the kinds of arithmetic calculations that people have the most trouble with.

MULTIPLYING NUMBERS ENDING WITH ZERO

In multiplying two numbers, if one or both of the numbers have zeros at the extreme right, place the zeros to the right of an imaginary line, multiply the numbers to the left of the line, and bring down the total number of zeros to the right of the line.

For example:

```
      4 7|                4 7|0 0              4 7|0
  × 2 3|0 0            × 2 3|              × 2 3|0 0
  -------              -------              -------
    1 4 1|              1 4 1|              1 4 1|
    9 4  |              9 4  |              9 4  |
  -------              -------              -------
  1 0 8,1|0 0          1 0 8,1|0 0        1,0 8 1|0 0 0
```

DIVIDING BY NUMBERS ENDING WITH ZERO

When the divisor is 10, 100, 1,000, etc., move the decimal point in the dividend one place to the left for each zero. Moving the decimal point one place to the left divides a number by 10; two places to the left, by 100; three places to the left, by 1,000; etc.

For example:

$14.2 \div 10 = 1.42$ $4,685 \div 1,000 = 4.685$
$231.7 \div 100 = 2.317$

$168.2 \div 20 =$

$2) \overline{16.82}$

8.41

When the divisor is 20, 400, 3,000, etc., drop the zeros in the divisor, move the decimal point in the dividend one place to the left for each zero, and divide by the remaining number 2, 4, 3, etc.

Other examples:

$$72.8 \div 400 =$$
$$4\ )\ .728$$
$$.182$$

$$6,729 \div 3,000 =$$
$$3\ )\ 6.729$$
$$2.243$$

USING DECIMALS

Some students find the use of decimals difficult. Knowing and following a few simple rules will help improve your calculations involving decimals.

1. Adding numbers with decimals — keep all decimal points in line.

For example:

Add:	84.25		34.7
	1.89		1.98
	625.00		362.
	16.93		.459
	728.07		16.16
			8.73
			424.029

2. Subtracting numbers with decimals — keep decimal points in line.

For example:

392.6 ←fill out spaces to the right with 0's→ 392.600

−8.794

$$-8.794$$
$$383.806$$

Subtract 9.876 from 74

$$74.000$$
$$-9.876$$
$$64.124$$

3. Multiplying numbers with decimals.

For example: Multiply 6.34 by 6.3

$$6.3\ 4$$
$$6.3$$
$$1\ 9\ 0\ 2$$
$$3\ 8\ 0\ 4$$
$$3\ 9.9\ 4\ 2$$

a. Keep right margin even.
b. Keep figures in line.
c. To locate decimal point, count all digits to the right of the decimal point in the two original figures — in this case *three* — count off that number of places from the right in the product, and set the point.

4. Always multiply by the simpler number.

For example: Multiply 2.4 × 375.1. This is the same as multiplying 375.1 by 2.4, which is simpler.

$$3\ 7\ 5.1$$
$$2.4$$
$$1\ 5\ 0\ 0\ 4$$
$$7\ 5\ 0\ 2$$
$$9\ 0\ 0.2\ 4$$

5. Dividing numbers with decimals.

First example: (Dividend) 129.54 ÷ .34 (Divisor) =

.34) 129.54

$$\begin{array}{r} 381. \text{ (Quotient)} \\ .34 \overline{)\ 129.54} \\ \underline{102} \\ 275 \\ \underline{272} \\ 34 \\ \underline{34} \end{array}$$

To the right of the decimal point in the dividend count as many places as are to the right of the decimal point in the divisor. Set the decimal point in the quotient at this point. Keep figures in line.

Second example: 420 ÷ 75 =

$$\begin{array}{r} 5.6 \\ 75 \overline{)\ 420.0} \\ \underline{375} \\ 450 \\ \underline{450} \end{array}$$

Decimal point is always at extreme right of whole number, although not shown. In dividing, a decimal point may be placed at the right of the dividend and 0's added as needed.

MULTIPLYING BY PRICE FIGURES

Dealers frequently price items for sale at such figures as 99¢, $4.98, $99.98, etc. This is done because a price of $99.98, for example, seems less to the prospective buyer than an even $100.

Let us assume that 27 items are purchased at $19.99 each.

The usual method of multiplication:

$$\begin{array}{r} \$\ 19.99 \\ \times\qquad 27 \\ \hline 13993 \\ 3998 \\ \hline \$539.73 \end{array}$$

A simpler method:

$$\begin{array}{r} 27 \\ \times\ \$\ 20.00 \\ \hline 540.00 \\ -\qquad .27 \\ \hline \$539.73 \end{array}$$

(1) Multiply by the next higher number containing zeros — in this case $20.00. (2) If the price figure ends in 99¢, subtract 1¢ for each item purchased — in this case 27¢.

Other examples:

If the price figure ends in 98¢, subtract 2¢ for each item purchased — in this case 64¢.
($.02 × 32 = $.64).

If the price figure ends in 97¢, subtract 3¢ for each item purchased — in this case $2.13.
($.03 × 71 = $2.13).

32 items at $4.98

$$\begin{array}{r} 32 \\ \times\ \$\ 5.00 \\ \hline \$160.00 \\ -\qquad .64 \\ \hline \$159.36 \end{array}$$

71 items at $9.97

$$\begin{array}{r} 71 \\ \times\ \$\ 10.00 \\ \hline \$710.00 \\ -\qquad 2.13 \\ \hline \$707.87 \end{array}$$

USING FRACTIONAL PARTS OF $1.00 IN MULTIPLYING

While merchandise may be priced at any figure, prices are frequently expressed in fractional parts of $1.00, $10.00, $100.00, etc., that can be calculated easily and quickly. For example, 50 cents is ½ of $1.00; 25 cents is ¼ of $1.00; 33⅓ cents is ⅓ of $1.00. Thus:

24 items selling for $1.00 each would cost	$24.00
24 items at 50¢ each would cost ½ of $24 or	$12.00
24 items at 25¢ each would cost ¼ of $24 or	$ 6.00
24 items at 33⅓¢ each would cost ⅓ of $24 or	$ 8.00

With a little practice, many similar calculations can be made mentally. While there are many fractional parts of $1.00, the ones shown below will be very helpful to you from time to time in making your arithmetic calculations.

Fractional Part of $1.00	Halves	Thirds	Fourths	Sixths	Eighths
¹/₈					$.12½
¹/₆				$.16⅔	
¹/₄			$.25		
¹/₃		$.33⅓			
³/₈					$.37½
¹/₂	$.50				
⁵/₈					$.62½
²/₃		$.66⅔			
³/₄			$.75		
⁵/₆				$.83⅓	
⁷/₈					$.87½

You already know several of the above fractional parts of $1.00, and with practice you will be able to use those and others quickly and accurately. Four different types of calculations are involved. Perhaps you will not be able to master all of them, but certainly you can master some of them.

First type:
1. Numerator of fractional part is "1," that is, ¹/₈, ¹/₆, ¹/₄, etc.
2. There *is no remainder;* that is, the calculations come to even dollars.

For example:
$24 \times .25 = \$6.00$

How to calculate:

24 items at $1.00 each would cost...$24.00
25¢ is ¼ of $1.00, hence at 25¢ 24 items will cost ¼
   of $24 or...$ 6.00

Other examples:
$32 \times \$.12½$ $(32 \times ¹/₈) = \$4.00$
$36 \times \$.16⅔$ $(36 \times ¹/₆) = \$6.00$

$48 \times \$.25$ $(48 \times {}^1/_4) = \$12.00$
$39 \times \$.33^1/_3$ $(39 \times {}^1/_3) = \$13.00$
$48 \times \$.50$ $(48 \times {}^1/_2) = \$24.00$

Second type:

1. Numerator of fractional part is "1."
2. There *is a remainder*; that is, the calculations will result in dollars and cents.

For example:

$33 \times \$.25 = \$8.25$

   How to calculate:

   33 items at \$1.00 each would cost...\$33.00
   25¢ is ¼ of \$1.00; hence at 25¢ 33 items will cost ¼
      of \$33 or \$8¼; ¼ of \$1.00 is 25¢, thus ....\$ 8.25

(*Note:* The fraction of a dollar obtained will always be one of the fractions illustrated on page 598 so that once these fractional parts are mastered there is nothing new to be learned.)

Other examples:

$41 \times \$.12^1/_2 = \$ \ 5^1/_8 = \$ \ 5.13 \ ({}^1/_8 = .12^1/_2$ changed to .13)*
$39 \times \$.16^2/_3 = \$ \ 6^3/_6 = \$ \ 6.50 \ ({}^3/_6 = {}^1/_2 = .50)$
$37 \times \$.25 \quad = \$ \ 9^1/_4 = \$ \ 9.25$
$28 \times \$.33^1/_3 = \$ \ 9^1/_3 = \$ \ 9.33*$
$25 \times \$.50 \quad = \$12^1/_2 = \$12.50$

   (* Since 1¢ is our smallest coin, if the final fraction is ½ or more, the last figure is raised 1 penny; if less than ½, the fraction is dropped. *Note:* Some retailers convert every fraction to 1¢, even if the fraction is less than ½.)

Third type:

1. Numerator is other than "1."
2. There *is no remainder*.

For example:

$48 \times \$.75 = \$36.00$

   How to calculate:

   Think of \$.75 as ¾ of \$1.00 and solve by cancellation.

$$48 \times \$.75 \ (\overset{12}{\cancel{48}} \times \frac{3}{\cancel{4}}) = \$36.00$$

Other examples:

$$24 \times \$.37\tfrac{1}{2} \ (\overset{3}{\cancel{24}} \times \frac{3}{\cancel{8}}) = \$ \ 9.00$$

$$32 \times \$.62\tfrac{1}{2} \ (\overset{4}{\cancel{32}} \times \frac{5}{\cancel{8}}) = \$20.00$$

$$36 \times \$.66\tfrac{2}{3} \ (\overset{12}{\cancel{36}} \times \frac{2}{\cancel{3}}) = \$24.00$$

Fourth type:
1. Numerator is other than "1."
2. There *is a remainder*.

For example:

$34 \times \$.62\frac{1}{2} = \$21.25$

How to calculate:

Think of $\$.62\frac{1}{2}$ as $\frac{5}{8}$ of $\$1.00$; but since 8 does not divide evenly into 34, first multiply by 5 and then divide by 8.

$$\$\ 34 \times 5 = \$170$$
$$\$170 \div 8 = \$\ 21^2/_8$$
$$\$\ 21^2/_8\quad = \$\ 21.25$$

$$34 \times \$.62\frac{1}{2}\quad (34 \times \frac{5}{8} = \frac{170}{8}) = \$21.25$$

Other examples:

$$61 \times \$.37\frac{1}{2}\ (61 \times \frac{3}{8} = \frac{183}{8}) = \$22.88$$

$$43 \times \$.66\frac{2}{3}\ (43 \times \frac{2}{3} = \frac{86}{3}) = \$28.67$$

$$21 \times \$.75\quad (21 \times \frac{3}{4} = \frac{63}{4}) = \$15.75$$

$$51 \times \$.83\frac{1}{3}\ (51 \times \frac{5}{6} = \frac{255}{6}) = \$42.50$$

$$23 \times \$.87\frac{1}{2}\ (23 \times \frac{7}{8} = \frac{161}{8}) = \$20.13$$

Note: You will observe that after the number is multiplied by the numerator, the remaining calculation is exactly like that in the *second type* above.

Fractional parts of other amounts.

To the student who is interested in developing greater skill in calculating fractional parts of other amounts, a few additional examples will demonstrate the large number of applications possible.

First example:

.05 is ½ of	.10	
.50 is ½ of	1.00	
5.00 is ½ of	10.00	Thus:
50.00 is ½ of	100.00	
500.00 is ½ of	1,000.00	

$$24 \times\ .05 = 1.20$$
$$24 \times\ .50 = 12.00$$
$$24 \times\ 5.00 = 120.00$$
$$24 \times\ 50.00 = 1,200.00$$
$$24 \times 500.00 = 12,000.00$$

Second example:

.02½ is ¼ of	.10	
.25 is ¼ of	1.00	
2.50 is ¼ of	10.00	Thus:
25.00 is ¼ of	100.00	
250.00 is ¼ of	1,000.00	

$$430 \times\ .02\frac{1}{2} = 10.75$$
$$430 \times\ .25 = 107.50$$
$$430 \times\ 2.50 = 1,075.00$$
$$430 \times\ 25.00 = 10,750.00$$
$$430 \times 250.00 = 107,500.00$$

FINDING PERCENTAGES AND INTEREST

What does *percent* mean?

Some students get confused when the term "percent" is mentioned. Actually the "percent" concept is very simple. Percent is derived from two Latin words, "per centum," meaning "by the hundred." This is why percent is easy — you are using a fraction whose denominator is always 100. The percent sign is %. Every percent figure can then be expressed as either a common fraction or a decimal fraction.

For example:

Percent		Common Fraction		Decimal Fraction
3%	=	3/100	=	.03
5%	=	5/100	=	.05
7%	=	7/100	=	.07

In fact, you never use the percent figure in calculating percent. You always change the percent figure to either a common fraction or a decimal fraction.

To find:

4% of $300: multiply $300 $\times \dfrac{4}{100}$ = $12.00; or $300 $\times$ .04 = $12.00

6% of $250: multiply $250 $\times \dfrac{6}{100}$ = $15.00; or $250 $\times$ .06 = $15.00

CALCULATING INTEREST

Interest is expressed as a percent; but in calculating interest, both the percent and the length of time are considered.

For example:

8% interest on $400 for 1 year = $400 × .08 × 1 = $32.00
5% interest on $550 for 3 years = $550 × .05 × 3 = $82.50

One method of calculating interest for less than one year is explained in Part 26 of this textbook; another method of calculating interest for less than a year is explained below.

THE 60-DAY, 6% METHOD OF FINDING INTEREST

Bankers and other business people often use a simple method of finding interest, known as the 60-day, 6% method. As this name indicates, the method is based on a period of time of 60 days and a rate of 6%. This method of finding interest will be explained through the use of several problems.

Problem 1. Find the interest on $100 for 60 days at 6%.

Step 1: Find the interest for one year.
$100 × .06 = $6

Step 2: Find the interest for 60 days.

In interest problems a year is considered to be 360 days.

Therefore $\frac{60 \text{ days}}{360 \text{ days}} = {}^1/_6$ of a year

$6 × ${}^1/_6$ = $1, the interest on $100 for 60 days at 6%

Since the interest on $100 for 60 days at 6% is $1, it will be observed that the interest on any amount for 60 days at 6% can be found simply by *moving the decimal point two places to the left.*

Examples: Interest on $100.00 for 60 days at 6% = $1.00
Interest on $550.00 for 60 days at 6% = $5.50
Interest on $275.50 for 60 days at 6% = $2.755, or $2.76

The 60-day, 6% method may be used when the time is not 60 days.

Problem 2. Find the interest on $1,000 for 30 days at 6%.

Solve for 60 days:
The interest on $1,000 for 60 days at 6% = $10

30 days is ½ of 60 days; therefore:
$10 × ½ = $5, the interest on $1,000 for 30 days at 6%

Problem 3. Find the interest on $500 for 90 days at 6%.

Break down the 90 days into 60 days and 30 days, as follows:
The interest on $500 at 6% for 60 days = $5.00
The interest on $500 at 6% for 30 days = 2.50
The interest on $500 at 6% for 90 days = $7.50

To find the interest for any number of days, break down the 60 days into periods of time that are simple fractions of 60 days.

Examples: 30 days = $\frac{1}{2}$ of 60 days
20 days = $\frac{1}{3}$ of 60 days
15 days = $\frac{1}{4}$ of 60 days
10 days = $\frac{1}{6}$ of 60 days

Problem 4. Find the interest on $420 for 105 days at 6%.

The interest on $420 at 6% for   60 days = $4.20
The interest on $420 at 6% for   30 days =   2.10
The interest on $420 at 6% for   15 days =   1.05
The interest on $420 at 6% for 105 days = $7.35

To find the interest for 1 day or for a few days, first find the interest for 6 days. Six days are $\frac{1}{10}$ of 60 days.

Examples: The interest on $720 for 60 days at 6% = $7.20
The interest on $720 for   6 days at 6% = $ .72 ($\frac{1}{10}$ of $7.20)

(Notice that the interest on any amount for 6 days at 6% can be found by *moving the decimal point three places to the left*.)

The interest on $720 for 1 day at 6% = $.12 ($\frac{1}{6}$ of .72)

The interest on $480 for 6 days at 6% = $.48
The interest on $480 for 1 day at 6% = $.08

The interest on $42 for 6 days at 6% = $.042
The interest on $42 for 1 day at 6% = $.007 = $.01

Problem 5. Find the interest on $412.50 for 97 days at 6%.

The interest on $412.50 at 6% for 60 days = $4.125
The interest on $412.50 at 6% for 30 days =   2.0625
   (carry to 4 decimal places)
The interest on $412.50 at 6% for   6 days =   .4125
The interest on $412.50 at 6% for   1 day =   .0688
   ($\frac{1}{6}$ of $.4125)
The interest on $412.50 at 6% for 97 days = $6.6688 = $6.67

The 60-day, 6% method may be used when the rate is other than 6%.

In order to find the interest on any amount at any rate of interest, first solve for 6%; divide by 6 to obtain the interest at 1%; then multiply by the desired rate.

Problem 6. Find the interest on $360 for 75 days at 10%.

First, solve for 6%:
The interest on $360 at 6% for 60 days = $3.60
The interest on $360 at 6% for 15 days =   .90
The interest on $360 at 6% for 75 days = $4.50

Next, find the interest at 1%:
$4.50 ÷ 6 = $.75, the interest at 1%

Then, multiply by the desired rate of interest:
$.75 × 10 = $7.50, the interest on $360 for 75 days at 10%

CALCULATION OF INTEREST ON INSTALLMENT LOANS

The method of calculating the rate of interest on installment loans presented in Part 26 is sufficiently accurate for most purposes. For a more exact calculation of interest, the following method is presented.

Problem. Martin B. Allen borrowed $120 from the small loan department of his bank and signed a note for $126. He agreed to pay back the balance in 8 equal monthly installments of $15.75. What annual rate of interest did he pay for the use of the $120 that he actually received?

Solution. The cost of the loan was $126 − $120 = $6. Assume that an interest rate of 12% a year, or 1% a month, was charged for the loan. On this basis the interest would have been:

$120.00 borrowed for 1 month @ 1% would cost.............. $1.20
−15.75 1st payment

104.25 borrowed for 1 month @ 1% would cost.............. 1.04
−15.75 2d payment

88.50 borrowed for 1 month @ 1% would cost.............. .89
−15.75 3d payment

72.75 borrowed for 1 month @ 1% would cost.............. .73
−15.75 4th payment

57.00 borrowed for 1 month @ 1% would cost.............. .57
−15.75 5th payment

41.25 borrowed for 1 month @ 1% would cost.............. .41
−15.75 6th payment

25.50 borrowed for 1 month @ 1% would cost.............. .26
−15.75 7th payment

9.75 borrowed for 1 month @ 1% would cost.............. .10
−15.75 8th payment

Interest cost if the money had been borrowed at 1% a month, or 12% a year $5.20

It will be observed that the interest was figured on the total $120 for the first month only, because the borrower had the use of the entire amount only during that month. During the second month the interest was figured on \$104.25, as \$15.75 was repaid at the end of the first month. The amount on which the interest was figured was decreased in a like manner for each month during the time of the loan.

At 1% a month, or 12% a year, the interest would have been \$5.20. The actual cost of the loan was \$6. How many times greater was this actual cost than \$5.20? This may be found by dividing \$6 by \$5.20:

$$\$6 \div \$5.20 = 1.1538$$

The amount actually paid was, then, 1.1538 times greater than the amount would be if the rate had been 1% a month, or 12% a year. Since interest rates are given on a yearly basis, the actual rate was:

$$12\% \times 1.1538 = 13.85\%$$

CALCULATION OF INTEREST ON INSTALLMENT PURCHASES

The method of calculating the rate of interest on installment purchases is similar to the method of calculating the rate of interest on installment loans.

Problem. Larry Simms bought a radio on the installment plan from Ace Radio Shop for \$102. A down payment of \$12 was made at the time of the purchase, and \$9 was paid at the end of each of the following 10 months. The radio could have been purchased for \$92 in cash. What rate of interest was paid for the privilege of buying on installments?

Solution. The amount that Larry paid for the privilege of buying on installments is found by subtracting the cash price of the radio from the installment price of the radio.

> \$102 the installment price of the radio
> −92 the cash price of the radio
> \$ 10 the amount paid for the privilege of buying on installments

The radio could have been purchased for \$92 in cash. A down payment of \$12 was made. The cash price was therefore \$80 more than the down payment. Larry could have bought the radio for cash if he had borrowed \$80 from some other source. He was, then, in reality borrowing \$80 from the Ace Radio Shop. This may be shown as:

> \$ 92 the price that would have been paid if the purchase had been for cash
> −12 the down payment at the time of the purchase
> \$ 80 the amount borrowed from the dealer

If Larry had borrowed \$80 from some other source at a rate of 1% a month, or 12% a year, the interest would have been found as follows:

$80 borrowed for 1 month @ 1% would cost............ $ .80
−9 1st payment

 71 borrowed for 1 month @ 1% would cost............   .71
−9 2d payment

 62 borrowed for 1 month @ 1% would cost............   .62
−9 3d payment

 53 borrowed for 1 month @ 1% would cost............   .53
−9 4th payment

 44 borrowed for 1 month @ 1% would cost............   .44
−9 5th payment

 35 borrowed for 1 month @ 1% would cost............   .35
−9 6th payment

 26 borrowed for 1 month @ 1% would cost............   .26
−9 7th payment

 17 borrowed for 1 month @ 1% would cost............   .17
−9 8th payment

  8 borrowed for 1 month @ 1% would cost............   .08
−9 9th payment

Interest cost if the money had been
borrowed at 1% a month, or 12% a
year $3.96

You will observe that the interest was figured on $80 for the first month only, since Larry had the use of this amount during that month only. During the second month the interest was figured on $71 because $9 was repaid at the end of the first month. The amount on which the interest was figured was decreased in a like manner for each installment paid.

At 1% a month, or 12% a year, the interest was $3.96. The actual cost for the loan was $10 ($102 − $92 = $10). How many times greater was this actual cost than $3.96? This may be found by dividing $10 by $3.96:

$$\$10 \div \$3.96 = 2.5252$$

The amount actually paid, then, was 2.5252 times greater than the amount would have been if the rate had been 1% a month, or 12% a year. The actual rate, then, was:

$$12\% \times 2.5252 = 30.30\%$$

Appendix D

USING THE METRIC SYSTEM

More and more of the world's people are using the metric system of measurement. Over 90 percent of the nations in the world now use or are changing to the metric system. Because of our great amount of trade with other countries, the United States is joining the rest of the world and moving to the metric system. Of course this will not happen overnight. The change to metric will be made gradually over a number of years. But some U.S. industries have already made the change, and you should begin to become familiar with the metric system.

There are some things about the metric system that are already familiar to you. For example, if you have been to a track or swimming meet or seen one on TV, you know that the distances are sometimes measured in meters, not in feet or miles. Food is often labeled to show amounts in grams as well as pounds or ounces. Meters and grams are examples of metric units of measurement.

BASIC METRIC UNITS

To use the metric system, you will measure weight (or mass), distance, volume, and temperature differently from the way you are used to. Once you become familiar with it, the metric system is actually simpler to use than the U.S. system. Metric has very few base units, while the U.S. system uses many base units. The following paragraphs tell you the metric base units that you need to know now.

The kilogram is the metric base unit of weight. A kilogram is equal to a little over two pounds. The kilogram and units based on the kilogram are used instead of ounces and pounds.

The meter is the metric base unit of distance. A meter is a little longer than a yard. The meter and a few other units based on the meter are used to measure things we now measure in inches, feet, and miles.

The cubic meter is really the metric base unit of volume. However, for most measurements of volume, you will use the liter. A liter is equal to a little more than a quart. You will use the liter in place of the fluid ounce, the pint, the quart, and the gallon.

The degree Celsius (named after the Swedish astronomer Anders Celsius), once called the centigrade degree, is used instead of the Fahrenheit degree to measure temperature.

Illus. D-1 gives you some idea of how these metric units of measure compare with U.S. units.

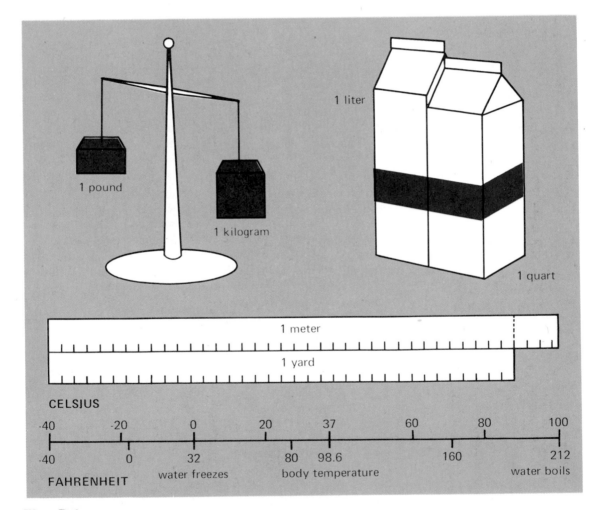

Illus. D-1

Some common units of measure in the U.S. and metric systems.

METRIC PREFIXES

Any measure can be expressed in the base units of the metric system. But this can be awkward if very large or very small numbers are involved. By using prefixes with the units of the metric system, you can express measurements in a more convenient way. Since the metric system is a decimal system (that is, it is based on the number 10), the prefixes all mean to multiply or divide the unit by 10, 100, or 1000. There are quite a few metric prefixes, but the ones which you use in this book and in most everyday measurements are:

> milli = one one-thousandth or 1/1000 or 0.001
> centi = one one-hundredth or 1/100 or 0.01
> kilo = one thousand or 1000

Prefixes are added to or taken away from the names of the base units to produce larger or smaller metric units. For example:

> 1 millimeter = 0.001 meter (about the diameter of a paper clip wire)
> 1 centimeter = 0.01 meter (about the width of a paper clip)
> 1 kilometer = 1000 meters (a little over half a mile)
> 1 gram = 0.001 kilogram (about the weight of a paper clip)

You may wonder why the kilogram, a base unit, has a prefix. Because the gram is extremely small, there was no way to measure it precisely when the standards for metric measurement were being set up. Therefore the kilogram is considered the base unit.

The metric base units and prefixes are shown with their abbreviations in Illus. D-2. Study this illustration until you are familiar with the units, the prefixes, and their abbreviations.

The abbreviations are combined in the same way that metric prefixes and units are combined. For example, millimeter is abbreviated mm; centimeter, cm; kilogram, kg; and kiloliter, kL. The prefixes are never used with degrees Celsius. The degree is the only unit of temperature.

Illus. D-2

These units and prefixes are the most commonly used ones in the metric system.

UNIT	ABBREVIATION	USE
kilogram	kg	weight
meter	m	distance
liter	L	volume
degree Celsius	°C	temperature

PREFIX	ABBREVIATION	MEANING
milli	m	1/1000
centi	c	1/100
kilo	k	1000

USING UNITS AND PREFIXES CORRECTLY

It would not mean much to say that a pill weighs 0.0001 kilogram or that the distance between two towns is 77 058 meters. That would be like telling someone that the distance to the next service station is 10,560 feet instead of 2 miles. (As you see here, in the metric system a space is used instead of a comma to show thousands when grouping five or more digits.)

You would not say that your bicycle weighs 12 000 grams, but that it weighs 12 kilograms. The kilogram is ordinarily used wherever we are used to using pounds. The milligram, a very small measure, is used a great deal in the medical and scientific fields. Pills prescribed by doctors are often measured in milligrams.

Meters are used where we are accustomed to using feet or yards, and millimeters usually replace inches for short measurements. Centimeters are used for some measurements such as the dimensions of household objects, for example towels and sheets, and personal measurements, for example your height.

The liter replaces the fluid ounce, the pint, the quart, and the gallon for small quantities. Gasoline in a car's tank would be measured in liters. But the amount of gasoline in a large storage tank would be measured in kiloliters. The milliliter is used to measure very small quantities such as medicine dosages or amounts of liquid ingredients in recipes.

CHANGING FROM ONE SYSTEM TO THE OTHER

To use the metric system well, you must learn to think in terms of metric units. However, until you get used to doing this, it is easier to convert the metric units into units you know. Illus. D-3 tells you how to convert some commonly used metric units to their U.S. equivalents and some U.S. units to their metric equivalents. The numbers that you are to multiply by have been rounded off to make them easier for you to use and remember.

Take a look at Illus. D-3; then study these examples.

If you buy a 6-ounce bag of candy, what is its weight in grams?

$$6 \text{ ounces} \times 28 = 168 \text{ grams}$$

If you have 9 meters of masking tape, how many yards of tape do you have?

$$9 \text{ meters} \times 1.1 = 9.9 \text{ yards}$$

What is the volume in liters of 5 quarts of oil?

$$5 \text{ quarts} \times 0.95 = 4.75 \text{ liters}$$

If the temperature is 77°F, what is the temperature in degrees Celsius?

$$77 - 32 = 45$$
$$5/9 \times 45 = 25°C$$

APPROXIMATE CONVERSIONS FROM U.S. TO METRIC AND METRIC TO U.S.

	WHEN YOU KNOW:	YOU CAN FIND:	IF YOU MULTIPLY BY:
DISTANCE	inches	millimeters (mm)	25
	inches	centimeters (cm)	2.5
	feet	meters (m)	0.3
	yards	meters (m)	0.9
	miles	kilometers (km)	1.6
	millimeters (mm)	inches	0.04
	centimeters (cm)	inches	0.4
	meters (m)	inches	39.4
	meters (m)	feet	3.3
	meters (m)	yards	1.1
	kilometers (km)	miles	0.6
WEIGHT (MASS)	ounces	grams (g)	28
	pounds	kilograms (kg)	0.45
	grams (g)	ounces	0.035
	kilograms (kg)	pounds	2.2
VOLUME	pints	liters (L)	0.47
	quarts	liters (L)	0.95
	gallons	liters (L)	3.8
	liters (L)	pints	2.1
	liters (L)	quarts	1.06
	liters (L)	gallons	0.26
TEMPERATURE	degrees Fahrenheit	degrees Celsius (°C)	5/9 (after subtracting 32)
	degrees Celsius (°C)	degrees Fahrenheit	9/5 (then add 32)

Illus. D-3

Table of approximate metric-to-U.S. and U.S.-to-metric conversions.

GLOSSARY

A

account: the record that a bank keeps of a customer's deposits

add-on plan: an installment plan in which the costs of all time purchases are grouped together in one monthly payment

allowance: an amount of money budgeted for savings or expenditures

alphabetical directory: a book listing all the people in an area who have telephones, arranged alphabetically

annuity: an amount of money that an insurance company will pay at definite intervals to a person who has previously deposited money with the company

application form: a form filled out by each job applicant showing information the employer wants to know

appraiser: an expert in estimating the value of property

appreciation: the amount of increase in the value of property

articles of partnership: a written agreement made by partners in forming their business

assessed value: the amount which property is determined to be worth for tax purposes

assets: everything of value that a person, family, or business owns

automated data processing: processing data by using automatic machines that require little human attention

automation: using electronic or mechanical equipment to produce goods, services, and information with a minimum of human effort

B

bank draft: a check that a bank draws on its deposits in another bank

bank money order: a form often purchased from banks for use in making small payments

bank reconciliation: a statement showing how the checkbook balance and the bank statement balance were brought into agreement

bank statement: a report given by a bank to a depositor showing the condition of his or her account

basic economic problem: the problem of satisfying unlimited wants with limited resources which faces individuals, businesses, organizations, and governments

basic health coverage: a combination of hospital, surgical, and regular medical expense insurance

beneficiary: the person named in an insurance policy to receive the insurance benefits

blank endorsement: an endorsement consisting of a name only

blue-collar workers: workers who perform work that requires physical skills and the operation of equipment

board of directors: a group of people elected by stockholders to guide a corporation

bodily injury liability insurance: insurance that protects you from claims resulting from injuries or deaths for which you are found to be at fault

bond: a printed promise to pay a definite amount of money, with interest, at a specified time

boycott: when union members refuse to transport and handle or buy the products of a business involved in a labor dispute

brand name: a special name given to a product by a manufacturer to distinguish it as being made by that particular firm

broker: a specialist in buying and selling securities

budget: a plan for saving and spending income

budget account: a credit plan which is similar to an open charge account but spreads payments over a few months

building and loan association: an organization that provides savings account services and makes loans to individuals, primarily for use in buying homes (*same as* savings and loan association)

business: an establishment that supplies us with goods and services in exchange for payment in some form

C

canceled check: a check that has been paid by a bank

capacity: the factor in credit that has to do with a customer's ability to earn

capital 1: tools, machinery, and other equipment used in producing goods and services (*same as* capital resources) **2:** the factor in credit that has to do with the property and money that a customer owns

capitalism: an economic system in which most of the economic resources are owned by individuals rather than by the government (*same as* free enterprise system)

capital resources: tools, machinery, and other equipment used in producing goods and services (*same as* capital)

career exploration: an important process that involves learning about yourself and about jobs in the world of work

career interview: a planned discussion with a worker to find out about the work that is done, preparation necessary, and feelings about that career

carrier: an individual or company that transports goods or people

cashier's check: a check that a bank employee draws on the bank's own funds

cash value: the amount that an insurance company will pay to the insured if a policy is given up

certificate of deposit: a special form of savings which requires a large amount of money to be invested and requires that the deposit be left for a certain period of time

certificate of incorporation: a document, generally issued by a state government, giving permission to start a corporation

certified check: a personal check that is guaranteed by a bank

character: the factor in credit that has to do with a customer's honesty and willingness to pay

check: an order written by a depositor directing a bank to pay out money

checkbook: a bound book containing blank checks and check stubs or a check register

checking account: a bank account against which a depositor may write checks

check protector: a machine that prints the amount of a check on the check form

check register: a separate form on which the depositor keeps a record of deposits and checks

check stub: the perforated end of a check on which a depositor keeps a record of deposits and checks

claim: a request for payment due to loss

class-action suit: legal action brought against a business by a group of consumers with a similar complaint about deceptive or dishonest practices

classified directory: a book listing all businesses which have telephones, arranged according to the goods or services they offer

clearance sale: using a price reduction to sell items that a merchant no longer wishes to carry in stock

clearing a check: returning a check to the drawer's bank to be paid and charged to his or her account

clearinghouse: a place where banks exchange checks to clear them

closed shop agreement: an agreement to employ only people who are already members of a union

coinsurance clause: a provision in which the insured agrees with the insurance company to pay a percentage of his or her medical expenses

collect call: a long distance call that is billed to the number that is called

collective bargaining: negotiations between an organized body of workers and an employer dealing with wages and working conditions

collision insurance: insurance coverage which pays for damages to the insured's car caused by collision or by turning over

commercial bank: a bank that handles checking accounts, makes loans to individuals and businesses, and provides other banking services (*same as* full-service bank)

commission: a fee paid to a broker for services in buying and selling securities

common stock: stock that has no stated dividend rate but shares in the profits of a firm

communication: the exchanging of information

communism: an economic system in which government owns most of the property and has tight control over the production and distribution of goods and services

competition: the rivalry among businesses to sell their goods and services to buyers

compound interest: interest added to the total invested before the interest is calculated

comprehensive physical damage insurance: insurance coverage which pays for damages to your car caused by events other than a collision or by turning over

compulsory insurance regulations: laws that say you may not register a car or obtain a license to drive without presenting proof of having the minimum amounts of insurance coverage

condominium: an individually owned unit of an apartment-like building or complex

consumer: one who buys and uses goods and services

consumer finance company: a company which specializes in making small loans to borrowers with weak credit ratings

consumer price index: a price index that shows the changes in the average prices of goods and services

consumers' cooperative: an organization of consumers who buy goods and services together

containerization: a shipping service in which specially designed containers can be carried on railroad flatcars, trucks, or ships

contract: an agreement to exchange goods and services for something of value

convertible policy: a term life insurance policy that may be changed into another type of insurance

cooperative: a business that is owned by the members it serves and is managed in their interest

copyright: the exclusive right of an author, composer, or artist to use or sell what he or she has produced for life and for 50 years after death

corporation: a business made up of a number of owners but authorized by law to act as a single person

cosigner: a person who guarantees to pay a debt if the person who obtained the loan cannot do so

credit: buying something today and agreeing to pay for it at another time

credit card: a card which identifies a person and gives him or her the privilege of obtaining goods and services on credit

credit memorandum: a written record the seller gives you when you return merchandise

creditor: one who sells or lends on another's promise to pay in the future

credit rating: a person's reputation for paying debts on time

credit references: firms or individuals who have given credit to someone in the past and can give information on an individual's credit record

credit union: a cooperative association which accepts savings deposits and makes small loans to its members

D

data: facts or information of all kinds

Data-Phone: a telephone that enables computers to send information over telephone lines

debtor: one who buys or borrows and promises to pay later

decreasing term insurance: term life insurance on which the premiums remain the same during the term but the amount of protection gradually decreases

deductible clause: a clause in an insurance contract that says the car owner agrees to pay the first $100 or $200 of damage to his or her car and the insurance company will pay the rest

deflation: a decrease in the general price level

demand: the amount of a product or service that consumers are willing and able to buy

dental expense insurance: insurance that pays for normal care of and accidental damage to teeth

deposit: money that is placed in a bank account by a customer

deposit slip: a form that accompanies a deposit and shows the items deposited (*same as* deposit ticket)

deposit ticket: a form that accompanies a deposit and shows the items deposited (*same as* deposit slip)

depreciation: a decrease in the value of property as it becomes older and wears out

direct distance dialing: a method of making a long distance call in which the caller dials the number and does not require help from the operator

disability income insurance: insurance that provides a worker with weekly or monthly payments when he or she is unable to work as a result of an illness or injury covered by the policy

discount: interest deducted in advance from the total amount borrowed

distribution: the activities that are involved in moving goods from producers to consumers (*same as* marketing)

dividend: the part of the profits of a corporation that each stockholder receives

division of labor: specialization by workers in performing certain portions of a total job

dollar vote: expressing approval of a product by buying it (*same as* economic vote)

domestic trade: the buying and selling of goods and services among people and businesses within the same country

down payment: part of the purchase price of an item that is paid at the time of buying

drawer: the person who signs a check

E

economic resources: the means or sources of help through which we produce the things we need and want (*same as* factors of production)

economic risk: the chance of losing the financial value of something

economics: the study of producing and making available products and services to help satisfy as many of our wants as possible

economic system: the plan that a nation has for making decisions on what to produce, how to produce, and how to distribute goods and services

economic vote: expressing approval of a product by buying it (*same as* dollar vote)

electronic data processing: the processing of data by electronic computers

electronic funds transfer: the transfer of money electronically from one account to another

eminent domain: the right of the government to purchase private property at a fair price for necessary public use

employee benefits: things of value which workers receive free or at very low cost from their companies

endorsement: a signature on the back of a check that transfers ownership of the check

endowment life insurance: a life insurance policy payable to the beneficiary if the insured should die or payable to the insured if he or she lives beyond the number of years in which premiums are paid

equity: the difference between what your house is worth and what you owe on your mortgage

estate tax: a tax on the total amount of property left by a person who dies

exchange: a special place of business where stocks and bonds are sold

excise tax: a federal tax on certain goods and services, generally included in the price quoted to purchasers

expenditure: an amount actually spent for food, clothing, or other items

exports: goods and services sold to another country

express money order: a form purchased from an express company for use in making payments

extended coverage: additional protection of property against losses from such causes as windstorms, hail, and smoke

extractor: a business that grows products or takes raw materials from nature

F

face value: the amount printed on the front of a bond

factors of production: the means or sources of help through which we produce the things we need and want (*same as* economic resources)

family income policy: a policy that combines a standard whole life insurance policy with decreasing term insurance

Federal Deposit Insurance Corporation: a federal agency that guarantees bank deposits up to $100,000 for each account

Federal Reserve System: a nationwide banking plan set up by our federal government to assist banks in serving the public more efficiently

Federal Savings and Loan Insurance Corporation: an organization that insures accounts in savings and loan associations up to $100,000

finance charge: the total cost of a loan

financial responsibility laws: laws providing that if you cause an accident and cannot pay for the damages through insurance or through your savings or property, your driver's license will be suspended or taken away

first-class mail: mail that includes handwritten or typewritten material that is sealed against postal inspection

fishyback: a shipping service in which loaded trailers are carried on ships

fixed expenses: expenses such as house payments and insurance payments that regularly occur and are for the same amount each time

flowchart: a first step in planning a computer program, written in diagram form

foreign trade: trade among different countries (*same as* international trade *and* world trade)

forgery: the crime of signing another person's name to a check without the authority to do so

fourth-class mail: mail that includes all packages weighing one pound or more that may be opened for postal inspection (*same as* parcel post)

fraud: when false information is given to a customer in an effort to make a sale

free enterprise system: an economic system in which most of the economic resources are owned by individuals rather than by the government (*same as* capitalism)

freight: goods that are transported (*same as* shipments)

freight forwarder: a firm which groups small shipments to make a full railroad carload

full endorsement: an endorsement including the name of the person to whom the check is transferred (*same as* special endorsement)

full-rate telegram: a telegram which is sent and delivered as quickly as possible

full-service bank: a bank that handles checking accounts, makes loans to individuals and businesses, and provides other banking services (*same as* commercial bank)

G

gift tax: a tax imposed on large amounts of property given away

goal: something that a person or family wants to achieve

goods: the tangible things you use in everyday life

government employment office: a government agency that helps persons find jobs and has information available about careers

grade: an indication of the quality or size of a product

gross national product (GNP): the total value of all goods and services produced in a country during a year

gross profit: the difference between the selling price and the cost price of an article (*same as* margin)

group health insurance: health insurance available to members of a group

group life insurance: life insurance issued to members of a group as a unit

guarantee: a promise that a product is of a certain quality or that defective parts will be replaced (*same as* warranty)

H

health maintenance organization: an organization which provides complete health care to its members for a fixed regular payment

homeowners policy: a package policy covering a wide range of risks for the owners of homes

hospital expense insurance: insurance that pays part or all of the charges for room, food, and other hospital expenses that the insured person incurs

house brand: a special name used for products sold by one particular store or chain of stores

human resources: the people who work to produce goods and services (*same as* labor)

I

import quota: a limit on the amount of a given type of product that may be imported within a given period of time.

imports: goods and services bought from another country

impulse buying: unplanned purchases you make when you see an item attractively displayed and suddenly decide to buy it

income taxes: taxes on the earnings of individuals and corporations

increasing term insurance: term insurance on which the premiums remain the same during the life of the policy but the amount of coverage increases

inflation: an increase in the general price level

inheritance tax: a tax on the amount inherited by an individual

input: the data that is fed into a machine for processing

installment credit: a type of credit in which a debt is repaid in a series of payments

installment loan: a loan repaid with interest in a series of payments

insurable interest: having some kind of financial benefit in the continued life of someone

insurance: the planned protection provided by sharing economic losses

insurance agent: a person who sells insurance

insurance commission: a state agency which acts to assure that insurance premium rates and practices are fair

insurance company: a business that makes insurance available to others

insured: the person for whom risk is assumed by an insurance company (*same as* policy-holder)

interchangeable parts: parts that are made exactly alike so that one can be used to replace another that is worn out or broken

interest: an amount paid for the use of money

international trade: trade among different countries (*same as* foreign trade *and* world trade)

inventory: a list of goods showing the cost of each item, when it was purchased, and how long it is expected to last

investment bank: a bank that handles the transactions of businesses that need to obtain large amounts of money

investment club: a small group organized to study stocks and invest members' money

investment company: a corporation that sells its own stock to the public and buys stocks and bonds of other corporations (*same as* mutual fund)

investments: savings that are put to work to earn more money

J

job title: the name that is given to a job

joint account: a bank account that is used by two or more people

L

label: a statement attached to a product giving information about its nature or contents

labor 1: the people who work to produce goods and services (*same as* human resources) **2:** all mental and physical effort directed toward the production of goods and services

letterhead: a sheet of paper with the name and address of a business printed on it

letter of application: a letter expressing interest in a job and selling the prospective employer on the qualifications of a job applicant

level term insurance: term life insurance on which the amount of protection remains the same during the term

liabilities: debts that a person, family, or business owes

liability insurance: the general term used to describe insurance you buy to protect yourself against financial loss if you injure someone else or damage someone else's property in an automobile accident

life-style: a person's way of living, judged in part by the goods and services used and by what the person likes to do for self-improvement, recreation, and entertainment

limited-payment policy: permanent life insurance on which premiums are paid only for a stated number of years

liquid investment: an investment which can be turned into money quickly

liter: the metric unit of volume

loan credit: credit that is used to borrow money

M

mailgram: a message service provided by Western Union and the U.S. Postal Service which gives next-business-day delivery to any location within the continental United States

major medical expense insurance: insurance that provides protection against the very large costs of serious or long illness or injury

manufacturer: a business that takes an extractor's products or raw materials and changes them into a form that consumers can use

margin: the difference between the selling price and the cost price of an article (*same as* gross profit)

market economy: a term used to describe the freedom of buyers and sellers to make economic decisions in our free enterprise system

marketing: the activities that are involved in moving goods from producers to consumers (*same as* distribution)

marketplace: any place where buyers and sellers exchange goods, services, and money

market value: the price at which a share of stock can be bought and sold

mass production: the production by machine of great numbers of the same kind of article

Medicaid: medical expense assistance provided by state governments to medically needy families

medical payments insurance: insurance coverage which provides medical expense protection for the policyholder, immediate family members, and guests while in the insured person's car

Medicare: health insurance provided by the federal government for aged and disabled people

metric system: a decimal measuring system used by most countries of the world

mobility: the willingness of a worker to move from one community to another

money management: getting the most for your money

monopoly: a firm which has control of the market for a product or service

mortgage: a legal paper giving a lender a claim against property if the principal, interest, or both are not paid as agreed

mortgage insurance: a life insurance policy that assures the payment of debts on real property if the insured dies

municipal bonds: bonds issued by city and state governments

municipal corporation: an incorporated town or city

mutual fund: a corporation that sells its own stock to the public and buys stocks and bonds of other corporations (*same as* investment company)

N

natural resources: raw materials supplied directly by nature

needs: those things we must have to stay alive, such as food, clothing, and housing

net income: the amount a person receives after taxes and other deductions are withheld from his or her earnings (*same as* take-home pay)

net profit: the amount left over after expenses are deducted from the gross profit

net worth: the difference between the assets and the liabilities of a person, family, or business

night letter: a telegram sent overnight for a relatively low rate

no-fault insurance: a plan in which people injured in auto accidents can collect for their financial losses from their own insurance companies no matter who is at fault

noninstallment credit: a type of credit in which a debt is repaid in one payment

O

one-time sale plan: an installment plan in which the cost of each item is paid for in separate monthly installments

open charge account: a credit plan in which a customer may charge a purchase at any time but must pay the amount owed in full at the end of a specified period

output: data that has been processed and put into some requested form

output per worker-hour: the amount of goods that one worker, on the average, can produce in one hour (*same as* productivity)

outstanding check: a check given to the payee but not yet returned to the bank for payment

overdrawing: writing checks for more money than is in one's account

ownership shares: deposits made to credit union savings accounts

P

parcel post: mail that includes all packages weighing one pound or more that may be opened for postal inspection (*same as* fourth-class mail)

partnership: an association of two or more people operating a business as co-owners and sharing profits or losses according to a written agreement

passport: an official government document identifying a traveler and giving that traveler permission to leave and return to a country

patent: the exclusive right given to an inventor to make, use, or sell an invention for a period of 17 years

payee: the person to whom a check is made payable

pension: payment made to a retired worker under a privately organized plan

per capita output: the figure that results from dividing the GNP of a country by the population of that country

personal data sheet: a written summary of a person's education, experience, and other information used in seeking employment

personal liability coverage: insurance to protect against claims arising from injuries to other people or damage to other people's property which are caused by you, your family, or your pets

personal property: property not attached to land

person-to-person call: a long distance call which is made to a particular person

picketing: when union members walk in front of a place of business carrying signs telling of their complaints against the firm

piggyback: a shipping service in which loaded trailers are carried on railroad flatcars

policy: a contract between one who buys insurance and the company which provides it

policyholder: the person for whom risk is assumed by an insurance company (*same as* insured)

postal money order: a form issued by a post office for use in making small payments

postdated check: a check dated later than the date on which it is written

preferred stock: stock that has preference in payment of dividends and in return of the investment

premium: the amount that a policyholder must pay

price index: a series of numbers showing how prices have changed over a period of years

principal: the amount you borrow when getting a loan

private carrier: a transportation unit used by its owner to move his or her own products

private enterprise: the right of individuals to choose what business to enter and what to produce

private property: the right to own, use, or dispose of things of value

proceeds: the net amount of money a borrower receives after the discount is subtracted from the principal

process: to change the form of data in some way

producers' cooperative: an organization which farmers form to market their products

productivity: the amount of goods that one worker, on the average, can produce in one hour (*same as* output per worker-hour)

profit: the difference between what it costs to run a business and the amount sales bring in

profit motive: the desire to benefit financially from investing time and money in a business

program: a set of step-by-step instructions, written in code, telling the computer what to do

programmer: a person who writes computer programs

promissory note: a written promise to repay borrowed money at a definite time

promotional sale: selling items below regular price to increase the sales of regular merchandise or to draw customers into the store

property damage liability insurance: insurance coverage which provides protection against claims if your car damages someone else's property and you are at fault

public carrier: a transportation firm that transports passengers and goods for others

public property: things owned in common by the people of a city, state, or nation

public utility: a business that supplies a service or product at prices usually determined by government regulation rather than by competition

R

raised check: a check on which the amount was increased by a dishonest person

rate of exchange: the value of the money of one country expressed in terms of the money of another country

rate of return: the percentage at which your savings earn money

real estate: land and anything attached to it

real property: property attached to the land

realtor: an expert in buying and selling real estate

rebate: a refund of finance charges when an installment agreement is paid off early

receipt: a written acknowledgment that payment was made

reference initials: the initials of the person who types a letter, placed in the lower left corner of the letter

regular medical expense insurance: insurance that pays part or all of a doctor's fees for nonsurgical care given in the doctor's office, the patient's home, or a hospital

renewable policy: a term life insurance policy that the policyholder can continue for more than one term without taking a physical exam

repossess: to take back what was sold on the installment plan if payments are not made as agreed

restrictive endorsement: an endorsement that limits the use of a check to a specific purpose

retail credit bureau: an organization which keeps records on people who have done business on credit

retirement, survivors, and disability insurance: government insurance that provides, among other things, for benefits to be paid to retired workers and their families

revenue: income that the government receives from taxes and other sources

revolving charge account: a credit plan in which purchases can be charged at any time and at least part of the debt must be paid each month

right-to-work laws: laws which forbid making union membership a requirement for employment

S

safe-deposit box: a box in a bank vault for storing valuables

sales credit: credit that is used to acquire goods and services and pay for them at a later time

sales tax: a tax on consumer purchases in general, added separately to the cost of the items taxed

savings account: a bank account on which interest is paid

savings and loan association: an organization that provides savings account services and makes loans to individuals, primarily for use in buying homes (*same as* building and loan association)

savings bank: a bank that mainly handles savings accounts and makes loans to home buyers

securities: another name for stocks and bonds

security: something of value pledged to insure payment of a loan

semiannually: twice a year

seniority rights: recognition by an employer of the length of time a worker has been with the company

service business: a business that does things for you instead of making or marketing products

service charge: a charge made by a bank for checking account services

services: those things that you pay others to do for you or to show you how to do

shareholder: a person who owns stock in a corporation (*same as* stockholder)

shipments: goods that are transported (*same as* freight)

shipper: the person or firm who ships something

signature card: a card, kept by a bank, that shows the signatures of persons authorized to draw checks against an account

signature loan: a small loan received by simply signing a promissory note

single-payment loan: a loan repaid with interest by one payment at the end of a definite time

socialism: an economic system in which the government owns and operates a number of basic industries and provides for some degree of private property and private enterprise

social security card: the document showing one's social security number

social security number: the number used to identify one's record of earnings under social security laws

sole proprietorship: a business owned by one person

source document: the first record made of a transaction

special endorsement: an endorsement including the name of the person to whom the check is transferred (*same as* full endorsement)

special-purchase merchandise: goods bought especially for a sale rather than marked down from regular stock

standard fire policy: a basic type of property insurance that protects against loss resulting from fire or lightning damage to a home

statement: a record of the transactions that a customer has completed with a business during a billing period (*same as* statement of account)

statement of account: a record of the transactions that a customer has completed with a business during a billing period (*same as* statement)

station-to-station call: a long distance call in which the caller will speak with anyone at the number called

stock certificate: a printed form that shows ownership in a corporation

stockholder: a person who owns stock in a corporation (*same as* shareholder)

stopping payment: instructing a bank not to pay a certain check

straight life insurance: permanent life insurance on which the insured pays unchanged premiums throughout his or her life

strike: when employees refuse to work until their demands are met

supply: the amount of a product or service that businesses are willing and able to provide at a particular price

surgical expense insurance: insurance that provides benefits to cover part or all of a surgeon's fee for an operation

T

take-home pay: the amount a person receives after taxes and other deductions are withheld from his or her earnings (*same as* net income)

tariff: a tax which a government places on imported products

technology: the use of scientific and technical knowledge to produce goods, services, and information

telegraphic money order: a message directing a certain telegraph office to pay an amount of money to a certain person

tenants policy: insurance on household goods and personal belongings for those who rent

term insurance: a life insurance policy that protects against risk only for a specified period of time

trade: the buying and selling of goods and services

trade association: an organization of firms engaged in one line of business

trademark: a word, letter, or symbol used in connection with a product and which indicates the origin or ownership of the product

transportation: the movement of goods from one place to another

travel: the movement of people from one place to another

traveler's check: a form sold by a bank, express company, or other establishment to take care of the financial needs of travelers

trust company: a bank that manages the money and property of others

turnover: the number of jobs that have to be filled because people leave their jobs

U

unemployment insurance: insurance that provides cash payments for a limited time to people who are out of a job

uninsured motorists protection: insurance coverage which protects the policyholder against losses resulting from injuries caused by a hit-and-run driver or by a driver who has no insurance or no money to pay claims

union shop agreement: an agreement requiring workers to join a union within a specified time after employment

unit pricing: showing the cost of one standard measure of a product for comparison of brands and sizes

upkeep: keeping property in good condition

V

variable expenses: expenses which occur infrequently, are for widely differing amounts, and are difficult to estimate

visa: permission granted by a government to enter its country

W

wants: those things which we can live without but which can add pleasure and comfort to living

warranty: a promise that a product is of a certain quality or that defective parts will be replaced (*same as* guarantee)

white-collar workers: workers who perform work that emphasizes mental skill and the ability to deal with people

whole life insurance: permanent insurance that extends over the lifetime of the insured

withdrawal slip: a written request for a bank to take money out of a savings account

word processing: the use of specially trained people, automated equipment, and organized procedures to handle business communications

work force: the total of all persons 16 years of age and older who either are employed or are looking for employment

worker's compensation: state government insurance that provides payments to employees for injuries or loss of income caused by accidents on the job

world trade: trade among different countries (*same as* foreign trade *and* international trade)

INDEX